Communicating in
the Classroom

This is a volume in

Language, Thought, and Culture: Advances in the Study of Cognition

A complete list of titles in this series appears at the end of this volume.

Communicating in the Classroom

Edited by
LOUISE CHERRY WILKINSON

DEPARTMENT OF EDUCATIONAL PSYCHOLOGY
UNIVERSITY OF WISCONSIN—MADISON
MADISON, WISCONSIN

ACADEMIC PRESS 1982

A Subsidiary of Harcourt Brace Jovanovich, Publishers

New York   London

Paris   San Diego   San Francisco   São Paulo   Sydney   Tokyo   Toronto

ACADEMIC PRESS, INC.
111 Fifth Avenue, New York, New York 10003

United Kingdom Edition published by
ACADEMIC PRESS, INC. (LONDON) LTD.
24/28 Oval Road, London NW1 7DX

Library of Congress Cataloging in Publication Data
Main entry under title:

Communicating in the classroom.

  (Language, thought, and culture)
  Includes bibliographies and indexes.
  1. Interaction analysis in education--Addresses,
essays, lectures. 2. Oral communication--Addresses,
essays, lectures. 3. Forums (Discussion and debate)--
Addresses, essays, lectures. 4. Language arts--
Addresses, essays, lectures. I. Wilkinson, Louise Cherry.
II. Series.
LB1033.C62   371.1'022   82-3877
ISBN 0-12-752060-0   AACR2

PRINTED IN THE UNITED STATES OF AMERICA

82 83 84 85   9 8 7 6 5 4 3 2 1

Contents

I

Theoretical Approach

1

Introduction: A Sociolinguistic Approach to Communicating in the Classroom 3

LOUISE CHERRY WILKINSON

5

Peer Learning in the Classroom: Tracing Developmental Patterns and Consequences of Children's Spontaneous Interactions   69

CATHERINE R. COOPER, ANGELA MARQUIS, AND
SUSAN AYERS-LOPEZ

6

Effective Speakers: Students' Use of Language to Request and Obtain Information and Action in the Classroom   85

LOUISE CHERRY WILKINSON AND STEVEN CALCULATOR

7

Discourse Rules for Literacy Learning in a Classroom   101

JOHANNA S. DE STEFANO, HAROLD B. PEPINSKY, AND
TOBIE S. SANDERS

8

Creating Communication-Rich Classrooms: Insights from the Sociolinguistic and Referential Traditions   131
W. PATRICK DICKSON

III

Contextual Diversity

9

Classroom Discourse as Improvisation: Relationships between Academic Task Structure and Social Participation Structure in Lessons   153
FREDERICK ERICKSON

10

Gaining Access to Learning: Conversational, Social, and Cognitive Demands of Group Participation   183
JUDITH L. GREEN AND JUDITH O. HARKER

11

Distributing and Directing Attention in Primary Classrooms   223

MARILYN MERRITT

12

Differences in Communicative Styles across Ability Groups   245

DONNA EDER

13

What Is Writing For? Writing in the First Weeks of School in a Second–Third-Grade Classroom   265

SUSAN FLORIO AND CHRISTOPHER M. CLARK

14

Instructional Language as Linguistic Input: Second-Language Learning in Classrooms   283

LILY WONG FILLMORE

15

Teachers' Interpretations of Students' Behavior   297

HUGH MEHAN, ALMA HERTWECK, SAM EDWARD COMBS, AND
PIERCE JULIUS FLYNN

16

Conclusion: Applications for Education   323

LOUISE CHERRY WILKINSON AND FRANCESCA SPINELLI

Contributors

Numbers in parentheses indicate the pages on which the authors' contributions begin.

SUSAN AYERS-LOPEZ (69), Austin, Texas 78712

STEVEN CALCULATOR (85), Department of Communication Disorders, Pennsylvania State University, University Park, Pennsylvania 16802

CHRISTOPHER M. CLARK (265), Institute for Research on Teaching, Michigan State University, East Lansing, Michigan 48824

SAM EDWARD COMBS (297), Department of Sociology, University of California, San Diego, La Jolla, California 92039

JENNY COOK-GUMPERZ (13), Institute of Human Learning, University of California, Berkeley, Berkeley, California 94720

CATHERINE R. COOPER (69), Departments of Home Economics and Psychology, University of Texas at Austin, Austin, Texas 78712

JOHANNA S. DE STEFANO (101), Program on Language and Social Policy, Mershon Center and the College of Education, Ohio State University, Columbus, Ohio 43201

MARIANNA DI PAOLO (49), Department of Linguistics, University of Texas at Austin, Austin, Texas 78712

W. PATRICK DICKSON (131), Child and Family Studies, and the Wisconsin Center for Education Research, University of Wisconsin—Madison, Madison, Wisconsin 53706

DONNA EDER (245), Department of Sociology, Indiana University, Bloomington, Indiana 47405

FREDERICK ERICKSON (153), Institute for Research on Teaching, Michigan State University, East Lansing, Michigan 48824

SUSAN ERVIN-TRIPP (27), Department of Psychology, University of California, Berkeley, Berkeley, California 94720

LILY WONG FILLMORE (283), School of Education, University of California, Berkeley, Berkeley, California 94720

SUSAN FLORIO (265), Institute for Research on Teaching, Michigan State University, East Lansing, Michigan 48824

PIERCE JULIUS FLYNN (297), Department of Sociology, University of California, San Diego, La Jolla, California 92039

CELIA GENISHI (49), Department of Curriculum and Instruction, University of Texas at Austin, Austin, Texas 78712

JUDITH L. GREEN (183), School of Education, University of Delaware, Newark, Delaware 19711

JOHN J. GUMPERZ (13), Department of Anthropology, University of California, Berkeley, Berkeley, California 94720

JUDITH O. HARKER (183), Andrus Gerontology Center, University of Southern California, Los Angeles, California 90007

ALMA HERTWECK (297), Department of Sociology, University of California, San Diego, La Jolla, California 92039

ANGELA MARQUIS (69), Department of Psychology, University of Texas at Austin, Austin, Texas 78712

HUGH MEHAN (297), Department of Sociology, University of California, San Diego, La Jolla, California 92039

MARILYN MERRITT[1] (223), Center for Applied Linguistics, Washington, D.C. 20007

HAROLD B. PEPINSKY (101), Department of Psychology, Ohio State University, Columbus, Ohio 43210

TOBIE S. SANDERS (101), Department of Early and Middle Childhood Education, Ohio State University, Columbus, Ohio 43210

FRANCESCA SPINELLI (323), Department of Communicative Disorders, University of Wisconsin—Madison, Madison, Wisconsin 53706

LOUISE CHERRY WILKINSON (3, 85, 323), Department of Educational Psychology, University of Wisconsin—Madison, Madison, Wisconsin 53706

---

[1]*Present address:* 3 Malcha Marg, Chanakyapuri, New Delhi 110021, India.

Preface

The impetus for this volume was a conference funded by the National Institute of Education and held at the University of Wisconsin, Madison, in October 1980. The purpose of the conference was to assess the impact of a "new wave" of multidisciplinary research on the functions of language in the classroom for theory, methods, and practice. This volume captures the spirit of the conference participants' free exchange of ideas and goes substantially beyond that event.

Within the last decade, a new paradigm of research has developed for the study of social interaction in the classroom: the sociolinguistic approach. This approach focuses on descriptions of students' and teachers' use of language in the classroom. These descriptions provide us with a richer understanding of realities in classrooms, revealing the diversity of students and the complexity of communication in this setting. These descriptions also serve as reference points for the improvement of, and/or evaluation of, specific educational programs. They can serve as sources of ideas for the investigation of the processes of teaching and learning.

This volume brings together recent work, both theoretical and empirical, on the use of language for communicating in the classroom. The research reported here focuses on the spontaneous communication of school-age children and their teachers in a variety of classroom settings. The introductory chapter provides a brief overview of the assumptions that underlie the research, followed by a discussion of factors that may influence communication in the classroom and their possible consequences. Fourteen separate chapters report theoretical and empirical work, and the last chapter provides a discussion of the implications of the research for educational practice, including teaching, learning, and assessment.

One unique feature of the volume is its multidisciplinary perspective: Among the contributors are psychologists, educators, linguists, sociologists, and anthropologists. Thus, the volume is of interest to students of several disciplines within the social sciences.

The chapters in this volume present different perspectives on the language used by teachers and students. Taken separately, they stand as significant theoretical and empirical advances in research on the functions of language in the classroom. Taken together, they are an affirmation of the essential role of multidisciplinary approaches to the study of language and education.

I gratefully acknowledge the contributions of all of the participants at the conference, who included the first authors of the chapters, John Gumperz, and the following people who served as discussants: Courtney Cazden, Robin Chapman, Richard Duran, Roy Freedle, Dell Hymes, and Marcia Farr (formerly Whiteman). Special thanks go to Bob Cavey, Janet Lindow, Jean Padrut, and Fran Spinelli, for their assistance during the conference and in the preparation of this volume.

I
Theoretical Approach

1

Introduction:
A Sociolinguistic Approach to
Communicating in the Classroom[1]

LOUISE CHERRY WILKINSON

Definition and Assumptions

Within the last decade, a new tradition of research has developed for the study of social interaction in the classroom: the sociolinguistic approach. This approach focuses on descriptions of students' and teachers' use of language in the classroom. These descriptions provide us with a richer understanding of the life in classrooms, revealing the diversity of students and the complexity of communicating in this context. The descriptions can serve as reference points for the improvement and/or evaluation of specific educational programs. They can also serve as a source of new ideas for investigating the processes of teaching and learning. This volume brings together recent work, both theoretical and empirical, on the use of language for communication in the classroom. Some of the implications of this work for educational practice, including teaching, learning, and assessment will be discussed in the last chapter of the volume.

Learning to use language in social situations is the focus of the language and communicative development of school-age children. Structural knowledge of language is largely developed by the time the child enters school (for first-language learners). Relatively little is known about the continuing development

[1] The preparation of this chapter was supported by a grant from the National Institute of Education to the Wisconsin Center for Education Research (NIE-G-81-0009).

3

of language and communicative knowledge of school-age children. The research that is reported in this volume focuses on the spontaneous communication of school-age children and their teachers in a variety of classroom settings. This introductory chapter provides a brief overview of the assumptions that underlie the research, followed by a discussion of factors that may influence communication in the classroom and their consequences. At the end of this chapter, there are abstracts of the other chapters.

Several assumptions underlie the sociolinguistic approach to the use of language in the classroom. First, interaction in classroom activities requires competence in both the structural and functional aspects of language. This second aspect has been referred to as communicative or interactional competence. Classroom communicative competence is an end in itself, as well as a means of achieving other educational objectives. It can serve both cognitive–academic and social–interpersonal goals. In order to participate effectively in the life of classrooms, children must have more than academic knowledge alone. As Mehan (1979) has stated so eloquently:

> Students not only must know the content of academic subjects, they must learn the appropriate form in which to cast their academic knowledge. . . . They must know with whom, when, and where they can speak and act, and they must provide the speech and behavior that are appropriate for a given classroom situation. Students must also be able to relate behavior, both academic and social, to varying classroom situations by interpreting implicit classroom rules [p. 133].

A second assumption is that the classroom is a unique communicative context. The kind of competence required is specific, although it may share some general characteristics with communicative competencies in contexts such as the home. For example, many communicative interchanges between teachers and students in the classroom are structured to facilitate the acquisition of academic information by students. Thus, the content of these exchanges may be more restricted and the students' contributions may be evaluated more frequently in this context compared with others.

A third assumption is that students differ in their communicative competence, particularly in aspects of competence that are vital in the classroom. We cannot assume that the special aspects of communicative competence that are required in classroom activities necessarily are taught or learned. Certainly, children come to primary classrooms already knowing something about using language and they may have certain expectations about adapting to the new classroom context. However, the special characteristics of the classroom may not be recognized by all students, and they may experience a discontinuity between this context and others, and some may learn slowly how to be an effective communicator in this new context.

The primary technique used by researchers in this area is descriptive and observational research, with specific tools that have been borrowed from the fields of psychology, linguistics, anthropology, such as naturalistic observation, linguistic field description, and ethnography and participant observation.

Major Findings and Themes

The major findings from this tradition of research are organized around three themes: (a) the complexity of social interaction in the classroom; (b) the diversity of students' learning and development; and (c) the central role of the teacher. The discontinuities between the classroom context and other contexts may present special problems for some students, interfering with their development of communicative competence, as well as their overall adjustment to school. Thus, the effects of students' not knowing the "rules of the game"— the standard ways—of communicating in the classroom are not limited to the obvious problems that these students face in their unsuccessful interactions with students and teachers in the classroom. In addition to such immediate problems, if some children do not understand the social situation and its communicative demands, then they may learn little from the classroom experiences in which they participate. Furthermore, accurate assessment of their achievement is unlikely, since access to their knowledge is predicated upon optimal communicative performance. Perhaps the educational failure of some students is caused, at least in part, by differences in the communicative patterns between students and teachers who come from different cultural backgrounds: for example, the misunderstanding that results from miscommunication across cultural barriers (Cook-Gumperz & Gumperz, Chapter 2, this volume). The role of teachers in facilitating the development of communicative competence and in resolving miscommunication is critical. Their decisions at the general level of the classroom and the specific level of microinteraction affect the opportunities students have to develop academic and interpersonal competence.

The sociolinguistic tradition is multidisciplinary and interdisciplinary. For example, linguists have studied the development of some communicative functions of primary school children (Shuy & Griffin, 1981); psychologists have investigated individual differences in language use and communication (Cooper, Ayers-Lopez, & Marquis, Chapter 5, this volume; Wilkinson, Clevenger, & Dollaghan, 1981; Cole, Griffin, & Newman, in press); anthropologists have studied verbal and nonverbal aspects of communicating within and between cultural groups (Cook-Gumperz, 1979; Erickson & Shultz, 1981; Florio & Shultz, 1979); sociologists have studied the regulation of social order through communicative processes such as turn-taking (Mehan, 1979; Merritt, in press); and educators have studied the organization of formal activities such as the lesson (Green & Wallat, 1981; Mehan, 1979; Sinclair & Coulthard, 1975).

Questions for Further Study

Several issues have not been examined adequately in recent research. We do not fully understand the complete range of language use in the variety of situations that students encounter, the origins of individual differences in this competence, and the causes and effects of differential competence in language usage in the classroom.

By far, the greatest amount of information that exists consists of descriptions of microprocesses of social interaction that are involved in specific classroom activities, such as the teacher instructing a "large group" lesson (e.g., Mehan, 1979). These descriptions do not exhaust the available instructional and noninstructional activities that take place in classrooms in which communication is required. Almost all previous research has examined teacher–student interaction, although some studies of peer interaction have been published recently (Steinberg & Cazden, 1979; Cooper, Ayers-Lopez, & Marquis, in press; Wilkinson & Dollaghan, 1979; Wilkinson, Clevenger, & Dollaghan, 1981).

Another issue not addressed adequately in previous research is the origins of individual differences in competence. Some researchers have suggested that there are differences between the language use at school and home (Heath, in press; Philips, 1972). It is argued that culturally diverse students do not receive an adequate explication of the "rules of the game" for classroom interaction, which can contribute to their failure to learn these rules. Direct teaching of the rules of classroom communication is one potential source of variation, as is the knowledge or "preparatory learning [Merritt, in press]" that students bring to the new situation. Most of the recent studies include descriptions of what students actually do in specific classroom contexts; some studies have attempted to relate their behavior in this situation to other contexts, such as the home (Cook-Gumperz, 1979). Further research is needed, however, to address adequately the causes of individual differences among students in their classroom communicative competence. This information would provide a basis for developing programs that promote students' development.

Another limitation of previous research is that it suggests, rather than tests, the relationship of social processes to intended and unintended outcomes. An example of an obvious and intended effect is learning the rules of the game of communicating in the classroom; an example of an unintended and subtle effect is educational failure as an indirect outcome of communicative failure.

Few quantitative studies have examined the effects of specific instructional decisions, such as peer tutoring, on students' development of classroom communicative competence (e.g., Wilkinson, Clevenger, & Dollaghan, 1981; Cooper et al., in press). Previous research suggests that teachers are a source of variability in students' learning. Their decisions are a component in creating the optimal conditions for learning of individually different students. However, experimental studies, which systematically vary teacher variables, such as accessibility (Merritt, in press) have not yet been conducted.

Some of the unintended effects of inadequate learning of the rules of classroom interaction are a lack of understanding and an inability to function adequately in that context. This pattern is demonstrated by students' misunderstandings of the curriculum, as well as the teacher's lowered expectations, which can then cause the teacher's differential interactions (Cherry, 1979; Eder, in press; Cook-Gumperz & Gumperz, Chapter 2, this volume; Gumperz, 1978; Mehan, Hertweck, Combs, & Flynn, Chapter 15, this volume; Morine-Dershimer & Tenenberg, 1980). However, this possible effect of misunderstanding has not been tested empirically (Koehler, 1978). An alternative hypothesis is that the communicative pressure that is generated in such situations actually may promote the child's development of communicative competence (Cherry, 1979).

All of the chapters in this volume contribute new information about the processes of communicating and the competence that is required of individuals in the classroom. The empirical work consists of descriptions of the use of language and nonverbal communicative behaviors that accompany the academic aspects of classroom interaction. These descriptions, which exist in a variety of forms and at a number of different levels, provide information about what is required of students in order to participate effectively in particular interactions with teachers and other students. Diversity among specific contexts in the classroom that require the use of language to communicate is also a major theme in this work. Contexts differ in many ways including participants, topic, setting, and goals (Ervin-Tripp, 1964). Another major theme is diversity among students in their use of language to communicate, particularly for students who do not speak a standard dialect of English or who are members of minority groups. The implications of these two themes are seen to be interrelated and of critical educational importance.

This volume consists of the reports of empirical studies and theoretical statements. The diversity of disciplinary concerns, observational methods, and analytical tools anchor these findings firmly in theory. We believe that this work may suggest ways to ameliorate the problems of inequality of educational opportunity. One thing seems clear: Just as learning can be viewed as a process, so can the mechanisms for its facilitation. Fully understanding the mechanisms that are amenable to positive intervention may be elusive at the present time. However, a major effort in the search for that understanding belongs here— communicating in the classroom.

Two groups of empirical studies are reported in this volume. One focuses primarily on diversity among teachers and students in their use of language to communicate in specific school-related situations (Cooper, Marquis, &

Ayers-Lopez; De Stefano, Pepinsky, & Sanders; Dickson; Ervin-Tripp; Genishi & Di Paolo; Wilkinson & Calculator). These studies concern the functions of the language for informational and interpersonal goals. A second group of studies focuses primarily upon diversity among specific situations in the classrooms which require teachers and students to communicate (Eder; Erickson; Fillmore; Florio & Clark; Green & Harker; Mehan, Hertweck, Combs, & Flynn; Merritt).

Overview of the Chapters

Cook-Gumperz and Gumperz (Chapter 2) provide a theoretical statement regarding communicative competence from an educational perspective. They believe that the problems of urban minorities are not sufficiently described by studies that simply demonstrate linguistic and cultural variation. The establishment of special programs, in which children are separated from the mainstream and taught in their own dialect and exposed to their own culture, raises questions about the equity of such programs for those children. They do not believe that communicative competence can be assessed in a context-free sense, as an abstract ability, but it must be examined as the use of language in specific contexts.

Ervin-Tripp (Chapter 3) examines the strategies that children use to control the acts of others and their ability to understand such acts by others. In describing observational and experimental data, she emphasizes the continuity for some children between their use of language in school and at home.

Genishi and Di Paolo (Chapter 4) analyze the structure of arguments among preschool children. They trace the complexity and sophistication in this special use of language. Their work illustrates one of the important qualities emerging from research in this area: the intersection of cognitive–academic knowledge and social–interpersonal knowledge.

Cooper, Marquis, and Ayers-Lopez (Chapter 5) examine peer exchanges among kindergarten and second-grade students. They identify seven types of episodes that occur during interaction, such as asking for help, "advertising" newly acquired knowledge, and pacing. Their analysis brings us closer to understanding how children are effective in achieving their interpersonal and informational goals through other students.

Wilkinson and Calculator (Chapter 6) examine first-grade children's use of requests and responses in peer-directed reading groups of differing ability levels. Aspects of requests predicted whether requests were effective in eliciting appropriate responses from intended listeners. Their results suggest that distinctive patterns of communication within groups may serve to maintain differences in reading achievement.

De Stefano, Pepinsky, and Sanders (Chapter 7) analyze interactive discourse between a teacher and three culturally diverse students in a single classroom during the process of literacy instruction. They identify differences between the children in their language knowledge and highlight their differential learning of discourse rules necessary for participating in literacy learning.

Dickson's (Chapter 8) research derives from the referential communication tradition, which is primarily an experimental psychological paradigm. He reviews the assumptions and investigatory techniques of this approach and also reports the results of a study in which students' use of language was assessed using dyadic communication games. This innovative use of an experimental task provides opportunities and motivation for students to practice and model specific language use, which may be generalized to other situations. The use of the microcomputer to create contexts that are rich in communication experiences is also discussed.

Erickson (Chapter 9) elaborates two theoretical distinctions that are implicit or explicit in several other chapters in this volume: social–interpersonal versus cognitive–academic competence; and rule-governed versus spontaneous–improvisational performance particular communicative situations. He presents a multilevel analysis of teacher–student interaction during a classroom lesson that exemplifies his theoretical contribution.

Green and Harker (Chapter 10) conceptualize teaching and learning as a communicative process, drawing on theoretical work in anthropological linguistics and cognitive and social psychology. As an application of this model, they present data from two classrooms that illustrate individual differences between the two teachers and among their students in using language to accomplish both social and cognitive goals in particular contexts.

Merritt's (Chapter 11) research provides an analysis of teachers' and students' attempts to signal and obtain attention from one another in different situations. The results show that teachers' attention is a scarce resource whose allocation is determined by an implicit set of rules shared by both teachers and students. Students' attention requires direction for adequate participation in the classroom.

Eder (Chapter 12) investigates differences in communication patterns within teacher-directed reading groups of differing ability levels. Her analyses provide evidence that initial differences in these processes occur as well as evidence that teachers perceive these differences. Teachers responded to interruptions by high and low group members differently, encouraging topical interruptions during reading turns in low groups, while discouraging all reading-turn interruptions in high groups.

Florio and Clark (Chapter 13) examine children's use of writing as communication in the classroom. Research in this area is rare. Florio and Clark analyze the written products of second- and third-grade children that reveals both the academic–cognitive and social–interpersonal functions that writing can serve and explain the teacher's role in facilitating the use of writing in school.

Fillmore (Chapter 14) examines teachers' use of language and students' learning of English as a second language in bilingual classrooms. She analyzes the organization of bilingual classrooms along two dimensions: the social structure (teacher-directed versus peer-directed), and composition of the classroom with regard to language ability of students (homogeneous versus heterogeneous). Fillmore's results suggest that bilingual students develop the second language, English, when their teachers rarely mix the languages of instruction. Both the composition and the social structure of classrooms affect this learning.

Mehan, Hertweck, Combs, and Flynn (Chapter 15) examine teachers' understandings of the classroom as a communicative context, and the interaction of their understanding with their perception of the communicative behavior that is displayed by students in specific situations. The data concern teachers' accounts of the reasons for referring particular students to special educational programs and their understanding of the students' behavior. Mehan *et al.* use a technique of the "viewing session" and interview with the teachers in order to elicit accounts so that inferences may be drawn about their implicit perspectives on students.

References

Cherry, L. A sociolinguistic approach to the study of teacher expectations. *Discourse Processes*, 1978, *1* (4), 374–393.

Cherry, L. The role of adult's request for clarification in the language development of children. In R. Freedle (Ed.), *New directions in discourse processing.* Norwood, N.J.: Ablex, 1979, 273–286.

Cole, M., Griffin, P., & Newman, D. Locating tasks in psychology and education. *Discourse Processes*, in press.

Cook-Gumperz, J. Communicating with young children in the home. *Theory into Practice*, XVIII, (4), 1979, 207–212.

Cooper, C., Ayers-Lopez, S., & Marquis, A. Children's discourse during peer learning in experimental and naturalistic situations. *Discourse Processes*, in press.

Eder, D. The impact of management and turn-allocation activities on student performance. *Discourse Processes*, in press.

Erickson, F., & Shultz, J. When is a context? In J. Green & C. Wallat (Eds.), *Ethnography and language in educational settings.* Norwood, N.J.: Ablex, 1981, 147–160.

Ervin-Tripp, S. An analysis of the interaction of language, topic, and listener. *American Anthropologist*, 66, (6), 1964, 45–61.

Florio, S., & Shultz, J. Social competence at home and at school. *Theory into Practice*, XVIII, (4), 1979, 234–239.

Heath, S. B. Protean shapes in literacy events: Evershifting oral and literate traditions. In D. Tannen (Ed.), *Spoken and written language.* Norwood, N.J.: Ablex, in press.

Green, J., & Wallat, C. (Eds.) *Ethnography and language in educational settings.* Norwood, N.J.: Ablex, 1981.

Koehler, V. Classroom process research: Present and future. *Journal of Classroom Interaction,* 1978, *13,* (2) 3–11.

Mehan, H. *Learning lessons.* Cambridge: Harvard University Press, 1979.

Merritt, M. Requests and reformulations in primary classrooms as windows on talk engagement. *Discourse Process,* in press.

Morine-Dershimer, G., & Tenenberg, M. *Participant perspectives of classroom discourse.* Final report to the National Institute of Education (NIE-G-78-0161), 31 July 1980.

Philips, S. Participant structures and communicative competence: Warm Springs children in community and classroom. In C. Cazden, V. John, & D. Hymes (Eds.), *Functions of language in the classroom.* New York: Teachers College Press, 1972.

Sinclair, J., & Coulthard, R. *Towards an analysis of discourse: The English used by teachers and pupils.* London: Oxford University Press, 1975.

Shuy, R., & Griffin, P. What they do at school any day: Studying functional language. In W. P. Dickson (Ed.), *Children's oral communication skills.* New York: Academic Press, 1981.

Steinberg, Z., & Cazden, C. Children as teachers—of peers and ourselves. *Theory into Practice,* XVIII, (4) 1979, 258–266.

Wallat, C., & Green, J. Social rules and communicative contexts in kindergarten. *Theory into Practice,* XVIII, (4) 1979, 275–84.

Wilkinson, L. Cherry, Clevenger, M., & Dollaghan, C. Communication in small instructional groups: A sociolinguistic approach. In W. P. Dickson (Ed.), *Children's oral communication skills.* New York: Academic Press, 1981.

Wilkinson, L. Cherry, & Dollaghan, C. Peer communication in first-grade reading groups. *Theory into Practice,* XVIII, (4) 1979, 267–274.

2
Communicative Competence in Educational Perspective[1]

JENNY COOK-GUMPERZ
JOHN J. GUMPERZ

In this chapter, we will review some of the thinking that led to the notion of communicative competence as originally proposed and discuss difficulties that arise in attempts to apply this notion to issues of modern urban education. Using concepts developed in our work on interethnic communication and classroom interaction, we will suggest that a detailed examination of the verbal cues emitted and received during classroom talk, the interpretive processes to which they give rise, and the evaluative criteria in terms of which they are judged can shed light on the underlying causes of many current educational problems.

The notion of communicative competence was originally proposed by sociolinguists to account for the fact that, to be effective in everyday social settings, speakers and listeners depend on knowledge that goes beyond phonology, lexicon, and abstract grammatical structure. Language usage, they argued, is governed by culturally, subculturally, and context-specific norms, which constrain both choice of communicative options and interpretation of what is said.

The significance of this concept and its application to the task of specifying what is involved in the ability to produce and comprehend messages, is best understood within the context of the academic atmosphere of the 1960s.

[1] Research for this chapter was supported by grants from NIE, NIMH, and The Institute for Advanced Studies, Princeton.

13

The then predominant theories of generative grammar drew a sharp distinction between **competence**, defined as the abstract knowledge that enables speakers to identify grammatical sentences and recognize structural relationships among them, and **performance** (i.e., what is actually said at any one time). Only the former was seen as rule governed and subject to formal analysis, whereas the latter was regarded primarily as a matter of personal choice or interindividual variation.

By applying the term **competence** to communication rather than to languages as such, ethnographers of communication advance the claim that there exist measurable regularities at the level of social structure, and social interaction, which are as much a matter of subconsciously internalized ability as are grammatical rules proper. Control of these regularities, they contend, is a precondition of effective communication (Hymes, 1974).

The difference between the generative grammarians' and the sociolinguists' view of language is of both theoretical and practical significance. It has important implications for our views of what counts as linguistic data and for the way these data are elicited through fieldwork and analyzed. The generative grammarians' method of operation is basically a deductive one in which linguists, using their own knowledge of abstract grammatical processes, construct sentences which **they** see as illustrating important theoretical issues. Native speakers' responses are elicited primarily to test the linguists' hypotheses. Ethnographers of communication, on the other hand, take an inductive, empirical approach starting with the description of natural speech in what is usually seen as a single social group, as it varies from speaker to speaker and situation to situation. Rather than accounting for their observations by postulating unitary systems of rules and categories that any one individual must control in order to speak the language, they tend to see grammar as the shared knowledge of the community of speakers. The basic claim is that such a community grammar consists of a range of subsystems, not all of which are known by all individual members. It is assumed that individuals must select among the options of the community's overall system in accordance with principles of linguistic and social etiquette specific to the speech situations in which they intend to take part or which they need to control in order to carry out their daily affairs. Variability thus becomes a communicative phenomenon to be accounted for as part of the linguist's analysis. Neither the range of linguistic variability nor the range of grammatical relations among sets of variants and the norms that govern their employment can be known beforehand. These must all first be discovered through ethnographic observation. Thus, in this view, any system of linguistic analysis relying primarily on linguists' use of their **own** necessarily limited knowledge to evaluate grammatical relationships is incapable of uncovering new, hitherto unknown facts about variation and thus risks ethnocentrism.

Sociolinguistic research of the 1960s and early 1970s was motivated in large part by the awareness that we lack reliable information about everyday speech. Existing descriptions had dealt either with the standard literary styles of the educated in complex societies or with the languages of small face-to-face tribal groups. Partly because of earlier linguists' preoccupation with language history and the analysis of abstract sentence structures, and partly because of the lack of reliable electronic recording equipment to capture the subtleties of verbal exchanges, information on language usage adequate for the sociolinguists' need had simply not been collected. Efforts to collect new data on variability concentrated on two types of situations, the speech of urban ethnic minority groups in industrial societies and that of rural and tribal peoples in Asia, Latin America, Africa, and the Pacific. Following the then current ethnographic practice, researchers tended to concentrate on the folk speech of groups who had remained relatively unaffected by our own Greco–Roman literary traditions. The search for sources of diversity led to an emphasis on such special speech events as ritual performances, verbal dueling, storytelling sessions, or formal speech-making that are diagnostic of particular cultural traditions and stand apart from everyday conversation.

During the last two decades, ethnographic work along these lines has helped document the diversity of folk communicative conventions throughout the world. We now have ample evidence to demonstrate the sociolinguist's contention that the criteria by which we evaluate what counts as persuasive, what is appropriate or what is even grammatical speech, are always context bound and can vary from setting to setting. A new fieldwork tradition has emerged that begins by isolating identifiable communities or subgroups in a region. Ethnography is then used first to describe the culture of such groups with special reference to values and norms relevant to speaking and second to isolate speech events characteristic of the group. Analyses of speech behavior concentrate on isolating time-bound sequences of interaction. These are characterized in terms of their sequential structure, participants' roles, rights, and duties and in terms of the communication and linguistic codes employed. Linguistic analysis can then be used to determine the phonological, syntactic, and lexical characteristics of constituent codes, so as to isolate both categorical or shared and variable, that is nonshared features. The goal is to determine the community level rules that determine what variants are used when, by whom, and under what circumstances.

Viewed in historical perspective, the early work in ethnography of communication was basically descriptive in nature and dealt with simple societies and folk cultures. The notion of communicative competence was developed to deepen the theoretical response to the complexities of culture and to the variety of communicative options, and so seemed particularly relevant to the educational arena. What the work on communicative competence has done for education is to question the standard language bias that in the past has shaped most research in education. For example, it has demonstrated that minority groups who do not do well in school had access to well-developed folk traditions and value systems of their own, which are internally consistent and systematic. Differences at the level of both language and culture now must be seen as instances of variability—not of inferiority—so that failure of the school system to incorporate these differences into curriculum, textbooks, and teaching strategies may be one of the causes that account for minority students' failure to achieve in school.

Focus on diversity has revealed, however, more complex sources of differentiation. There is a growing body of evidence that as soon as we begin to apply the qualitative ethnographic techniques that led to the discovery of differences in discourse conventions to examine more general questions concerning the acquisition of knowledge, we also begin to notice additional cultural differences in patterns of learning and in cognitive styles. Anthropologists and comparative cognitive psychologists, working in nonliterate and literate, but economically simple societies have called attention to informal or experiential learning processes, that is the context-bound procedures by which members acquire the locally valued skills and knowledge needed to carry on their daily affairs (Cole & Scribner, 1974; Elsasser & John-Steiner, 1977; Goody, 1978; Greenfield, 1972).

These informal styles differ from known classroom learning processes in several important respects. The outside observer will note relatively little in the way of direct verbal instruction. Skills tend to be acquired through observation and imitation. Evaluations, criticism, or other types of immediate verbal feedback are rare. It seems to be taken for granted that the child is able to learn and that progress will eventually be made, so adults do not expect to test for progress at various stages of acquisition. The details of such experiential learning processes vary for different societies and in relation to different tasks, yet all experiential learning takes place against a background of shared, but for the most part nonverbalized, communicative conventions and shared understandings of what goals are to be achieved.

In our own society also, strategies for participating in everyday learning situations outside the school context seem to show at least some of the characteristics of experiential learning and thus reveal significant discrepancies from what our psychological models of the learning process would lead us to expect. To the extent that this is true, we need to account for the possibility that there are many paths to the acquisition of skills and knowledge. The very nature of the interaction situations that constrain the acquisition process and the participant structures by which we recognize that learning is taking place and that progress has been made are subject to cultural variation.

We can go some way toward recognizing differences of discourse style and cultural norms in classroom practices if, in addition, we admit the validity of the claim that strategies of learning differ. Then, however, the problem of dealing with cultural difference in schooling becomes more difficult. The recently republished 1920s studies by Luria with isolated groups in Soviet Asia (1976) and Scribner and Cole's work in Africa (1978) have demonstrated that in societies where formal schooling is a new experience, even a little schooling—as little as 6 months or a year—makes a critical difference, both in strategies of learning and understanding. Yet these findings are not directly transferable to western urban settings. All sectors of western society, where the presence of minority groups is seen as an educational problem, have by now had more than 100 years of experience with formal education and mass literature, and as a result have already acquired their own attitudes about the knowledge and practice that make up schooling.

In comparing minority group achievers with majority group achievers we are thus not dealing with a simple distinction between people who **do** and who **do not** have certain types of abstract knowledge, but rather with systematic differences in notions of what learning is about and differences in criteria for estimating and evaluating achievement. If simple differences in knowledge were involved, how could we explain the fact that differences in achievement as measured by formal tests are relatively small at the onset of education when children first enter school, but reach a maximum after several years of formal schooling? A simplistic cultural difference model along the lines suggested by ethnographers' of communication empirical studies, in which cultures, contexts, and codes are seen in purely descriptive terms as separate, isolable entities, is not sufficient to deal with the problems of urban minorities in modern educational systems.

Critical for any consideration of communicative competence is the need to see the sociolinguistic practices of speaking and interacting within the wider context of the educational assumptions and ideologies held by members of the society. That is, almost all members of modern societies, parents, administrators, and children have assumptions and expectations about the purpose and goals of the educational process. These assumptions find expression in their immediate activities and attitudes toward schooling. As Patricia Graham (1980) has commented recently in an historical article on the goals of equity in American education:

> For a variety of reasons, school officials traditionally made tacit assumptions about attitudes, habits and talents that children brought with them to the classroom. Generally teachers believed that children from properous families did better than those from poor unstable families. There were always some exceptions to the general rule, but research findings and conventional wisdom supported these beliefs about school achievement measured in conventional ways through teacher-made tests, standardized tests and course grades. **The job of the teacher and the school was to move the children into the curriculum which was also organized along these assumptions** [p.120; emphasis added].

Graham's analysis supports the view already current in Britain and France that the curriculum of schools, widely defined as **the things to be learned and the ways of learning**, can be seen as part of the process of what Bourdieu calls the social transmission of knowledge (Bourdieu, 1973; Young, 1971). The study of classroom practices either tacitly or explicitly must take into account the ways in which the curriculum presents and constrains the social and cognitive options available to the classroom participants. School curricula in other words are not just task oriented, they are also socioculturally shaped (Lawton, 1980).

Recent work in educational sociology, particularly in Britain, France and some other European countries (Karabel & Halsey, 1977) that has looked at the acquisition of specific cultural practices and information through schooling has seen this acquisition process as central to the way in which schools legitimize the passage of social knowledge across generations, as the transmission of accumulated **cultural capital**. It follows that what counts as knowledge in the classroom and in the school system must become an area of enquiry and is not to be taken for granted. One of the values of such approaches is to emphasize that the strategies and content of learning are not universal but specific to the experience of any particular groups' accumulated "cultural capital."

Although the notion of knowledge as cultural capital has recently been adopted in educational theory (Bourdieu & Passeron, 1977), the idea is one which has long been implicit in the educational practice of many societies. In fact, traditional education systems everywhere selected those who were educable on grounds of social origin. Twentieth-century western educational systems by contrast aim to redress the imbalance of educational opportunity. There has been an almost determined effort to assume that judgments of ability can be made culturally neutral. But as we apply our understanding of sociolinguistic difference and its effect on interactive and evaluative processes to the analysis of classroom communication, we come to recognize that neither the curriculum nor the opportunity to learn can be regarded as equally available to all children.

To the extent that the cultural capital is encoded in language, as it must be in our modern education systems where words are what is taught and evaluated, it was necessary for specific institutions of schooling to be set up to transmit this capital. If we adopt this approach the following emerge as issues for research: (a) How are school systems organized in response to the need for a smooth transition across generations of the accumulated capital of any group?; (b) How are such requirements and capital transformed into specific curricular programs?; (c) How do classrooms, as bounded interactional units, put into practice this transmission process?

It is in this third research area that much of the work on sociolinguistic processes in the classroom in the United States finds its wider social relevance.

Although many of the studies of classrooms made within the linguistic tradition extensively explore different linguistic models of acquisition and understanding, the ultimate significance of much of the work is its potential for understanding the processes of social transmission.

One of the most enduring problems in the study of all forms of schooling is how the practices of students and teachers and the shaping of the curriculum can provide a means to achieve equity of educational experience; or how these practices result in the undermining of this aim and a continued imbalance in educational opportunity. In this connection we can note a recent wry comment by A. H. Halsey who has suggested that "education is in danger of becoming like a 'posh' hotel, in principle anyone can enter only the poor don't [St. John-Brooks, 1980, p. 446]."

The question thus remains one of how the problems of the urban poor and minorities can be studied apart from merely demonstrating that cultural variation exists. How the working out of these differences can be seen in the forms of different strategies of speaking within the context of a mass education system, and how these differences may still result in a continued failure of normal school learning techniques, must be further explored. However, in such an attempt serious problems arise when **communicative competence** is used as one of a battery of context-free skills to be measured within a school setting. Communicative competence is an analytical construct that has served to bring a new perspective into the study of language and has broadened the range of phenomena considered by linguists; yet it cannot be given a set of two-dimensional values. We should no more attempt to measure communicative competence than we should attempt to devise a single test that would capture everything meant by the linguists' notion of grammatical competence. Rather than use communicative competence as a basis to devise tests of "language competence," this concept is better used as a diagnostic notion to sharpen and focus the basically qualitative tools of ethnography. Its value lies in its potential for deepening our understanding of the complexities involved in ensuring the transmission of knowledge as **a process of conversational experience and communicative understanding** that is essential to interactive sociolinguistics.

From this perspective we can see that by building on the notion of the social transmission of cultural capital and on the sociocognitive difference in learning strategies we are aware that both the curriculum and its specific skills are not merely available to all children through exposure alone. The process of transmission of knowledge, the form that knowledge takes, and access to it, is both socially defined and socially constrained. We cannot assume therefore that the problem of cultural variability in the classroom can be solved by changes in language code or discourse style or even teaching strategies **if these are taken as single factors to be manipulated out of context.** The task of exploring the cultural transmission of knowledge as communicative competence requires us to see the interactional face-to-face relationship of teacher to student as embedded interactively within a context of the procedures of classroom practices within schools, which themselves are part of an institutional system of educational policies and ideology. This perspective requires the intermeshing of the two research traditions we have outlined in this chapter, the more European-based tradition of looking at the generation of systems of educational knowledge and the more American-oriented tradition of interactional socio-linguistics and ethnography of communication.

If we are to accept and develop the argument set out in this chapter, that the communicative context of school classrooms is determined in large part by the hidden curriculum, which itself is a part of the social transmission of knowledge, then we must ask again how the workings of this curriculum can be studied. The European approach has been to outline the symbolic, culture-specific character of the school system at a very general level. Another approach, more revealing of the actual mechanisms that give rise to the symbolisms, is to use the microethnographic approaches to classroom interaction. As we suggested earlier, we must bring together these two traditions.

In this attempt our particular concern is with the specifics of the linguistic and sociolinguistic practices that publicly aim to achieve equity of educational experience, yet generate a socially differentiated interpretive process and result in differential learning within educational settings. In doing this we can notice that formally in their practices mass education systems do not, and cannot, take into account the nonstandardizable experiential learning practices of different groups. Mass education systems focus on readily accessible information and accountable means of evaluating skills and educational achievement. This results in a focus on specific aspects of verbal learning skills as the medium of education. Further, although the attempt in a modern educational system is to construct a value-free, context-free notion of basic skills, the discourse style differentiation that sets off subgroups within the population of any large-scale society, inevitably results in, to some extent, a cultural pluralism of styles. The teacher in many modern educational situations is put into the position of being a "cultural broker" between different styles of discourse and different implicit or explicit theories of learning.

As Basil Bernstein has suggested recently, modern education experience consists of three **message systems** that are inextricably intertwined, "the curriculum defines what counts as valid knowledge, pedagogy defines what counts as valid transmission of knowledge and evaluative techniques define what counts as the valid realization of knowledge on the part of the taught [1971, p. 203]." Bernstein, however, does not point out that it is the teacher whose activities through actual communicative practices within actual classroom settings produce the working out of these message systems as day-to-day reality. Teachers' activities are inextricably involved with attempts to evaluate the potential of children for education or to measure their success, which involves using tests that must necessarily express a specific **model of educability**. That is, these tests predict the potential of individuals for successful participation in established programs of instruction, where these programs themselves are social expressions of the goals of education and of the transmission of specific societal capital. Any curriculum built around these skills is more likely to reflect one social group's view of the goals of education or of its model of educability. Conversely, tests that reflect one model have a tendency to become self-fulfilling prophecies (Rosenthal & Jacobsen, 1968).

Our tasks as ethnographers of communiction in modern education are both to chart the process by which these models of educability are put into daily practice and to uncover the implicit theory of learning that informs our notions of educability and often underlies apparently simple communicative choices. Both our work and that of others in this volume are concerned with the American tradition and the different ways teachers and pupils together in classrooms construct a day-to-day reality. This reality can in general terms be summarized as the process of **social transmission of knowlege**, but the main aim of both is to break down the generality by looking at the actual mechanisms of daily communication in school settings and showing how these processes relate to the wider system of knowledge creation. In conclusion we will explore briefly how this can be achieved in practice. Although not wishing to give a simple answer to a very complex set of questions, we can point to some uses of the notion of communicative competence as a diagnostic tool and to some ways we consider the teacher to be in a position of an everyday "ethnographer of communication."

A central aim of work in ethnography of communication is to isolate definable speech events that stand out as figures from the ground of everyday conversation. These events have characteristics that can be understood and described by both ethnographers and participants. Second, these speech events are common to groups of people; they are not occasional occurrences, but have a place in the daily conduct of affairs of groups. From this perspective, language in the classroom can be seen as part of the language of the school setting. Characteristics of a particular classroom setting of different ages of children are seen to have a regular occurrence as isolable speech events held together through the daily routines of teachers and students. Work on the "functions of language in the classroom [Cazden, John, & Hymes, 1972]" and on the detailed ethnographies of particular classrooms in different age grades (e.g., Florio, 1975) shows regularity of speech event occurrences and norms that govern these isolable events. Speech events can be further explored through looking at participant structures, which are the norms of participation existing in different cultural groups and governing the type and quantity of interaction that make up the event.

An ethnographer of communication can reveal the key speech events that make up the communicative economy of any group or setting, such as a school classroom or series of classrooms within a school, by examining the patterns of events over time and space: that is, in different settings, schools, or classrooms. It is possible to see that these events, however, although a critical part of the structuring of social life, do not constitute the whole communicative experience of members of a school classroom setting. The work in this volume builds on the ethnography of communication strategy of isolating key speech events in classrooms, to reexamine in detail the occurrence of events and to focus on the processes by which definable events are recognized as special sequences within the stream of activities and speech making up daily interaction. For members of classrooms, the daily movement through time, event to event, is part of the essential communicative knowledge—of when an event is happening, how a shift in activity is taking place and is recognizable as such, and how such a shift becomes a new context in which to reference and relate talk as conversation. Work on this process of conversational inferencing and interpreting (Gumperz, 1977) and on the recognition of verbal and nonverbal cues that **contextualize** the stream of daily talk activity, recognizes speech events as a wider, externally definable sequence of speech within which contexts are signaled and created by participants to act as frames for each other's situated meanings. Such cues can be verbal and nonverbal and together make up a nexus of meaning by which conversation progresses through the transitions between specially recognizable events. These transitory and transitional conversational phenomena, while having a situated and localized meaning reference, also provide a continuing thematic thread by which participants across time build up a specific inferential chain of understandings.

It is by means of this analytic apparatus for exploring conversational inference and contextualization of meaning that we can link the actual specifics of classroom practice in face-to-face interaction between teacher and student to some of the longer time characteristics of teachers' practices and educational outcomes. Several chapters in this volume illustrate how this can be accomplished. For example, Mehan, Hertweck, Combs, and Flynn (Chapter 15, this volume) in special interview sessions, after a period of natural observation in classrooms, work with teachers to review videotapes of naturally occurring sequences of classroom interaction. Such a research strategy is able to explore the daily face-to-face communicative processing that develops across time and the social perceptions that can then become retrospective categories for interpreting and evaluating further behavior. A similar finding is made by DeStephano, Pepinsky, and Sanders (Chapter 7, this volume) by means of a rather different research strategy. Concentrating on direct, linguistically oriented discourse analysis of classroom talk, they demonstrate that the usual linguistic measures fail or cannot account for the author's own ethnographic observations of differential learning and evaluation. The microprocesses accounting for differential learning are the subject of Eder's chapter (Chapter 12, this volume). By building on McDermott's (1978) earlier nonverbal analysis, she finds that the verbal control process with which the teacher instructs high and low achievement groups differs, with the result that the two kinds of groups are exposed to quite different learning environments.

Recent studies completed by our own Berkeley research group apply methods based on the linguistic analysis of conversational inference, to show how results such as those reported by DeStephano et al. and Eder can be generated as the natural outcome of automatic—subconscious—processes of interpretation common to conversational interactions of all kinds (Collins, in preparation; Collins & Michaels, 1980; Gumperz & Cook-Gumperz, in preparation; Michaels & Cook-Gumperz, 1979). The assumption behind such detailed analysis is that communicative competence is to be demonstrated daily and achieved as a shared understanding that satisfactory communication and learning have taken place. In this way we can see that communicative competence is more than the application of rules or norms for appropriate speech; it is the interactive realization of communication within contexts that are themselves coded as part of that communication. At the level of sociocultural experience, there is selection of discourse strategies such that the recognition of appropriate, or at least feasible, strategies acts as a frame for further interpretation and action (Goffman, 1974; Tannen, 1979). It is hoped that such analyses as those cited here, if part of an ethnographic–sociolinguistic study of different settings, can go some way toward demonstrating how participants' (i.e., teachers' as well as students') cultural presuppositions interact with other kinds of knowledge and processing strategies to generate different interpretations of what is intended at any one time. Across time such interpretative mechanisms build up to result in different views of the learning process that can affect both the teaching and assessment of students. If used in this way, communicative competence becomes a means of extending our knowledge of the interactive uses of language into modern urban issues in settings and ways that provide new insights into possibly stalemated problem situations.

References

Bernstein, B. *Class, codes, and control: Theoretical studies towards a sociology of language* (Vol. 1). London: Routledge & Kegan Paul, 1971.

Bourdieu, P. Cultural reproduction and social reproduction. In R. Brown (Ed.), *Knowledge, education, and cultural change.* London: Tavistock Press, 1973.

Bourdieu, P., & Passeron, J. C. *Reproduction in education, society, and culture.* London and Beverly Hills: Sage Publications, 1977.

Cazden, C., John, V., & Hymes, D. *Functions of language in the classroom.* New York: Teachers College Press, 1972.

Cole, M., & Scribner, S. *Culture and thought.* New York: John Wiley and Sons, 1974.

Collins, J. Differential treatment in reading instruction. In J. Cook-Gumperz (Ed.), *Beyond ethnography,* in preparation.

Collins, J., & Michaels, S. The importance of conversational discourse strategies in the acquisition of literacy. *Proceedings of the Sixth Annual Meetings of the Berkeley Linguistics Society,* Berkeley, California, 1980.

Elsasser, N., & John-Steiner, V. P. An interactionist approach to advancing literacy. *Harvard Educational Review,* 1977, *47,* 355–369.

Florio, S. *Learning how to go to school.* Unpublished doctoral dissertation, Harvard University, 1975.

Goffman, E. *Frame analysis: An essay on the organization of experience.* New York: Harper and Row Publishers, 1974.

Goody, E. N. Towards a theory of questions. In E. N. Goody (Ed.), *Questions and politeness: Strategies in social interaction* (Cambridge Papers in Social Anthropology Series No. 8). Cambridge, England: Cambridge University Press, 1978.

Graham, P. Whither the equality of educational opportunity. *Daedalus,* 1980, *109* (3), 115–132.

Greenfield, P. M. Oral or written language: The consequences for cognitive development in Africa, the U. S., and England. *Language and Speech,* 1972, *15,* 169–177.

Gumperz, J. Sociolcultural knowledge in conversational inference. In M. Saville-Troike (Ed.), *Linguistics and anthropology* (Georgetown University Roundtable on Language and Linguistics). Washington, D.C.: Georgetown University Press, 1977.

Gumperz, J., & Cook-Gumperz, J. Manuscript in preparation to appear in J. Cook-Gumperz (Ed.), *Beyond ethnography,* in preparation.

Hymes, D. *Foundation of sociolinguistics.* Philadelphia: University of Pennsylvania Press, 1974.

Karabel, J., & Halsey, A. H. *Power and ideology in education.* New York: Oxford University Press, 1977.

Lawton, D. *The politics of curriculum.* London: Routledge & Kegan Paul, 1980.

Luria, A. R. *Cognitive development.* Cambridge: Harvard University Press, 1976.

Michaels, S., & Cook-Gumperz, J. A study of sharing time with first grade students: Discourse narratives in the classroom. *Proceedings of the Fifth Annual Meetings of the Berkeley Linguistics Society,* 1979.

McDermott, R. Relating and learning: An analysis of two classroom reading groups. In R. Shuy (Ed.), *Linguistics and reading.* Rowley, Mass.: Newbury House, 1978.

Rosenthal, R., & Jacobsen, L. *Pygmalion in the classroom: Teacher expectation and pupils' intellectual development.* New York: Holt, Rinehart, & Winston, 1968.

St. John-Brooks, B. Sociologists and education: A for effort, B for achievement. *New Society,* 1980, *53,* 443–446.

Scribner, S., & Cole, M. Literacy without schooling: Testing for intellectual effects. *Harvard Educational Review,* 1978, *48,* 448–461.

Tannen, D. What's in a frame?: Surface evidence for underlying expectations. In R. O. Freedle (Ed.), *New directions in discourse processing* (Advances in Discourse Processes: Vol. 2). Norwood, N.J.: Ablex, 1979.

Young, M. F. D. *Knowledge and control: New directions in the sociology of education.* London: Collier-Macmillan, 1971.

II
Individual Diversity

3
Structures of Control[1]

SUSAN ERVIN-TRIPP

In a program of research in families and through work with comprehension–interpretation experiments, we have recently been exploring the verbal strategies used by children for controlling the actions of others, which we call **social control acts**, and their ability to understand such acts. We have chosen to study strategies of control because they constitute a substantial proportion of interactional events in young children; their effectiveness is relatively easy to observe; they matter to speakers; and they are likely to be sensitive to social relationships since they impose on others.

What is the relevance of social control acts to the classroom? Teachers must of course accomplish rather considerable feats to control activities. Students engage in peer activity openly in activity-centered classes, as hidden agenda in teacher-focused classrooms, and on the playground. Differences between children in styles of interpersonal control probably affect both their acceptability as social partners and their effectiveness in getting what they want from peers and adults at school. Teachers, too, can be misunderstood by children whose family and peer experience are quite different. Teachers could easily misread such children as uncooperative.

In this chapter, I will discuss our research on the production and comprehension of social control acts by children in the age range of 2–8 years. Rather than treat this as a conventional data report, however, I want to raise

[1] Work on this chapter has been funded by Grants MH 26063 and NSF BNS-7826539.

27

many methodological issues along the way. The focus will be more on problems in doing this kind of research than on immediate results.

Methods

DATA SOURCES

Natural Family Interaction

We used three methods in the research to be discussed here. One was videotaping unstructured natural interaction in families. We chose five white, middle-class families because they were cooperative and came from a milieu familiar enough to allow us some initial methodological work. Each family had 2 or 3 children between the ages of 1.3 and 7.3 years at the outset: of the 14 children, 3 were over 5 years old, 6 were 3 and 4 years old, and 5 were under age 3. The study went on for varying periods in each family, ranging from 4 to 14 months, allowing some developmental changes to be observed. Our intention was to record natural conversation with siblings, parents, friends, and adults such as the experimenters. Because of our interest in natural conversation, we did not try to structure the scenes, but we did plan to include a range of partners. In retrospect, a more deliberate situation sampling and a wider search for families with a particular age and sex structure would have allowed better quantitative studies. The videotapes have been transcribed and coded.

Comprehension Experiments

Picture stories. We developed both picture-story and video-scene methods of assessing interpretive processes and getting judgments of appropriateness from children. The picture-story methods were used first because they were flexible and took less technical skill. We developed a narrative with pictures, using minimal simple language. The 10 picture sets showed family scenes in which a problem arises. For instance, a mother or child arrives at a closed front door with a load of groceries, while other children watch. Maybe nothing is said. Maybe the mother or the child says, *Is the door open?* This we will call the **crisis point act**. We can vary who speaks, whether silence occurs, what is said, and how it is said. In other stories, the children are committing a breach of family rules, by fighting or making a mess for instance. At the crisis point there may be a visible mother or child, or they may just hear a voice. A voice might, for example, say *Are you fighting?* We used verbal acts at the crisis point in which there was no explicit mention of the activity the speaker wanted.

Having started a dialogue by the speech act at the crisis point, we asked the subjects what the children in the story would say and do. Then we questioned them about the event—what the speakers meant or wanted to say, why they spoke, how the child's own mother would have done it, and so on. We wanted to find out how the children interpreted the utterance at the crisis point, how much they relied on knowledge of context (hence the control group in which nothing was said), and what they thought was appropriate.

Realistic directives. During the picture stories, we have used realistic directives of various sorts to children, sometimes going to the extreme of mentioning desired objects in an anomalous way. For example, during an experiment, I might say *Oh, my purse,* which is not anomalous. Often with an older child, if the purse is nearer the child than me, this will be successful as a directive. Or I might say *My purse is white,* which is successful less often. It is anomalous as a directive since it is in full view of both of us, the only purse around. If I only want the purse, I have given too much information.

In this "realistic" requesting, we systematically rotated the object requested and the form, including anomalous, elliptical mention, and various degrees of explicitness up to *Can you get . . . .*

Structured Eliciting

A third method, developed by David Paul Gordon in our research team (Gordon, Budwig, Strage, & Carrell, 1980) involved giving children drawing tasks and building into the tasks occasions when they were likely to give warnings, make offers, make requests, and so on, with peers or adults.

ANALYSIS OF VIDEOTAPED CONVERSATIONS

Speech Act Types

We have been interested in a variety of methods of studying natural conversation. Ethnographic analysis of some of our material has been reported by Jenny Cook-Gumperz, who collaborated in this work (Cook-Gumperz, 1981). Another approach, leaning more heavily on coding categories, is in my view less revealing of the real structure of the episodes. But it will serve to summarize some of the contrasts we have seen. In one of our coding systems, we were primarily concerned with issues such as how the form of the speech varied with the social characteristics of the addressee, the speech event context, and the gestural accompaniments. A central feature of our coding was identifying control acts, that is moves in which there was a clear intention to influence the activities of the partner. In each such episode, we chose the most explicit form and called it the **head act,** which might be accompanied with supporting explanations, attention getters, vocatives, and polite markers; we indicated each of these.

> Have you got a red marker?
> Mine's run out. It doesn't work.
> I really need one.

In this example, the first utterance is an implicit question or condition, which specifies an external obstacle to what the speaker wants the hearer to do. In the second utterance, a problem condition is mentioned. In the third utterance, an explicit statement occurs of the familiar **I need** variety. In such a sequence, if it occurred in one episode with no refusals between, the head act would be the third utterance because it is the most explicit. However, if the child had said Give me a red marker, I really need one, we would code the imperative as more explicit since it specified the desired act of the hearer.

We coded additional information of various sorts, such as whether it was a first or second try, whether refusing, complying, or ignoring occurred, whether gestural supports were used, and so on.[2]

Problems in the Analysis

Speaker's focus. We assumed that control acts can be defined by **activity sought in the addressee or in goal states.** Thus we regarded a head act that was a directive as explicit if it was an imperative such as *Bring me some water*, or a desire statement *I want some water*, or mentioned the act that was wanted *Can you eat some.* Other forms were seen as either elliptical or not explicit. Yet such a view does not take into account the intent of participants. Sometimes the speaker's interest is in the consequences of getting an object, not in the means, or in a problematic state, not in the solution. So if one says, My *throat is really dry* or *It's a dry day*, one might not be making a tactful request at all, but simply indicating a problem. Such attention to aversive states may be due to several causes, not just discretion.

Multiple functions. Every social control act is potentially effective on several planes of change at once; our focus was on altering physical activity. These acts also always communicate social relationships and feelings. Thus, they can be considered, at a minimum, dual messages. Although we initially concentrated only on activity, it would be equally appropraite to consider the social message as primary since many children do.

Even when social control acts do not give new information about relative rank or age (e.g., adult–child, teacher–pupil), which are already known, they

---

[2] Garvey (1975) has discussed some aspects of the sequential internal structure of request episodes.

confirm that information. In the rare extreme, for instance, a shout for help when drowning is social nuance neutralized or subordinated to an activity goal.

But as Mitchell-Kernan and Kernan (1977) first pointed out, children may be primarily concerned with manipulating social face. They can use social control acts to manage social relations; thus, activity outcomes are secondary. The response to a social control act sometimes makes clear what is being addressed by the partner. For example, a brother may state, *Stop sucking your thumb*, and receive the reply, *You're not the boss of me*. In adult speech, too, some social control acts, such as the cliché, *Do you have a match*, may be used primarily to establish attention and start talk or for other social goals.

To make action central is to betray a traditional bias of task-centered adults. It is quite likely that children are capable of juggling several agenda at once, such as schemas for physical activity, declaring rights, and power. Overlooking second agenda might result in missing major determinants of choice, both in the decision to issue a control act and in the form it takes. In the same way we could misconstrue success. If a child says, *Don't speak to me again, stupid*, the insult may succeed even if the recipient does speak.

Level of analysis. This has proven to be a difficult problem in conversational analysis. If several agenda can coexist, it is because a longer sequence exists at several levels that affects not only what happens next, but how any event is realized. A child may be working to get a particular toy, and try various strategies, such as demanding, pretending, or proposing joint play. The purpose of getting the toy may underlie each strategy without any obvious similarity among them. Or, at a deeper level, a child may repeatedly make moves to direct the activity of other children though surface activities may be quite different. These sequences can be interrupted and recovered—see for instance the examples in Garvey's work on contingent queries (Garvey, 1977). They may be imbedded. The work of Labov and Fanshel (1977) revealed an almost infinite regress in the origins and consequences of particular events, if one chose to push the analysis. At each level one can see an act as a means to realize a move at a higher level. On the other hand, for the social versus activity analysis, a move may be codetermined at a higher level. Only in the youngest children do we see sequences that are rather beadlike, lacking complex imbedding, so that act A occurs before act B, but is not projected as a means.

We are aware of this problem, but have not found easy ways to solve it. Most existing interactional codes are relatively shallow in the strata of analysis they address by not seeing moves as realizations of larger plans. Since the comprehension of speech acts depends critically on action schemata, we need to know more about activity contexts. We have not progressed far enough in finding out their properties to project expectations that will help develop theories of production or comprehension. A model of this kind of enterprise, which relies on the ideal-typical analysis, was Sinclair and Coulthard's (1975) work on traditional classrooms. Ethnological work suggests that in fact children do know something of this structure as described by Sinclair and Coulthard: that it is virtual and tacit implicitly in form, even if sequences do not fit the precise format described. Because tasks in homes are more complex, we cannot expect to find so orderly a scheme. But their work does provide an example of an attack on the problem of levels in terms of a phrase structure model in which each construct has systematic realizations at a lower level.

Speech acts are hypothetical constructs. A speech act is not identifiable by the activity or goal in view or by the words used. Yet the notion of a speech act comes from common language; the speech act is clearly a commonsense notion, a category in everyday thinking about what we do. The categories we used in coding were in part these commonsense categories, such as offering, warning, threatening, and giving permission, and in part combinations, such as directives, prohibitions, ownership claims, and intentions. But because these are inferred categories, we began to notice that the inferences are based on complex social factors.

If A says to B, *Can I help you*, most of us, out of context, would assume this was an offer. However, we have seen such utterances from adults **after** beginning the helping action, so the child had no chance to refuse. Children have told us that offers are different from other control acts because they permit you to refuse. Thus, although the utterance takes the overt verbal form of a typical offer, we coded it as a statement of intention or a directive, depending on circumstances, when the other could not refuse.[3]

Further, if a small child comes to an adult doing a complex task and says, *Can I help you?* we might interpret it as a permission request, such as *Can I cross the street?* or *Can I have a cookie?*. The difference between an offer and a permission request here lies in the assumed capacities of adult versus child in the task at hand. If the petitioner has greater or equal ability to provide help, we might think it an offer, if very little, an intrusion calling for permission.

This example is given to show that the same words, indeed the same ultimate action, can be considered different at the interpretive, speech act level by virtue of differences in assumptions about relative skills, power to refuse, and relative benefit. When we code and when we report past experiences

[3] Other approaches to these problems include treating certain constellations of form and social features as central or normal and others as defective, an approach common in speech act analyses. We had to decide that form and speakers' intention were analytically separate, in order to discover what was interesting about strategic choices of form. It is statistically true that certain forms predominate for certain acts.

in everyday life, we are making such assumptions. And of course, two con-versational partners could very easily make different assessments of these social elements and therefore classify the same act differently, without the difference being visible in the interaction.

So our coding by speech acts, both those involving action by the addressee (warnings, directives, prohibitions, and ownership claims), and those involving action by the speaker (offers, promises, permission requests, and intentions), rests on complex social inferences. We did not know this when we began.

Because of earlier work on the social nuancing of requests, I had assumed that social information about role, rank, distance, cost of task, and so on would be manifested in two ways. One would be in the major verbal form chosen for the head act. An example would be, *Bring me a drink* versus *Could you bring me a drink?*. A second way would be through nuancing by markers, such as saying *please*, using slang, address forms, minimizers, conditionals, or past tense. For instance, *Could you lend me a little sugar?* or *I wanted to ask you . . ..*

By opening up our analysis beyond requests to other forms of social control acts, we found that exactly the same activity goals might be served by different speech acts: A child might drink juice after an offer or a directive. But we are not sure of the importance of this difference. We are not sure whether the social classification of acts that we make as coders, as observers, corresponds to a major level of decision making by participants. And we are not sure whether it makes any difference that we have included both natural-language categories such as **offer** and invented categories such as **directive**. We are calling attention to the problem of the analytic status of speech acts since it is bound to affect research until a successful theory of action is developed.

Summary of problems. The methodological focus of this work makes it important to be candid about problems. I have explained reservations about the observational work, because many of these are general issues affecting classroom observations as well. To summarize, in our analysis and coding, we concentrated on sequences of social control acts, which made activity con-sequences primary and social information secondary. We assumed a common— and indeed a single—focus on the action of the other. We have not solved the problem of the larger contexts, sequences, and options within which the speech act level is imbedded. We found that the speech act was hypothetical, resting on social assumptions by the coders at least.

Having classified a speech act type, we identified an event context and verbal form, and various accompanying characteristics of each social control act. The results of this analysis are indicated in the following.

Results

CONVERSATIONAL TEXTS

Verbal Forms

A second major system of classification, which we saw as a scheme of realization for speech acts (Table 3.1), was to classify by verbal form (Table 3.2). This scheme was based on considerable experience with the observation of adult directives (Ervin-Tripp, 1976) and some theoretical notions about relevant dimensions. The scheme is based on a division between **explicit** forms, which mention what is wanted, and **implicit** verbalizations, which do not. (We have avoided the term **indirect**. This is commonly used to refer to explicit forms that are not imperatives, but are used to express directives, such as, *Can you get off my foot, please.*) What is explicit depends on the speaker's purpose. Warnings state a hazard, ownership claims identify an owner of property or place; directives, prohibitions, and intentions state an act and goal–object. Explicit statements identify the object desired plus a desire or need verb. Implicit wording includes statements that could be linked by a *therefore* to an explicit form, statements of discomfort, or questions about preconditions: *I'm hungry., It's lunchtime., Are there any apples?* The transcripts included many ellipses and gesturing or crying, which could be interpreted only by context.

Crosscutting the dimension of explicitness was the linguistic dimension, imperative–statement–question, important because of its consequences for response. Tables 3.1 and 3.2 show the frequency of these categories in coded

Table 3.1
Control Act Types by Children[a]

Inferred speech act	Example	Percentage
Directives	*Can I have some of yours?*	59
	I need those scissors.	
	Give me that.	
Prohibitions	*Quit it.*	17
	Use your own fork.	
Offers	*Here.*	10
	I'll do it for you.	
Solicit permission	*Can I go outside?*	6
Ownership	*This one is yours.*	4
	Mine.	
Intentions	*I'm gonna sit in your lap.*	3
	Here goes your tower!	
Warnings	*Look out!*	1

[a] Data base 911 acts in families.

Table 3.2
Form of Head Control Act by Children[a]

Verbal form of act	Example	Percentage
Explicit forms		
Imperatives	*Get off me!*	32
Explicit questions and tagged forms	*Do you want some?*	11
	Could you lift this?	
	Bring it, will you?	
Explicit statements	*I want some too.*	25
	That's mine.	
Permission questions	*Can I have your brush?*	5
Permission statements	*You can play with that if you want.*	3
Ellipsis (no verb)	*No. Here. Mine.*	16
Implicit forms		
Cries and gestures only		2
Implicit questions	*Where are your shoes?*	1
Aversive state	*I'm cold. John hit me.*	1
Conditions or consequences	*I finished.*	5

[a] Data base 911 acts in families.

family samples totaling 10,000 lines (911 child control acts), in 4 white, middle-class families in California.

Context

We improvised activity context categories for our work. It became obvious that there were major differences in every way between activity settings, which was hardly surprising.

Context categories (in boldface). **Mealtimes** differed a great deal from family to family. In some cases there was a considerable amount of activity management. In the control acts, more permission requests occurred than elsewhere, even though directives to act dominated the control acts, especially in statement form such as, *I want more ice cream.*

The construction of play illustrated more interesting differences. Others have observed stages in play, such as negotiation, stage setting, and enactment. These of course can be recycled any time. **Negotiation** was typically verbal, so prohibitions were rare, but future-oriented acts such as intent statements, offers, and requests for permission were increased.

M2   *Let's play choo-choo train.*
F4   *No.*
M2   *Yeah.*
F4   *No. I don't want to.*

M2   *Yeah. Yeah. Let's play choo-choo train.*
(M2)   *Could we play choo-choo train?* (to adult)
Adult   Uh, yeah. Why don't you play, uh, choo-choo train?

In this negotiation, the little brother's directive was refused repeatedly, until he asked permission of the adult who finally gave a directive in his behalf.

Stage setting is identified by its focus on roles, props, and territory, and by its high frequency of ownership claims, directives, and prohibitions. Because actual places and props are involved, ellipses are frequent. Disputes lead to an especially high rate of refusals, as the details of play are negotiated. Younger children are so involved in negotiation of objects and territory that the play may be ended after stage setting and never reach enactment.

We divided organized play into construction, role playing, and other structured play. **Construction,** including cooking, necessarily involves many materials, sequences of action, and allocation of goods. There was a high frequency of disputing about where to put objects and who was to do it. Prohibitions were higher than in any other context, directives to act were common, and children often were so preoccupied they ignored each other. Ellipses, of course, were very frequent.

Role playing is the opposite of construction. It is primarily verbal with props invented through fantasy. Ellipsis is rare since the language makes roles, props, and actions clear, *Now I'm washing the dishes.* Directives to act were unusually high—77% of control acts. They are an important vehicle for signaling roles, both in terms of their frequency and their form. Imperatives were more common than elsewhere, as were explicit questions (polite requests), which can indicate deference. Both Andersen (1978) and Mitchell-Kernan and Kernan (1977) found that role-playing directives differed in frequency and form according to role. "In many cases the sheer density of these directives, that is, their rapid delivery in an extended and uninterrupted series, often at the beginning of the role-playing episode, indicates that their broader function in these instances was to establish a relationship of dominance-submission betweeen the characters in the play [Mitchell-Kernan & Kernan, 1977, p. 201]." In addition, cooperation in the game required submissiveness to control acts (unless the game called for rebellion) and, of course, the children did not ignore directives properly issued in a role. Since both refusing and ignoring were substantial in other contexts, this high compliance rate is unusual. Of course, one could say these are "mock control acts."

Structured play is a mixture including ownership claims, offers, prohibitions, and directives. A rather high refusal rate occurred in comparison to other play enactment.

Activity structure. Like semantic categories, these structures cut across language and persist even when there are serious obstacles, such as primitive

knowledge of a language. In the following text recorded in France, playing
with a French child a child who had spoken French about 3 months set up
a classroom scene with herself as "maîtresse." This 8-year-old child was so-
phisticated at role-playing behavior. Although the sequences are often strange
for a classroom, the phrases alone clearly have the intonation of a teacher
(T = "teacher"; C = child).

1. T: *Les enfants! Tu viens ici!* [both giggle] *Oui! Et quoi, c'est quoi,
   toi le- c'est le- c'est quoi le nom à toi?* (Children come here! Yes!
   And what, what is it, you- it- what is the name of you?
   . . ..)
2. C: *Sylvie* [giggles] . . . .
3. T: *Sylvie quoi? . . . Allez. Vite.* (Sylvie what? Hurry up.)
4. T: *Sylvie. Tu pas comprends ça, aujourd'hui. Mais, tu comprends? Tu
   pas comprends ça. Mais tu comprends. Mais pas comprends donc
   ça, à l'école. Tu comprends?* (You not understand, today, But,
   you get it? You not understand this. But **you** do. Not understand
   this in school. Understand?)
5. C: *Oui.* (Yes.)
6. T: [as she writes on slate] *C'est trois comme ça. C'est comme ça.
   C'est . . Bon, alors c'est sept francs. Bon alors, c'est sept francs.
   Sept. Sept francs. Sept. Bon alors, sept francs.* (It's three like this.
   It's like this. It's, good, then it's seven francs. Okay, it's seven
   francs. Seven. Seven francs. Seven, okay seven francs.)
7. C: *Regarde.* (Look.)
8. T: *Sept. Attends, attends. C'est ça. Bon. Mais deux fois. Deux fois
   sept égale, égale.* (Seven. Wait, wait. That's it. Good. But two
   times. Two times seven equals, equals.)
9. C: *Quatorze.* [giggles] (Fourteen.)
10. T: *Ou.* (Or.)
11. C: *Sept fois sept.* (Seven times seven.)
12. T: *Sept fois deux égale quatorze.* [long pauses between words as she
    says them while writing them on slate] *Tu comprends?* (Seven
    times two equals fourteen. Understand?)
13. C: *Oui.* (Yes.)
14. T: *C'est ça et c'est ça.* [writing] *C'est quatorze. Bon, c'est à toi.*
    (That's it, and that. It's fourteen. Good, it's your turn.)
15. C: *C'est pas comme ça.* (That's not it.)
16. T: *Sylvie mais tu comprends, eh?* (Sylvie, but you understand?)
17. C: *Oui. Comme ça.* [goes toward corner of room] [giggles] (Yes.
    Like this.)
18. T: *Non, tu viens là! Tu- tu- tu es pas là! Sylvie!* [crossly] *Sylvie!
    Allez, vite.* [giggling of Sylvie as Maîtresse pursues her with a

little stick] (No, you come here! You- you- you don't go there! Sylvie, Sylvie! Hurry up!) [both giggle]

In Turn 4 the teacher tries, in her primitive French to explain that her partner should pretend to be more ignorant. She has the pupil sit in front of her on the floor while she sits on the bed, up front like a traditional teacher, writing on her blackboard. She arranges what presumably is a traditional demonstration of commutation. To liven the proceedings, the "pupil" rebels, giggling to show she is still cooperative, but having a joke of the game, which gives the "maîtresse" a chance to use a cross tone of voice and threaten her with a stick. (On her first day in the French school the "maîtresse" had been very disturbed by the tears of a classmate who was struck by the teacher.) Her representation of a French maîtresse contains information on how the teacher gives orders, how she teaches, and how she punishes.

Role playing provides evidence of children's representations of "proper" roles. They can be at considerable variance with individual experience with such roles in the family, for example, in cases where a child's culture teaches a norm. There may also be some evidence of a personal experience because of the lack of exposure to French play norms. The role playing displays the child's beliefs about activity structure in classrooms.

Social Meaning

By the time they were of school age, the children in our sample could deploy a full range of verbal means to express control wishes toward others, including implicit acts or hints. There are a number of determinants besides social meaning, such as expression of solidarity or politeness, as discussed in the literature on speech acts and politeness (Brown & Levinson, 1978; Ervin-Tripp, 1976).

Frequency and social relations. Children do not choose randomly among potential partners. The frequency of moves to control specific others may be a result of possession of the desired resources, familiarity, cooperativeness, submission to coercion, or importance to the child as a potential partner for social needs.

Factors affecting verbal form of control acts. Choice of form for a control act can be determined by both nonsocial and social factors. These include:

1. **The attention or concern** of the speaker of the moment. The speaker may focus on the problem condition: *I'm hungry.* The speaker may focus on the goal object: *I want an apple.* Or the speaker may focus on the partner's projected activity: *Hand me an apple.* Although these changes in focus may be strategically selected so that focus on a problem may be more subtle than

focus on the partner's act, they may also arise from attention. These two sources may be indistinguishable.

2. **Projected contextual factors or probable external obstacles.** An imaginative or well-practiced partner knows what obstacles there are to achieving a goal. A focus on these obstacles can be a spontaneous concern, or it may be a device to relieve the addressee of responsibility. For example: *Are there some blue markers? Is Mrs. Nellermoe there?*

3. **Formal status marking** for high rank addressees or strangers. Some speakers use this routinely and conventionally even for easy requests. For example: *Pardon me, could you . . .?*

4. **Social marking addressed to anticipated internal resistance** by the addressee. The form the marking takes varies. The anticipated resistance itself can be focused on by conventional forms such as, *can you, would you, would you mind, would you care to.* There may be payments by vocatives, *please,* and minimizers and grammatical devices for diverting directness. These include passives, past tense, and conditionals (e.g., *If you wanted to Xerox these.*). The social factors stimulating these payments have been described as recompense for face-threatening acts by Brown and Levinson (1978). They were found by Ervin-Tripp (1976) to include physical distance, territory, rank of addressee, high cost or effort called for, and preoccupation of the addressee with other activities. Formal status marking may arise from the assessment of anticipated internal resistance, or it may be independent.

5. **Emotional tone of the speaker.** This can affect intonation, increase explicitness, or produce sarcasm. And, of course, there is ample evidence that social features such as rapport can be signaled, for instance, by humorous allusion through hints, which imply shared assumptions.

6. **Abbreviation or conventionalization from common use.** When a particular constellation of circumstances occurs often, it becomes possible to index the speech act very economically. There can be ellipses, or such allusions as, *It's noon."* Because certain external obstacles are recurrent, reference to them can become the conventional directive and lose the social advantages of not being explicit. In Brown and Levinson's (1978) terms, *Is the boss in?* ceases to be off-record since its purpose is obvious. The inferential process is abbreviated by common use.

7. **Activity.** The activity context indirectly affects the forms of social control acts, because the context changes (*a*) the focus of the speaker; (*b*) probable external obstacles; (*c*) roles and rights expected, and therefore what is seen as an infringement or cost; and (*d*) what is frequent from repeated use, hence abbreviated or conventionalized. Activity contexts lead to differences in the kinds of speech acts children address to peers as compared to adults. For example, stage setting is a characteristic of young children's peer play that is not usual in interaction with adults. Stage setting is marked by a high

frequency of both ownership claims and prohibitions. Both of these speech acts are rare in children's speech to adults, perhaps as a result of the types of activities in which they are partners.

Formal variation in conversation. Do children use formal variation for social purposes? As I have shown, formal variation can arise out of attention or concern. However, I pointed out in an earlier study (Ervin-Tripp, 1977) that by the age of 2.5 years children employ indirect requests in the form of explicit questions or imbedded imperatives such as *Can you help me?* to their seniors, more than to peers. (And clearly, of course, they understand such forms by that age.) What we found rare then was evidence of the use of hints or implicit forms that do not mention the desired act, which are of course quite frequent in adult use.

Our data from the 911 social control acts in this sample indicate the two types of acts that are strongly differentiated by addressee are explicit questions (polite requests or permission requests) and hints (conditions or consequence statements and questions). Controlling for speech act by looking only at directives, we find that 3- and 4-year-old children do not hint to younger children, but do hint (implicit requests) to adults. The children also differentiate between parents and researchers, asking more explicit questions (polite requests) to the researchers, giving more hints or explicit statements of desires or needs to parents (Table 3.3).

Mitchell-Kernan and Kernan (1977) reported that in peer speech, polite requests seemed to be used to disarm resistance to different tasks, or to maintain social distance or coolness. If this is the case in our sample, we might explain our findings that polite requests are overall the least effective in getting compliance. If polite requests are particularly used on occasions when internal resistance is expected, they would be least successful. Compliance is higher when older children address younger children than the reverse; that is, compliance directly reflects social power. The polite request as a social marker of age and rank implies expected failure.

Formal variation in elicitation experiments. How are these social effects on form reflected in speech in more controlled conditions? In an experiment described earlier (Gordon et al., 1980), children made requests to an unfamiliar adult for marker pens or for a letter to take home to parents. We found that the children in K–2 and those in Grades 3–5 differed in the forms selected. None used either direct or imbedded imperatives to solicit from unfamiliar adults. Instead, the younger children expressed needs (as they did to the mother in the family study) or asked locations (*Where's the letter?*) more often than the older children. The older children asked permission (*Can I have . . .?*), identified obstacles to compliance (*Are there any . . .?*; *Do you have . . .?*),

Table 3.3

Form of Directives by Age of Speaker and of Addressee (in percentage)

	2-year-olds			3-year-olds			4-year-olds			5- to 8-year-olds		
	O	P	R[a]	O	P	R	O	P	R	O	P	R
Ellipsis	10.3	11.1	(11.1)[b]	—	16.3	—	2.5	20.8	18.0	11.1	7.9	—
Imperative	33.3	25.9	(11.1)	(70)	7.0	55.1	52.5	47.2	52.0	74.1	39.5	(100)
Explicit question (polite request)	—	—	(22.2)	(30)	2.3	28.6	12.5	9.4	22.0	—	10.5	—
Explicit statement (need or want)	50.0	63.0	(55.6)	—	72.1	10.2	32.5	13.2	6.0	14.8	26.3	—
Implicit	3.3	—	—	—	2.3	6.1	—	9.7	2.0	—	15.8	—
N	30	27	9	10	43	49	40	53	50	27	38	7

[a] O = older children; P = parents; R = researchers.

[b] Percentages based on unusually small Ns are in parentheses.

or displaced responsibility (*She told me to get* . . .) more often than the younger children. They often combined several of these strategies. For instance, *Do you have a blue marker I can use?* (obstacle plus permission). The older group used strategies that are more other-centered. They conventionally give to the listener the right or the excuse not to comply.

Compliance

Do children learn polite requests and hints because they are more successful? Do they learn by reinforcement? In the natural conversations we videotaped we were strongly impressed that the major determinants of success were grossly unrelated to form. They seemed to depend on many other variables. For instance, many demands were inconvenient or impossible to carry out. Some children kept asking to go outside the camera range, for instance. A major factor in success was the relative age of the speaker and listener. Older children complied only 27% with control acts of their juniors, whereas compliance was 60% in the reverse case (rejecting ambiguous cases).

Older listeners were less attentive to the interventions of little children. As children mature, their contributions become more relevant, but even when relevance is controlled, older speakers have an advantage in gaining attention (Ervin-Tripp, 1979). Younger children are more restricted in their means of expressing purposes. On second tries, they simply repeat what they said before, which turns off listeners. School-age children are more likely to try new tactics, or change the addressee to seek the most effective means. Older children more often figure out what the opposition is about and provide supporting explanations; these are needed primarily when persuading junior partners.

The most telling evidence, however, that compliance is related to social power rather than to the means deployed, is that polite requests are the least successful form in terms of total figures. We also found that there is no increment in success probability for the same difficulty of demand, when hints or polite requests are offered (Ervin-Tripp, O'Connor, & Rosenberg, in press).

Comprehension Experiments

If 3-year-olds begin to use hints when speaking to adults, then hints might also be intelligible to them. We have been studying children's interpretations of experimentally situated directives that are merely hints. We used pictures and real-life situations as described earlier. The clearest finding was that as soon as children have a strong sense of action sequence and right and wrong behavior, any mention of a prohibited act suffices, if it comes from the mother. When it came from peers it was less effective. Children regarded hints as odd. For instance, if children were pictured painting all over the living room, *Are you painting on the walls?* seemed a somewhat weak way for a mother to talk. However, the children, as early as age 3, knew what was to be done, even when no one spoke or said something so silly.

In cases where real help was needed, the youngest children were less used to helping adults and less informed about what should happen next. In getting them to help, explicit forms such as, *Can you get me my purse?* were needed at 3 years old, though less so later. We found that for school-age children, any mention of a needed object, except the most anomalous, got cooperation— even *Oh, my pencil.*

One interpretation of these results is that children develop pragmatic intelligence. By calling attention to a problem situation, the speaker sets off a train of inference to correct the situation. For example, *Oh, my purse* calls attention to the separation of the purse from its owner. *The door's closed* calls attention to an obstacle in getting the groceries into the kitchen. Pragmatic intelligence can be used with relatively little linguistic information, if the situation is familiar.

In our recent work we have tested second-language learners in order to separate pragmatic sophistication from linguistic skill. We used the same picture stories and real requests for help described earlier, with a group of English-speaking children of primary-school age, who were in French schools. Although the full study is not yet completed because we are compiling control group data, we have observed some results that differ from our American samples. In the case of hints to help such as, *Is my purse there?* a surprising number of Swiss seemed to be attentive just to the literal processing of the sentences. They answered questions, but did not offer help.

We also introduced a new procedure. For the "forbidden act" pictures such as fighting and making messes, we experimentally proposed sarcastic remarks by the mother. A common maternal strategy in Europe is a rebuke such as *Oh that's really great* or *Go right on, keep it up.* European children recognize such phrases as criticism.

We introduced such sarcastic remarks to second-language learners to see if their pragmatic intelligence would override the opposite literal meaning. In many cases it did not. The children in such cases found the sarcasm confusing. Some said the mother was lying. The children who heard the sarcasm as rebuke reported that their teachers talked that way too. The children had relatively little access to French families, so if they had not heard sarcastic teachers they were puzzled. We have not yet analyzed all the French data, so we do not know why pragmatic reasoning takes priority in some children and linguistic processing in others, in the artificial conditions of experiments.

What is most striking to us about the discussions with the children following the English experiments, is that they do not necessarily think about motives. When we asked what the mother wanted in the picture stories, the children went back to look, as if they considered motive for the first time. In many children, estimations of the consequences of various responses and the learning of effectiveness of different strategies do not depend on imputing purposes. What takes on much greater importance is the child's understanding of patterns of events. Sinclair and Coulthard (1975) implied such a control method; they pointed out that any mention of a required or prohibited act could function as a directive in a classroom. We might call this control by routine. However, it applies very broadly, since it seems to explain why 3-year-olds open the door to the mother with groceries even when they do not think *Is the door open?* means she wants it opened. Compliance in such cases is not cooperation with the speaker's intent. Children take action to keep a situation normal, to make an event follow an expected course.

Discussion

MUTUAL COMPREHENSION IN CLASSROOMS

Communication in a school or family that depends heavily on cooperation and on an understanding of routines in the normal course of events can easily be disrupted. The teacher may consider children who fail to do what is expected uncooperative, but there may be other causes. A newcomer unfamiliar with routines, or an unattentive child who does not notice abbreviated cues, or a child who expects a social style with more explicitness would have trouble appearing cooperative. Teachers may find it irritating to have to call the children's attention constantly and to develop explicit control forms for such children. Among adults, explicitness implies distance or unfriendliness (Ervin-Tripp, 1976). We can only surmise that ethnic and social class differences in social control styles could lead to misunderstanding whenever there is ambiguity about the normal course of events.

Some ethnic groups rely on explicit polite requests to mark status differences. Some use them upwards, but not downwards in rank and age. Some groups rely heavily on allusion and hints (e.g., Greek-Americans studied by Tannen, 1979) and some carefully train children to understand hints from infancy (e.g., the Japanese).[4] We might expect an easier enculturation into a classroom relying on hints and allusions for Japanese children than for children from families relying on explicitness in adult speech to children. On the other side, of course, children taught to hint may not be understood by their teachers or their peers from other ethnic groups.

---

[4] Patricia Clancy, from a manuscript prepared for a book on comparative studies of language development to be edited by Dan Slobin.

SOCIAL MEANING

Since the signaling of social differences by children seems to start as early as the third year, we may look for factors entering into the development of diverse communicative strategies varied by context. One frequently proposed explanation is reinforcement. That is, polite requests are more effective. We know that parents consciously teach children certain polite forms such as *please* though they themselves usually rely on more complex ways to be polite. It is our impression, however, that the granting of requests by and large depends on factors other than verbal form. Although a fine-tuned testing of this finding depends on better controls, we would suggest a competing or at least complementary hypothesis. Like the learning of grammar, learning of social styles arises partly out of children's interest in sounding appropriate. The dramatic evidence we see in role play, when children simulate teachers or parents for instance (Andersen, 1978), cannot be based on any obvious direct reinforcement history.

Summary

Our work has focused on the understanding of the development of children's strategies for getting other people to do what they want and for interpreting the speech of others. Such a focus puts activity at the center and makes information of interest only when it serves to persuade. We have developed several methods of studying these processes, which include analysis of natural conversations, elicitation, and structured interpretation experiments. These experiments differ from earlier work on speech evaluation in that they put the critical item in a context of activities and of people with social properties, so that we could find how social factors affect understanding and judgment.

The findings regarding comprehension indicate a heavy reliance on routing knowledge and pragmatic intelligence. They imply that young listeners are more attuned to proceeding with the normal action than with trying to figure out speaker's intentions—unless something unusual or discordant occurs.

Our work on family interaction has uncovered some serious conceptual difficulties in the analysis of speech acts. These include multiple functions, levels of analysis, and, in the role of the hypothetical construct, the speech act itself, in language use. In examining speech acts, we saw that confirming or altering social relationships can be done simultaneously with conveying information about desired activities through social control acts. The argument has been made that social meanings such as rapport and deference are conveyed by the frequency and type of control act chosen, the verbal form of the act, and nuancing by various markers.

Children make use of the possibilities of form variation appropriately very early. The growth in their flexibility and ability to supply supporting arguments continues in the school years. Between early and late primary school, social control acts to strangers shift focus from being ego-based on what is wanted to being other-based on potential obstacles, permission, and responsibility. We have argued that the development of competence in social control acts may depend only partially on direct reinforcement, but may, like grammar, come from close observation of others. Polite requests were more often ignored or refused than other forms, so they were not, on the whole, rewarded. Social differences between groups in the explicitness of social control moves influence the success of classroom communication.

Acknowledgments

The data collection and analysis owe a great deal to David Paul Gordon, Georgette Stratos, Ruth Bennett, Catherine O'Connor, Amy Strage, Nancy Budwig, Susan Gelphman, and Miriam Petruck. David Gordon provided valuable criticism of the draft.

References

Andersen, E. *Learning to speak with style*. Unpublished doctoral dissertation, Stanford University, 1978.

Brown, P., & Levinson, S. Universals in language usage: Politeness phenomena. In E. N. Goody (Ed.), *Questions and politeness: Strategies in social interaction* (Cambridge Papers in Social Anthropology Series No. 8). Cambridge, Mass.: Cambridge University Press, 1978.

Clancy, P. Acquisition of Japanese. In D. Slobin (Ed.), *The cross-linguistic study of language acquisition*. Hillsdale, N.J.: Lawrence Erlbaum Associates, in preparation.

Cook-Gumperz, J. Persuasive talk: The social organization of children's talk. In J. Green & C. Wallat (Ed.), *Ethnography and language in educational settings*. Norwood, N.J.: Ablex, 1981.

Ervin-Tripp, S. M. Is Sybil there? The structure of some American–English directives. *Language in Society*, 1976, 5, 25–66.

Ervin-Tripp, S. M. Wait for me, roller-skate. In S. Ervin-Tripp & C. Mitchell-Kernan (Eds.), *Child discourse*. New York: Academic Press, 1977.

Ervin-Tripp, S. M. Children's verbal turn-taking. In E. Ochs & B. Schieffelin (Eds.), *Developmental pragmatics*. New York: Academic Press, 1979.

Ervin-Tripp, S. M., O'Connor, C., & Rosenberg, J. Language and power in the family. In C. Kramerae & M. Schulz (Eds.), *Language and power*. Champaign: University of Illinois Press, in press.

Garvey, C. Requests and responses in children's speech. *Journal of Child Language*, 1975, 2, 41–59.

Garvey, C. The contingent query: A dependent act in conversation. In M. Lewis & L. Rosenblum (Eds.), *Interaction, conversation, and the development of language: The origin of behavior* (Vol. 5). New York: John Wiley and Sons, 1977.

Gordon, D. P., Budwig, N., Strage, A., & Carrell, P. *Children's requests to unfamiliar adults: Form, social function, age variation*. Boston University Conference on Language Development, October 1980.

Labov, W., & Fanshel, D. *Therapeutic discourse.* New York: Academic Press, 1977.

Mitchell-Kernan, C., & Kernan, K. Pragmatics of directive choice among children. In C. Mitchell-Kernan & S. Ervin-Tripp (Eds.), *Child discourse.* New York: Academic Press, 1977.

Sinclair, J., & Coulthard, R. M. *Towards an analysis of discourse: The English used by teachers and pupils.* London: Oxford University Press, 1975.

Tannen, D. *Ethnicity as conversational style* (Working Paper No. 55). Austin, Texas: Southwest Educational Development Laboratory, 1979.

4

Learning through Argument in a Preschool[1]

CELIA GENISHI
MARIANNA DI PAOLO

Sociolinguists have taken a variety of approaches to studying the form and content of children's discourse. Some have analyzed particular speech acts, such as directives and requests (Wilkinson & Calculator, Chapter 6, this volume; Ervin-Tripp, 1976), whereas others have looked at speech events, such as narratives (Kernan, 1977) and arguments (Boggs, 1978; Brenneis & Lein, 1977; Eisenberg & Garvey, 1981). Neither speech acts nor events have been investigated extensively, and work on theoretical and methodological problems in studying children's discourse is just beginning. In this chapter, we focus on a speech event, the argument, as it appears in the spontaneous speech of seven preschoolers, 3–5 years old. We attempt to analyze the children's arguments in terms of children's knowledge as it is reflected in the content and structure of their arguments. The following questions are addressed:

1. What kinds of arguments do children have in the naturalistic setting of an informal preschool?
2. What do arguments show about children's knowledge and learning?
3. How are the children's arguments structured?

[1] The research reported here was funded by a Spencer Foundation Seed Grant to the senior author.

49

Related Research

Literature related to children's arguments, also called quarrels, conflicts, and adversative episodes, is not abundant. Early investigators asked what nursery-school children between the ages of 2 and 5 years argued about, how often they argued, and what the effect of arguments was on social development. Dawe (1934) analyzed 200 spontaneous quarrels in a thorough descriptive study of 40 children between 25 and 65 months. Children were observed during free play in nursery school. The average duration of a quarrel was 23 seconds; boys quarreled more than girls; quarrels decreased as children got older; and the majority of quarrels started over questions of object possession. Green (1933a, 1933b) focused on the relationship between preschoolers' friendships and quarreling and between the kind of group play and quarreling. One of her conclusions was that quarrels could be socially beneficial since they encouraged children to be "good sports."

The cognitive benefits of arguments or conflicts have been emphasized by Piagetians. Piaget (1959) points out the importance of children's social interactions in developing their ability to reason. His interest is in "genuine arguments" that occur only when a speaker can take the viewpoint of the listener and offer reasons or explanations to argue for fair solutions. According to Piaget, children are unlikely to have genuine arguments until age 7 or 8. In the Piagetian tradition, recent investigators (e.g., Botvin & Murray, 1975; Miller & Brownell, 1975) have tested the effect of arguing on 6- to 9-year-olds' ability to conserve. Botvin and Murray suggest that social conflicts over the solution to a conservation problem are no more effective in inducing conservation than is modeling. Miller and Brownell found that conservers arguing in a conservation task with nonconservers are more persuasive than nonconservers.

In contrast, sociolinguists have been interested in children's arguments as a discourse phenomenon. Brenneis and Lein (1977) and Lein and Brenneis (1978) have done a comprehensive analysis of role-played arguments of first through eighth graders in three speech communities: white American, black American, and Fiji Indian. Children were asked to argue about "whose ball it is" and "who is the strongest or smartest." The investigators analyzed prosodic features, sequencing, and content of the arguments and concluded that role-played arguments in all three groups of children share common elements. Arguments did not represent a breakdown in communication but, instead, were rule-governed and cooperatively constructed by participants. Argumentative sequences were made up of utterances that could be described by 13 content categories (e.g., threat, insult, moral persuasion, simple assertion, nonword vocal signals). In addition, the arguments followed three basic patterns: (a) repetition, in which speakers simply repeat their utterances in successive turns; (b) escalation, in which successive statements are more powerfully stated than previous utterances; and (c) inversion. Inversion involves an utterance, such as an assertion, and its inverse, such as a denial.

CHILD 1: *You're dumb.* (assertion)
CHILD 2: *No, I'm not.* (denial, or inverse of assertion)
CHILD 1: *Yes, you are.*
CHILD 2: *No, I'm not.*

Most relevant to the focus of our study is the investigation of spontaneous arguments by Eisenberg and Garvey (1981) and Boggs (1978). Because our analysis builds on their studies, their analytic methods are presented in some detail. Like Brenneis and Lein, Eisenberg and Garvey recorded arguments of dyads videotaped in a laboratory playroom. The 108 subjects in the latter study, however, were of preschool age, ranging from 2 years, 10 months (2:10) to 5 years, 7 months (5:7). Eisenberg and Garvey were concerned with sequencing of discourse within a particular context, which they called an adversative episode or conflict. This was defined as "the interaction which grows out of an opposition to a request for action, an assertion, or an action [p. 3]." The episode ends with a resolution of conflict; resolution is the interactive goal.

The uniqueness of Eisenberg and Garvey's analysis was its focus on the resolution of conflict and on the strategies by which children reach resolutions. Unlike Brenneis and Lein (1977) and Boggs (1978), who viewed arguments as cultural conventions or routines, Eisenberg and Garvey treated an argument primarily as a problem that is jointly solved through discourse and, secondarily, as an interactive ritual. Their perspective was both sociolinguistic and Piagetian. Solutions to arguments could be analyzed as more or less adaptive, depending on how well a child takes the viewpoint of the other and whether a compromise is reached.

According to Eisenberg and Garvey, the structure of a conflict can be described by the nature of the "initial opposition" (the utterance that begins the conflict) and the "strategies" that follow the opposition (pp. 15–21). The five kinds of initial opposition are (a) a simple negative (e.g., *no*); (b) a related reason or justification; (c) a countering move or alternative proposal; (d) temporizing; and (e) evading or hedging. The nine strategies that can follow are

1. Insistence: Support for a previous utterance that adds no new information
2. Mitigation or aggravation: Paraphrase of previous request that either increases or decreases in politeness
3. Reasons

4. Counter: An alternative proposal
5. Conditional directives: Two linked complex propositions—the first is a promise, and the second, a directive
6. Compromise: Proposal for some form of sharing
7. Requests for explanation
8. Physical force
9. Ignores

This episode contains an example of the fourth strategy, counter.

> CHILD 1:   0. *I have to drive the truck.*
> CHILD 2:   1. *No. I'm gonna drive it.*
> CHILD 1:   2. *You could play with this. This could be a snake. But this could be a snake.* (holds out snake)
> CHILD 2:   3. (getting off) *Ok.* [p. 160]

Utterance 0 is called the antecedent event; utterance 1 is the initial opposition; utterance 2, the counter; and utterance 3, the resolution.

Eisenberg and Garvey concluded that their preschool subjects did not rely only on simple strategies, such as insistence; they also used reasons and requested explanations or justifications for behavior. More than any other, the strategy of giving reasons led to the successful termination of conflicts.

Boggs (1978) presented another view of sequencing in part-Hawaiian children's arguments. Although he focused on a "contradicting routine," his data seemed similar to ours, perhaps because the disputes were recorded in naturalistic group situations. Among 4- and 5-year-olds, the contradicting routine was simple in structure and initiated by one child saying *Not!*. The simplest and most common sequence for Boggs's corpus was what he termed **Sequence I**.

> assertion, claim, or allegation → (followed by) contradiction → repetition of assertion, claim or allegation
> *or*
> supporting argument, allegation, or appeal to authority

Sequence I may be followed by Sequence II.

> (Sequence I →) challenge → supporting argument, allegation, or appeal to authority

Either Sequence I or II may be followed by Sequence III.

> (Sequence I or II →) insult → counter-insult, threat or trial (pp. 330–332)

In the data for 4- and 5-year-olds, claims on desired objects, status, or an attribute (e.g., age) often led to a contradiction. Exclaiming, *Not!*, seemed to be a stylized response that initiated a serious dispute. Children seldom resolved the resulting conflict satisfactorily although older children (10- and 11-year-olds) seemed to end disputes by joking and laughing. Boggs concluded that part-Hawaiian children develop the ability to engage in the contradicting routine as a playful exchange and that adults induct children into the routine by teasing them at an early age. Similarities and contrasts between the categories we present and those of Boggs and others will be included in the next section.

Method

DATA COLLECTION

The data for this study were audiotaped in a small, church-affiliated private school in Austin, Texas, for eight white middle-class 3- to 5-year-olds. Parents of the children were college-educated and professionals. We chose this small group so it would be possible to record an appreciable amount of talk from all children and the teacher without the excessive background noise of a larger classroom. There were three girls and five boys. Ages at the beginning of data collection were: Tessa, 5 years; Jennifer, 5 years; Lee, 4 years; Billy, 5 years; Rhett, 4 years; John, 3 years; Stewart, 3 years; and Tom, 3 years. Tom was often absent and seldom spoke when present so analyses were based on the arguments of the other seven children. The teacher was a woman who had previously taught in preschools and kindergartens for 10 years.

One observer, a graduate student in early childhood education, audio-taped most of the 20 hours of data over a 3-month period. The second author, a graduate student in linguistics, made occasional visits to familiarize herself with the children as she transcribed the audiotapes. The group of children met twice a week, and recordings were made in the morning when children were most active and talkative. In general, audiotapes were made of these activities: free play, in which children could select among several activities; a teacher-directed lesson that lasted from 10 to 15 minutes; cleanup time; singing; and snacks. Teacher-directed lessons occurred once during the morning. Topics were related to science, for example, dinosaurs, bones, and grubworms. The bulk of the children's time was spent in free play.

The main observer focused on one child at a time or on the teacher for 30-minute segments. Her recording equipment consisted of a Sony TC-142 cassette tape-recorder and a unidirectional microphone, placed on a Sony PBR-330 parabolic disc to eliminate as much background noise as possible. She took notes on the context of talk as well as on concurrent nonverbal behaviors, and was an unobtrusive, not a participant observer. Although the classroom was small (less than 400 sq. ft.), children's behavior seemed to be unaffected by the observer's presence and by the use of recording equipment. The teacher noted before observations began that the children were used to visitors' observing. Even the introduction of the parabolic disc, which resembles a miniature radar screen, brought few questions from the children who were generally preoccupied with their own play.

DATA ANALYSIS

The second author began the analysis of data by transcribing entire observations. Because some of what was recorded was not related to arguments, we decided to transcribe only the interactions that might be defined as arguments, along with interactions relevant to the arguments and their interpretation. Our criterion for an argument was derived from Eisenberg and Garvey's (1981) definition of an adversative episode, an interaction that grows out of opposition to a request for action, an assertion, or an action. According to their definition, an argument has three essential parts: an antecedent event, an initial opposition, and a resolution. The following, then, would be an argument.

> A: *That's mine.* (antecedent event)
> B: *No, it's not.* (initial opposition)
> A: *Oh, OK.* (resolution)

In our data, we identified the antecedent events as well as the initial oppositions, but resolutions were not always clear. Our arguments could consist of two turns, an antecedent event followed by an initial opposition. There are two possible reasons for the lack of resolutions. One may have been our use of audiotape only. No video record of nonverbal resolutions was available (e.g., a child hands something to another child to resolve a conflict). The more powerful reason for the small number of resolutions is the nature of the situation in which the data were collected. In Eisenberg and Garvey's study, dyads were videotaped in a playroom. The investigators pointed out that a resolution was necessary because interaction between the pair could not continue without one. In our naturalistic classroom setting, arguments tended to become diffused because of distractions from children outside the arguing dyad or because of the teacher's intervention.

Arguments were marked by both authors in the transcripts. Reliability was established informally by discussing interactions on which we disagreed. A source of unreliability was a tendency to code negative statements as beginnings of arguments when the statements were not "oppositions." In these cases the interactions were not coded as arguments.

All arguments were then categorized by content. Seven themes were identified. Arguments about possession usually started with a claim on a desired object, status, or attribute. There were more arguments of this kind than any other. The category called number was defined by explicit use of cardinal numbers. Arguments about conduct had to do with children's perceptions of correct or appropriate behavior. They often contained requests for action. The truth category referred to disagreements over assertions, such as *Jaguars are friendly*. Arguments over role were similar to arguments over possession and started with claims on a desired role in dramatic play. Oppositions to requests were arguments in which children refused to comply with requests of the form, *Stop doing* X. Finally, the exclusion category had to do with children's limiting activities to select individuals. The frequency counts for content categories are presented in the following section of this chapter.

To answer our question about the structure of arguments we relied on the coding systems of Boggs (1978) and Eisenberg and Garvey (1981). These are the categories we applied:

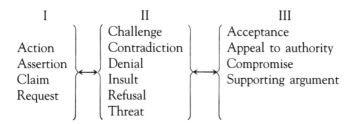

Categories under I function as Eisenberg and Garvey's antecedent events; categories under II, as initial oppositions; and categories under III correspond roughly to resolutions. See Table 4.1 for definitions and examples. The double arrows show that utterances categorized under II can be followed by utterances categorized under I or III and so on. The categories we adapted are chiefly those of Boggs, who collected his data in naturalistic, small-group situations. In our attempt to apply Eisenberg and Garvey's system, which included giving reasons, temporizing, and evading, we found it difficult to distinguish reliably among some of the categories. Eisenberg and Garvey's subjects may have had more complex and developed arguments because they interacted in dyads. The arguments of children in our study were often interrupted or terminated by others.

We assigned the mutually exclusive categories to all utterances in the arguments. An utterance was analogous to a sentence, an idea, or a proposition. Arguments with simple structures were separated from those that were complex. Simple arguments were essentially repetitious. Once the initial opposition occurred, speakers added no new information to the argument. Our definition of a complex argument was one that included an acceptance, appeal to authority, compromise, or supporting argument (in Group III in the preceding

Table 4.1

Definitions and Examples of Categories Applied to Utterances in Arguments

_____

Group I

Action: A nonverbal behavior (e.g., grabbing another's toy; sitting down).

Assertion: A statement, not related to possessing a desired object (e.g., *Rhett wrote all over the place*).

Claim: A statement related to possessing a desired object, status, role, or attribute (e.g., *I was playing with this!*).

Request: An elicitation for goods, services, or information, or for regulating another's behavior (e.g., *And don't talk mean to me any more; can I have the big one?*).

Group II

Challenge: A calling into question, often of a claim (e.g., *You're stronger than my brother?*).

Contradiction: An assertion that opposes the previous speaker's utterance (e.g., *You're not the mother*).

Denial: A negation of the previous utterance that begins with a negative form and may precede a contradiction (e.g., *No, it's not*).

Insult: An affront (e.g., *I don't like you*).

Refusal: A negative form used in response to a request (e.g., *No, I don't want to*).

Threat: A statement of intention to retaliate (e.g., *I'm gonna tell the teacher*).

Group III

Acceptance: An agreement to comply (e.g., *OK*).

Appeal to authority: A reference to an authority's rules or an utterance directed to an authority, usually the teacher (e.g., *She said two can play; teacher, she's had it a long time, and I didn't have it*).

Compromise: An alternative proposal that implies sharing or give-and-take (e.g., *I won't play— I'm just watching*).

Supporting argument: A fact or reason that adds new information to previous utterances (e.g., *I'm stronger than you 'cuz I even can lift my dad up*).

_____

diagram). These kinds of utterances were complex because they indicated that children were attempting a resolution. Instead of repeating themselves, they tried to go beyond the stalemate, add supportive information, or end the argument. As with the analysis of content, our objective in studying structure was to see how arguments reflected what children knew or were learning.

Results

There were 189 arguments in 10.5 hours of audiotape, the recordings in which children, not the teacher, were the focus. The mean number of arguments per half hour was 9; the range per half hour was 1 to 17. Only about 28% (41) of the arguments were complex in structure; the others (148) were simple. Table 4.2 shows the frequency of the 7 kinds of arguments identified by content.

Table 4.2
Frequency of Occurrence of Major Themes in Arguments

Major themes	N	Percentage
Possession	59	31
Number	29	15
Conduct	28	15
Truth	24	13
Role	22	11.5
Opposition to request	22	11.5
Exclusion	5	3
Total	189	100

The first part of this section is an analysis of arguments in the category called number. As they use numbers in conversation, children show both academic and social knowledge. Questions about the structure of arguments are addressed throughout.

ARGUMENTS INVOLVING NUMBERS

We identified 29 arguments involving numbers and subcategorized these according to content. Of these 29, 17 reflected the idea that "more is better." A second category was exclusion, or how many were allowed to join a group. This does not overlap with the exclusion category in Table 4.2. A "miscellaneous" category consisted of a range of themes, including time of day and temperature. Table 4.3 shows the frequency of occurrence for each category.

The seven children's abilities to count or manipulate numbers in conversation varied from child to child, but even the youngest child attempted to use numbers in arguing. The children drew on their academic knowledge to make social points. For example, in the arguments demonstrating that "more is better," numbers helped the speaker assert superiority. Example 1 is part of the longest argument we recorded and shows that age is an important indicator

Table 4.3
Frequency of Occurrence of Themes Related to Number

Themes related to number	N	Percentage
"More is better"	17	59
Exclusion	5	17
Miscellaneous	7	24
Total	29	100

of status. Turns of the argument are numbered. Turn 0 is the antecedent event; turn 1 is the initial opposition. Unnumbered utterances are included to provide context. A description of the argument's structure is on the right.

(1)   "More is better" (Older is better)
      JOHN: I'm (goin' on?) 10! How old
                   are you, Tom?
      TOM: 0. (inaudible—must be 4)   0. Claim
      JOHN: 1. Really?   1. Challenge
      TOM: 2. I'm gonna be 4—3.   2. Claim
      JOHN: 3. Are you really 3?   3. Challenge
      TOM: 4. Just 4.   4. Claim
      JOHN: 5. Are you really 4?   5. Challenge
      TOM: 6. I'm only 4 years old.   6. Claim
      CHILD: 7. You're not!   7. Contradiction
      (CHILD: I'm 2.)
      JOHN: 8. You're not really 4!   8. Challenge
      TOM: 9. Yes.   9. Claim
      JOHN: 10. No. My mom's 20—28.   10. Denial–
                   She's older than you   supporting
                   ('cuz?) she's bigger.   argument

                        . . .
      JOHN: No. She's 7—she's 750.
      LEE: Seven, 90, 50—20 pounds.

Here John appears to know that older is better, and 4 years old is more than 3 years old. Tom, who has just had his fourth birthday, seems unable to convince John that he is 4 and therefore older than John, who is 3. Tom stops talking about his age, and Lee later unsuccessfully tries to participate in the argument by using what she believes are big numbers. Unsuccessful attempts like this one seemed to lead to the end of arguments.

The structure of this argument up to Turn 9 is simple and repetitious. It is essentially: claim ↔ challenge. At Turn 10, John adds a supporting argument by introducing new information. The basic structure is typical of many of the arguments involving numbers and of the arguments in general.

Example 2 is a brief argument that, like Example 1, is complex by our definition since it contains a supporting argument.

(2)   "More is better" (Possession)
      LEE: We've got three cookie
                   cutters.
                0. So we have more than y'all.   0. Claim

| TESSA: | 1. *Well, I have four!* | 1. Contradiction |
| RHETT: | 2. *And four is more than three.* | 2. Supporting argument |

Rhett's supporting argument provides a resolution to the argument at the same time that it shows his understanding of an elementary relationship between numbers.

Under the category of exclusion, in which more is not better, children manipulate numbers to keep someone from joining their group. In many cases, they make up ad hoc rules. Here, for example, only two people can make ballerinas.

(3) Exclusion

STEWART:	0. *What y'all makin'?*	0. Request
JENNIFER:	1. *We're makin' those ballerinas. And* **you** *can't play.*	1. Assertion–request
JOHN:	2. *Only two people!*	2. Supporting argument
JENNIFER:	3. *Yeah! So shoo!*	3. Request
STEWART:	4. *Oh, I'm watchin'.*	4. Acceptance

The teacher in the classroom placed limits on the number of children who can play in the housekeeping corner or at given centers, but children adapt that policy for their own purposes. Examples 2 and 3 also show that children, here Rhett and John, sometimes help others build or resolve arguments.

Another kind of exclusion has to do with who can play particular roles in dramatic play. This argument is made up of several "rounds" or subarguments, beginning at Turns 0, 3, and 9, all related to who will play mother. Number is involved at the point where the teacher intervenes.

(4) Exclusion

LEE:	0. *I'm the mother.*	0. Claim
TESSA:	1. *I'm the mother!*	1. Contradiction
LEE:	2. *Un unh, I'm the mother! I'm the mother. She said I'm the mother.*	2. Claim–appeal to authority
TEACHER:	3. *You can have two mothers.*	3. Compromise
LEE:	4. *No, we have to have one mother.*	4. Contradiction
TESSA:	5. *Two.*	5. Contradiction
LEE:	6. *One.*	6. Contradiction
TESSA:	7. *Two.*	7. Contradiction
TEACHER:	8. *Lee, in our house we can have two mothers.*	8. Compromise
TESSA:	9. *I can be the grandmother.*	9. Compromise

Lee:	10. *No, we don't need a grandmother.*	10. Contradiction
Tessa:	11. *Ye-e-s.*	11. Contradiction
Tessa:	12. *You and me can be a sister, you and me can be sisters, and Lee's the mother, OK?* (addressed to Jennifer)	12. Compromise

This is one of the most complex and clearly developed arguments in our corpus. Tessa's compromises are adaptive in Eisenberg and Garvey's sense since she is proposing alternatives that might be acceptable from Lee's point of view. What is impressive about the argument is Tessa's persistence, Lee's effective resistance, and Tessa's ability to progressively compromise, based on her knowledge of family structure. In the end, Lee maintains a superior position as the only mother, and Tessa is her daughter. Although this argument is atypical in its complexity, it is typical in its focus on negotiation of status. As in the many arguments about possession of desired objects, Tessa and Lee may be more concerned about who is "one-up" than about who ultimately plays which role.

An example from the miscellaneous category has to do with temperature. This argument also consists of more than one subargument, one beginning at Turn 0 and the other at 2, and it illustrates the range of knowledge the children displayed.

(5) Miscellaneous (Temperature)

Billy:	0. *Doctor, doctor, nurse, nurse. I just took my temperature and it was 109!*	0. Assertion
Tessa:	1. *I'm not a doctor.*	1. Contradiction
Billy:	2. *Nurse, I just took my temperature, and it was 109!*	2. Acceptance– assertion
Tessa:	3. *OK, that's not very much.*	3. Assertion
Billy:	4. *Yes, it is. I know about temperatures, for **real**.*	4. Contradiction– supporting argument
Tessa:	5. *You're gonna have to lay down, right on the floor.*	5. Acceptance.

Billy is the son of an accountant and presumably learned how to count at home. He not only knows which numbers are more or less than others, but also what constitutes a very high temperature. In conversations and arguments in which he could introduce numbers, he had the position of power. Although Billy did not participate in more arguments involving numbers than other children, he introduced numbers in general conversation more than others.

The arguments involving number are the best evidence that social knowledge and academic content are integrated. Children's efforts to get what they want, their ideas about social dominance and status are translated into expressions of knowledge about number and size. Children can embed the vocabulary of lessons in naturally occurring, noninstructional contexts.

SOCIAL KNOWLEDGE IN COMPLEX ARGUMENTS

According to our definition, complex arguments contained an acceptance, appeal to authority, compromise, and/or supporting argument. Of the 41 complex arguments in the corpus, one group had to do with conduct. Children in this preschool already knew or were learning rules of conduct or appropriate behavior. Children demonstrated their knowledge when they reminded each other of some "rules of the game" of school. We saw earlier that they imposed limits on the number of children who could join an activity as the teacher sometimes limited the number allowed at a center. Here we present examples that demonstrate the children's knowledge of appropriate conduct in and out of school. There is at least one example of a child who uses the teacher's phrasing for, *Don't be so loud.*

> **(6)** Conduct
>
> BILLY: 0. *Mine!!* (yelling) *Teacher!* 0. Claim–appeal to authority
>
> JOHN: 1. *Billy, don't yell!* (yelling) *That's an outside voice.* (Billy stops yelling.) 1. Request– assertion
>
> JOHN: 2. *Billy, don't yell!* 2. Request

That's an outside voice is part of many preschool teachers' repertoire of regulatory euphemisms, and John knows when to use it.

Another routine that Billy especially has learned is that of singing to tell the children what the appropriate behavior is. This teacher sings regularly at two times, cleanup time (*Oh, do you know what time it is? . . . It's cleanup time*) and a time similar to circle time (*Everybody, sit down, sit down. . . . Everybody sit down on the rug*). Billy occasionally sings these songs at the correct time and at other times apparently as a joke. The following interaction shows how he can initiate the "sit down" routine and later argue about whether he will follow the directions in the song. The episode takes place during the transition time between free play and story telling when the children sit together on the rug.

> **(7)** Conduct
>
> BILLY: *Everybody sit down, sit down, sit down. Everybody, sit down on the rug* (singing).

Lee:	Everybody fold your legs, fold your legs, fold your legs. Fold your legs, fold your legs, on the rug (singing the next part of the song).	
Billy:	0. You don't fold your legs, Lee.	0. Assertion
Lee:	1. Yes, you do.	1. Contradiction
Billy:	2. I don't.	2. Assertion
Lee:	3. Well, you're supposed to.	3. Appeal to authority

It is not clear whether Billy is joking when he tells Lee not to fold her legs, but Lee eventually ends the brief argument with a vague appeal to authority, as if to say, "That's the rule."

Some of the arguments about conduct occur in dramatic play and reflect knowledge about how things work outside of school. For example, Tessa and Billy have the following exchange while playing "doctor."

(8)   Conduct

Billy:	0. The aspirin (doesn't it?) (laughs)	0. Action
Tessa:	1. No, don't laugh because doctors do not laugh.	1. Request with supporting argument
	2. (Billy keeps laughing.)	2. Refusal (action)
Tessa:	3. Billy, quiet! Teacher, I thought Billy was a doctor. Do not laugh (to Billy).	3. Request–appeal to authority
Teacher:	Do you hear their words, Tessa? I mean Billy?	
Billy:	Yep.	

Another brief argument also develops while the children play doctor.

(9)   Conduct

(Jennifer and Lee are calling Tessa into the doctor's office from the waiting room.)

Jennifer:	Play like you wanna (call) Tessa, please. Tessa, please!	
Lee:	Tessa, please!	
Jennifer:	Now play like you (inaudible) on the bed.	
Tessa:	OK.	
Jennifer:	0. You have—you go—play like you went ahead and laid down on the bed.	0. Request

TESSA: 1. *No, you know what? It takes*   1. Refusal–
              a long time for people to—   supporting
              uh—come in the room. So   argument
              it's gonna take a long time
              for me.

Examples 8 and 9 both include supporting arguments that show how much
these girls know about doctors' behavior and the waiting room. Tessa knows
that doctors are serious people and that to enact a visit to the doctor realis-
tically, one must sit for a long time in the waiting room.

A final example, although not about conduct, is based on Billy's knowledge of how fathers behave.

(10)   Possession (Turn-taking)
       BILLY: 0. *I have to call business.*   0. Claim
       LEE: 1. *Let me call somebody.*   1. Request
       BILLY: 2. *I have to call business first.*   2. Claim
       TESSA: 3. *We have two phones.*   3. Compromise

Tessa intervenes at Turn 3 to offer a compromise and a resolution to the
argument. Since she considers the viewpoints of the other children to make
the compromise, her strategy is adaptive.

The five arguments presented in this section are all complex, but they
illustrate an increasing complexity in terms of children's strategies. Examples
6 and 7 show children citing rules the teacher has established. In Examples
8 and 9 children include supporting arguments implying, "That's how things
are supposed to be," based on what they have experienced, not on another's
authority. In Example 10 Tessa demonstrates that she can formulate a simple
but fair solution for her friends in a situation she has presumably not experienced
before.

Discussion

This section consists of our conclusions and a discussion of possible
reasons for our findings. Effects of teacher intervention and the social significance of arguments for these children are considered, along with practical
implications of the study. We conclude from our results, first, that the children
in this preschool were argumentative. There were 189 arguments recorded; the
mean number per half hour of audiotaped talk was 9. Second, the arguments
seldom included compromises or solutions reflecting give-and-take. Most of the
arguments were simple in structure. The vast majority (148) did not contain
utterances that functioned to terminate the argument, add new information,

or show the speaker was taking others' viewpoints into account. Third, many
of the arguments, whether complex or simple, did reflect children's social
knowledge about how to behave in school. Arguments also reflected knowledge
about out-of-school roles, such as family member, doctor, or patient, as children
attempted to regulate each other's behavior and assert their own importance.

The first conclusion may be explained in part by the nature of the
children. Most of them were talkative and assertive so they showed no re-
luctance to argue. In addition the teacher's attitude toward arguing may have
contributed to the large number of arguments. While children played, she was
nondirective and generally responded to children's questions or to their arguments only when the arguments became loud or "violent" or when children
directly appealed to her. There was no prohibition against arguing, and brief
arguments took place without the teacher's intervention. This is typical of
many simple arguments in which the teacher did not intervene.

   (11) Possession

BILLY:	0. *Mine!*	0. Claim
JOHN:	1. *This is yours.*	1. Contradiction
BILLY:	2. *No, it's not. This is mine.*	2. Denial–claim
	This *is mine.*	
JOHN:	3. *No, it's not.*	3. Denial–
		Contradiction

A similar argument is also about possession.

   (12) Possession

BILLY:	0. *Gimme my baby!!* (yelling)	0. Request
JENNIFER:	1. *No!!* (also yelling) *I had*	1. Refusal–
	this first.	supporting
		argument
TEACHER:	*Billy, Jennifer would like*	
	to have a turn with it now.	
	When she's through, you may	
	have another turn.	

This example becomes complex at Turn 1 when Jennifer adds a supporting
argument (*I had this first*). The teacher then intervenes, probably because the
children are yelling, to remind them that they need to take turns.

Arguing loudly, then, seemed to be unacceptable. Physical aggression
was also forbidden. While talking to the first author about her educational
goals, the teacher said, *We do a lot with social skills.* One important skill was
getting things without hitting, or negotiating verbally. According to the
teacher, the nursery school had a policy of telling the children to *use your
words.* The teacher of the group of 2-year-olds also used this policy. A number

of times the teacher we observed reminded children to *use your words.* Her question, *Do you hear their words?* in Argument 8 is an example. *Talk about it,* is a more direct form that she used. The following example shows another variation of the reminder.

(13) Truth

BILLY:	0. *I need to see what size your jogging shorts are.*	0. Request
JOHN:	1. *They're not jogging shorts.*	1. Contradiction
TEACHER:	*Billy, we're having a story now—leave John alone.*	
JOHN:	2. *They're not jogging shorts.*	2. Repeats contradiction
BILLY:	3. *What are they?*	3. Request
JOHN:	4. *They're big-boy pants.*	4. Assertion
TEACHER:	*OK.*	
BILLY:	5. *Jogging shorts **are** big-boy pants.*	5. Supporting argument
TEACHER:	*That's what some people call them, John. Let's try again. Billy, Billy. John, I don't want you bothering him.*	
JOHN:	6. *Teacher, teacher.*	6. Appeals to authority
TEACHER:	*Would you please leave him alone? Tell him.* (to John)	
JOHN:	*Leave me alone.* (pause) *Leave me alone. Leave me alone.* (Billy ignores these requests.)	
TEACHER:	*Billy. Billy. Either leave John alone or move over here.*	
BILLY:	*I'll move over here.*	
TEACHER:	*OK, thank you.*	

After Turn 6 the teacher says, *Tell him* in order to end the aggression. This technique had the effect of making arguments shorter and less intense. It might also have decreased physical actions and increased the number of verbal arguments in general.

The second conclusion that the arguments were simple in structure may also be related to the teacher's presence. As we said in the second section, we suspect her behavior helps explain the contrast between our results and those of Eisenberg and Garvey (1981). Like us, these investigators found their

3- to 5-year-old dyads engaged most frequently in what we call simple arguments but they call a strategy of insistence, one of repetition. In contrast, however, their children's second most frequent strategy was the use of reasons; reasons were used to terminate arguments more often than any other strategy. Our children's supporting arguments, which seem analogous to Eisenberg and Garvey's reasons, occurred rarely. The small number of supporting, and complex, arguments in our data may be associated with the teacher's availability, suggestions, and compromises that made it unnecessary for children to formulate their own solutions to conflicts.

Since Eisenberg and Garvey's subjects interacted in dyads, they had no access to an adult who could help resolve conflicts. As noted earlier, the dyadic situation also made resolution of conflicts necessary. Whereas the children in our study could walk away from each other to end an argument, children placed in dyads are compelled to resolve arguments verbally, which then contain reasons, so that interaction can continue.

Another explanation for the small number of complex arguments in our data lies outside situational factors. Perhaps our children are less intelligent than Eisenberg and Garvey's subjects. Although this is possible, the content of many of the arguments shows that these children have little difficulty expressing themselves verbally and that their thinking, whether or not they are arguing, can be complex and imaginative. In the classroom situation where children and teacher share a small space, it is natural for the teacher to attend to children's arguments and for children to appeal to the adult who is clearly in charge. In fact, **for that situation,** appealing to the teacher seems the sensible and intelligent behavior.

Although the arguments of these seven children do not demonstrate that they generally formulate solutions, our third conclusion was that they nevertheless possess and are learning about various kinds of social knowledge. This social knowledge at times intersects the display of academic knowledge, as in the arguments involving numbers, but social negotiation seems to be the primary reason for arguing. Except for the arguments about truth (13%), the arguments refer in some way to possession of a desired object, role, or turn, or to appropriate or desired behavior. The children's goal often seems to be not the fair resolution of the argument but the control of another's behavior. In other words, their arguments contain many examples of "social control acts" (Ervin-Tripp, Chapter 3, p. 27, this volume). According to Ervin-Tripp, children may have more than one objective in using such acts: They may want to manipulate others' actions at the same time that they enhance their own status. Asserting one's importance or superiority may matter as much to the child as changing another's behavior. This may be why the children in our study spend much of their time doing what Ervin-Tripp calls "stage setting," focusing on roles, objects, and territory. Negotiation of roles for dramatic play may, for example, be done more to establish who is "one-up" than to ensure a well-cast play.

Our findings suggest two practical implications. First, teachers who wish to encourage children's formulation of their own solutions might intervene in arguments less often. In addition, whether or not children reach resolutions, a teacher may avoid intervening so children can fulfill their own social objectives. For them the act of arguing or negotiating may be more important than its termination. The technique of nonintervention may, however, be unrealistic for those teachers who only intervene when arguments become "disruptive," that is, loud or violent. Second, our findings support what early childhood practitioners have long believed: Nursery schools without a formal curriculum are fine places for the socialization of young children. The teacher in the class we observed stated that her general goal was to help the children to become aware of "things going on around them." The conversations we recorded show that the children are learning elementary facts about numbers and science, but more often they are reflecting what they know about how people behave in and out of school, as well as how they should behave. Along with an awareness of themselves, these children are developing abilities to assert power and status and to control the behavior of others through argument.

Summary

The content and structure of 189 audiotaped arguments of seven white middle-class 3- to 5-year-olds were analyzed from a sociolinguistic perspective to see what they show about the children's knowledge and learning in an informal preschool. There were seven major themes, including possession, which occurred most frequently, and number. The arguments in which children used cardinal numbers were the best evidence of their integration of academic and social knowledge. The majority (148) of arguments were simple in structure. Whether arguments were simple (repetitious) or complex (containing attempts to end or resolve the conflict), children seemed to have two equally important goals in arguing: to control the behavior of others and to assert their own importance. Resolution of the argument did not seem primary. The common-sense belief that traditional nursery schools are productive places for socialization seemed to be supported by our study. Children were learning some academic facts, but the bulk of their learning may have been social. Learning how to negotiate through argument was for these preschool children not trivial, but absorbing and socially valuable.

Acknowledgments

We would like to thank Carol Davis for collecting the data.

References

Boggs, S. T. The development of verbal disputing in part-Hawaiian children. *Language in Society,* 1978, *7,* 325–344.

Botvin, G. J., & Murray, F. The efficacy of peer modeling and social conflict in the acquisition of conservation. *Child Development,* 1975, *46,* 796–799.

Brenneis, D., & Lein, L. "You fruithead": A sociolinguistic approach to children's dispute settlement. In S. Ervin-Tripp & C. Mitchell-Kernan (Eds.), *Child discourse.* New York: Academic Press, 1977.

Dawe, H.C. An analysis of 200 quarrels of preschool children. *Child Development,* 1934, *5,* 139–157.

Eisenberg, A., & Garvey, C. Children's use of verbal strategies in resolving conflicts. *Discourse Processes,* 1981, *4* (2), 149–170.

Ervin-Tripp, S. Is Sybil there? The structure of some American English directives. *Language in Society,* 1976, *5,* 25–66.

Green, E. H. Friendship and quarrels among preschool children. *Child Development,* 1933, *4,* 237–252. (a)

Green, E. H. Group play and quarrelling among preschool children. *Child Development,* 1933, *4,* 302–307. (b)

Kernan, K. T. Semantic and expressive elaboration in children's narratives. In S. Ervin-Tripp & C. Mitchell-Kernan (Eds.), *Child discourse.* New York: Academic Press, 1977.

Lein, L., & Brenneis, D. Children's disputes in three speech communities. *Language in Society,* 1978, *7,* 299–324.

Miller, S. S., & Brownell, C. A. Peers, persuasion, and Piaget: Dyadic interaction between conservers and nonconservers. *Child Development,* 1975, *46,* 992–997.

Piaget, J. *The language and thought of the child* (3rd ed.). London: Routledge & Kegan Paul, 1959.

5

Peer Learning in the Classroom: Tracing Developmental Patterns and Consequences of Children's Spontaneous Interactions[1]

CATHERINE R. COOPER
ANGELA MARQUIS
SUSAN AYERS-LOPEZ

In recent years, social scientists have recognized the heterogeneity of values and expectations about schools among parents, children, and teachers, and they are now beginning to discern the impact of these differences on children's learning. In doing so, many investigators have begun to search for resources children may use to master not only academic tasks, but also the interpersonal demands of the classroom (e.g., Mehan, 1979). This chapter focuses on how children turn to one another in the process of learning. The work is based on a view that peers can serve as resources for one another in cognitive development (e.g., Piaget, 1959), which differs from a common attitude that peers are a source of "only" social skills, or only inferior intellectual and linguistic stimulation. Recent Piagetian research and examples from countries such as China, the Soviet Union, and Great Britain indicate that peers may offer genuine and substantive benefit in cognitive growth, but relatively little is known about how children's interactive capacities develop (e.g., Ervin-Tripp & Mitchell-Kernan, 1977; Flavell, 1977).

This chapter addresses three basic questions about peer learning. The first involves the form and function of spontaneous peer learning exchanges. What roles do children assume and how are they enacted? In conventional teacher–child interactions, the asymmetries of status, knowledge, and power

[1] The research for this chapter was supported by Contract No. NIE-6-78-0098 from the National Institute of Education to the senior author.

69

are readily apparent. Current analyses of teacher–child discourse reflect the responsibilities of teachers to maintain social order in the classroom by elicitation of behavior from students, allocation of turns, and regulation of access to the teacher's time and attention (Eder, in press; Mehan, 1979; Merritt, 1979). In peer relationships, the relative ambiguity of status makes the often explicit negotiation of dominance hierarchies an important function of interaction (Gumperz & Herasimchuk, 1972). How are the asymmetrical roles of teacher and learner negotiated? Current developmental sociolinguistic work in classrooms (e.g., Cherry, 1978; Genishi, 1979; Steinberg & Cazden, 1979) suggests that the differential status of children seeking or offering information in the classroom would require modification of speaking styles to achieve their learning goals, and that depending on the social status of the child, the learning outcome may vary significantly (Garnica, 1981). Although some current work has concentrated on peer learning that is initiated by an adult request (e.g., Allen, 1976; Carrasco, Vera, & Cazden, 1981; Cazden, 1979) in the form of "instructional chains," we still need to know about spontaneous peer learning, by children in both the teaching and in the learning role.

The second basic issue of this investigation concerns developmental trends in peer learning exchanges. During the early school years, for example, we have clear evidence of qualitative and quantitative changes in how children manage their attentional resources, categorize and sort their experiences in physical and social domains, and consider and reflect upon not only their own thoughts, but also the thoughts of others (Clark & Delia, 1976; Flavell, 1977; Mueller, 1972). Relating such developmental themes to classroom communication is essential to understanding how individual children may best be served in the classroom. Unfortunately, very little developmental data exist in this area (Genishi, 1979; Schachter, Kirshner, Klips, Friedricks, & Sanders, 1974).

Our third question involves identifying characteristics of effective peer learning discourse among kindergarten and second-grade children. We examine these issues using a framework derived from research in speech or conversational act analysis (e.g., Dore, 1977; Searle, 1971), in which information exchange transpires when a speaker first captures the attention of a listener, then provides an instrumental statement, such as a question, command, or pertinent descriptive comment. The listener has the opportunity to respond; the exchange may then be evaluated. Examining these speech events and the outcome of the children's conversations allows us to assess the degree to which such factors as general attentional support and referential specificity are necessary for effective communicative exchanges between younger learners.

To answer these questions, we have used two approaches. In order to investigate the various forms of peer learning, we have been open to unanticipated patterns in the data. And by adapting a more predetermined framework for examining the sequence of speaker elicitation–listener response–speaker evaluation used by many students of classroom discourse (e.g., Bellack, Klie-bard, Hyman, & Smith, 1966; Cook-Gumperz, 1977; Mehan, 1979; Sinclair & Coulthard, 1975), we could discern patterns across individual learning ep-isodes. In addition, we could trace both developmental differences in the early school years and the effectiveness of different discourse patterns in achieving the goals of teaching and learning within the peer network.

Method

SUBJECTS AND SETTING

Observations were conducted in a kindergarten classroom of a public school and a second-grade classroom of a private parochial school. The kin-dergarten class consisted of 27 children—16 girls and 11 boys—and the second-grade class included 22 children—12 girls and 10 boys. Both groups of children came from working- and middle-class families.

Since open organization of kindergartens is common, locating a suitable group was a straightforward matter. However, our selection of the parochial school was made after several unrewarding attempts to find a school in the public system that housed a genuinely open second-grade classroom. Several schools had been recommended within the system, when in fact their openness referred merely to architectural features of the building (absence of walls di-viding classes of the same grade level), while children were expected to follow traditional "don't-talk-to-your-neighbor" rules of peer interaction. Thus it was with a great deal of relief that we finally located a classroom in a parochial school where peer interaction was "legal" and consistently encouraged as a way for children to master classroom learning activities.

A further distinction must be made, however, between a classroom in which children learn primarily by working collaboratively with peers on group learning projects, and a classroom in which children are allowed and encouraged to work together, helping and seeking help from one another, on activities with outcomes primarily in the form of individual achievements, including workbooks, stories, spelling sheets, or cursive exercises. The second-grade class-room we observed was of the latter sort.

The data from these rooms were collected by research assistants. One joined each classroom as a participant observer, helping the teachers and their aides by answering the children's questions, distributing materials, and helping supervise some classroom activities, but mostly remaining free to move around the classroom to observe. They chatted with the children, but did not cultivate the role of teacher so the children would not rely on them for help when they could assist one another. In the kindergarten the assistant remained somewhat more distant to avoid distracting the children from peer learning activities. The children were introduced to the research assistant as someone who would be helping in the room and also using a tape recorder because "she was interested in how they did their school work."

The physical organization of the kindergarten classroom was distinguished by eight different learning areas: math, reading, art, dramatic play, science, instructional records, and two block areas, with tables or floor space set aside for each area. Children worked at large tables rather than at desks. Children moved from area to area, depending on how rapidly they completed their projects. The teacher or aide would instruct children on a particular project, usually math or art, and children could then instruct or help others as they were engaged in the project.

The physical organization of the second-grade classroom was distinguished by the presence of five working tables, science and math learning areas, and only two pairs of student desks. The children spent much of their day working at the group tables on individual assignments, while the teacher or aide worked with individuals or small groups.

PROCEDURES

For both age groups, the sampling of children's instructional episodes was as systematic as possible, given the variability of the amount of time children associated in groups. The research assistants identified periods when children were working at their tables on class assignments by observing daily activities for a week. During the subsequent weeks each observer placed a small audio recorder on the children's tables as they worked, encouraging them to continue with whatever they were doing. Children who were sitting alone or talking with the teacher or aide were not recorded.

Recordings were made on a continuing basis through the weeks of April 1980 for the kindergarten class, and during late April and May 1979 for the second-grade class. Supplemental field notes described nonverbal behaviors, seating arrangements, and other pertinent contextual information. The tapes were reviewed and indexed for the occurrence of instructional episodes (similar to the instructional sequence units of Green & Wallat, 1981). Seven episode types became apparent as we examined them. They occurred when children either (a) asked for the help of a peer (**learner bid**); (b) spontaneously offered to help (**teacher bid**); (c) referred only to the rate of work or attending of others without teaching (**pacing**); (d) made evaluative statements (**evaluative**); (e) attempted to join a learning group (**joining**); (f) attempted to manage others' behavior (**behavior management**); or (g) participated in cooperative learning by taking turns or pursuing a common goal (**collaborative**).

The episodes were analyzed in the following sequence. Research assistants first checked the transcripts of the conversations, marking where topics of conversation began and ended. The episodes that contained no explicit teaching or learning bids were coded into pacing, joining, behavior management, and evaluation categories. If the exchange involved speech events such as questions or directives (with or without one or more of the preceding functions), then the episode was classified as a teaching situation, and categorized as a teacher bid, learner bid, or collaborative episode. The distinction between the teaching and learning bids depended on the first move in the conversation. If its function was to request aid, information, or materials from another child, it was considered learner-initiated. If the first move involved requesting action, offering help, or giving information to another, it was considered a teaching bid. Collaborative episodes were distinguished by descriptive comments or by alternating moves, such that both children were making teaching and learning statements. Interrater reliability of coding for each item was established at above .80 and monitored throughout coding.

Results

The earliest analyses concerned the patterns of contact among the children. The records of the seating arrangements of the children indicated which children each child would have as potential learning partners. For the kindergartners, few stable learning groups occurred. Although some children regularly worked in pairs, most approached many other children during the observation periods. A small number of children remained in observer or isolate roles. In contrast, the second-grade class contained more stable learning groups, as well as others who worked in close proximity to other children, but did not seem to exercise deliberate choosing of "neighbors." Still others remained fairly isolated from any peer association, as they were observed with almost no other children on these occasions. The observations illustrate a developmental phenomenon with implications for school learning: Young children tend to have more ready access to others in their class, but by second grade this access is limited, with most peer learning occurring within a network of close friendships (Corsaro, 1979; Rubin, 1980).

FUNCTIONS OF THE INSTRUCTIONAL EPISODES

The remaining analyses involved the coding of the instructional episodes. The entire code is summarized in Table 5.1, and the frequency and percentages of each episode type by age is given in Table 5.2. Distributions of these forms of peer learning indicate that younger children engaged in a greater proportion

I. **Learning episode functions**
  A. Teacher bid: Child spontaneously offers information, *Did you know that lions sleep in the daytime?*
  B. Learner bid: Child seeks information from another child, *How do you do this?*
  C. Pacing: Child refers only to the rate of work or attending of others without providing subsequent teaching or elaboration on the same topic, *Hurry up, you guys.*
  D. Management: Child attempts to control general behavior of others, *Stop it.*
  E. Self-evaluation: Child makes either positive or negative statement about self, *What a good fish, I'm having trouble.*
  F. Joining: Child attempts to join another child in learning activity, *Can I sit here?*
  G. Collaboration: Child participates in either an explicitly cooperative task structure or an alternation of teacher and learner roles within an activity, *O.K., you read one page and I'll read one page.*

II. **Utterance functions** (coded for teacher and learner bid episodes)
  A. Attention focusing: Alerting or orienting another child to the learning task, (*hey, look,* and saying the child's name).
  B. Moves, including:
    1. Directives or requests for action: Either direct (*Put a G here*) or indirect (*Why don't you do the ones on page 8?*).
    2. Questions or requests for information: *What is the capital of Rhode Island?, Tell me the answer to number 4.*
    3. Request for help: Rather than specific information, *Could you help me?*
    4. Relevant comments: Descriptions that are not coded as other moves or responses, *This sure is a long story.*
    5. Irrelevant comments: Playful use of language, or other off-task comments, *Nanu nanu shazbat.*
  C. Responses or consequences of moves:
    1. Informative responses (+): Complete answer to a question or directive, including agreement or appropriate nonverbal response.
    2. Uninformative response (−): An incomplete or nonspecific answer.
    3. Acknowledgments (+): Response indicating listener is attending without providing substantive information, *Bill?, Yes.*
    4. Responses as question or directive (0): *Where's my spelling?, Why are you doing that one?* These are moves as well.
    5. Arguments or corrections (0): A counterassertion providing information discrepant from that just given may follow a move by learner or teacher, *It's time for art, We don't have to go today.*
    6. No response (−): Includes no verbal response, irrelevant response, explicit rejection of the role solicited, *I sure need help on this, Who cares?*
  D. Evaluative statements:
    1. Praising another child: *You put the right one in.*
    2. Criticizing another child: *You're a dum-dum.*
    3. Praising self: *I'm the greatest.*
    4. Criticizing self: *I blew it.*
    5. Task evaluative comments: Relating to the procedures or subject matter rather than to other children, *This puzzle is cinchy, I like the Z's the best.*

III. **Referential specificity** (coded for directives and questions)
  A. Specific: Child refers to materials or topic so that listener knows, through verbal or nonverbal means, what is described.
  B. Nonspecific: Referent not specified in description, *this one.*

Table 5.2
Frequency and Percentage of Peer Instructional Episode Types by Age Groups

Episode type	Kindergarten		Second grade	
	N	Percentage	N	Percentage
Teaching bids	53	(30.0)	88	(14.0)
Learning bids	45	(25.4)	146	(24.0)
Pacing	5	(2.8)	22	(3.6)
Management	12	(6.8)	12	(1.9)
Self-evaluation	35	(19.8)	82	(13.5)
Joining	8	(4.5)	20	(3.2)
Collaborative	7	(4.0)	174	(28.7)
Others not analyzed[a]	12	(6.7)	48	(7.9)
Total	177		592	

[a] Includes episodes in which the adult teacher was involved, no known response occurred; a child without parental permission to record was speaking; speech to self; fragments; "blends" of teaching bids, learning bids, and collaborative episodes.

of teaching bids, attention managing, and self-evaluation (primarily self-praise), and that older children exceeded younger ones in the frequency of collaborative interactions, whereas the numbers of learning bids, joining, and pacing were similarly distributed in the two groups.

Our experience in coding these episodes suggests these functions could be viewed as a continuum of activities, beginning with a child's awareness of his or her own state of understanding (Markman, 1977). A child might be pleased with a new accomplishment and express a positive self-evaluation (*What a good fish!*). If no acknowledgment is received, the child might repeat the message with an attention-focusing statement (*Hey, this is a big fish*) or in an indirect form (*Do you know I can cut this fish with one hand? I hope whoever gets this fish will like it*). A continuum might also operate from negative self-evaluation (*I'm having trouble.*), leading to joining (*Is anyone sitting here?*), to explicit learning bids (*How do you do this?*).

This framework illuminates the developmental differences observed between the two age groups. Younger children were more likely than older ones to make teaching statements to other children: $\chi^2(1) = 5.82$, $p < .05$. They also used their pacing statements to draw attention to their own activity (*Look at mine.*) and seemed to seek to manage behavior for its own sake (*Sit down, Stop it!*); in contrast, the 7-year-olds used pacing and managing embedded in teaching or learning sequences to help achieve their learning goal (*Hurry up, these will be checked at two o'clock.*), and exceeded the younger children in collaborative episodes: $\chi^2(1) = 18.71$, $p < .01$.

To examine the possibility that self-evaluations and teaching "announcements" may function similarly to elicit acknowledgment of the teacher's competence, we compared the way children became engaged in the teaching role. Some children initiated their teaching episodes (whom we dubbed the "advertisers"), whereas others became engaged in the teaching role primarily in response to the questions of other children (these we called the "consultants"). It is notable that the most active teachers, those most frequently engaged in teaching episodes, were the consultants rather than the advertisers. Similarly, some children in the learner role were taught spontaneously by other children, whereas others articulated their needs explicitly. In this second-grade classroom, the two children who received the most unsolicited information from their peers were also the ones most frequently sought as consultants. This pattern suggests that a small number of children may be at the crossroads of learning exchanges, and are both contributing to and benefiting from these interactions, whereas others miss both the challenge of questions and the benefit of instruction from their peers.

CONSEQUENCES OF DISCOURSE PATTERNS

We examined individual utterances in the teaching and learning episodes to assess whether patterns of discourse were predictive of the outcomes of these episodes. A sample of 50 episodes of each type for each age group were coded for the frequency of utterances reflecting typical conversational acts in the teaching–learning exchange, including attention focusing (e.g., Hey, Bill!), requesting action, requesting or offering information, requesting help, relevant comments, irrelevant comments, and evaluative comments. Each request for action or information was also coded for its referential specificity. Distinctive patterns in using these communicative behaviors have been associated with effectiveness on more structured experimental tasks of peer learning (Cooper, 1980; Cooper, Ayers-Lopez, & Marquis, in press).

The responses to these utterances provided the basis for evaluating the outcomes of the episodes. Chi-square analyses were conducted to assess the contingencies between the use of each utterance function and the outcome of the episode. Learner bids were considered effective when they elicited an informative reply. Teaching bids were judged effective when learners accepted the offered information either by acknowledging, elaborating, or making appropriate nonverbal response. Finally, both teaching and learning bids were considered failures if the listener responded by rejecting, giving an irrelevant response, or ignoring the speaker.

THE LEARNER ROLE

In order for a learner bid to be successful, the potential teacher must not only accept the teaching role, but must also be able to provide the information requested. Among both age groups, successful learners used questions, as opposed to indirect statements, such as this one's too hard for me, $\chi^2(1)$

= 15.16, $p < .01$, and $\chi^2(1) = 11.64$, $p < .01$, for younger and older groups, respectively, and referred to the materials or the problem involved. Kindergarten children's use of attention-focusing statements typically met with failure, perhaps because they were frequently expressed without accompanying instrumental statements (e.g., *Jody!*), leaving the listener with no idea of what response was expected or desired. The prospective child-teacher was often engaged in other activity and unless instructed as to what was needed, would simply ignore the bid. The success of pairing attention-focusing statements with other moves either in the same round or later in the conversation was reflected in the overall ratings, in which attention-focusing statements were highly associated with positive outcomes, $\chi^2(1) = 12.96$, $p < .01$. In contrast, effective second-grade children used attention-focusing to precede their questions, and on many occasions, first elicited an acknowledgment that the listener was willing to respond (*Hey Bill, are you busy?—No.—What is this called?*). When used, they were always associated with effectiveness.

Not only was the rise of references associated with effectiveness $\chi^2(1) = 26.78$, $p < .01$, and $\chi^2(1) = 16.85$, $p < .05$, for the two groups, but so was the use of nonspecific references, $\chi^2(1) = 29.70$, $p < .01$, and $\chi^2(1) = 19.73$, $p < .01$, respectively. The degree of referential specificity did not appear to influence the outcome of these learner bids: If the first bid was not understood, the learner could provide either verbal or nonverbal clarification, especially since learners typically asked about tasks to which they could point.

L: *What does that say?*
T: *No, wait . . . let me look. Oh. "Questions."*

* * * * *

L: *Can I use your thing?*
T: *This?*
L: *Yeah.*

Learners expressed very few evaluative statements. Usually they requested information involving the process or task at hand, rather than feedback about their own performance. Finally, after initial failure to elicit a response, learners engaged in a variety of strategies that were ultimately fruitful, ranging from simply repeating the initial bid; bargaining, shaming, pleading, or threatening; increasing the specificity of the reference; or seeking another child or the adult teacher. Kindergarten children frequently reformulated bids more directly, whereas second graders more typically adopted more indirect or "polite" forms.

THE TEACHER ROLE

Unlike learner bids for information, child teachers did not always elicit a response. The child teacher needs the learner to accept the role as well as the information being offered, by acknowledging (*Oh, yeah*), elaborating, or making an appropriate nonverbal response. The child cast in the learner role may accept it but dispute the veracity of the information and correct it, or reject the teacher altogether (*Who cares?, Bug off!*). Of course, these "failures" may ultimately result in learning as the learner corrects the teacher, or as both generate a new solution.

Attention-focusing statements were not used frequently in teaching bids in either age group. Kindergarten children were most effective when conveying information through direct requests for action (*Don't let it drip, Take the colors back, Do "fist"*), $\chi^2(2) = 7.67$, $p < .05$. Older children may have a greater tolerance for indirectness. Descriptive comments simply announced on the first bid had an equal chance of success or failure, but when used later in conjunction with other kinds of statements, were highly associated with success $\chi^2(2) = 11.73$, $p < .01$, 11.67, $p = .01$, for younger and older children, respectively. The basic gloss of these descriptive statements seemed to be "I know this now" (e.g., *Fish have feet. I found out.*), and after the listener had had an opportunity to question or clarify such statements, they were typically acknowledged.

Referential specificity was highly associated with the success of the teaching episodes, $\chi^2(2) = 11.44$, $p < .01$, and 11.67, $p = .01$, respectively, although even 5-year-olds seemed able to repair the ambiguity of nonspecific bids.

T: *You're supposed to be doing that page.*
L: *Which page?*
T: *This one.* (points)

Finally, role negotiation continued implicitly throughout these instructional episodes. A child teacher might "lose his or her job" if the child seeking information detected that it was not correct. However, arguments were more likely in teacher-initiated episodes when a reluctant learner, who already knew enough to reject the proferred information or advice, did so.

Role switching was also observed among both kindergarten and second-grade children who were frequent companions. A child in the teaching role in a friendship pair might encourage the child who was typically a learner to be a teacher, whereas the first child took the role of the learner. In cases when this was observed, the more experienced child–teacher might provide an answer book so the learner did not have to depend on his or her own knowledge. This was seen with both riddle books and spelling word lists. It appears that the child-teachers can tolerate sharing the status of teacher with their friends. In general, the collaborative role was one utilized most by the children who worked together in stable friendship groups, since it seemed to require finely tuned reciprocated interaction, whether for turn taking (*Okay, you read one* page and I'll read one page), or a common goal (Sure, you can copy . . . what are friends for?).

CONTENT

To consider the function of learning and teaching bids in the broader context of classroom learning, the episodes were coded (following Bellack et al., 1966) as concerned either with instructional issues involving procedures for activities (e.g., What page are we on?), or substantive issues referring to the subject matter under study (Can penguins fly?). Issues considered substantive by kindergartners might have been viewed as procedural for the second graders: Learning how to cut paper with one hand was the goal discussed among several 5-year-olds, but it was simply the means of achieving other goals for a group of 7-year-olds. Much of the kindergartners' interaction involved mastering such skills, whereas second-graders' activities focused on the rules governing their activities such as cheating, helping, or pacing their work.

Discussion

In the open classroom, children's access to one another is not extensively regulated by any central figure. Mehan has observed that "while teacher-directed lessons are dominated by elicitation of information, peer instruction is characterized by the giving and receiving of information. While the teacher relies on the verbal modality to a great extent, students demonstrate their instructions, cooperatively complementing tasks together [1979, p. 200]." Our observations suggest, however, that admission to peer learning exchanges is not as automatic as we might suppose. Children are involved to widely varying degrees in this giving and receiving process as it occurs within the complex stream of classroom interaction. These differences in how children bridge the gap from the individual tasks of mastery to participation in the interpersonal life of the classroom can be seen as some children only bemoan to themselves their frustrations and failures, whereas others advertise their new insights, offer unsolicited corrections, and coordinate apprenticeships, partnerships, or arguments.

Our findings of differences between kindergarten and second grade in the peer learning episodes reflect basic developmental changes occurring during this period in children's ability to reflect on their own understanding and behavior as well as the knowledge of others. Children become more aware, for example, of the relative states of understanding between themselves and others sitting at a table, so that a child may work slowly while waiting for a friend, or bargain with a potential teacher to obtain help. These developmental data extend the observations of preschool children reported by Schachter *et al.* (1974). Together the data indicate that from 3 to 7 years, explicitly ego-enhancing statements and simple announcements increase and then decline, while collaborative exchanges increase. As language is used with increasing skill to coordinate self with others, children learn to use attention focusing and behavior management to negotiate and sustain their partner's involvement in interaction, and the one-round encounters lengthen to become multiround arguments, practice sessions, and discussions.

Multiple sources of evidence point to the significance of the role relationship between the two children who enter into a learning partnership. From a different perspective, observations in the classroom confirmed the significance of the acceptability of the peer learning relationship to its participants. Children's effectiveness in these coordinations is seen when they can approach and engage a listener, and when they can make their purpose clear. Classroom patterns of consultation and teaching were highly differentiated, and the importance of the acceptability of didactic and learner roles was clearly demonstrated when either the teacher's offers were rejected or when learners needed to be persistent and ingenious to secure the help of another child.

Evidence affirms the significance of informativeness in effective peer learning. Children who were spontaneously selected as teachers were those capable of providing clear and informative feedback, although requests for clarification were frequent and successful (Glucksberg, Krauss, & Weisberg, 1966; Pratt, Scribner, & Cole, 1977).

The importance of attentional factors was also apparent. In the classroom, the competing distractions of nearby children working on different tasks made attracting and maintaining the attention of the listener a key component of the instructional episodes. When attentional focusing was linked to requests, when a request was direct rather than hinted, and when an initially vague reference could be made less ambiguous, then children were more successful in achieving their goals.

Among the many directions for future research are several significant issues. Developmental work in classrooms will illuminate the relation between both cognitive and social skills and the form, function, and outcome of the negotiation of peer-assisted learning. Additional experimental work is also necessary for clarifying the components of the teaching and learning process. For example, what are the developmental patterns by which children monitor their own state of understanding and that of their listener, in order to offer help or seek it effectively? How do they communicate this information (Markman, 1977)? The role of sequencing appears to be a distinguishing one in the teacher role; frequently younger children guided their partners on a step-by-step basis, whereas older teachers provided orientation, both procedural and substantive, in an opening monologue (Cooper, Marquis, & Ayers-Lopez, in press). Future sociolinguistic work in classrooms is needed to illuminate the relationship between peer learning and adult-child and child-adult interactions (e.g., Merritt, 1979), as well as the role of instructional context in communicative style. Our observations in both experimental and classroom contexts demonstrate, sometimes poignantly, that children differ in their access to one another as resources and in their effectiveness in communicating their learning needs or in offering help (e.g., Cooper, Ayers-Lopez, & Marquis, in press). By identifying the skills associated with effectiveness, remediation of these skills can be achieved.

The work reported here sheds a new light on issues of current interest in the area of cooperative learning in classrooms. In two recent reviews, Slavin (1980) and Sharan (1980) summarize the extensive evidence that cooperative task structures in elementary and secondary classrooms enhance not only academic achievement, but also self-esteem, relationships among black, white, and Mexican–American groups, and liking of school. It is notable that, for the most part, current work in the area of cooperative learning addresses neither developmental changes in peer learning patterns nor the role of the process of peer interaction itself in peer learning outcomes. By demonstrating the existence and consequences of striking developmental and within-group individual differences in peer learning, and identifying features of the communicative process associated with effectiveness, this study contributes to the identification of ways children's access to learning opportunities can be rendered more equitable.

Implications for the Classroom

The findings from this study have significant implications for enhancing children's learning, and especially for improving equity of learning opportunities in classrooms. The implications of this research spring from our findings of striking individual differences in the abundance and quality of involvement in peer learning. Not only have we found that the children who learn are those that can ask, but we also see indications that the children who give information are likely to be the ones who receive it. Sociologists who study group process speak of "expert power," which individuals accrue as a function of their perceived competence rather than by dominating or coercing others. We see that those children who are known to be competent are approached by others not only to be asked questions, but also to be informed of new learnings by other, knowing children.

In our discussions with teachers, several questions recurred. Some teachers have wondered how peer learning activities can succeed if not every child has knowledge desired by others. Teachers can enhance peer learning by allowing children to develop areas of individual expert power or expertise and helping them demonstrate this competence to others. (The conventional "show and tell" format seems unlikely to be an appropriate means for showcasing all kinds of talent.) For example, an isolated child in the kindergarten class we observed was very skilled in designing mobiles. The teacher encouraged him to demonstrate how to make cuttings on paper to produce them, and within a short time all the children in the class had constructed their own mobiles, and were able to view this child as possessing valued knowledge. Teachers can engender and recognize expertise among their students in many ways. One major area concerns the instructions teachers give for daily activities, such as cooking, science, or writing assignments. With an "instructional chain" (Cazden, 1979) one child can be taught how to do an activity and then given the responsibility for teaching others. The teacher could rotate children as "experts of the week." Other teachers use the "jigsaw" technique (Aronson, 1978) by dividing assignments into interlocking pieces, which must all be combined for any one child to succeed.

Another question concerns how peer learning can first be introduced into a classroom. One primary-grade teacher uses a gradual approach by starting her class in September with a more highly structured format. She gives children their assignments for the morning, then allows them to talk together, at first on a trial basis for a brief period, such as 15 minutes. If the children can work smoothly under these circumstances, she increases the peer learning time, but if they cannot work well with that much responsibility, she drops back to a shorter length of time after a few days.

Especially by the second grade, teachers need to be aware of the nature of the social network of their group to facilitate the functioning learning centers or any learning group. For example, a child may be unwilling to take the learner role with someone who is not trusted, whereas an empathetic child–teacher can improvise face-saving "teaching" activities for a less competent friend. Feelings of jealousy that some children may have toward children considered the experts can be reduced when more children have an opportunity to have this role on a regular basis.

In summary, our findings indicate the significance of the age and the relationships among children who enter into learning partnerships. Such developmental findings complement and extend investigations of Cazden (1979), Mehan (1979), Merritt (1979), and others who have focused on single-age samples or adult–child classroom interactions, and provide significant implications for teaching, not only in the open classroom, but in mainstreamed groups (e.g., Guralnick, 1978), newly integrated rooms, or simply in enriching the potential resources of any child in a group.

Acknowledgments

The authors would like to express their appreciation to Victoria Carow, Alison Schockner, and Stephanie Odell, who assisted in the collection and analysis of the data reported in this chapter; and to Robert G. Cooper and Hugh Mehan, for productive discussion of this work.

References

Allen, V. L. Children as teachers. New York: Academic Press, 1976.

Aronson, E. The jigsaw classroom. Beverly Hills: Sage, 1978.

Bellack, A. A., Kliebard, H. M., Hyman, R. T., & Smith, F. L. The language of the classroom. New York: Teachers College Press, 1966.

Carrasco, R. L., Vera, A., & Cazden, C. B. Aspects of bilingual students' communicative competence in the classroom: A case study. In R. Duran (Ed.), Latino language and communicative behavior. Discourse processes: Advances in research and theory (Vol. 4). Norwood, N.J.: Ablex, 1981.

Cazden, C. B. "You all gonna hafta listen": Peer teaching in a primary classroom. In W. A. Collins (Ed.), Children's language and communication: 12th Annual Minnesota Symposium on Child Psychology. Hillsdale, N.J.: Lawrence Erlbaum, 1979.

Cherry, L. J. A sociolinguistic approach to the study of teacher expectations. Discourse Processes, 1978, 1, 373–393.

Clark, R. A. & Delia, J. G. The development of functional persuasive skills in childhod and early adolescence. Child Development, 1976, 47, 1008–1014.

Cook-Gumperz, J. Situated instructions: Language socialization of school age children. In S. Ervin-Tripp & C. Mitchell-Kernan (Eds.), Child discourse. New York: Academic Press, 1977.

Cooper, C. R. Collaboration in children: Dyadic interaction skills in problem solving. Developmental Psychology, 1980, 16, 433–440.

Cooper, C. R., Ayers-Lopez, S., & Marquis, A. Children's discourse during peer learning in experimental and naturalistic situations. Discourse Processes, in press.

Corsaro, W. A. "We're friends, right?": Children's use of access rituals in a nursery school. Language in Society, 1979, 8, 315–336.

Dore, J. "Oh them sheriff": A pragmatic analysis of children's responses to questions. In C. Mitchell-Kernan & S. Ervin-Tripp (Eds.), Child discourse. New York: Academic Press, 1977.

Eder, D. The impact of management and turn-allocation activities on student performance. Discourse Processes, in press.

Ervin-Tripp, S., & Mitchell-Kernan, C. Child discourse. New York: Academic Press, 1977.

Flavell, J. H. Cognitive development. Englewood Cliffs, N.J.: Prentice-Hall, 1977.

Garnica, O. Social dominance and conversational interaction: The Omega child in the classroom. In J. Green & C. Wallat (Eds.), Ethnography and language in educational settings. Norwood, N.J.: Ablex, 1981.

Genishi, C. Young children communicating in the classroom: Selected research. *Theory into Practice*, 1979, *18*, 244–250.

Glucksberg, S., Krauss, R. M., & Weisberg, R. Referential communication in nursery school children: Methods and some preliminary findings. *Journal of Experimental Child Psychology*, 1966, *3*, 333–342.

Green, J. L., & Wallat, C. Mapping instructional conversations: A sociolinguistic ethnography. In J. L. Green & C. Wallat (Eds.), *Ethnography and language in educational settings*. Norwood, N.J.: Ablex, 1981.

Gumperz, J., & Herasimchuk, E. Conversational analysis of social meaning: A study of classroom interaction. In R. Shuy (Ed.), *Sociolinguistics: Current trends and prospects*. Washington, D.C.: Georgetown University Press, 1972.

Guralnick, M.J. *Early intervention and the integration of handicapped and non-handicapped children*. Baltimore: University Park Press, 1978.

Markman, E. M. Realizing that you don't understand: A preliminary investigation. *Child Development*, 1977, *48*, 986–992.

Mehan, H. *Learning lessons*. Cambridge: Harvard University Press, 1979.

Merritt, M. *The view from service-like events: Teaching as managing linguistic (/communicative) participation*. NIE conference on Teaching as a Linguistic Process, Fredericksburg, Virginia, July 1979.

Mueller, E. The maintenance of verbal exchanges between young children. *Child Development*, 1972, *43*, 930–938.

Piaget, J. *Judgment and reasoning in the child*. Paterson, N.J.: Littlefield Adams, 1959.

Pratt, M. W., Scribner, S., & Cole, M. Children as teachers: Developmental studies of instructional communication. *Child Development*, 1977, *48*, 1475–1481.

Rubin, Z. *Children's friendships*. Cambridge: Harvard University Press, 1980.

Schachter, F. F., Kirshner, K., Klips, B., Friedricks, M., & Sanders, K. Everyday preschool interpersonal speech usage: Methodological, developmental, and sociolinguistic studies. *Monographs of the Society for Research in Child Development*, 1974, No. 156, Vol. 39, No. 3.

Searle, J. What is a speech act? In J. Searle (Ed.), *The philosophy of language*. New York: Oxford University Press, 1971.

Sharan, S. Cooperative learning in small groups: Recent methods and effects on achievement, attitudes, and ethnic relations. *Review of Educational Research*, 1980, *50*, 241–272.

Sinclair, J., & Coulthard, R. M. *Towards an analysis of discourse: The English used by teachers and pupils*. London and New York: Oxford University Press, 1975.

Slavin, R. E. Cooperative learning. *Review of Educational Research*, 1980, *50*, 315–342.

Steinberg, Z. D., & Cazden, C. B. Children as teachers of peers and ourselves. *Theory into Practice*, 1979, *18*, 258–266.

6

Effective Speakers: Students' Use of Language to Request and Obtain Information and Action in the Classroom[1]

LOUISE CHERRY WILKINSON
STEVEN CALCULATOR

Students' and teachers' use of language to request and obtain action and information is central to teaching and learning in the classroom. The classroom is an interactional context in which teachers and students meet to exchange information; teachers provide evaluation of students' performance, and the interpersonal behavior of students is regulated by both teachers and other students. Communication through language is crucial for learning in the classroom, since it is the means of accomplishing educational objectives that are embedded in teaching and learning activities. In addition, the development of communicative competence is an educational objective for students whose language background differs from the language of instruction in the classroom. In this chapter, we introduce the concept of **effective speakers** to refer to speakers who use their knowledge of language forms, functions, and contexts to achieve their goals in interaction, such as obtaining materials from others, and securing informative responses to their requests for information.

The goals of this chapter are (a) to propose a definition of effective speakers and apply this concept to students' language use in a specific classroom activity; (b) to propose a predictive model of effective speakers' use of requests to obtain action and information; (c) to test this model against data collected from first-grade students' interactions in peer-directed reading groups; and (d)

[1] The preparation of this chapter was supported by a grant from the National Institute of Education to the Wisconsin Center for Education Research (NIE-G-81-0009).

85

to discuss individual differences among speakers (students) who vary in effectiveness. The relationship between students' use of language to request and obtain information and action and their structural knowledge of their language will also be assessed.

Strategies of Research

Our model of effective speakers' use of language to request and obtain action and information is derived from some specific notions about pragmatic knowledge of language that have been introduced by sociolinguistic theorists. Before considering these ideas, we believe it is important to introduce the perspective we hold regarding the ways of examining children's language development. The researcher may adopt an adult-oriented strategy, whereby the child's system can be viewed as a progressive approximation of the adult system. Alternatively, the researcher might adopt a child-oriented strategy, in which the child's language development is viewed in terms of a progressive mastery of a particular functional or structural potential. This latter view suggests that the child has a linguistic system prior to actually producing words and syntactic structures, thus conforming to the arbitrary social norms governing the use of language in adult interaction (Ervin-Tripp & Mitchell-Kernan, 1977). The perspective we will take in this analysis relies heavily on the former strategy, since we have found it to be instructive in examining the extent to which children's knowledge of language is similar to adult norms. However, in the following analysis the introduction to some of the theoretical constructs of children's speech will be described, whether or not they conform to the arbitrary social and linguistic norms that have been introduced by the sociolinguistic theorists.

Requests and Responses: Bases of the Model

Effective speakers use their knowledge of language forms, functions, and contexts to achieve their goals in interaction. For example, in the case of requests, effective speakers obtain compliance from listeners. Searle (1969) introduced the idea that speakers perform actions with their speech whereby they attempt to communicate their intentions to listeners. We may assume, then, that effective speakers are successful in having their listeners recognize the speakers' intentions. Grice (1967) believes that conversations are cooperative efforts between speakers and listeners, each of whom recognizes, to some extent, the shared goals and direction of the interaction. He has proposed four rules that, when implemented, result in the successful application of cooperation. This, in turn, will result, in the case of requests, in speakers obtaining responses. The four rules refer to the informativeness, truth, relevance, and clarity of the speech.

Linguistic expressions differ in their degree of clarity and in the inferencing required for a particular intention to be recognized. According to Grice (1967), speakers are able to perceive that a particular speech act has been communicated, despite its indirectness or heavy reliance on inference. Listeners may integrate the form and content of the utterance itself with the social context and the shared cooperative principle to achieve an accurate recognition of the speaker's intention. If speakers desire clarity in their communication, they may attempt to minimize ambiguity and multiple interpretations of the same utterance through explicitly stating the agent, action, and object in the utterance, using **direct forms**, and specifically **designating** a particular listener to which a request is addressed.

Several researchers have noted that preschool and early school-age children tend to prefer using the direct form of a request, such as the imperative and either the wh- or yes–no question form in producing a request, as opposed to using one of the more indirect forms, such as "a need statement" or declarative (Ervin-Tripp, 1976; Read & Cherry, 1978). In the classroom, requests that are *on-task*, that is, those which refer to the shared activities in teaching and learning situations, are probably most likely to be understood mutually by teachers and students.

Labov and Fanshel (1977) offer a model that represents the shared understanding between speakers and listeners when requests are made. The preconditions of their model specify the action, purpose, and need for the request; the ability and obligation of the listener to comply with the request; and the right of the speaker to make the request. One implication of the model is that for a request to be effective, these conditions should be met (i.e., **sincere**) by speakers when they make requests. The preconditions are frequently referred to by speakers producing indirect requests or mitigating–aggravating requests. According to Labov and Fanshel, the demands of face-to-face social interaction require speakers to use various mitigating techniques to soften their requests in such a way as to avoid offending their listeners. These mitigated forms present the listener with a number of options in responding besides presenting the listener with a choice to comply or not. A request is aggravated when the force of the request is strengthened by repeating the same request in the same way. Effective speakers should be flexible in issuing their requests, particularly when compliance is not obtained initially. **Revising** their initial request by providing additional information may be more effective than merely repeating the same request.

In sum, we expect that certain characteristics of students' requests for action and information in the classroom will increase the likelihood that an appropriate response will be obtained. These include: on-task, direct form, sincere, designated to one particular listener, and revised (if there is an initially unsuccessful request).

This brief discussion of effective speakers provides some indication of the complex nature of knowledge that may underlie communicative competence. It is not sufficient for the child acquiring communicative competence to know merely about the issues that have been discussed here. Often, the separate knowledge included in different aspects of speech appear to be inconsistent and may even compete with one another.

Consider the directive or the request for action. Emphatic, direct, and explicit forms of expression for requests for action are probably the most effective means of communicating intention to listeners. This is, however, not the only consideration in choosing the form. Succinct directives may not always be successful in obtaining compliance with either child or adult listeners. They do not provide listeners with options in responding and may not result in listener compliance, particularly if the listener perceives them as rude (Read & Cherry, 1978). Thus, an apparent paradox is evident: There may be competing tendencies for speakers and their production of directives. They may have learned that the probability of a listener's **understanding** a directive is maximized when the directive is phrased clearly and emphatically, yet the probability of a listener's **compliance** is also maximized when a directive is phrased politely or given indirectly.

Thus, the task of acquiring communicative competence for the child must seem formidable. Not only must the individual acquire the structural and the functional knowledge that will enable him or her to produce speech, but also, the social norms that govern the use of language to secure compliance from listeners. There are some areas in which the children's speech may be incompletely developed (e.g., accountings for refusals; Wilkinson & Dollaghan, 1980). Goffman (1963) has referred to children as "communication delinquents," since often they violate the adult rules. In the present study, many of the concepts introduced in this review will be elaborated in light of new evidence provided by the study of first-grade students' use of requests and responses in their all-student reading groups.

Method

SUBJECTS

The subjects were 30 first-grade students who comprised 6 reading groups in the first-grade unit of one school. According to the teachers, the students' reading abilities and reading readiness at the beginning of the school year differed in the groups, even though no formal assessment of these skills was used. All of the students were Caucasian, native speakers of English, from middle-class families, and ranged in age from 6 to 7 years. They attended the school for the entire academic year. No students were diagnosed as having learning disabilities or any language problems. There were 13 males and 17 females. Parents' permission was obtained for the students' participation in the study.

DATA COLLECTION

Recording the Reading Event

A reading activity was the unit of sample for data collection. Reading activity typically began at 9:00 and lasted until approximately 9:40 in each of the classrooms; teachers announced both the beginning and ending of the activity. Students chose their seats at the reading tables designated by the teacher. The teachers often provided instructions for the reading groups when the students were in the whole-group formation; however, some of the teachers provided instructions after the students had formed their small reading groups. In either case, the completion of the instructions marked the beginning of the reading event.

The reading activities were audio- and videotaped in each of the classrooms for each of the reading groups. Data were collected every day for a period of 3.5 weeks; the days were regarded as typical by the classroom teachers. Each reading group was taped during one period defined by the teacher as the reading group time.

Two portable video cameras (Sony Portapak®) were used to record the reading activity of each group; cameras were visible to the students and were positioned across from one another so that nearly full-face views of all of the students would be on one or the other camera. Two microphones (Electra Voice 635A) were placed in the middle of each group's table.

Prior to, during, and following the recording, two observers prepared descriptions of the ongoing events in the group, including the behavior of the students, to supplement the recordings with relevant contextual information that may not have been included on the tapes. These two observers were also in the room and were visible to the students. Thus, along with the members of the research team who operated the cameras, there were four adults in addition to the students, teachers, and school staff. According to the principal, videotaping of both teachers and students was routine in these classrooms. The subjects were familiar with the presence of several adults in the classroom in addition to their teachers. These adults included student interns, nurses, parent aides, and various specialist teachers.

Data were collected in the fall, for 3.5 weeks at the end of September and beginning of October, and again in the spring for 3.5 weeks in April. There were 4 separate tapings for each reading group in each season for a total of 8 samples for each group; there were approximately 32 hours of recordings.

The reading groups were determined by the teachers prior to the study; there were between four and six subjects per group. The organization of the reading group was very similar to the organization revealed during a small-scale study conducted in the same school a year earlier (Wilkinson & Dollaghan, 1980). All of the groups were similar in the way that the reading activity was initiated, maintained, and terminated. Initially, there were instructions presented by the teachers; the teacher then left the reading group and the students functioned as a group in order to accomplish the individual tasks the teacher had presented to them. In all cases, the task was the same for all members of the group for that particular reading activity (e.g., a worksheet or a workbook page). The final phase of the reading group included another teacher-directed period occurring shortly before the group disintegrated, where the teacher often provided evaluation.

All of the groups were seated at small tables within the classrooms that also contained other groups of students as well as the teachers. Therefore, background noise and general environmental characteristics appeared to be comparable among the groups. The dominant activity during the reading group was reading—either silently or aloud. And all of the groups performed one or more activities requiring a written response, such as completing worksheets, drawing a picture of events the students had read about, or printing sentences from the stories.

The reading groups with which we were concerned were organized around individual tasks, so that each member had the same task; each student was encouraged to cooperate with the other students in the completion of the tasks. Rewards were individually distributed by the teacher, yet attainment of a reward for meeting the goal by one student did not preclude reward attainment by another student, as in the competitive situation. Also, in addition to individual task rewards, the group could be reprimanded and/or rewarded as a whole for its behavior.

Individual Assessment

Information concerning each student's language ability and reading achievement was collected by individual testing in the fall and in the spring; the assessments typically lasted for 45 minutes.

A free speech sample consisting of approximately 50 spontaneous utterances from each student was obtained during an informal conversation in which an experimenter posed open-ended questions regarding topics presumed to be of interest to the children, such as television, friends, and so on. Grammatical complexity was assessed by segmenting each child's transcript into a series of communication units (an independent clause plus all of its modifiers), then computing the average number of words per unit using a procedure based on Loban (1963, 1976). Unlike Loban, we did not score responses limited to yes–no replies, or "okay" as communication units because the conversational framework of our speech sample did not ensure narrative responses to the extent of Loban's elicited procedures. In addition, 40, rather than 30, communication units were used to increase the reliability of the scores.

Students' grammatical comprehension was assessed by their performance on the Miller–Yoder Test of Grammatical Comprehension (Miller & Yoder, 1975). This test, which consists of 84 items, requires the student to point to the picture, given a choice of four stimuli, that depicts the meaning of each utterance read by the experimenter. Various syntactic structures are tested, including prepositions, subject and object pronouns, possessives, and tenses.

Transcription of Tapes

The videotapes collected for each group were transcribed by a member of the research team who had been present during that day's data collection. The relatively long segment of all-student interaction for each group was chosen for detailed analysis in this study (10–30 minutes). During this segment, the teacher was not present in the group; typically, she was in the classroom assisting other students. Transcripts were rechecked against both tapes. Percentage agreement on these data had been previously established for word and utterance boundaries; they exceeded 80%. Following transcription, the videotapes were viewed for relevant nonverbal and spatial information that was included on the transcripts.

Two transcripts, one coded previously by the same observer, the second by an associate, were randomly selected and recoded by the second author. Intraobserver agreement, represented as the proportion of coding agreements divided by the number of agreements plus disagreements, was then computed with respect to each of the variables included in this study. Percentage agreement ranged from 88–100%.

Coding

The samples of data selected for analysis were coded according to the following categories.

1. **Utterance:** A string of words communicating one idea, usually bounded by a pause of 1 second or more.
2. **Requests for action or directives:** Attempts by speakers to obtain actions performed by listeners.
3. **Requests for information or questions:** Attempts by speakers to obtain information from listeners.

All requests were coded as having or not having the following characteristics.

1. **On-task:** Related to the academic content and/or procedures and materials of the assignment.
2. **Designated listener:** Directed verbally and/or nonverbally and un-ambiguously to a student.
3. **Sincere:** Meeting Labov and Fanshel's (1977) preconditions for requests.
4. **Revision:** A restatement of a request previously made by the same speaker to the same listener who had not responded appropriately.
5. **Direct form:** For requests for action, the imperative; for requests for information, the wh-, yes–no, or tag question.
6. **Appropriate response:** The requested action and/or information was given, or else a reason was given why the action and/or information could not be given.

Measures

The following measures were computed for each student. The quantity of speech was computed for each student as the number of utterances. Relative rates were: all requests divided by all utterances, appropriate responses obtained divided by all requests produced, revisions of requests divided by nonresponses to requests, direct forms of requests divided by all requests, on-task requests divided by all requests, and sincere requests divided by all requests.

Results and Discussion

The data base included 5055 utterances, of which 1025 (19%) were requests, with 443 requests for action and 582 requests for information.

RELATIONSHIP BETWEEN CHARACTERISTICS OF REQUESTS
AND APPROPRIATE RESPONSES AND ASSESSED LANGUAGE KNOWLEDGE

One standardized score for language knowledge was calculated, based on the scores from the two separate tests administered in the fall and spring. The correlations between language knowledge and the aspects of requests and re-sponses were not statistically significant.[2]

Characteristics of Requests and Appropriate Responses

The data for the characteristics of requests and appropriate responses are displayed in Figure 6.1. These displays are an adaptation of Tukey's (1977)

[2] Rank order correlations were used since they are as powerful as Pearson correlations, but are less likely to be biased by extreme cases, which occurred occasionally in these data. For a sample of 40, a Kendall's tau rank order correlation of .20 is the equivalent to a Pearson correlation of about .30, whereas a tau of .30 is equivalent to a Pearson correlation of about .45.

"box and whisker" diagram, which has the advantage of displaying all the data and variability. The following information is given for each variable: the lowest value in the sample (black circle); the 10th percentile (dash bar); the 25th percentile (solid bar); the median (solid bar); the 75th percentile (solid bar); the 90th percentile (dash bar); and the highest value in the sample (black circle). The "box" represents the interquartile range, or middle half of the sample.

Two kinds of variables are represented in Figure 6.1. One group of variables, represented on the extreme left-hand side of the figure, shows high medians and small interquartile ranges (.10 to .14), indicating low spread and "ceiling effects." This group of variables, which includes designated listener, on-task, and sincere requests, suggests a common competence among the students on these aspects of their communication. The second group of variables, which can be seen on the extreme right-hand side of the figure, shows medians in the middle range with moderate interquartile ranges (.15 to .27), indicating medium spread. On this group of variables, which includes direct forms, revisions, and appropriate responses to requests, these measures show enough variation among the children to suggest genuine individual differences.

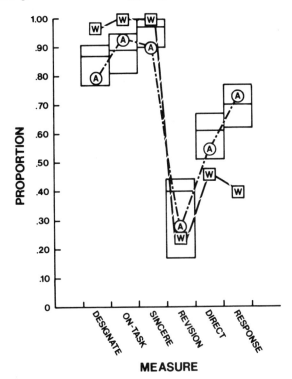

Figure 6.1. Characteristics of requests and appropriate responses.

Overall, the data show that this group of first graders were effective in obtaining appropriate responses to their requests for action and information more than two-thirds of the time. The typical student usually made requests that were direct, sincere, on-task, and to a designated listener. In cases where the listener did not respond appropriately, the typical student tried again only two-fifths of the time. The data suggest a pattern of language use for requests that places a premium upon explicitness, directness, and assertiveness. These findings are consistent with those of Ervin-Tripp (1976), Read and Cherry (1978), and Montes (in press). However, the findings contrast with the pattern of language use associated with adults, who express cooperation and politeness through use of indirect forms, and show a tendency to soften and elaborate requests when initial noncompliance occurs (Ervin-Tripp, 1976; Lakoff, 1973).

The stability of differences in characteristics of requests and appropriate responses. With some exceptions, the patterns concerning both requests for information and requests for action were stable from fall to spring. Wilcoxon Matched Pairs Signed Ranks Tests were used to examine the significance of differences between fall and spring, and between the two types of requests. There was only one significant difference between seasons. On-task requests for action ($z = -3.10$, $p \leq .01$) were used more often by the students in the fall than in the spring.

There were several differences between the two types of requests. Requests for information were significantly more likely to be used than requests for action (rate of requests: $z = -1.96$, $p \leq .05$). Requests for information were more likely to be of a direct form ($z = -4.47$, $p \leq .01$) and sincere ($z = -3.81$, $p \leq .01$), and they were more likely to obtain an appropriate response ($z = -4.07$, $p \leq .01$), compared with requests for action. In contrast, requests for action were significantly more likely to be designated to a particular listener ($z = -2.34$, $p \leq .02$) and on-task ($z = -1.93$, $p \leq .06$).

This pattern of differential language usage for requests for information and action reflects increasing sophistication in language usage. In contrast, adults' requests for action, typically, do not take a direct form, which is considered to be rude and impolite. For the students in this study, the probability of listener understanding may be increased by use of the characteristics of designated listener and by reference to the topic at hand. On the other hand, the probability of listener understanding and compliance seems to be increased by the use of sincere requests of a direct form.

Predicting appropriate responses to requests. An analysis was conducted to address the question: "Do selected characteristics predict whether an appropriate response will be obtained?" This question was addressed by classifying requests in a multidimensional contingency table defined by the following dimensions:

response, direct form, designated listener, on-task, sincere, revision, and request for action–information. Log linear models were fit to this table in an effort to find the simplest model that adequately predicted the frequencies observed in the table (Bishop, Fienberg, & Holland, 1975).

In the simplest model, it was assumed that the six characteristics of requests were completely independent of each other. This model was rejected: $\chi^2(120) = 354.88$, $p \leq .01$. In a more complex model, it was assumed that appropriate responses depended on the other characteristics, but that these other characteristics did not depend on each other. This model was rejected, $\chi^2(114) = 250.96$, $p \leq .01$, but it was a significant improvement over the first model, $\chi^2(6) = 103.92$, $p \leq .01$. In a still more complex model, it was assumed that there were associations between every pair of characteristics, but no higher order associations. This model did fit the data: $\chi^2(99) = 85.77$. Moreover, it fit better than the preceding model in which it was assumed that **only** appropriate response was associated with other characteristics, $\chi^2(15) = 165.19$, $p \leq .01$. Finally, this model fit better than one in which it was assumed that all pairs of characteristics were associated **except** pairs involving appropriate responses, $\chi^2(6) = 82.92$, $p \leq .01$. The major conclusions, therefore, are (a) that characteristics of requests are correlated, and (b) that whether a request received an appropriate response depended on other characteristics of the request. This latter effect received support from two sources: The goodness of fit improved when the effect was added to the model and worsened when it was removed.

Because the observations are dependent, the significance levels that were obtained are not completely trustworthy. One solution to this problem is to select a statistic which measures an effect of interest and to jackknife that statistic by groups (Mosteller & Tukey, 1977).[3] The log linear effect of each characteristic on appropriate responses was computed and jackknifed by reading groups. The results suggested that three characteristics predicted appropriate responses. Requests were more likely to obtain appropriate responses if they were for information instead of action, $t(5) = 4.63$, $p \leq .05$; if they were of a direct form, $t(5) = 2.35$, $p \leq .07$; and if they were to a designated listener, $t(5) = 2.48$, $p \leq .06$.

Individual differences. Overall, the individual differences among the students are represented in Figure 6.2 showing the distribution of the various measures. In this section, we will consider two selected examples: one student who is high on the measure of effective speakers and one who is low on the measure.

[3] Jackknifing is a method for assessing the degree to which an effect estimated from the data for all subjects persists when a subgroup of subjects is deleted from the analysis. In the present analysis, the subgroups were reading groups.

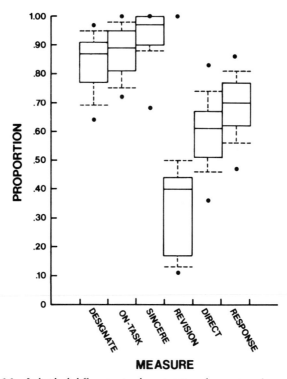

Figure 6.2. Individual differences in characteristics of requests and appropriate responses.

Student A is a good example of the typical profile identified in the previous section for the effective speaker. Amy is usually successful in obtaining compliance to her requests (.73). She uses a broad repertoire of request forms according to shifting situational demands. But, in particular, she displays that unique characteristic of effective speakers, persistence in continuing to seek responses to her requests when confronted with a noncompliant listener (17 revisions).

In the following example, Amy interacts with two fellow students, Joe and Dave. Amy has been successful in obtaining help from Dave in doing her assignment in the previous 15 exchanges between the two of them. For some reason, Amy then shifts her attention to another child, Joe, in an attempt to enlist his help. Joe is not able to help her, so Amy shifts her attention once again to Dave, by requesting his help for completing an answer to a particular question. At first, Dave is reluctant to help and resists Amy's initial request, which is interrupted by Joe's joining in to request the answer. However, Amy persists and Dave eventually submits to this pressure by supplying her with an answer to the question. Both Dave and Amy then continue to work together on the assignment, which consists of Amy's requesting information and action from Dave, who is the provider of both. The following exchange occurred in late September, during the initial taping of the reading group of these children.

AMY: *Okay, what, what's that word?*
JOE: *Don't ask me.*
AMY: *Ah, I'll ask him.*
   (to Dave) What's that word?
JOE: *Dave, do you know what we should write, like here?*
AMY: *Right here.*
   (several seconds elapse)
   I want you to look at my paper.
   (several more seconds elapse)
   Listen to this.
   I've got these words.
   I keep gettin' mixed up Dave.
   Dave, I keep gettin'
DAVE: *r, the, the*
   (The words Amy has requested are provided by Dave.)

In the spring, Amy continues to show characteristics of effective and appropriate speakers. One unusual strategy that appears quite effective with some children is an attempt to sustain a cooperative relationship with their listeners. In the following exchange, Amy is successful in securing Dave's cooperation by suggesting he may have something to gain by reviewing his work with her.

AMY: *Dave, let's go back and do, and see, what we, what words we missed.*
   Like I missed all of them.
DAVE: *Yeah, yeah, yeah, yeah.*

However, this strategy does not always prove successful as is illustrated in the following exchange:

AMY: *Let's do it together.*
   What is it?
ROY: *Don't look at mine Amy.*

Amy is an individual who frequently produces adjuncts designating the needs for her requests, and underlying the listener's obligation to respond, as illustrated in the following excerpts.

AMY: *Mindy, can I have the pen? I need the eraser for it.*
   I did something wrong.
   (Mindy turns over the eraser to Amy.)

Another taping session:

AMY: *Oh great.*
           Can I use your eraser for a minute Sandy?
           I made a boo-boo.
SANDY: *Oh, that is a boo-boo* (giving the eraser to Amy).

And later in the transcript:

AMY: *I forgot a word.*
MINDY: (no response)
AMY: *You, you know you could get me in trouble.*
           I really forgot this word.
           Mindy, Mindy, now I forgot this word.

Will, shown as W in Figure 6.2, illustrates an ineffective speaker. At an initial glance, Will seems to conform to the profile of the effective and appropriate speaker, with his high scores on sincerity, on-task, and designated requests. But, we notice that this child has a relatively low rate of compliance to his requests (.40), tends not to use direct requests initially, and is not as likely as the other children to revise his requests when noncompliance occurs. One explanation for Will's low rate of compliance could be that his initial requests, which are indirect, are also often inexplicit. It is likely that his listeners may not understand exactly what he wants, and thus may respond inappropriately or not at all. In the following example, the students are working in their workbooks and, at this point in the interaction, are discussing the progress each is making. While looking directly at the child next to him, Will produces a request that does not receive a response; it is unclear to the children as well as to the authors exactly what he meant.

JAKE: *I'm still on "shut the door."*
JEBB: *I'm not.*
KRISTY: *I'm on 9 and 10.*
WILL: *I wonder when we can?*
JAKE: *I'm right here (pointing).*

Summary and Conclusions

In this chapter, we have applied the concept of effective speakers, who use their knowledge of language forms, functions, and contexts to achieve their communicative goals in interactions, to students' language use in a specific classroom activity. Specifically, we are interested in students' use of language to request and obtain action and information that is central to the functioning of first-grade reading groups. In our examination of the language of 30 students in peer-directed reading groups during the course of one academic year, we have tested our model of requests. This model states that requests that have the following characteristics are likely to obtain appropriate responses: on-task, direct form, sincere, to a designated listener, and revised (if initially unsuccessful in obtaining a response). We see this work as a contribution to our understanding of the social and language skills that are necessary, even central, to the interactional process of teaching and learning. Our work is similar to several of the chapters in this volume, but most particularly to Cooper, Marquis, and Ayers-Lopez (Chapter 5). Further research should address differences in these aspects of communicative competence (e.g., developmental and second-language learning) and their role in mediating the process of teaching and learning in the classroom.

References

Bishop, T., Fienberg, S., & Holland, P. *Discrete multivariate analyses: Theory and practice.* Cambridge: M.I.T. Press, 1975.

Ervin-Tripp, S. Is Sybil there: The structure of some American English directives. *Language and Society,* 1976, *5,* 25–66.

Ervin-Tripp, S. & Mitchell-Kernan, C. Introduction. In S. Ervin-Tripp & C. Mitchell-Kernan (Eds.), *Child discourse.* New York: Academic Press, 1977.

Goffman, E. *Behavior in public places.* New York: Free Press, 1963.

Grice, P. *Logic and conversation.* Unpublished William James Lectures, 1967.

Labov, W., & Fanshel, D. *Therapeutic discourse.* New York: Academic Press, 1977.

Lakoff, R. Language and woman's place. *Language in Society,* 1973, *2*(1), 45–79.

Loban, W. D. *The language of elementary school children* (Research Report No. 1). Champaign, Ill.: National Council of Teachers of English, 1963.

Loban, W. D. *Language development: Kindergarten through grade twelve* (Research Report No. 18). Champaign, Ill.: National Council of Teachers of English, 1976.

Miller, J. F., & Yoder, D. E. *The Miller–Yoder Test of Grammatical Comprehension: Experimental Edition,* Madison, Wis., 1975.

Montes, R. Extending a concept: Functioning directly. In R. Shuy & M. Griffin (Eds.), *Children's functional language in the early years.* Washington, D.C.: Center for Applied Linguistics, in press.

Mosteller, F., & Tukey, J. *Data analysis and regression.* Reading, Mass.: Addison-Wesley, 1977.

Read, B., & Cherry, L. J. Preschool children's production of directive forms. *Discourse Processes,* 1978, *1*(3), 233–245.

Searle, J. *Speech acts.* New York: Cambridge University Press, 1969.

Tukey, J. W. *Exploratory data analysis.* Reading, Mass.: Addison-Wesley, 1977.

Wilkinson, L. J. Cherry, & Dollaghan, C. Peer communication in first-grade reading groups. *Theory Into Practice,* 1980, *4*(XVIII), 267–274.

7
Discourse Rules for
Literacy Learning in a Classroom[1]

JOHANNA S. DE STEFANO
HAROLD B. PEPINSKY
TOBIE S. SANDERS

The expansion of communicative competence is one of the most important kinds of socialization that can occur among the young (Cook-Gumperz
& Gumperz, Chapter 2, this volume; DeStefano, 1978; Florio & Clark, Chapter
13, this volume; Hymes, 1974). Within the school systems students are supposed to be taught and, in turn, to learn how to become acceptably literate.
In schools, as in the rest of society, then, considerable importance is attached
to literacy—the demonstration of the ability to read, write, and spell "correctly"
(DeStefano, Pepinsky, & Sanders, 1980; Hoover, 1975).

In first grade, competence in the rudiments of literacy is often synonymous
with success and is used as a major criterion for promotion to second grade.
In fact, the student who fails to satisfy this criterion as defined by the teacher
may fail the first grade.

Rates of failure in learning to be literate appear disproportionately high
among native English-speaking students in the inner-city schools of large cities
throughout North America. Many children from inner-city black and Appalachian cultures attend these schools. Children from these cultures, which
have traditionally placed value on oral rather than written means of communication, often have problems in learning to become literate according to
the rules of mainstream culture with which they come in contact in school.

[1] This chapter is based on research conducted under NIE Grant No. G-70-0032 from the
National Institute of Education and the Mershon Center for Programs of Research and Education
in National Security, Leadership and Public Policy.

This fact is widely documented and a reason for parent action in public arenas such as the courts.

For several years, research on the apparent mismatch between these children and their schools and their subsequent failure in the schools has centered on the language of inner-city black children and, to a lesser extent, on that of Appalachian children. The greatest emphasis has been on the formal features of language used by members of these groups. One helpful insight to come from this research was that phonological and syntactic differences among the varieties of American English used by these children have less effect on the students' demonstrated ability to become literate than the teachers' attitudes toward those differences (Williams, Whitehead, & Miller, 1977).

A major question remains unanswered, however. Why does this apparently widespread lack of success in becoming literate persist among members of these groups? Literature dealing with this question has not emphasized the interaction between such students and their teachers in the classroom. Although teachers may have been asked how they feel about the children's language (as in attitude studies such as those of Williams *et al.*, 1977), they usually have not been observed while teaching. Or the children's language may have been studied, but usually not in relation to educational tasks. Infrequently, measures of reading (Labov & Robins, 1973) have been obtained, but under more restricted conditions than those found in the classroom during reading instruction. Currently, however, more studies are focusing on such settings, as in the classroom language project at the Center for Applied Linguistics (Shuy & Griffin, 1978), Cook-Gumperz and Gumperz (Chapter 2, this volume), Eder (Chapter 12, this volume), Mehan, Cazden, Coles, Fisher, and Maroules (1976), and Mehan, Hertweck, Combs, and Flynn (Chapter 15, this volume).

A reason for centering attention on the context in which children are exposed to literacy instruction is that language is explicitly used to teach and learn about language and there is emphasis placed on competence in verbal communication, both receptive and productive. During lessons on literacy, teachers tend to concentrate on students' verbal behavior and to evaluate in a highly prescriptive manner their verbal initiations and responses. As Cicourel, Jennings, Jennings, Leiter, MacKay, Mehan, and Roth (1974) observed, the teacher is evaluating the children's developing "interactional competence [p. 15]."

In this chapter, we have elected to work within the context of interaction between student and teacher. A few preliminary words about our intent should clarify both the kinds of questions we have raised in the investigation and the methods used to deal with them. We begin with the postulate that teaching in a classroom, like counseling or over-the-counter saleswork, exists as a process of social influence (Strong, 1978) in which treatment policies are both made and implemented, primarily through the medium of language (Meara, Pepinsky, Shannon, & Murray, 1981). We assume that teaching success requires concerted actions on the part of teacher and students to further their attainment of common knowledge and understanding between them. The process thus entails the "social construction of reality" in which agreements are negotiated about what is taking place and for what purpose (cf. Berger & Luckmann, 1966; Garfinkel, 1967).

In this view of things, students and teacher come to the classroom with prior intentions and expectations. Through their use of language, they signal their expectations, influence one another reciprocally, and establish ground rules that define social policies to guide them further in their interactions. Ideally in the process, they attain a common knowledge and understanding that enable them to work together to minimize perceived discrepancies between actual and desired states-of-affairs (after Pepinsky & Patton, 1971). For a parallel statement and evidence about what occurs during counseling or psychotherapy, see Meara *et al.* (1981).

Quite apart from expert testimony that outsiders may gather to describe and interpret classroom teaching and its outcomes, then, it is the phenomenally perceived realities of students and teacher who interact there that define for them what is happening and how it is to be evaluated. As we have already suggested and shall document in the following, the teacher in our study served as gatekeeper in using available information to record for future reference how well each student performed and to decide who was or was not to be promoted by the end of the year.

Hence, in this research, we chose to deal with the teaching and learning of literacy in the classroom as a context in which natural language was employed and modified. The study of language thus used by teacher and students, we reasoned, would help us identify rules of discourse to be taught and acquired. We wanted to know, particularly, whether and how children with diverse cultural backgrounds—including the cultural mainstream in North America— might differentially identify and acquire rules of discourse appropriate to becoming literate.

Method

To describe rules of discourse operating within the framework of literacy instruction, we centered this study on the actual language among teacher and students, recorded within selected periods of literacy learning in a desegregated classroom of first graders.

SETTING

The research site was a self-contained classroom of first graders in a midsized school in the immediate ring surrounding the inner-city area of a large midwestern city. The cultural mix of the neighborhood is mainly inner-city black and Appalachian. As part of the school system's program of desegregation, put into effect the year we conducted this research, the school had been paired with an adjoining area comprised of middle-to-low income families of whites and blacks from the cultural mainstream. For the first time in the history of the system, children from the adjoining area were bused in.

SUBJECTS

The teacher in this study was a woman from mainstream culture and had 6 years of teaching experience, all in the site school where our research was conducted. She was more experienced in working in her classroom with students from the black and Appalachian cultures than with those who shared her cultural background. The self-contained classroom is typical of many in the school system, although less traditional settings exist in various areas of the city. A basal reading series was used for primary instruction in reading.

In addition to the teacher, three children served as subjects in the research. Each of these subjects was a male first grader with the usual kindergarten experience of students in the city's schools, consisting of half-day sessions primarily concerned with "readiness" and socialization. One child, Harry, was from the cultural mainstream; one we called Dick, from inner-city black culture; and one we named Tom, from the Appalachian culture. Cultural membership was determined via family history and performance on sentence repetition tasks, revealing use of black English, an Appalachian dialect such as South Midland, or a less marked form of American English. Males were selected because research indicates they have more difficulty becoming literate than females in North America (DeStefano, 1978).

All males from the Appalachian culture in the first grade (five classrooms) were repeaters, except for two students taking daily behavior-modifying medication. Therefore, we had to select a subject from the Appalachian culture who was repeating the first grade. The selected child's retention had been attributed to prolonged absence during the previous school year.

DATA COLLECTION

Discourse of the teacher and the three principal student subjects, during the teaching and learning of literacy, was collected via audiotape and videotapes. The use of lavalier wireless microphones made it possible to collect the student subjects' subvocalizations as well as their interactive language in the classroom. The individual audiotapes facilitated careful transcription and examination of interactional discourse. Videotaped records were available to provide a check against the audiotapes and the opportunity to examine elements of nonverbal interaction as well as verbal interaction. Classroom observation notes were collected and served as yet another check upon the accuracy of information collected and analyzed in this research.

Data were collected on 3 consecutive days during the third week of school, after conclusion of the first grading-period (before Christmas), and at the beginning of the second semester of that year. The periods of data collection consisted primarily, but not exclusively, of time when literacy instruction occurred. The periods were interspersed with other business, such as explanations of seatwork, time structuring, and language used to control individuals and groups of children.

This schedule for collecting data was used because the first, few weeks of school were crucial for identifying problem areas in the initial acquisition of literacy, as defined by the teacher. Also during this period, concepts, classroom values, and social expectations tied to the learning of literacy were introduced by the teacher. By the second collection period, the children had been exposed to approximately 3 months of instructional discourse in the classroom. At that time, the children were academically assessed in their progress of becoming literate. By late February, they had been assessed three times in their progress, after being further exposed to instruction and experiencing the Christmas holiday break. This holiday period was a major interruption in the school year, providing the subjects with some reisolation in their respective cultures.

DISCOURSE ANALYSIS

Discourse recorded each day during the three periods of observations was first carefully transcribed. Representative samples of these texts were then examined independently by three different methods, to provide analyses within and over occasions (a) of interactions among our subjects, (b) of cohesion within and among their utterances, and (c) of their grammatical structuring.

Interactions and other activities in the classroom were examined following methods introduced by Sinclair and Coulthard (1975; see Chapter 3 in *Towards an Analysis of Discourse*) and Mehan (1979). Use of Mehan's (1979) analytic framework displays both student- and teacher-initiated talk as well as their replies to talk initiated by others. In addition, the teacher's evaluative statements are identified and displayed. Exchanges between talkers are treated as basic interactional units in this form of analysis. Sinclair and Coulthard (1975) offer a complementary mode of analyzing activities in the classroom, much like

Mehan's in that each interaction is organized into three parts: an initiation of some type, a reply, and a follow-up. But, by contrast, this approach concentrates on academic rather than social interaction, emphasizing teacher initiation of talk and the teacher's control of discourse. Also, it is based on a relatively traditional organization of behavior within the classroom.

Cohesion has to do with internal consistency among the component parts of a set of texts. (See Halliday & Hasan, 1976, pp. 333–339, for a summary of cohesion analysis and a description of the coding scheme.) Cohesion analysis was designed to make explicit a speaker's or reader's ability to know whether a given sample of discourse is or is not to be comprehended as a unified text (adapted from Halliday & Hasan). In our research, Halliday and Hasan's method of analyzing cohesion in text was used to determine whether the teacher's and the students' talk were interrelated, and whether over the periods of instruction in literacy, there was a tendency for the contents of the students' talk to become even more related to the teacher's. Moreover, we could determine the extent to which the contents of each subject's talk cohered with each other over time. Although Mehan's (1979) and Sinclair and Coulthard's (1975) analytic systems were designed specifically for use in the classroom, Halliday and Hasan's (1976) system is applicable to a variety of situations.

Grammatical structuring of our subjects' talk was identified and interpreted by means of CALAS, acronym for a Computer-Assisted Language Analysis System (Hurndon, Pepinsky, & Meara, 1979; Meara et al., 1981; Pepinsky, 1974, 1980; Strong, 1974). Like cohesion analysis, CALAS was designed to be more generally applicable in the analysis of text. Its use is predicated on the assumption that people produce and interpret communicable written or spoken language by a structuring process of naming perceived things and of relating the named things to each other (Hicks, Rush, & Strong, 1977; Pepinsky, 1974, 1980). To account for that process, CALAS postulates the existence of a surrogate language with which the original words of a text can be assigned grammatical equivalents (Strong, 1974; for a brief description of CALAS, see Appendix A, pp. 125–127).

Sampling of the data generated in each period when data were collected was determined by (a) the presence of all three subjects, (b) clearly audible recordings that could be readily transcribed, and (c) actual meetings of reading groups to which our subjects had been assigned during the second (November) and third (February) periods of observation. Data analyzed by recourse to CALAS and to cohesion analysis were further restricted to actual interactions among the teacher and the other three subjects.

Comprehensiveness of the analysis was enhanced in several ways. First, as indicated, the analyses of discourse centered on different aspects of the texts. The focus on interactions between our subjects provided evidence concerning the social organization of the classroom. The analysis of cohesion furnished information about the internal consistency of discourse within the classroom. Structural changes in the patterns of talk could be inferred from the grammatical analysis of the discourse. Second, the levels of inquiry ranged from macroscopic, in the analyses of cohesion and discourse across subjects, to relatively microscopic, in the analysis of grammatical changes within and among clauses.

Results

In examining our findings, one should keep in mind changes in the organization of reading instruction that occurred within the classroom over the three periods of data collection. During the first period (September), all students participated together in a general program of instruction in reading readiness. By the time of the second observational period (November), the students had been divided into three reading groups: the one most advanced, a middle group, and a third least advanced. At that time, Harry, the student from mainstream culture, and Tom, representing the Appalachian culture, were in the middle group. Dick from the black culture of the inner-city, was in the least advanced group. By the third period (February), Harry and Tom were still in the middle group, but Tom was also participating in the higher of two subgroups in the least advanced category. Dick remained in the least advanced group, but was now in the lower of the two subgroups.

SUCCESS IN LEARNING TO READ

In this study, we also looked at a variety of measures of reading success. One of the most overt measures is reading group membership, which was determined by the teacher and was described in the preceding section.

Harry, the child from the cultural mainstream, received a satisfactory reading progress report on his report card. At the end of the year, the teacher expressed no concern about promoting him to the next grade. By then, he was still a member of the middle reading group. The teacher observed that "He did not really try very hard in the group" and "wasn't applying himself," but basically was progressing at the predetermined rate. He had also successfully passed the reading series criterion-referenced test of progress for moving from level to level. Using a measure of progress devised by Marie Clay (1972), we ascertained that his performance on her *Concepts About Print Survey* increased only two points from the first to the third administration, whereas the stanine score remained the same. And when asked in an interview to explain "how to read" to someone like Mork from Ork, he responded with essentially an understanding that reading was word recognition.

Although there was evidence of reading at frustration level—that is, the material had become so difficult for him that he was restive in responding to it—Tom, our Appalachian subject, nonetheless volunteered frequently in his groups, continued to self-select books during his free time, and made fairly accurate approximations of text contained in those books. Also, he passed the reading series criterion-referenced test required for his placement in the middle group. Reviewing his performance on Clay's *Concept About Print Survey* (1972), we find Tom's score to have remained the same from the time of administration at the first observation period to that of the second administration 5 months later. When interviewed about how to explain to someone how to read, he responded *You read to somebody* and *I'd teach him how to read*, but could offer no more explanation than that. Tom's teacher was aware of some of his difficulties and prescribed repetition of reading levels he had already gone through. As a repeater of first grade already, he was not in danger of being retained.

Though Dick, the black inner-city child, ended the year in the lowest reading group, he seemed to have maintained enthusiasm for becoming literate and displayed an awareness of his own growth, as evidenced in part by comments made during the last administration of the *Concepts About Print Survey* (Clay, 1972). Also, when interviewed about what it is to read, he first responded with *We mark stuff*, which in his experience is a very accurate observation. When probed, however, he finally answered that he *thought* and then *sounded the word out*. He went on to say that *You have to know the sounds so you could sound the word so you could know it*. This is the most insightful and complicated explanation offered by any of our students—and it came in the second observation period at the beginning of the third month of the school year.

Despite his enthusiasm and progress, Dick received a "needs improvement" on his progress report at the end of the first semester. In fact, the teacher had expressed concern to his parents that he might have to be retained in first grade, though he finally was placed in, but not promoted to second grade. Dick's score on the *Concepts About Print Survey* (Clay, 1972) increased enough to move him from the middle of the fourth to the top of the fifth stanine on the test, although he remained one stanine below the other two boys.

INTERACTIVE PATTERNS OF DISCOURSE

Social Organization in the Classroom

Mehan's (1979) system isolates for analysis interactive turn taking in the discourse, which is partitioned into categories of initiated talk, reply, or evaluation. In overview, 77% of all turns allocated by the teacher across the three periods of data collection were individual nominations to respond. In other words, for the majority of times she elicited a response from the students, she called on a specific child. Only 23% of the total turns were in an "open bid" category; that is, open to anyone's responding.

Initiation of discourse was begun by the teacher over 90% of the time during reading instruction. Thus, the students initiated exchanges only about 9% of the time. Mehan's (1979) research had suggested that teachers typically used directives to make the opening and closing of lessons. He also noted that behavioral directives were not typically found within the body of an academic lesson. Our teacher did use directives, however, within lessons during all of the observational periods.

Collection period 1. During the first period of observation, the teacher used two types of allocated turns: (*a*) individual nominations and (*b*) open bids. Both individual nominations and open bids were in the category of speech acts known as product elicitations. In each case, that is, there evidently was a specific answer or product that the teacher "had in mind" when she allocated a turn for discourse to a student. Also, the teacher made individual nominations almost 25 times as often as she made an open bid for a response from a group of students.

During this period, our student subjects demonstrated differential patterns of initiation of exchanges with the teacher. Harry, the mainstream culture student, initiated talk five times; the teacher responded with a turn or two before "binding off" his talk. In one case, she rejected his initiation. Tom, the Appalachian child, initiated talk only one time, whereas Dick, the black child, did no initiating at all. The teacher used directives throughout the whole class reading lesson for purposes of controlling student behavior.

Collection period 2. During the second collection period, the teacher again used individual nominations and open bids for allocating turns. And, as before, both procedures were used to elicit specific answers in the students' responses. In this sample, individual nominations outnumbered open bids seven to one, representing some lessening of the almost exclusive use of individual nominations in the first period.

During this collection period, we found more student-initiated exchanges. For example, Harry, the mainstream culture subject, initiated talk seven times whereas the Appalachian subject, Tom, initiated talk with the teacher a total of five times. Accepting all the latter's initiations, the teacher carried on reading instruction procedures, commonly called synthetic phonics, exceeding four turns in the discourse. In each case, they were in response to Tom's saying he was "stuck" on a given word in his reading text. Finally, Dick, the child from the inner-city black culture, initiated talk with his teacher four times during this period, which she accepted, replied to, and bound-off each in one turn.

The majority of the children's initiations were oriented to the task set by the teacher in each reading group. If they were not, she terminated their responses quickly or simply told them they were not on the topic. Again, the teacher interspersed directives throughout the lessons with both reading groups in which our subjects participated. However, directives were used differentially in that she used them to control behavior in the middle ability group's lesson, while using them to direct activity in the lowest ability grouping. In the latter group, her instruction utilized worksheets and flash cards, both of which drew out extensive directions for their use.

Collection period 3. During the third data-collection period, after the midpoint of the school year, the teacher continued to use individual nominations and open bids to allocate turns. In this sample, individual nominations outnumbered open bids at a ratio of five to one; this represented another diminution, although a less dramatic one than previously, in her calling on specific students. Thus, turn-taking had become more open than at the beginning of the school year. Both procedures, however, were again used to elicit specific products, or responses, she evidently had in mind.

Student initiations of discourse increased in this data-collection period. Harry initiated talk eight times in this sample, but only half of his initiations were accepted by the teacher. The other four times she did not acknowledge his bid, thus not allowing him access to the discourse via his bid.

Tom also initiated turns eight times, but half of those were requests to go to the bathroom, so these were materially different from either Harry's or Dick's initiations. The other four were procedural questions such as *Are we going to read this whole page?* Tom volunteered no personal or content-oriented initiations. The teacher accepted all his bids, responded by one turn, and then bound them off.

Dick initiated talk seven times, each being accepted by the teacher and responded to by up to three turns. His initiations largely involved the material in the reading text; his were the most task-oriented initiations.

During this collection period, the teacher used no directives with the middle-ability reading group, but continued to do so with the lowest ability group of which Dick was a member.

The Organization of Academic Work

In this section, the results of analyzing our data following Sinclair and Coulthard (1975) are reported. First, the total number of teacher- and student-initiated exchanges were determined and compared. Across all the data-collection periods, teacher-initiated exchanges accounted for almost 80% of total exchanges, whereas student initiations made up the remaining 20%. The range of teacher-initiated exchanges was from a low of 71.5% for the last low reading group sampled to a high of 92% in the first data-collection period. The student-initiated exchanges mirror that range. There appears, however, to be no consistent change in the pattern of teacher-initiated exchanges over time in our sample of reading lessons and they remain the majority of the exchanges.

The patterns of the various exchange types found in the data are displayed in Table 7.1. It is evident that all exchange types found in the discourse are utilized primarily by the teacher, except for the one called listing. However, when the students engaged in that type of exchange, it was only under the circumstances of playing a word recognition game called "Around the World." And although a child did call out a word to initiate the exchange, the game was controlled by the teacher who nonverbally allocated the turns. The other major student-initiated category is that of inform. This occurred especially when students either volunteered information about themselves or when they initiated a control sequence in which informing could almost be taken literally; its more informal name is tattling.

Table 7.1
Types of Exchanges (in percent)

Type	Teacher-initiated	Student-initiated
Elicit[a]	87	13
Direct[b]	100	0
Inform[c]	71	29
Reinitiate[d]	82	18
Check[e]	100	0
Repeat[f]	100	0
Listing[g]	0	100

Source: After Sinclair & Coulthard, 1975
 [a] An elicit exchange type is headed by an elicitation or question functioning to request a language response.
 [b] A direct exchange type is headed by an imperative functioning to request an action, nonlanguage response.
 [c] An inform exchange type is headed by utterances designed to be informative, to impart information to listener(s).
 [d] A reinitiate exchange type is headed by utterances designed to reestablish the line of discourse which a teacher or student feels may have gotten "off the track." It is often shown by teachers calling sequentially on students.
 [e] A check exchange type is headed by an actual question seeking unknown information, such as *Are you finished?*
 [f] A repeat exchange type is headed by an utterance designed to elicit again an utterance made by someone, such as *What did you say? I didn't hear you.*
 [g] A listing exchange type is often headed by an utterance that "demands" students' actually listing items as the response.

The data identify the teacher as the only one to initiate directive exchanges during the reading lessons sampled. She was also the only one to use checks, which are actual questions for unknown information. In Sinclair and Coulthard's (1975) analytic framework, elicitations may be in question form, but are not actual questions because the teacher already knows or has in mind how a student should respond. However, a check is an actual question to which the answer is not known by the questioner. Repeats were also used only by the teacher in our samples.

Analysis of the predominating exchange types for the teacher reveals discourse elicitations comprised virtually half of her total exchanges. Directives were over 20%, reinitiations were over 18%, whereas informative discourse was only 8.5%. Checks, actual questions, made up only 1% of her total production of exchanges, and repetitions constituted less than 1%. The inform exchanges impart information on the topic and tend to be highly instructional in nature.

Teacher reinitiations consisted largely of individual acts labeled clues, prompts, and nominations. Nominations were calls to individual children to respond. Clues were found predominantly in certain sections of the lessons, usually during silent reading times when children asked for help in decoding a word. And prompts were often directives for action such as *You read Ben's part now.*

The predominant type of exchange involving the students was listing at 43%. If we consider those more under the control of the student, however, we find elicitations to be the second most prevalent in our data at 28% of all student-initiated exchanges. Reinitiations comprised 15.5%; informatives were at the bottom at 13%. In our sample, the students produced no checks and no repetitions.

Consequently, the overall most prevalent type of exchange for both teacher and students was elicitation. Other than that, the two sets of major exchange types were not similar, as the teacher made different kinds of initiations than the students.

Looking at each collection period, and then across them, we analyzed the predominant types of exchanges in each for the teacher and the students. In the first period, we found the number of teacher elicitations and directives to be very close—36.5% and 33.3%, respectively. Much further behind came reinitiations at 16% and informative exchanges at 14%. Directives, in the Sinclair and Coulthard (1975) framework, serve to elicit a nonverbal reaction, so in this period of reading instruction the teacher was giving many directions for the children to follow nonverbally. Student-initiated exchanges were very few in number in the first period—only 9 out of over 100 total exchanges. Among those few, elicitations and informatives predominated about equally. They were almost entirely produced by one child, Harry, the middle-class boy from the cultural mainstream.

In the second data-collection period, in the middle reading group of which Harry and Tom were members, the dominant teacher-initiated exchange type was elicitation at 41%, with reinitiations following at 33%. These latter were mostly clues and prompts in response to elicitations for help in decoding. Directives were 17%; informatives 5.5%; and checks 3%. The children produced, as had the teacher, predominantly elicitation exchange types at 52%; listing was 44% as they played "Around the World." Informatives comprised the remaining 4%.

In the least advanced reading group of which Dick was a member, the teacher produced mostly directives (52%), reflecting the fact that they were working with worksheets and flashcards and not reading from a text. This was typical of the reading instruction lessons during that time of the year for that group. Elicitations comprised most of the rest of the exchanges, with informatives and real questions—checks—being almost negligible. As "Around the World" was played within the sample, listing accounted for 68% of the student-initiated exchanges. The rest were elicitations and reinitiations.

During the last data-collection period, as shown in Table 7.2, both reading groups were making use of reading texts, and the teacher's patterns of exchanges were similar for both. Although directives and reinitiations were reversed for the two groups, the patterns and percentages of exchanges were quite similar. This did not hold as much for student-initiated exchange types (see Table 7.3).

In the low reading group, "Around the World" was played again, but not in the middle reading group. For the latter, elicitations comprised the single largest exchange type, whereas for the low reading group, it was the smallest. Reinitiations for both were similar in proportion and were largely comprised of the children carrying the exchange forward by reading aloud from the text as instructed by the teacher. However, both elicitations and informative exchanges accounted for 74% of the exchange types in the middle reading group, but for only 18% in the low reading group.

An analysis of how the teacher interacted with each of our subjects revealed for Dick, the black child in the low reading group, an early pattern of virtually no student-initiated exchanges. During the last period of data

Table 7.2
Period 3 Teacher Exchange Types (in percent)

Exchange type	Middle reading group	Low reading group
Elicit	57	61
Direct	18	11
Reinitiate	14	17
Inform	10	11

Source: After Sinclair & Coulthard, 1975.

Table 7.3
Period 3 Student Exchange Types (in percent)

Exchange type	Middle reading group	Exchange type	Low reading group
Elicit	48	Listing	59
Reinitiate	26	Reinitiate	24
Inform	26	Inform	11
		Elicit	7

Source: After Sinclair & Coulthard, 1975.

collection, however, he initiated half as many as the teacher did with him. But at that point in the study, this group consisted of three lower-class black males; also they were reading in a book, not doing worksheets. By contrast, both Harry and Tom, in the much larger middle reading group, initiated exchanges during all three periods.

On the whole, the teacher evaluated their replies to her initiations favorably, with positive evaluations outweighing negatives by at least two to one. Such evaluation was similar for each of our subjects. Moreover, most of the children's replies were either evaluated or accepted, but not ignored by the teacher, which was generally consistent behavior on her part.

COHESION IN THE DISCOURSE

From each period of instruction in literacy, the interactive discourse between the students, Tom, Dick, and Harry, and the teacher was selected for cohesion analysis, thus deleting discourse between the teacher and other students, or among the students themselves. Such selection allowed us to focus on the degree of interrelatedness of the teacher's talk and that of our subjects. Also, because of the capabilities of the microphones and their placement, other students' discourse was frequently unintelligible.

Density of the cohesion was established by determining the mean number of cohesive ties per utterance. In *Cohesion in English*, Halliday and Hasan (1976) define a tie as being "best interpreted as a *relation* between the two elements," the two elements being "the cohesive element itself . . ." and an element "which is presupposed by [the tie] [p. 329]." The average number of ties per utterance was one, with the range from a high of 1.5 ties per utterance in one reading group session to a low of .5 ties per utterance in another. Across the data-collection period, little in the way of change was noted, either in terms of increase or decrease in density of cohesion.

Predominating types of cohesion used both by the teacher and by Tom, Dick, and Harry were also determined. See Table 7.4 for three major types to emerge from the data.

Table 7.4
Types of Cohesion (in percent)

	Total cohesive ties	Teacher ties	Student ties
	Lexical cohesion		
Period 1	61.5	75	62.5
Period 2			
Middle reading group	56	57.5	50
Low reading group	50	50	33.3
Period 3			
Middle reading group	53	66	19
Low reading group	68	85	36
Total ties produced			
across all periods	58	67	40
	Ellipsis cohesion		
Period 1	17	11	18
Period 2			
Middle reading group	12	6	39
Low reading group	17	0	33.3
Period 3			
Middle reading group	23	5.5	64
Low reading group	19	5	64
Total ties	17.6	5.5	44
	Reference cohesion		
Period 1	21	14	15
Period 2			
Middle reading group	30	34	11
Low reading group	33.3	50	33.3
Period 3			
Middle reading group	25	28	17
Low reading group	13	100	0
Total ties	24	45	15

Lexical Cohesion

As can be seen in Table 7.4, slightly over half of all the ties produced by both the teacher and the three students were lexical ties. However, lexical ties accounted for 67% of the teachers' total ties, whereas for the students, this type did not account for their predominant tie type, which was cohesion through ellipsis. In fact, by the third data-collection period, in the middle reading group, lexical cohesion dropped to a low of 19%.

The predominating type of lexical cohesion used was that of identical item—repetition of a word used earlier in the discourse. For example, the teacher often said something such as:

*Is that **Bob**?*
*Yes, it does look like **Bob**.*
*Where does . . . it look like **Bob's** going to?*

In that case, the identical items producing this cohesion are all **Bob,** rather than her saying "*Is that Bob? Yes, it does look like him. Where does it look like he's going?*

Ellipsis Cohesion

Cohesion via ellipsis was, overall, not a predominant type of cohesion, but did account for about 44% of the ties made by the three students. This type of tie was achieved primarily through propositional ellipsis in which all the propositional element is omitted to yield a *Wh*- question answer. A typical example is

    TEACHER: *What do those letters say?*
    DICK: *Lion.*

In fact, ellipsis of this and other sorts to achieve an answer to a **Wh**-question or a **yes-no** question is the predominating type, reflecting in part the structure of the reading lessons that yielded the data we analyzed. By the third data-collection period, this type of cohesion accounts for 64% of all cohesive ties for all three of our subjects. This reflects, again, the structure of the reading lessons.

Reference Cohesion

About 45% of the teacher's total ties consisted of cohesion through use of reference. This was achieved predominantly through use of pronouns and demonstratives as referents, usually in the form of **that**. Across time little change in this pattern was found. This type of cohesion was rarely used by the three students, representing only 15% of their total cohesive ties.

According to Halliday and Hasan's (1976) scheme for the coding of cohesive elements, five major types of cohesion are possible. Two types, substitution and conjunction, almost never appear in our data. Within the three types we find in the data, relatively few of the possible subtypes detailed by Halliday and Hasan (1976) were used either by the teacher or the students. For example, there are at least 12 types of reference ties in the coding scheme, but in our data, only the pronominals and a few demonstratives predominate. (See Halliday & Hasan, 1976, pp. 333–339, for the coding scheme.)

Taking the distance of the ties and their presuppositions into account, we found the majority of ties, about 63%, to be what Halliday and Hasan call "immediate," that is, the presupposed item for the tie is in the preceding utterance, no matter who uttered it. This percentage held relatively constant across the data-collection periods. The second most predominant distance was what Halliday and Hasan call "mediated," with utterances in between, but having the same presupposition. These were often produced by the teachers' tieing with themselves, usually to make a pedagogical point as in:

TEACHER   *No. Bob. -b.*
DICK: *-b.*
TEACHER: *A -b sound. It begins with a -b sound, and it ends with a* **b** *sound.*

Relatively few ties were what Halliday and Hasan call remote, nonmediated, which means the reference is not in the discourse sequence analyzed or is far back in the sequence. There were virtually no cataphoric ties at all.

Domination of ties was also determined. A tie was considered teacher-dominated if (a) any of the three boys tied to her discourse, or (b) if she tied to her own discourse. Student-dominated ties were those in which (a) the teacher's discourse tied to what any of the boys had said previously, or those in which (b) the students tied to their own discourse. Table 7.5 indicates the majority of ties were teacher-dominated. However, the range is from a low of 60% in the first period to a high of 86% in the low reading group during the second data-collection period. To account for this range, we looked at the pattern of ties with each of the three boys.

Harry, the boy from the cultural mainstream, accounted for the majority of ties with the teacher in the first collection period. This was achieved largely through his domination of ties by introducing several topics into the discourse. The other boys did not initiate during this period, but did contribute in such a way that the teacher did tie to some of their responses that were oriented to the reading lesson material. Again, in the second period, Harry dominated more ties with the teacher than Tom, the boy from the Appalachian culture. And in his small reading group, Dick, the black inner-city child, dominated

Table 7.5
Tie Domination (in percent)

	Teacher-dominated	Student-dominated
Period 1	60	40
Period 2		
Middle reading group	64	36
Low reading group	86	14
Period 3		
Middle reading group	77	23
Low reading group	66	34
Total ties	71	29

only 14% of the ties with the teacher. In the third period of data collection, Harry again initiated more ties with the teacher than Tom, but Tom was also tied more to by the teacher than Harry. This seems to emerge as a pattern for Harry: more discourse interaction with the teacher than Tom, either ties to or elicits from the teacher. On the other hand, Dick made a change in his pattern of ties in the reading group by the third data-collection period. At that time, he actually dominated 34% of all the cohesion produced, and he also initiated topics with the teacher.

Continuing to analyze the three subjects' cohesion, we looked at predominating types of cohesion for each of them. The results are displayed in Table 7.6. For all three students, lexical cohesion predominates in the first data-collection period, but begins to give way to ellipsis by the last period. Nor, for any of these boys, does there appear to be a consistent preference across time for a particular type of cohesive tie. We suspect that, in large part, the type of student-generated tie is more dependent on the teachers' conduct of the reading lesson than on the student's choice from a wide range of possible ties.

GRAMMATICAL STRUCTURING OF DISCOURSE

Results of applying CALAS (the Computer-Assisted Language Analysis System) to our data are presented in this section. Table 7.7 displays results of the analysis of verb usage by the four subjects for the three periods of data collection and for all periods combined. Each cell exhibits a proportion of the

Table 7.6
Students' Cohesion Types (in percent)

	Dick	Harry	Tom
Period 1			
Lexical	75	50	62.5
Ellipsis	25	16.6	12.5
Reference	0	33.3	12.5
Substitution	0	0	12.5
Period 2			
Lexical	33.3	60	40
Ellipsis	33.3	30	48
Reference	0	10	12
Substitution	33.3	0	0
Period 3			
Lexical	35.5	8	31
Ellipsis	64.5	72	55.5
Reference	0	20	13.5
Substitution	0	0	0

Table 7.7
Proportionate Use of Verb Types (in percent)

Verb type[a]	Basic				Mixed experiential				Benefactive				Total			
	C	H	D	T[b]	C	H	D	T	C	H	D	T	C	H	D	T
Collection period 1 (no. of verbs = 71)																
State	15	8			6	1				1			21	11		
Action	37				10				1				47		1	1
Process	8				8				1				17			
Total	61	9			24				1	1			86	11	1	1
Collection period 2 (no. of verbs = 86)																
State	7				12				2				21			
Action	38	1		2	15			2	2	2			56	3		5
Process	7				3	3			1				12	3		
Total	52	1		2	30	3		2	5	2			89	6		5
Collection period 3 (no. of verbs = 293)																
State	27	1	2	1	9	1			1				37	2	2	
Action	14	2	1		9	1							25	3		
Process	11	2	2		12		1		1				25	2	2	
Total	52	5	4	1	31	2	1	1	2				86	8	5	1
All collection periods (no. of verbs = 450)																
State	21	2	1	1	9	1			1				31	3	2	1
Action	22	2	1		11				1				34	2	2	1
Process	10	2	1	1	10	1			1				21	3	2	5
Total	54	6	3	2	30	2		1	3				86	8	4	2

Note: Percentage totals across columns and rows may not be identical because of rounding off.

[a] For definitions and discussions of basic and mixed verb types see Meara et al. (1981) (adapted from Cook, 1979).

[b] C = Ms. Cook (teacher), H = Harry, D = Dick, T = Tom.

total frequency with which verb phrases are used on any given occasion. Each of the tabular displays is further partitioned by research subject. For example, we note that in the first collection period, Ms. Cook, the teacher, accounts in her discourse for 15% of the total use of state verbs, whereas Harry, the white male from the cultural mainstream, only accounts for 8% of the total of verbs used in that period.

The table itself has been adapted from Cook's (1979) "Matrix Model of Case Grammer," whose construction resides on the assumption that there are essential and inherent relations between verb and noun phrases in the deep structure of the English language. Following Meara et al. (1981), we also have redefined these verb phrases (see Appendix A, pp. 125–127).

The results are strikingly consistent over the three periods of observation. Ms. Cook, the teacher, uses nearly 9/10 of the verbs employed (86% in Period 1, 89% in Period 2, and 86% in Period 3, with an overall average of 86%). Table 7.8, which contains a similar kind of tally for phrases other than verb phrases, indicates the teacher consistently uses nearly 9/10 of these (89%, 86%, and 88%, with an overall frequency of 87%). In Table 7.7, we also note the teacher uses most of the "basic" verbs of state, action, or process (61% in Period 1 and more than 50% in Periods 2 and 3).

Again, most of these are action verbs in the first two periods (37% and 38%); by Session 3, however, she is using mostly verbs of state (27% as compared to 14% for action verbs in the third period). The contrast becomes even sharper when we add the other verb types: She uses action verbs 47% of the time in Period 1 and 56% in Period 2; by Period 3, however, her relative frequency of action verbs has decreased to 34%. An examination of the text reveals that she is spending much of her time in the first two periods demanding action, including nominating persons to read aloud.

Note in Table 7.7 that proportionately little of her talk (8%, 7%, with an overall average of 10%) is devoted to process—things happening to people or things. By and large, the people in her talk either are or are not supposed to be doing something. They do have experiences (45%, 30%, 31%, with an overall average of 30%), but mainly because the teacher admonishes her students to be reading aloud or otherwise saying something, or to be looking at or seeing something. Table 7.8 shows that the teacher uses mostly nouns among the phrases other than verbs, and that most of these identify the objects, rather than the agents, experiencers, or beneficiaries of a state, action, or process.

Some embellishment of her talk is revealed in the proportion containing adverbial or prepositional phrases (27%, 22%, 23%, with an overall average of 25%). In the main, however, her talk remains singularly uncomplicated over the three occasions. As Table 7.9 reveals, she uses on the average only 2.06 phrases other than verb phrases per clause, including noun phrases, slightly more (2.56) in the first session, but less than two (1.89, 1.98) in the second and third sessions.

Table 7.8
Proportionate Use of Phrases Other Than Verb Phrases

	Collection period																			
	1 (N=209)					2 (N=213)					3 (N=647)					4 All (N=1069)				
Type of phrase	C	H	D	T^a	Total	C	H	D	T	Total	C	H	D	T	Total	C	H	D	T	Total
Noun																				
Agent	7	1			8	13	1			14	8	1			9	9				9
Object	28	3			32	23			1	24	38	3	1	1	43	33	2	1	1	37
Experiencer	7				7	6			1	7	6				6	6				6
Beneficiary				1	1	1				1	1				1	1				1
Adverb–preposition	27	2			29	22	2			24	23	1	1		25	23	1		1	25
Conjunction–subordinator	5	1			6	2			1	3	2				2	3				3
Phrase not in clause	14	1	1	1	17	19	1	7		27	11	1	2	1	14	12	1	3	1	17
Total	89	8	1	2	100	86	4	7	3	100	88	6	5	3	100	87	6	4	2	100

Note: Numbers in parentheses are raw frequencies. Percentage totals across columns and rows may not be identical because of rounding off.

^a C = Ms. Cook (teacher); H = Harry; D = Dick; T = Tom.

Table 7.9
Proportionate Use of Phrases Other Than Clauses (= Verb Phrases) as Measure of Stylistic Complexity[a]

Type of phrase	Collection period																						
	1					2					3					4							
	C	H	D	T[b]	Total	C	H	D	T	Total	C	H	D	T	Total	C	H	D	T	Total			
Clauses (verb phrase)	86	11	1	1	100	89	7		5	100	86	8	5	1	100	86	8	4	2	100			
	(61)	(8)	(1)	(1)	(71)	(76)	(6)		(4)	(86)	(251)	(22)	(16)	(4)	(293)	(383)	(36)	(17)	(9)	(450)			
All other phrases	89	8	1	2	100	86	4	7	3	100	88	6	5	3	100	87	6	4	3	100			
	(186)	(16)	(2)	(5)	(209)	(184)	(9)	(14)	(6)	(213)	(560)	(41)	(30)	(16)	(647)	(933)	(66)	(46)	(27)	(1069)			
Phrases not in clauses	81	8		11	100	70	5	25		100	70	9	14	7	100	72	8	15	5	100			
	(30)	(3)		(4)	(37)	(40)	(3)	(14)		(57)	(63)	(8)	(13)	(6)	(90)	(133)	(14)	(27)	(10)	(184)			
All other phrases in clauses [2–3]	91	8	1		100	92	4		4	100	89	6	3	2	100	90	6	2	2	100			
	(156)	(13)	(2)	(1)	(172)	(144)	(6)		(6)	(156)	(497)	(33)	(17)	(10)	(557)	(797)	(52)	(19)	(17)	(885)			
Ratio of AOPIC/C [4/1]	2.56	1.63	2.	1.	2.42	1.89	1.		1.5	1.81	1.98	1.5	1.06	2.51	1.90	2.06	1.44	1.12	1.89	1.97			

Note: Numbers in parentheses are raw frequencies. Percentage totals across rows and columns may not be identical because of rounding off.

[a] For discussions of stylistic complexity see Hurndon et al. (1979) and Meara et al. (1981) (adapted from Cook, 1979).

[b] C = Ms. Cook (teacher); H = Harry; D = Dick; T = Tom.

By comparison, our student subjects have relatively little to say in any or all of their discourse with the teacher, as they do not have much chance. In their whispering (not discussed here), however, they reveal themselves able both to say more and to do so in a more complicated manner.

Discussion

In our introductory remarks, we conceptualized teaching in the classroom as a process of social influence in which, optimally, teacher and students act in concert to reduce what each perceives to be a discrepancy between an actual and a desired state of affairs (cf. Pepinsky & Patton, 1971). We alluded further to teaching as a process in which social policies are not only implemented but may be reformulated. Meara et al. (1981) advance a similar argument about counseling as a policymaking process, which suggests that phenomena such as teaching and counseling have common formal properties. In that sense, what either set of participants perceives as a discrepancy that must be reduced may also act as a contingency that demands that something be done. In the present case, teaching policy becomes "a general premise in the form of ground rules that either presuppose—or are presupposed by—a category of social actions [Pepinsky, Hill-Frederick, & Epperson, 1980, pp. 54–55]."

In his *Pre-view of Policy Sciences*, Lasswell (1971) described the policy sciences as properly employing a variety of methods, as being rooted in explicit social contexts, and, within any such context, as being alert to problems arising in that context. We have followed these guidelines in this research, being aware of the problems occurring in public schools in a large urban setting where children with diverse cultural backgrounds come into contact with one another in a classroom. They are confronted here by demands arising from within the dominant culture of the city. We recognized the problem would be more severe in a newly desegregated school system. In the school and classroom where our research was conducted, white and black children were being bused in from an adjacent neighborhood whose members were identified as being in the cultural mainstream. We hoped to describe what impact this setting would have on three male students representing diverse cultures. We chose three discrete methods of analyzing talk in the classroom between these students and their teacher, again in a manner consistent with Lasswell's (1971) exhortation.

The results of our various analyses tell a remarkably consistent story. Mehan's (1979) form of analysis revealed that over time there were relatively few open bids on the teacher's part for initiating talk in the classroom. Most of the students' discourse consisted of their responses to nominations by their teacher to have them talk. Our teacher continued to issue procedural directives within lesson times and over all periods of observation. An almost identical pattern of teacher-initiated versus student-initiated exchanges of talk was found when Sinclair and Coulthard's (1975) method was employed. At the same time, there was relatively little cohesion in the talk, either of the teacher over time or between the teacher and her students, except the latter tended to cohere as requested to particular demands, queries, or comments on the part of the teacher. Mainly, however, these took the form of propositional ellipses in which the teacher asked questions with particular, largely one-word answers in mind. The teacher did use a reference form of cohesion entailing the use of pronouns and demonstratives, particularly **that**, as referents.

Spontaneous bids on the students' part—for example, Harry's earlier bids for ties with the teacher—tended to be relatively infrequent among the students. Even Harry's talk evolved into making ties with what the teacher had said rather than with what he elicited from her. Saliently, as indicated in the first two sets of analyses and by CALAS, the teacher talked by far the most and on all occasions. Mostly, the talk centered on states or actions, with a relatively heavy, accompanying reference to objects. There was rarely talk about processes—things happening to people or things, the experiences people have, or the benefits they might gain from these experiences. None of the respondents, including the teacher, was stylistically complicated in his or her utterances. The teacher, for the most part, demanded, commanded, questioned, and exhorted, eliciting largely single words in response from the students.

As far as a mutually devised "social construction of reality" is concerned, in this culturally diverse classroom, there does not appear to be much reciprocity between the teacher and students in minimizing perceived discrepancies. The teacher clearly controlled the discourse during the three data-collection periods, as shown by amount of talk, percentage of teacher-initiated exchanges, and percentage of teacher-dominated cohesion ties. Despite their cultural diversity, the three students, in turn, seemed to have learned this as a major rule of discourse. By the third data-collection period they were volunteering virtually no personal information in the form of student-initiated exchanges. Instead, they responded to her initiations with one-word answers that were the product responses she was apparently seeking. Each of the student subjects had learned to respond appropriately through his discourse during periods of literacy instruction, although each was different with regard to how effectively he was learning to read. Their interactional competence, as defined and shaped by the teacher, appeared to be developing well.

Whatever else these culturally diverse students might have learned in the classroom about how to be literate seemed to have been overshadowed, in the teacher's judgment, by her own perspective on the course of events. Our analyses of the students' and teacher's discourse suggest she was remarkably adept at modifying and shaping the students' verbal behavior over the three periods of observation. As discussed elsewhere (DeStefano et al., 1980), she was preoccupied with laying down and enforcing, as matters of policy, two sets of ground rules in her classroom: (*a*) how students should behave in an orderly manner (**procedural policy**); and (*b*) how they should become literate (**substantive policy**). The students' interactive discourse indicates them to have learned these rules, but masked their relative success, defined by other criteria and by independent measures of their accomplishment, in becoming literate.

Given all of the available evidence, we can infer that evaluative judgments about the teacher, as good or bad, are premature. Given the tense circumstances of court-ordered racial desegregation in the school system, there was a singular absence of disruptive behavior among her students throughout the school year. In fact, an end-of-year party, which several of us attended, was characterized by frequent and widespread marks of affection toward her by her students. On the other hand, her teaching seemed narrowly focused on rules of conduct and on learning how to be literate. We found no substantial evidence that her students were being helped to perceive and comprehend as coherent text the words, phrases, or sentences to which they were being exposed one at a time.

At this stage of knowledge about analyzing discourse in a classroom, we believe it is more important to show how such discourse may be sensibly identified and interpreted by reference to three case studies in the context of interactive behavior within a single classroom, than to attempt a definitive investigation of how culturally different children are taught and learn to be literate. We have sought rather to offer a methodological contribution to the analysis of discourse itself, and to use our comparative analysis in raising questions that need to be asked before one leaps to conclusions about what is happening and what ought to be done. For now, we can leave off with the question of whether changes in the school system—the larger organizational context within which any single teacher attempts the task of teaching students to be literate—may be more critical than changes in the behavior of any single teacher. This issue becomes more central if students' opportunities to become literate take into account their potential unhampered by the masking effects of cultural backgrounds. More to the point, a recognition of such cultural differences may result in a redefinition of what it means to become literate and to adapt successfully to societal demands.

Appendix A: Description of the Computer-Assisted Language Analysis System (CALAS)

The explicit paradigm for CALAS is a form of case grammer whose informational unit is the clause. By definition, the clause contains one and only one verb phase, which, in turn, defines an essential relation (e.g., of state, action, or process) within the clause. Nonessentially, adverbial or prepositional phrases may occur within clauses to define peripheral relations (e.g., of cause, manner, time, purpose); similarly, conjunctions and subordinators may occur to define relations between clauses. Use of the paradigm entails both a syntactic analysis of word strings as they occur linearly in the text, and a nonlinear, semantic analysis of essential and peripheral relations within clauses and blocks of clauses (cf. Cook, 1979, adapted from Chafe, 1970; Fillmore, 1968).

To accomplish this kind of analysis, CALAS was constructed as an interactive system, the principal components of which are persons and a computer's "hardware" and "software." The software includes four sets of programs that operate in three stages of analysis. In stage 1, the computer reads a text in the English language and displays its word-for-word, grammatical equivalents (e.g., noun, verb, adverb). Because there remain fine, perceptual discriminations of structure-within-context to be made, beyond the foreseeable ken of computers (cf. Marr & Nishihara, 1978), CALAS prescribes for editing of the transformed text by human monitors and at each stage of analysis. Editing of the computer's relatively few "errors" revealed in the display may be accomplished directly and on-line, or off-line from a printout of the display.

At stage 2, the edited output of stage 1 is transformed into phrases (e.g., noun phrase, verb phrase, prepositional phrase). Its edited output is then aggregated into clauses. Finally, the verb phrases are identified as **case markers** (defining essential relations of state, action, process, experience, benefaction), in terms of which noun phrases are assigned **case roles** (as agents, objects, experiencers, or beneficiaries of an essential action, process, or state, cf. Pepinsky, Baker, Matalon, May & Staubus, 1977; Meara et al., 1981; Pepinsky, 1980; adapted from Rush, Pepinsky, Landry, Meara, Strong, Valley, & Young, 1974).

Information exhibited in the edited output of stage 3 is now ready for quantification and further statistical analysis. At present, these analyses have centered on two sets of phenomena, providing measures (a) of stylistic complexity (e.g., numbers of words, phrases, clauses used by any or all speakers; number of clauses per independent clause, number of phrases per clause, cf. Hurndon et al., 1979; Meara, Shannon, & Pepinsky, 1979, adapted from Cook, 1979) and (b) of essential relations within clauses (e.g., relative proportions of different verb-types employed by any or all speakers, cf. Bieber, Patton, & Fuhriman, 1977; Meara et al., 1981; Patton, Fuhriman, & Bieber, 1977). We present results of both kinds of analysis, comparing our informants in terms of their relative proportions of phrases to clauses as a measure of stylistic complexity, and of their proportionate uses of any and all types of verbs to yield measures of semantic communication. After Cook (1979) and

Meara *et al.* (1981), the system is based on postulation of the existence of three primary or fundamental types of verbs. The adapted definitions follow:

> **State** verbs define a particular, non-causal relation between persons or things, or state or property of such an object.
> Examples: *I am happy. The wood is dry.*
> **Process** verbs define a causal relation in which something is happening to a person or a thing.
> Examples: *I was burned. The wood dried.*
> **Action** verbs define a causal relation in which a person or thing does something (optionally, to somebody or something).
> Examples: *May hit John. The boy ran.*

When any of the three inherent semantic features of state, process, or action is present in simple form, the verb phrase is termed **basic**. In addition to these basic types, Cook (1979) proposed three other categories of verbs, which only exist interactively with the fundamental types, forming compounds of them. This second set, of interactive types, includes experiential and benefactive verbs. **Experiential** verbs define relations in which states of feeling, sensing, or knowing, are attributed, or acts of consciousness or awareness are imputed, to a person or thing. **Benefactive** verbs define a relation in which persons or things are identified as beneficiaries of a state, an action, or a process. The latter verbs connote ownership or possession of, or that someone or something has benefitted from, somebody or something. The adapted definitions and examples of the interactive verb-types are as follows:

> **State–experiential** verbs define cognitive or affective states.
> Examples: *I knew the answer. I wanted a drink.*
> **State–benefactive** verbs define states of ownership.
> Example: *I have four daffodils.*
> **Process–experiential** verbs define the experiencing of a sensory–perceptual activity.
> Examples: *I heard a cat. I felt the pain.*
> **Process–benefactive** verbs define an activity that is of benefit to someone or something.
> Examples: *I received a new job. The forest is reclaiming the land.*
> **Action–experiential** verbs define an action that provides an experience to a person or thing.
> Examples: *I spoke to them. She tells me everything.*
> **Action–benefactive** verbs define an action that benefits someone or something.
> Example: *I gave him some money.*

References

Berger, P. L., & Luckmann, T. *The social construction of reality.* Garden City, N.Y.: Doubleday, 1966.

Bieber, M. R., Patton, M. J., & Fuhriman, A. J. A metalanguage analysis of counselor and client verb usage in counseling. *Journal of Counseling Psychology*, 1977, *24*, 264–271.

Chafe, W. L. *Meaning and structure of language.* Chicago: University of Chicago Press, 1970.

Cicourel, A., Jennings, K., Jennings, S., Leiter, K., MacKay, R., Mehan, H., & Roth, D. *Language use and school performance.* New York: Academic Press, 1974.

Clay, M. M. *A diagnostic survey and concepts about print test, sand.* Aukland, N.Z.: Heinemann Educational Books, 1972.

Cook W. A. *Case grammer: Development of the matrix model (1970–1978).* Washington, D.C.: Georgetown University Press, 1979.

DeStefano, J. S. *Language, the learner, and the school.* New York: Wiley, 1978.

DeStefano, J. S., Pepinsky, H. B., & Sanders, T. S. *Making policy: A preliminary note on the language of cultures-in-contact in the educational domain.* Paper presented at the International Conference on Language and Power, Bellagio, Italy, April 1980.

Fillmore, C. J. The case for case. In E. Bach & R. T. Harms (Eds.), *Universals in linguistic theory.* New York: Holt, Rinehart & Winston, 1968.

Garfinkel, H. *Studies in ethnomethodology.* Englewood Cliffs, N.J.: Prentice-Hall, 1967.

Halliday, M. A. K., & Hasan, R. *Cohesion in English.* London: Longman, 1976.

Hicks, C. E., Rush, J. E., & Strong, S. M. Content analysis. In J. Belzer, A. G. Holzman, & A. Kent (Eds.), *Encyclopedia of computer sciences and technology.* New York: Marcel Dekker, 1977.

Hoover, M. E. *Appropriate use of black English by black children as rated by parents* (Technical Report 46, SCRDT). Stanford: Stanford University, 1975.

Hurndon, C. J., Pepinsky, H. B., & Meara, N. M. Conceptual level and structural complexity in language. *Journal of Counseling Psychology*, 1979, *26*, 190–197.

Hymes, D. *Foundations in sociolinguistics, an ethnographic approach.* Philadelphia: University of Pennsylvania Press, 1974.

Labov, W., & Robins, C. A note of the relation of reading failure to peer-group status in urban ghettos. In J. S. DeStefano (Ed.), *Language, society and education: A profile of black English.* Worthington, Ohio: Charles E. Jones, 1973.

Lasswell, H. D. *A pre-view of policy sciences.* New York: Elsevier, 1971.

Marr, D., & Nishihara, H. K. Visual information-processing: Artificial intelligence and the sensorium of sight. *Technology Review*, October 1978, 28–49.

Meara, N. M., Pepinsky, H. B., Shannon, J. W., & Murray, W. A. A comparison of semantic communication in and expectations for counseling across three theoretical orientations. *Journal of Counseling Psychology*, 1981, *28*, 110–118.

Meara, N. M., Shannon, J. W., & Pepinsky, H. B. Comparison of the stylistic complexity of the language of counselor and client across three theoretical orientations. *Journal of Counseling Psychology*, 1979, *26*, 181–189.

Mehan, H. *Learning lessons, social organization in the classroom.* Cambridge: Harvard University Press, 1979.

Mehan, H., Cazden, C. B., Coles, C. L., Fisher, S., & Maroules, N. *The social organization of classroom lessons.* CHIP Report 67, December 1976.

Patton, M. J., Fuhriman, A. J., & Bieber, M. R. A model and a metalanguage for research on psychological counseling. *Journal of Counseling Psychology*, 1977, *24*, 25–34.

Pepinsky, H. B. A metalanguage for systematic research on human communication via natural language. *Journal of the American Society for Information Science*, 1974, *25*(1), 59–69.

Pepinsky, H. B. *Differentiating among texts to be comprehended.* Part of a symposium on "Application of semantic grammars to individual difference research," V. M. Rentel, Chair. Presented at the Annual Convention of the American Educational Research Association, Boston, Mass., April 1980.

Pepinsky, H. B., Baker, W. M., Matalon, R., May, G. D., & Staubus, A. M. *A user's manual for the Computer-Assisted Language Analysis System.* Columbus: Group for Research and Development in Language and Social Policy, Mershon Center, Ohio State University, November 1977.

Pepinsky, H. B., Hill-Frederick K., & Epperson, D. L. *The Journal of Counseling Psychology* as a matter of policies. In J. M. Whiteley (Ed.), *The history of counseling psychology.* Monterey, Calif.: Brooks/Cole, 1980.

Pepinsky, H. B., & Patton, M. J. Informative display and the psychological experiment. In H. B. Pepinsky & M. J. Patton (Eds.), *The psychological experiment: A practical accomplishment.* Elmsford, N.Y.: Pergamon, 1971.

Rush, J. E., Pepinsky, H. B., Landry, B. C., Meara, N. M., Strong, S. M., Valley, J. A., & Young, C. E. *A computer-assisted language analysis system* (Computer and Information Science Research Center, OSU-CISRC-TR-74-1). Columbus: Ohio State University, 1974.

Shuy, R., & Griffin, P. (Eds.). *The study of children's functional language and education in the early years.* Washington, D.C.: The Center for Applied Linguistics, 1978.

Sinclair, J. C. H., & Coulthard, R. M. *Towards an analysis of discourse: The English used by teachers and pupils.* London: Oxford University Press, 1975.

Strong, S. M. An algorithm for generating structural surrogates of English text. *Journal of the American Society for Information Science,* 1974, *25*(1), 10–24.

Strong, S. R. Social psychological approach to psychotherapy research. In S. L. Garfield & A. E. Bergin (Eds.), *Handbook of psychotherapy and behavior change.* New York: Wiley, 1978.

Williams, F., Whitehead, J., & Miller, L. *Attitudinal correlates of children's speech characteristics* (USOE Research Report, Project No. 0-0336). 1977.

8

Creating Communication-Rich Classrooms: Insights from the Sociolinguistic and Referential Traditions[1]

W. PATRICK DICKSON

The purpose of this chapter is to discuss the translation of research on children's communication into practice: specifically, the use of referential communication activities derived from research to create communication-rich experiences for children in classrooms. Some issues in the assessment of the communicative competence of individuals will also be examined. I begin by placing this work in the context of research on children's oral communication.

Much research on children's oral communication has been conducted in one of two rather separate research traditions, which for convenience may be labeled the "referential" and the "sociolinguistic" (Dickson, 1981a). Research in the sociolinguistic tradition is exemplified in other chapters in this volume and need not be reviewed here, but a brief description of referential communication research and some assumptions guiding this research may be useful.

Research in the referential tradition has focused on children's skills in giving directions in standardized tasks. Typically, one child is designated as the speaker and another child the listener. The children are usually separated by a visual barrier. The speaker attempts to describe one of a set of objects or pictures such that the listener can select the one described. Typical referential

[1] This chapter is based in part upon work supported by the U.S. National Institute of Education under Grant Number NIE-G-81-0009. Any opinions, findings, and conclusions or recommendations expressed in this chapter are those of the author and do not necessarily reflect the views of the Institute or the Department of Education.

131

tasks include giving directions on a map or describing how to assemble a model from separate parts. The primary dependent measure in this research has been the accuracy of the listener's choices and, in contrast to the sociolinguistic research, scant attention has been given to the actual language used in transcripts of the children's language itself.

Referential communication tasks are useful in research because they provide experimental control for intention and yield unambiguous measures of communicative accuracy. The referential task controls for questions concerning the speaker's intention by defining the task for the speaker and designating the target referent to be communicated. In addition, by having the listener make an overt response that can be unambiguously judged as correct or incorrect, questions about the listener's understanding are circumvented. This control is obtained, however, at the cost of having created a rather artificial situation, but as Piaget commented in defense of the utility of such tasks, "We can only reply that we found no other way of solving the problem [1926, p. 80]" (of experimental control). Complete reviews of referential communication research can be found elsewhere (Asher, 1979; Dickson, 1981b, 1982).

Despite the somewhat artificial nature of the referential communication situation, an argument can be made that such situations have considerable face validity. Information giving and receiving are clearly important components of communicative competence when more broadly defined (see Allen & Brown, 1977, p. 250, for one taxonomy). These settings can be considered representative of naturally occurring situations, such as giving directions to one's own house, following directions in class, telling another person how to put something together, and so on. In addition, although the focus on the communication is on exchanging information, the actual process calls into play many other communicative functions, including cognitive monitoring (Flavell, 1981), comprehension monitoring (Markman, 1981), active listening and questioning (Patterson & Kister, 1981), as well as the formulation of informationally explicit descriptions (Whitehurst & Sonnenschein, 1981). In short, the validity and communicative richness of the referential communication situation should not be underestimated, as will be illustrated with protocols from these situations later in this chapter.

In my introduction to a recent book that included writings by representatives of both the sociolinguistic and referential traditions, I discussed ways in which the two traditions differed and noted that the two traditions have much to learn from each other (Dickson, 1981a). Research in the sociolinguistic tradition has highlighted the importance of studying communication in natural contexts and in so doing, has emphasized a broad definition of communicative competence. Careful study of children in natural contexts has revealed many instances in which children are highly competent communicators. The referential communication research tradition, on the other hand, has given greater attention to interventions aimed at training communication skills, but, as a metaanalysis of this work revealed, the experimental contexts have tended toward increasingly artificial and restricted tasks, rendering their validity and generalizability questionable (Dickson, 1981b).

Translation of Research into Practice

The ways in which research influences practice tend to be quite indirect and uncertain (Kerlinger, 1977). Such a conclusion seems especially true of the oral communication curriculum. The limited impact of research in the sociolinguistic and referential communication traditions on educational practice can be attributed to at least four reasons. First, research in each tradition has characteristics that limit the applicability of its finding to practice. Second, neither research tradition has produced educationally useful measures of communication competence. Third, the implementation of a communication-rich curriculum must take into account organizational constraints faced by teachers. Fourth, few basic researchers have attempted actually to implement ideas generated in their research. In this chapter, each of these impediments to implementation are discussed briefly, followed by a description of a study of the use of communication games in classrooms.

PARADIGMATIC WEAKNESSES

One strength of the sociolinguistic tradition is its emphasis on ecological validity (Bronfenbrenner, 1979) and the unobtrusive observation of natural contexts. As a consequence, however, training and the evaluation of communicative competence in the classroom has rarely been carried out in sociolinguistic research.

On the other hand, research in the referential tradition has increasingly included training studies, and these training studies have been successful in modifying children's communication performance on experimental tasks (Dickson, 1981a). As of yet, however, the training studies within the referential tradition appear to have had little impact on the oral communication curriculum, perhaps because of the artificiality of the experimental tasks used in this research. In short, both the sociolinguistic and referential traditions have features that enable them to claim educational relevance, yet neither tradition appears to have had major, direct influence on the day-to-day language arts experiences of young children in classrooms.

MEASURING INDIVIDUAL COMPETENCE

A second major impediment to increased attention to oral communication in the curriculum is the lack of instruments for assessing individual competence.

Neither the sociolinguistic nor the referential tradition has produced instruments suitable for use by teachers in assessing individual children's communicative competence. And this is unfortunate, for, despite the legitimate concerns about misuses of testing, the fact remains that teachers need some way of diagnosing what individual children know in order to prescribe an appropriate curriculum. In addition, in the absence of ways of measuring children's learning in the oral communication curriculum, teachers (and school administrators and parents) will be reluctant to allocate precious class time to oral communication activities. Sociolinguistic and ethnographic research has amply instantiated acts of communicative competence, such as responding appropriately in different contexts, turn-taking, and attention getting. Sociolinguistic research has led us to have a more favorable view of the competencies many young children have, and this, in itself, is a major accomplishment, bringing to mind Cronbach's remark that "our abstract concepts perform a great service in altering the prevailing view of man [1975, p. 123]." But educational practice must go beyond the celebration of instances of competence observed on occasion in a few individual children. It is one thing to accentuate the positive competencies of children, especially those children suffering under the stereotype of linguistic deficits (Labov, 1969); it is quite another to ensure that individual children acquire and display essential communicative competence in formal contexts such as the school and work place.

The fact that many sociolinguistic studies have focused on the communicative behavior of only a small number of children has contributed to this neglect of the question of individual differences in communicative competence. An interesting exception in the sociolinguistic literature appears in a study by Wilkinson, Clevenger, and Dollaghan (1981), where they make use of exploratory data analysis techniques to display the relative tendency of individual children to address their requests to same-sex versus cross-sex peers. This visual display highlights the large individual variability on this single dimension.

One might expect that research in the referential communication tradition would have led to more standardized techniques for assessing certain aspects of children's communication competence, because referential tasks typically do yield numerical scores in terms of referents correctly communicated or adequately described. But a comprehensive literature review (Dickson, 1982) revealed scant attention to the internal consistency of these measures, their generalizability of communication performance across referential tasks, or the validity of referential communication performance for assessing communicative competence in more natural settings. A few assessment instruments have been described that make use of referential communication tasks (Aaronson & Schaefer, 1971; Cazden, 1971; Chandler, Greenspan, & Barenboim, 1974; Wang, Rose, & Maxwell, 1973), but there is little evidence that these instruments are valid or that they have been used in classrooms. What evidence exists supports the view that dyadic performance in referential communication tasks does generalize across tasks (Baldwin & Garvey, 1973; Dickson, 1979). In addition, referential communication performance (Dickson, Hess, Miyake, & Azuma, 1979) and early development of referential specificity (Nelson, 1981) appear to be related to cognitive and linguistic development. Nevertheless, no standardized and normed instruments for assessing referential communication performance have been developed. A task force of the Speech Communication Association is presently reviewing various approaches to assessment of oral communication competence, but it is clear that considerably more work is required in this area.

CLASSROOM CONSTRAINTS

The third major impediment to the creation of a communication-rich classroom lies in the organizational and administrative constraints on what teachers do. Cazden (1972) and others have long advocated the centrality of the communicative uses of language in the language arts curriculum. Communication skill, as with other complex skills, must be learned through practice to the point that the performance is automatic (Cazden, 1972, pp. 236–239). Although I share Cazden's belief in the importance of the communicative uses of spoken and written language, the stubborn fact remains that it is the rare classroom where this belief is realized in practice. This reality deserves more serious consideration than it has been given by scholars interested in the oral communication curriculum, for if we cannot find ways of implementing a communication-rich classroom that is acceptable and appealing to average teachers, our best research will come to naught. An example is to be found in an editorial note in the *National Elementary School Principal*, describing the Houghton Mifflin Interaction Program, which was guided by the writing of Moffett and Wagner (1976). According to the article, the program was a coherent point of view and "is based on the knowledge, guesses, and hunches of well-informed researchers and theorists in the fields of child development, language development, psycholinguistics, and instruction in the language arts. The program emphasizes the student as a producer of meaningful ideas ["A Success That Failed," 1978, p. 29]." Yet the program failed to gain even a minor share of the market. A number of reasons for the failure are offered in the article, including the developers' belief that it was sufficient simply to place good materials in the hands of students, accompanied by an aversion to "developing teacher manuals, sequences, and structures that would help teachers use the program." The absence of techniques for demonstrating that children were learning anything from the curriculum, I suspect is another factor. The limited success of this nine million dollar program should give us pause.

Perhaps the biggest obstacle to the implementation of a curriculum emphasizing oral communication lies in the difficulty such a curriculum poses for
the teachers' need to structure and organize children's activities during the day.
Speaking skills can probably best be learned by practicing speaking to a real
listener in contexts where one can judge the effectiveness of one's performance.
Within the classroom, the way to optimize opportunities to speak to a real
listener is to pair up all children in the classroom and have them alternate
in speaking and listening roles in communication activities.

But the classroom is a noisy place when these activities are in progress.
Teachers and principals must be tolerant of a high noise level for such speaking
and listening activities to be used. In addition, the teacher cannot be present
beside each pair of children to provide structure for their interaction, so the
structure must derive from the nature of the game itself, otherwise the activity
may reduce to simply having an opportunity to talk that does not differ in
educationally significant ways from talk that takes place outside the classroom.
In short, we must find activities that require minimal direct teacher supervision,
engage children in complex communication, and yield credible evidence that
the children are learning something from the activities (Dickson & Patterson,
1981).

FOLLOWING RESEARCH THROUGH TO IMPLEMENTATION

I have come to the view that the quality of both research and practice
would be improved by reducing the gulf between researchers' and practitioners,
although the reward structures for the two groups are so different that such
a vision is only a hope. There have been some exceptional efforts in this
regard. Cazden (1979) bravely ventured to teach in the classroom and drew
useful insights from the experience. A project at the Center for Applied
Linguistics led to some suggestions, such as the provision of videotape protocols
for discussion by teachers (discussed in Shuy & Griffin, 1981), but little documentation of the actual use and effects of these materials is available. A few
researchers in the referential communication tradition have given some suggestions for teachers of this research (Dickson & Patterson, 1981; Foorman,
1980; Patterson, 1978), though these suggestions are rarely based on actual
involvement of the researchers with classrooms. Referential communication
type games appear frequently in language arts programs favorably reviewed in
a book edited by Cazden (1972, pp. 19–20; 25–27). This book includes a
chapter by Gleason (1972) showing effects of referential communication activities on children's communicative ability.

Unfortunately, it is still rare for researchers and teachers to collaborate
over extended periods of time on the development of curriculum materials,
and these promising research results have had limited impact in education.

We must not assume that basic research will directly influence educational practice. One of the clearest examples I know of comes from a different domain. Guided by respected theory, basic research on mnemonic techniques has thoroughly established that a number of these techniques can dramatically increase the retention of information. The translation of this well-replicated finding into educational practice, however, turns out not to be a simple task. Joel Levin contrasted some commercial materials with his own, developed and refined over an extended period of research in the Wisconsin Research and Development Center. He found that the commercial materials, despite the use of mnemonics, were hardly better than no mnemonics at all (Levin, Kessler, Miller, & Bartell, 1981). The point is that extensive evaluation and revisions of curriculum materials are required, even in domains where the basic research principles are quite well understood (Levin & Pressley, in press).

Communication Games in the Classroom

Guided by the belief that a closer integration of research and practice would lead to better research practice, I have begun studying communication activities that can be used in the classroom. In the remainder of this chapter, I will describe a study involving several of these games in four elementary school classrooms.

Three communication games were used in this study; two of them involved the entire classroom at the same time; the other more suitable for a "learning center" where single pairs of children would use them on their own. The study was aimed at two related questions. First, are individual children's speaking and listening scores as observed in these games stable across trials, partners, and tasks? Second, is there qualitative and quantitative evidence to indicate that children are learning something from these activities?

The selection of games to be used in the study was guided by an earlier analysis of communication games available through commercial sources or described in the research literature (Dickson & Patterson, 1981). Eight criteria were developed for evaluating such games. We noted that tasks designed to measure children's oral communication skills encourage them to interact in a way that taps their speaking, listening, and questioning skills. Similarly, the rich verbal interaction seen in referential tasks requires different types of communicative skill, such as clarification, specification, producing utterances that are highly contingent on the previous speakers', and choosing appropriate vocabulary.

The process of evaluating games and watching children playing them highlighted the importance of allowing children to work in pairs. In order to improve speaking and listening skills, children must have opportunities to talk with each other. There will be more opportunities for verbal interaction if only two children play a game, rather than six or eight. It is also important that these games allow pairs of children to communicate without direct teacher supervision, both to reduce demands on teachers and to allow natural child–child interaction. Although children may get opportunities for listening, such as when the teacher gives the whole class directions for a project, this listening is of a different nature than that which demands listening for a specific purpose or when the child is expected to respond to the speaker.

THREE COMMUNICATION GAMES

Three different communication games were used. Two of the games were administered to intact classrooms: a notebook game and a worksheet game. The notebook game consisted of a notebook positioned upright between 2 children; on each side of the notebook were pages that contained rows of 4 pictures. On the speaker's side, one of the pictures in each row was marked with an "X" that designated it as the target. The speaker's task was to describe the target and the listener placed a mark on the one he or she thought the speaker was describing. There were a total of 20 sets of 4 referents.

The worksheet game was similar to the notebook game, but consisted of 12 pairs of rows of 4 pictures; 6 on the front and 6 on the back of the worksheet. Two pairs of rows from the worksheet are shown in Figure 8.1. On the speaker's copy of the worksheet, a target referent in one row was connected with a target referent in a second row. The speaker's task was to tell the listener how to draw a corresponding line on the listener's worksheet.

The third game used Lego® block models as referents. The Lego block game was administered by an experimenter to individual pairs of children outside the classroom. In this task, the speaker was given a model built from Lego blocks and asked to tell the listener how to assemble the model from loose blocks.

A total of 100 children from 4 elementary school classrooms were involved in the study. The children were predominantly white and middle-class. Two of the classrooms combined first- and second-grade children and 2 of the classrooms combined third- and fourth-grade children. The children were paired and the pairs seated at desks in a circle around the edge of their classroom. An older and younger child from the same class were paired. The mean age for the dyads in the two younger classes was 7:5, and the mean age for dyads in the two older classes was 9:3. Half of the pairs were same-sex and half were cross-sex.

The children were told they were going to play a game where they would talk to each other about some pictures. The instructions emphasized the importance of working cooperatively. One child in each pair was designated as

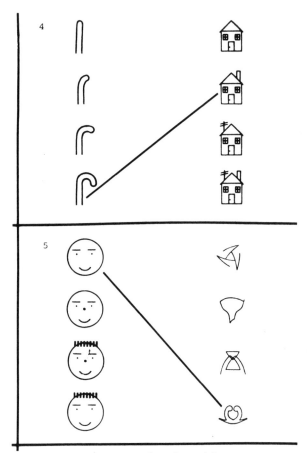

Figure 8.1. Two items from the worksheet game.

speaker. In order to be sure the game was understood, the experimenters modeled playing the game in front of the class, demonstrating the need for the speaker to be explicit in descriptions and for the listener to ask questions when uncertain.

Certain procedures were the same for all three games. Each game consisted of four trials, with the children alternating as speaker and listener across trials. In the notebook and worksheet games, one member of each pair rotated after the second trial, whereas in the Lego-block task the same pair completed all four trials. For all trials the children were allowed 3 minutes; the score for the pair for the trial was the number of correctly placed blocks for the Lego-block task, with points being given for both correctness of block and correctness of placement. (Details of scoring are given in Dickson, Patterson, and Tracy,

The same children who had been paired on trial one and two of the notebook game were again paired on the block model task. The notebook and worksheet games were administered on separate days, approximately 1 week apart; the block model game was administered over the next 2 weeks following the worksheet game.

In summary, by the end of the study, each child had served as speaker on six trials (two each on three tasks) and listener on six trials. Half of these trials had been with the same partner (trials one and two of the notebook game and trials one through four of the block model game), and half had been with a different partner.

RESULTS

For both theoretical and practical purposes, one of the most interesting questions is whether speaking and listening performance is stable. Indeed, to talk about communicative competence is to imply the existence of some set of behaviors that individuals possess to varying degrees. Yet, as noted earlier, remarkably little evidence has been gathered testing whether communication performance is stable. For the construct of communication competence (or communication skill) to be of theoretical or practical utility, some stability of individual's performance across occasions, settings, and partners must be shown to exist.

The data permit us to address this question, though the statistical analyses are somewhat complex. Each score on each trial must be treated as the speaking score for one child and the listening score for the other child in the dyad. In addition, because scores improved over trials, it is necessary statistically to partial out the effects of order of speaking and listening, so as to adjust the scores of individuals according to whether they were speakers on trials one and three or trials two and four. Having done that, scores for individuals were created, combining various subscores in ways that take advantage of the logic built into the experimental design.

The pattern of results is best discussed in terms of the display in Figure 8.2, where correlations among various subscores within each of the 4 classes are shown, plotted from -1.00 to $+1.00$. The bottom row of Figure 8.2 displays 12 correlation coefficients, representing the correlations between individuals' listening scores across tasks for each of the 4 classes. Each of these listening scores is the sum of the listening scores on the 2 trials within each task. In other words, for each class we compute the correlation between individuals' listening score on the notebook game with the worksheet game, the notebook game with the Lego block game, and the worksheet game with the Lego block game, yielding a total of 3 correlation coefficients. For the 4 classrooms, this yields a total of 12 correlation coefficients. Inspection of the

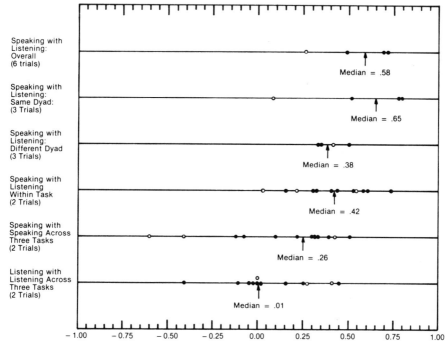

Figure 8.2.   Display of correlation coefficients among various subscores. Each circle represents one correlation. Open circles designate the class with anomalous data.

distribution of correlations reveals little evidence that listening skill, as measured by these activities, is stable. The median correlation is almost zero.

The second row from the bottom of Figure 8.2 displays the correlations between speaking and speaking scores across the three tasks, corresponding to the listening score correlations just discussed. Inspection of the distribution of these correlations reveals evidence that speaking performance is somewhat stable, with a median correlation of .26. One anomaly was found in the data for which no explanation has been found. In one of the four classes, strong negative correlations were found between speaking scores on one task (the worksheet) and speaking scores on the other two tasks. Despite exhaustive explorations of the data, no explanation can be found for this improbable result. The data from this class are indicated in Figure 8.2 as open circles, and though the data from this class on this one measure weaken the overall estimates of stability, the median correlation is not strongly affected by the extreme values from this class.

The third row from the bottom of Figure 8.2 shows the correlations between speaking and listening scores within task, as distinguished from the preceding analyses across task. Inspection of these data suggests considerable stability of the overall communicative performance within a given task, with a median correlation of .42.

The experimental design was such that for one half of the trials each individual was paired with the same partner, and for one half of the trials each individual was paired with a different partner. A comparison of correlations for these two conditions permits us to examine the relative stability of speaking and listening scores across partners and across tasks. The fourth row from the bottom of Figure 8.2 displays the correlations between speaking and listening scores in the four classes on the three trials where individuals were paired with different partners. The median correlation is .38. These data can be contrasted with those in the fifth row from the bottom of Figure 8.2, showing correlations between speaking and listening scores on the three trials where individuals were speaking to the same partners. Here the median correlation is .65.

Finally, looking at the top row of Figure 8.2, we see the correlations between individuals' overall speaking and listening scores based on six trials as speaker and six trials as listener. The median correlation is .58.

The pattern of correlations in Figure 8.2 tells us a number of important things. First, individual differences in speaking and listening skills, as tapped by these referential communication tasks, do appear to show considerable stability. Further, the stability of performance is greater within a given pair of children than across partners. In other words, communication performance is very much a product of the interaction of two individuals. In a real sense, we should think in terms of the communicative competence of dyads rather than the communicative competence of individuals. The data verify the common experience that individuals communicate well with certain individuals, but not with other individuals. Finally, although speaking scores for individuals correlate across tasks, listening scores do not. This finding is important and deserves comment.

The lack of correlation between listening scores suggests that individual differences in listening skill contribute less to dyadic performance than individual differences in speaking skill. This interpretation is supported by the results of a standardized listening test administered following each classroom activity, in which an adult gave fully adequate descriptions of referents similar to those used in the notebook and worksheet. Children in all classrooms performed almost perfectly on this task, suggesting that most of the variability in dyadic performance is in the adequacy of the speaker's descriptions.

The second major research question was whether quantitative and qualitative evidence indicated that the children were learning from the activities. Analyses of variance across trials for all three games revealed statistically significant increases in the children's scores across trials. Not surprisingly, the older children had higher scores than the younger children. There were no differences in performance between pairs according to sex pairing (male–male, female–female, female–male). Details of these statistical analyses are given elsewhere (Dickson et al., 1981).

Turning to qualitative evidence of the educational value of these communication game activities, several observations may be made. The teachers and children involved in the research were enthusiastic about the activities and asked that we return with more communication activities. During the 3-minute trials the classrooms buzzed with intense communication among all of the children. Despite the background noise, the children within each pair seemed to have no difficulty hearing each other—testimony to children's ability to communicate in distracting environments!

Excerpts from transcripts of children engaged in these referential communication games may convey something of the richness of the verbal and social interaction that occurs in this context. In the following excerpt, two 10-year-old girls complete two items on the worksheet format. The first item has four pictures of an abstract shape on the left and four pictures of a house with attributes that are present or absent. The second item has four faces with systematically varying features on the left and four abstract line drawings on the right. The speaker is designated with an "S" and the listener with an "L."

S:	*It goes out but then it sort of curves in a little bit.*	(1)
L:	*Is it like . . . pointy?*	(2)
S:	*It's not pointy, really.*	(3)
L:	*Does it go up, then curves in?*	(4)
S:	*Yeah.*	(5)
L:	*It doesn't point?*	(6)
S:	*No, it doesn't point, really. It's a full candy cane.*	(7)
L:	[The listener nods, nonverbally indicating comprehension.]	(8)
S:	*And then the house **does** have a chimney, but it doesn't have an antenna.*	(9)
L:	*OK.* [She correctly draws a line between the two pictures.]	(10)
S:	*The person doesn't have hair and it doesn't have a nose.*	(11)
L:	*Umhm.*	(12)
S:	*This one sort of looks like two fingers coming up.*	(13)
L:	*Like two worms in a sled?*	(14)
S:	*Yeah.*	(15)
L:	[Correctly draws a line between the two pictures.]	(16)

This brief excerpt, consisting of only 16 turns and lasting less than 60 seconds, illustrates the richness of the communication elicited by these tasks. Detailed analyses of the children's language are not of interest here, but using some commonly applied categories, we find four requests for more information (Lines 2, 4, 6, 14); two affirmations (Lines 5, 15); two denials (Lines 3, 7); three uses of metaphoric language (Lines 7, 13, 14); eight uses of analytic language (Lines 1, 2, 3, 4, 6, 7, 9, 11); one use of stress for emphasis (Line 9: *does have*); and two uses of conjoint logical operations (Lines 9 and 11: docs and does not). Of particular interest is the negotiation of a shared nomenclature observed in the sequence from lines 2 through 7, where the listener persists in her hypothesis that the referent is *pointy*. The speaker denies that description a second time and then shifts from an analytic mode to a metaphoric mode and succeeds by aptly characterizing the referent as a *full candy cane*. Notice, too, that the listener is a fully active partner in the game.

In the following excerpt, two 7-year-old boys are communicating about faces that differ only by the presence or absence of binary features (eyebrows, hair, ears, noses). Yet notice the richness with which they embue the activity.

L:	[After completing the previous item.] *OK, now describe the faces.*	(1)
S:	*It's a boy . . . happy . . . but he doesn't have a nose.*	(2)
L:	*How can he be happy without a nose?* (laughter) *Does he have hair?*	(3)
S:	*No, he doesn't.*	(4)

I have included this example to suggest that even referents that may appear on the surface to be uninteresting often evoke interest in young children. Similar examples are found in transcripts of descriptions of pictures showing a monkey in various spatial locations relative to a cage. As experimenter and educator, my focus was on establishing contexts in which young children exercise their capacity to convey spatial relations; the transcripts are rich in this regard. But, in addition, the children enrich the game with fantasies never anticipated. A child says, *It looks like he's lifting the cage,* where I had constructed the referent sets from the logical intersection of binary characteristics, inside–outside and top–bottom.

The creativity of children in these interactions exemplifies an interesting dilemma for one attempting to translate sociolinguistic and referential research into educational practice. Sociolinguistic research on naturally occurring contexts has done much to sensitize us to the powerful influence of context (the "situation") on behavior, but the priority accorded observation in natural contexts in this tradition resulted in inattention to intervention through the creation of new contexts. On the other hand, communication contexts have been deliberately created in referential research, but the priority accorded experimental control has led to the creation of contexts that deliberately limit the "richness" of children's interaction because it would create error variance in experiments. These paradigmatic "blind spots" must be kept in mind as we seek to bring insights from sociolinguistic and referential communication research to bear on the design of educational settings that elicit from children higher frequencies of various speech acts serving specific communicative functions than would occur naturally in other classroom contexts.

Consider a recent analysis of requests for action and information in 3 first-grade reading groups, containing a total of 15 first-grade children (Wilkinson et al., 1981). The 3 reading groups were videotaped for a total of 78 minutes during which the 15 children made 65 requests for information. About a third of the requests were aimed at obtaining a particular piece of information needed in the academic task, a type of request similar to the 4 requests for information produced in approximately 1 minute of interaction in the communication activity described in the previous excerpt. The 20 or so requests for specific information observed in the reading groups were produced by 15 children, compared to 2 children in the communication game context. As a rough approximation, we can say that an individual child in the communication game context would make over 100 requests for specific information per hour, whereas an individual child in a reading group would make about 4 such requests per hour.

I would hasten to add that the point is not that more is better. Nor is the point that communication games are more important than reading groups. The point is that different contexts elicit different amounts of different types of communicative competencies. For example, the reading group setting is richer in its demands for persuasion techniques (among them, indirect forms of requesting information), whereas the rules of the game in the communication activity establish a context in which compliance with requests for information is expected. Although sheer amount is not as critical as quality of interaction, amount must count for something. Most advocates of increased peer communication in classrooms would view it as undesirable if children had almost no opportunities to exercise their skills in requesting information.

This brings us to the question of individual differences. My analysis of the data on requests for information in the preceding reading groups led to the conclusion that the **average** child made four requests for specific information per hour. But average children do not exist. Further examination of the data in Wilkinson et al. (1981) highlights the enormous individual variability in requesting information. Of the 65 requests, 3 children produced 41 (63%). Of the remaining 12 children, 2 made no requests for information, 3 made one request, and the others ranged from 2 to 5 requests for information. Thus, for about half of the children in these three reading groups, the estimate is that they would make about one request for specific information per hour in reading groups. Although the data give evidence of communicative competence in the children, the performance of these communicative acts is quite unequally distributed among them.

If one is concerned that individual children be given opportunities to exercise the manifold communicative functions identified by sociolinguists, the widely unequal distribution of requests evident in this analysis suggests the importance of attending to individual differences in performance and creating communicative contexts in the classroom where all children have the opportunity to give directions and ask questions. Dyadic tasks, such as referential communication settings, have the advantage of giving all children the opportunity to communicate actively—not just the verbally assertive.

Merging Research and Practice

The approach taken in the research described in this chapter is aimed at reducing the gulf between research and practice in the domain of children's oral communication skills. I have attempted to draw on the strengths of both the sociolinguistic and referential research traditions and bring them to bear on educational practice. The research was carried out largely in classrooms, as is commonly done in sociolinguistic research, using contexts created with deliberate experimental purposes, as is commonly done in referential research. But the specific activities were designed with their potential educational application in mind, however, leading to the use of communicative contexts richer in the opportunities for interaction between the children in the study and richer in the types of referent sets than has been common in recent research in the referential communication research (see Dickson, 1981b). This approach to research begins with considerations of the reality of the classroom and seeks to design experimental activities that offer the possibility of implementation in the classroom. Results from research with such activities are more likely to have educational impact than research using tasks less representative of the domain of activities that might be used in the classrooms. One need not worry so much about far transfer, when the tasks used in the research have this representativeness.

Extending my earlier recommendation that sociolinguistic and referential research traditions might profit from the exchange of insights, I would like to mention two other lines of research that appear to me to be relevant to our efforts at improving the school curriculum in the area of children's communication skills.

The first is research on children's cooperative learning. The cooperative contexts used in this research have many features in common with referential communication contexts. Communication games are, by their very nature, cooperative. They involve a joint activity with a well-defined outcome that depends on the sharing of information. Reviews of research on cooperative learning present convincing evidence that cooperative learning in various game and team contexts can lead to higher achievement, improved cross-race and cross-sex interaction, as well as improved attitudes toward school (Johnson, Maruyama, Johnson, Nelson, & Skon, 1981; Sharan, 1980; Slavin, 1980). Examining the literature, however, one cannot help but be struck by the lack of detailed information on the small group processes in the cooperative activities used in this research. More detailed analyses of the small group interaction by sociolinguists could enlighten this work. Similarly, much of the interaction in the types of cooperative activities contexts used in these studies is referential in nature, yet no linkages have been created between these two domains of research.

Foreign language instruction is the second body of research that appears to offer an opportunity of integration with research on children's oral communication skills. Recent developments in foreign language instruction, characterized as the "notional–functional" approach to foreign language instruction (Munby, 1978; Wilkins, 1976), have placed great emphasis on the use of communication activities similar to those used in referential communication. Related work in the teaching of English as a second language also makes use of communication games, many of which are referential in nature (Palmer, 1981). Fillmore's chapter in this volume suggests that the rate of acquisition of English by children whose primary language is not English is strongly influenced by the extent to which these children interact with English-speaking children in the classroom. One way to increase the extent to which such interaction occurs is to increase the frequency of cooperative small group activities in classrooms and ensure that these small groups are composed of children from different linguistic backgrounds.

Given the pressures on schools to achieve multiple objectives, among which social and communication skills are central, we need to create learning activities that offer rich opportunities for acquiring these skills. These activities can engage an entire classroom at one time, as with the notebook and worksheet games, or they can be set up in a learning center in the corner of the classroom, as in the Lego block game. Microcomputers also hold considerable promise as learning centers for creating deliberately structured interaction between children. We are presently conducting research and development on a referential communication game that runs on an Apple® microcomputer. The game presents pairs of children with arrays of referents, automatically designating the speaker and listener roles and scoring the listener's choices. Melodic feedback is given to distinguish correct and incorrect choices and scores are recorded for each pair. Considering Fillmore's evidence on the acquisition of English, one extension of the microcomputer communication game would be to program it to "recommend" to the teacher the pairing of limited English-speaking children with English-speaking children in the classroom who have been found to be skillful communicators in this game. Our work to date suggests that microcomputers offer almost unlimited potential for the creation of social interactions between children.

Referential communication activities of the type discussed in the present chapter do create rich interaction between children and at the same time yield educationally useful diagnostic information about the children's speaking and listening skills. Such referential communication activities deserve careful consideration as one component of a more comprehensive oral communication curriculum.

References

Aaronson, M., & Schaefer, E. S. Preschool preposition test. In O. G. Johnson & J. W. Bommarito (Eds.), *Tests and measurements in child development: A handbook.* San Francisco: Jossey-Bass, 1971.

Allen, R. R., & Brown, K. L. (Eds.). *Developing communication competence in children.* Skokie, Ill.: National Textbook Co., 1977.

Asher, S. R. Referential communication. In G. J. Whitehurst & B. J. Zimmerman (Eds.), *The functions of language and cognition.* New York: Academic Press, 1979.

Baldwin, T. L., & Garvey, C. J. Components of accurate problem-solving communications. *American Educational Research Journal,* 1973, 10, 39–48.

Bronfenbrenner, U. *The ecology of human development: Experiments by nature and design.* Cambridge: Harvard University Press, 1979.

Cazden, C. B. Evaluation of learning in preschool education: Early language development. In B. S. Bloom, J. T. Hastings, & G. F. Madaus (Eds.), *Handbook on formative and summative evaluation of student learning.* New York: McGraw-Hill, 1971.

Cazden, C. B. *Child language and education.* New York: Holt, Rinehart & Winston, 1972.

Cazden, C. B. Forward. In H. Mehan, *Learning lessons.* Cambridge: Harvard University Press, 1979.

Chandler, M. J., Greenspan, S., & Barenboim, C. Assessment and training of role-taking and referential communication skills in institutionalized emotionally disturbed children. *Developmental Psychology,* 1974, 10, 546–553.

Cronbach, L. J. Beyond the two disciplines of scientific psychology. *American Psychologist,* 1975, 30, 116–127.

Dickson, W. P. Referential communication performance from age 4 to 8: Effects on referent type, context, and target position. *Developmental Psychology,* 1979, 15, 470–471.

Dickson, W. P. Introduction: Toward an interdisciplinary conception of children's communication abilities. In W. P. Dickson (Ed.), *Children's oral communication skills.* New York: Academic Press, 1981. (a)

Dickson, W. P. Referential communication activities in research and in the curriculum: A meta-analysis. In W. P. Dickson (Ed.), *Children's oral communication skills.* New York: Academic Press, 1981. (b)

Dickson, W. P. Two decades of referential communication research: A review and meta-analysis. In C. J. Brainerd & M. Pressley (Eds.), *Progress in cognitive development research. Vol. 2. Verbal processes in children.* New York: Springer-Verlag, 1982.

Dickson, W. P., Hess, R. D., Miyake, N., & Azuma, H. Referential communication accuracy between mother and child as a predictor of cognitive development in the United States and Japan. *Child Development,* 1979, *50,* 53–59.

Dickson, W. P., & Patterson, J. H. Evaluating referential communication games for teaching speaking and listening skills. *Communication Education,* 1981, *30,* 11–21.

Dickson, W. P., Patterson, J. H., & Tracy, K. *Classroom communication games for teaching speaking and listening skills.* Paper presented at the meeting of the American Education Research Association, Los Angeles, April 1981.

Flavell, J. H. Cognitive monitoring. In W. P. Dickson (Ed.), *Children's oral communication skills.* New York: Academic Press, 1981.

Foorman, B. R. Language development in the K–3 classroom: Using the referential communication paradigm. *Psychology in the Schools,* 1980, *17,* 278–283.

Gleason, J. B. An experimental approach to improving children's communicative ability. In C. B. Cazden (Ed.), *Language in early childhood education.* Washington, D.C.: National Association for the Education of Young Children, 1972.

Johnson, D. W., Maruyama, G., Johnson, R., Nelson, D., & Skon, L. Effects of cooperative, competitive, and individualistic goal structures on achievement: A meta-analysis. *Psychological Bulletin,* 1981, *89,* 47–62.

Kerlinger, F. N. The influences of research on education practice. *Educational Researcher,* 1977, *6,* 5–12.

Labov, W. The logic of non-standard English. In J. E. Atatis (Ed.), *Linguistics and the teaching of standard English.* Monograph Series on Languages and Linguistics, No. 22. Washington, D.C.: Georgetown University Press, 1969.

Levin, J. R., Kessler, J., Miller, G. E., & Bartell, N. P. *More on how (and how not) to remember the states and their capitals* (Working Paper No. 306). Madison: Wisconsin Research and Development Center for Individualized Schooling, 1981.

Levin, J. R., & Pressley, M. Understanding mnemonic imagery effects: A dozen "obvious" outcomes. *Educational Technology,* in press.

Markman, E. M. Comprehension monitoring. In W. P. Dickson (Ed.), *Children's oral communication skills.* New York: Academic Press, 1981.

Moffett, J., & Wagner, B. J. *Student-centered language arts and reading, K–13* (2nd ed.). Boston: Houghton Mifflin Co., 1976.

Munby, J. *Communicative syllabus design.* Cambridge, Mass.: Cambridge University Press, 1978.

Nelson, K. Individual differences in language development: Implications for development and language. *Developmental Psychology,* 1981, *17,* 170–187.

Palmer, A. S. Measurements of reliability and concurrent validity of two picture description test of oral communication. In A. S. Palmer, P. J. M. Groot, & G. A. Trosper (Eds.), *The construct validation of tests of communicative competence.* Boston: TESOL (Teaching English as a Second or Other Language), 1981.

Patterson, C. J. Teaching children to listen. *Today's Education,* 1978, *67,* 52–53.

Patterson, C. J., & Kister, M. C. The development of listener skills for referential communication. In W. P. Dickson (Ed.), *Children's oral communication skills.* New York: Academic Press, 1981.

Piaget, J. *Language and thought of the child.* New York: Harcourt, Brace, 1926.

Sharan, S. Cooperative learning in small groups: Recent methods and effects on achievement, attitudes, and ethnic relations. *Review of Educational Research,* 1980, *50,* 241–272.

Shuy, R. W., & Griffin, P. What do they do at school any day: Studying functional language. In W. P. Dickson (Ed.), *Children's oral communication skills.* New York: Academic Press, 1981.

Slavin, R. E. Cooperative learning. *Review of Educational Research,* 1980, *50,* 315–342.

A success that failed. *National Elementary School Principal,* 1978, *57,* 28–29.

Wang, M. C., Rose, S., & Maxwell, J. *The development of the language communication skills task.* Pittsburgh: University of Pittsburgh, Learning Research and Development Center, 1973.

Whitehurst, G. J., & Sonnenschein, S. The development of informative messages in referential communication: Knowing when versus knowing how. In W. P. Dickson (Ed.), *Children's oral communication skills.* New York: Academic Press, 1981.

Wilkins, D. A. *Notional syllabuses.* Oxford: Oxford University Press, 1976.

Wilkinson, L. C., Clevenger, M., & Dollaghan, C. Communication in small instructional groups: A sociolinguistic approach. In W. P. Dickson (Ed.), *Children's oral communication skills.* New York: Academic Press, 1981.

III
Contextual Diversity

9

Classroom Discourse as Improvisation: Relationships between Academic Task Structure and Social Participation Structure in Lessons

FREDERICK ERICKSON

Talk among teachers and students in lessons—talk that is not only intelligible but situationally appropriate and effective—can be seen as the collective improvisation of meaning and social organization from moment to moment. How this improvisation happens, and what the pedagogical significance of improvisation may be, are the topics of this chapter.

I will first discuss some general points: (*a*) academic and social aspects of the task structure of lessons as learning environments; (*b*) the role of timing in the social and academic organization of interaction in lessons; (*c*) cultural patterning of interaction; and (*d*) the implications of the previous three for our understanding of the conduct of teaching and learning as socialization. Then I will present specific examples from a mathematics lesson taught in a first-grade classroom. I will conclude with discussion of the pedagogical and sociolinguistic implication of a frame of reference and an analysis that considers school lessons as encounters, and considers interaction in lessons as situational variation on general sociocultural themes.

Learning Task Environments

Teachers and students engaged in doing a lesson together can be seen as drawing on two sets of procedural knowledge simultaneously; knowledge of the **academic task structure** and of the **social participation structure**. The

153

academic task structure (ATS)[1] can be thought of as a patterned set of constraints provided by the logic of sequencing in the subject-matter content of
the lesson. The social participation structure (SPS) can be thought of as a
patterned set of constraints on the allocation of interactional rights and obligations of various members of the interacting group (see Erickson & Shultz,
1977, 1981; Shultz, Florio, & Erickson, in press).

The academic task structure governs the logical sequencing of instructional "moves" by the teacher and students. Consider, for example, the following problem in addition:

$$\begin{array}{r} 14 \\ + \ 8 \\ \hline 22 \end{array}$$

In solving this equation in "old math" style (and in teaching the steps in its
solution) it is necessary to begin (a) with the rightmost column (the "1s");
(b) add the numbers in that column; (c) since the sum of that column is
greater than 10, "carry" the 10 units into the column next to the left (the
"10s" column); and (d) add the two 10s in that column. The sequence of steps
is constrained by the logic of computation; one does not know that two 10s
must be added in the "10s" column until one has first added the numbers in
the "1s" column. Thus the steps in adding stand in "adjacency pair" relationships to one another that are analogous to the adjacency pair relationships in
conversation that have been discussed by conversational analysts (Sacks, Schegloff, & Jefferson, 1974), for example, question–answer sequences. Both in
conversation and in computation these are invariant relationships of series
position, hierarchically and sequentially ordered.

There are at least four definable aspects of academic task environment
in a lesson: (a) the logic of subject matter sequencing; (b) the information
content of the various sequential steps; (c) the "meta-content" cues toward
steps and strategies for completing the task; and (d) the physical materials
through which tasks and task components are manifested and with which tasks
are accomplished. These four aspects together manifest the academic task
structure of the lesson as a learning environment.

The social participation structure governs the sequencing and articulation
of interaction; it involves multiple dimensions of interactional partnership
according to which interactional work is divided up in sets of articulated
communicative roles, for example, listener roles in relation to speaker roles.[2]
Considered as a whole pattern, a participation structure can be thought of as

---

[1] It should be noted that this is a much more specific sense of the term than that used
by Bossert (1979), whose "Task Activity Structure" is a much more general notion of task, and
derives from a very different theoretical frame of reference.

[2] Role here refers to a set of rights and obligations vis à vis others.

the configuration of all the roles of all the partners in an interactional event (see the discussion in Erickson & Shultz, 1977, 1981). Some aspects of these role relationships involve patterns in the ways interactional partners exchange turns at speaking, tie pairs of turns together semantically in question–answer sequences, and coordinate listening behavior in relation to speaking behavior.

Paralleling the four aspects of the academic task environment of a lesson are four definable aspects of the social task environment: (a) the social gate-keeping of access to people and other information sources during the lesson; (b) the allocation of communicative rights and obligations among the various interactional partners in the event; (c) the sequencing and timing of successive functional "slots" in the interaction; and (d) the simultaneous actions of all those engaged in interaction during the lesson. Taken together, these four aspects manifest the social participation structure of the lesson as a learning environment.

Aspects of social participation structure have been studied by conversational analysts and by ethnographers of communication (e.g., Sacks et al., 1974, on turn allocation; Schegloff, 1968 on question–answer sequences; and Duncan & Fiske, 1977, Erickson, 1979, and Kendon, 1967, on listener–speaker coordination).

All this work presumes a definition of the **social** in Weber's terms as action taken in account of the actions of others (Weber, [1922] 1978). Social **action** is distinguished from asocial **behavior** in that it is articulated with and oriented to what others are doing in the scene as well as to what others may be doing outside the immediate scene at hand. Occasions of social interactions are in Goffman's terms **encounters**; focused gatherings in which the focus is on what others are doing there (Goffman, 1961). The boundary between the encounter and the world outside it is not impermeable; outside influences do impinge on it. But the action inside the encounter takes on, to some extent, a life of its own. It is, in part at least, immediately social. The place in which what ethnomethodologists term "local production" is done; the action situated in its immediate locale.

In encounters, the actions of the various interactional partners are articulated in immediately social ways both sequentially and simultaneously. Reciprocal actions are articulated sequentially, for example, in question–answer pairs, in which the question asked by one conversational partner obliges an answer by another in the next successive "slot" in the conversation. Complementary actions are articulated simultaneously, for example, in listener responses such as nods that may occur in the same moment as the speaker's speech. In short, action that is immediately social is seen as radically cooperative and interdependent.

Sequential and simultaneous aspects of the social organization of interaction in classrooms have been considered recently by a number of researchers, notably, Bremme and Erickson (1977), Erickson and Mohatt (1982), Gumperz and Cook-Gumperz (1979), Mehan (1979), Merritt (Chapter 11, this volume), Michaels & Cook-Gumperz (1979), Shultz et al. (in press), Sinclair and Coulthard (1975), and Wilkinson, Clevenger, and Dollaghan (1981). Only the authors of the most recent work have begun to consider the social and academic aspects of lesson tasks together (see Au, 1980; Collins & Michaels, 1980; Cooper, Marquis, & Ayers-Lopez, Chapter 5, this volume; Griffin, Cole, & Newman, in preparation; Mehan & Griffin, 1980). This is necessary, as I have argued elsewhere (Erickson, 1980), if we are to develop an interactional theory of cognitive learning and teaching in social occasions (such as lessons) that are interactional learning environments.

Some earlier classroom research has emphasized the cognitive task environment of lessons (Smith, n.d.; Taba, 1964), while ignoring the social task environment. One notable attempt was made by Bellack, Kliebard, Hyman, and Smith (1966) to combine aspects of social and academic organization in the study of lessons. But in the years since then, sociolinguistically oriented researchers have studied mainly the social participation structure of lessons, whereas curriculum researchers and cognitive psychologists have concerned themselves primarily with the academic task structure of lessons. It is necessary to consider both aspects of organization as mutually constitutive. As Mehan puts it succinctly, for a student to give a right answer in a lesson, the answer must be "right" both in academic content and in social form (Mehan, 1979, p.1).

To the extent that talk in a lesson concerns subject matter, successful participation in the lesson involves knowledge of subject matter information and its logical organization, as well as knowledge of discourse and its social organization.

Time and Sequence in the Coordination of Social Interaction

If face-to-face interaction is a radically cooperative enterprise, "locally" produced in terms of locally situated actions and their significance, then interactional partners must have means available for establishing and maintaining interdependence in their collective action. These means appear to be patterns of timing and sequencing in the performance of verbal and nonverbal behavior. The patterns function as a signal system—a social steering mechanism—by which interactional partners are able to tell each other what is happening from moment to moment. I will begin this discussion by considering different functions and behavioral manifestations of coordination signals and then will discuss the organization of these signals in the real-time duration of interaction.

The signals are both explicit and implicit. They may communicate information about a moment that is past, this moment now, and/or the moment coming next. Explicit signals can be found in the literal meaning (referential content) of talk. The last sentence of the previous paragraph is an instance of this in written discourse; it points the expectations of the reader to what is coming next in the text.

In lessons some of this orienting is done explicitly in talk. Often that talk has to do with subject matter content and the ATS. Consider the addition problem discussed earlier. If the teacher were demonstrating the solution of this problem to the class, the lesson discourse might go something like this as the teacher pointed to the various numbers and columns on a chalkboard:

1. TEACHER: *What's four plus eight?* (pointing to the "1s" column)
2. CLASS: *Twelve.*
3. TEACHER: *Right, so we write the two here* (Teacher does so) *and then what?*
4. CLASS: (no answer)
5. TEACHER: *What did I say last time?* (i.e., in the previous problem)
6. CLASS: *Carry.*
7. TEACHER: *Carry the 10 over to the 10s column and add the two 10s there . . . so the answer is . . .*
8. CLASS: *Twenty-two.*
9. TEACHER: *Very good. Now "seven plus five"* (Teacher moves on to the next problem).

The question in turn 1, *What's four plus eight?* (even if not accompanied by the nonverbal action of pointing to the chalkboard), explicitly identifies and focuses attention on the step in the academic task structure that is being done in **this moment now**. In addition, the question form also signals that an answer is due in **the moment coming next**; hence the question not only allows the class to identify what is happening in the current moment but to anticipate, through prospective interpretation, what should happen in **the moment to come**. Turn 5 explicitly points to the need for retrospective interpretation by the class, asking for recall of what was taught about "carrying" in the previous problem.

Signals pointing to a particular sequential stage in the lesson can be even more explicitly formulated than in the previous illustration. For example, the teacher could have preceded the question in turn 1 with the statement, *Let's begin by adding the numbers in the '1s' column.* This would have pointed explicitly to the sequential stage in the ATS itself, before getting into the computational operation necessary at that stage. Explicit formulations of this type may occur at the very beginning of the lesson, as in the following hypothetical example: *Now we will have our spelling test. First take out a sheet of paper, write your name in the upper right hand corner, and then I will begin to read the words you are to spell.* (This is the same sort of function performed by the sentence at the end of the first paragraph of this section, *I will begin this discussion by considering different functions and behavioral manifestations of coordination signals and then will discuss the organization of these signals in the real-time duration of interaction.*)

The same kind of orientation to sequence position in a lesson can also be signaled through ellipsis. Elliptic signals can be used successfully because of familiarity with sequential routines of classroom procedure. An example is found in Turn 9 of the previous illustration. There one word plus a pause, *Now . . .* can function as a formulation of sequential position that is equivalent to the whole phrase, *Let's begin by adding the numbers in the '1s' column.* Through ellipsis, the first word of Turn 3, *Right,* points retrospectively to the correctness of the answer in Turn 2. The semantic pointing is elliptic, but is still explicitly communicated in the lexical item, *Right.*

Pointing to sequence position is also done more implicitly. This function can be accomplished both by words and syntax, and by paralinguistic and nonverbal cues. An example of a lexical cue is found in Turn 3, in which the word *Right* functions explicitly to signal that the previous answer was correct. It also functions implicitly to signal prospectively that, since the previous answer was correct, the teacher is about to move on to something new in the **next moment.** A syntactic cue accomplishes a similar prospective pointing function at the end of Turn 7, in which a pause interrupts the completion of the verb phrase: *so the answer is . . . .*[3]

Implicit prospective and retrospective pointing can also be done by so-called "suprasegmental" patterns of nonverbal and paralinguistic behavior; so-called because they are sustained across smaller phonological and syntactic units in the speech stream. Changes in postural position and interpersonal distance often mark the ending of one discourse unit and the beginning of another (see Erickson, 1975; Scheflen, 1973; and the analysis of postural positioning in classroom lessons by McDermott, 1976). Changes in pitch register and in speech prosody (pitch, stress, volume stress, tempo) can also signal the completion of one connected series of discourse "chunks," as in the successively falling pitch levels in the "listing intonation" found in this hypothetical example:

TEACHER: What did the ancient Greeks consider to be the essential material elements?

CLASS:

$$E^{arth} \quad A^{ir} \quad F^{ire} \quad Wa_{ter}$$

---

[3] The aspects of sequence-position signaling discussed so far have all been noted by other researchers, notably Sacks *et al.* (1974); Schegloff (1968) (see the discussion in Mehan & Wood, 1975), and in applications of speech act theory to lesson discourse, as in Sinclair and Coulthard (1975).

Here not only does the final pitch fall at the end of "water" signal the end of the list, but the slight rise of pitch in "air" and "fire" signals the end point is yet to come.

Gumperz (1977) uses the term **contextualization** *cues* to refer to all the surface–structural means by which communicative intent and interpretive form are signaled. Contextualization cueing procedures are learned and their usage is shared within speech communities. Cues of this general class point to various contexts of interpretation, not only to the aspects of sequential context discussed here, but to other aspects of context as well. These include **keying** of irony, sincerity, politeness, and **framing** as speaking activities of particular connected sets of communicative functions; for example, chatting about the weather, changing the subject, ordering a meal in a restaurant. (See Goffman, 1974, and Tannen, 1979, on the notions of keying and framing. See also Schank & Abelson, 1977, for a more idealized notion of frame, plan, and expectation.) Tannen and Gumperz assume that context is not merely given in the scene of action. The scene is too complex and broad to be informative by itself. Specific features of context must be pointed to continually and sustained through communicative behavior. The cues are manifested across many levels of organization of speech and nonverbal behavior, in syntax, lexicon, stylistic register of speech, in speech prosody, in body motion, gaze, postural position, and interpersonal distance.

The ability to "read" the signal system of contextualization cues is a crucial aspect of what Hymes (1974) terms **communicative competence**, that is, contextualization cueing and the inferential processes by which the cues are read are a fundamental requisite for performing communication that is not only intelligible, but appropriate and effective in its use.

The particular aspects of contextualization cueing that I want to emphasize here are those of (*a*) pointing to the sequentially functional place of the moment at hand and the next moment to come and (*b*) pointing to the location in real time of the moments now and next.

We have been reviewing the importance, for interactional partnership, of all the participants in an interactional event being able to point one another to the sequentially functional "slots" in interaction as it unfolds. This is important both at the level of the immediately adjacent slots, such as those of noun phrase and verb phrase within a sentence, or in question and answer pairs across turns at speaking. It is also important to know where one is in the sequence of larger "chunks," the connected sets of functional slots at hierarchically higher levels of sequential organization; for example, knowing when one has come to the end of a "topically relevant set" of semantically tied question and answer pairs within a lesson, knowing the preparatory phase of the lesson is ending and the instrumentally focused phase of the lesson is about to begin (see Erickson & Shultz, 1977, 1981), or knowing that the point of instructional climax—the "punch line" in the academic task structure—has arrived (see Shultz et al., in press).

These matters of sequencing in the ordering of sequential, functional slots and chunks define the time of "now" and "next moment" in a special sense; that of **strategic time**, in contrast to that of **clock time** (see the discussion in Erickson, 1981).

The ancient Greeks made a distinction between strategic and clock time. The former was termed **kairos**; the right time, the appropriate time. This is the time of human history, seasons, and weather. The latter kind of time was termed **chronos**; the time of literal duration, mechanically measurable. The anthropologist Hall makes a similar distinction between kinds of time, terming kairos as **formal time** and chronos as **technical time** (Hall, 1959).

In face-to-face interaction, both kairos and chronos must be clear to the interactional partners if they are to be able to coordinate their action socially, taking account of one anothers' actions simultaneously and sequentially. The partners must be able to anticipate that a functionally significant slot is about to be arrived at in the **next moment**; they must also be able to anticipate the **actual point in real time in which that next functional moment can appropriately happen**. This is done through contextualization cues of a special sort, which form patterns of what can be called **verbal and nonverbal prosody**. Points of emphasis in the speech stream—shifts in pitch, volume, and tempo, the onset and offset of syntactic junctures—appear at regularly periodic intervals. Points of emphasis in the stream of nonverbal behavior cooccur with those of the speech stream, or substitute for the verbal channel in marking the "next" rhythmic interval in the series. These points of emphasis occur in the change of direction of motion in hand gesture, in nodding, in the onset or offset of gaze involvement, and in changes of postural position and interpersonal distance. Taken together across the verbal and nonverbal channels, these points of emphasis outline an interactional rhythm that is almost, but not quite, metronomic.

In short, the same communicative means are used to delineate the semantic **content** with its sequential slots of kairos organization, and the rhythmic **form**, consisting of regular periods of chronos organization. Points in real time, as well as points of series position in a sequence relationship, are essential to the "context" of practical action and decision making that is being created and sustained in the conjointly articulated verbal and nonverbal behavior of the interactional partners. The maintenance of predictable patterns of convergence between kairos organization and chronos organization can thus be seen as fundamentally constitutive of the social coordination of face-to-face interaction, in Weber's ([1922], 1978) sense of the term.

(For additional discussion and examples of interaction among adults, see Erickson & Shultz, 1981; and Scollon, 1981. For discussion of the role of rhythm in organization of interaction between newborn infants and their care-takers, see Brazelton, Koslowski, & Main, 1974; Condon, 1974; and Stern & Gibbon, 1979. Although particular interaction rhythms and articulation patterns appear to be culture-specific, the constitutive function of the rhythm as a social organizing device appears to be a human universal; see Byers, 1972.)

Improvisation as Strategically Adaptive Action in Lessons

Although the predictability of kairos and chronos defines the potential opportunities for social action by a teacher and students in a lesson, the actual opportunities arise not only in the times and functional places that can be formally modeled, but in points of fortuitous happening that are not amenable to formal modeling. This is because school lessons, considered as environments for learning and teaching, are social occasions that are distinctively charac-terized by fortuity. Considered in terms of the ethnography of speaking, lessons stand at a midpoint on the continuum between highly ritualized, formulaic speech events, in which all the functional slots and their formal contents are prespecified, and highly spontaneous speech events, in which neither the suc-cessive slots nor their content is prespecified. Considered in terms of social theory and socialization theory, school lessons are of special interest because they are anomalous in the paradigms at either theoretical extreme; that of social or psychological determinism on the one hand, and that of radical contextualism on the other hand. I will first discuss the special character of lessons as social occasions and then discuss the implications of this for social theory and socialization theory.

Lessons are first of all occasions for learning and teaching. What this means for the smooth and felicitous conduct of interaction is that lessons are especially tricky local places, since they are situations in which it is certain that mistakes will be made and correction and assistance will be provided. Indeed, mistakes and hesitations by students and adaptive responses by teachers are the lesson's raison d'être.

Mistakes are inevitable, since the students are learners; learning is by definition the acquisition of mastery, not the possession of it. The opportunity to learn is the opportunity to make mistakes. Moreover, student mistakes provide the teacher with the opportunity to teach. The student's level of mastery is revealed by the level of difficulty in academic task at which mistakes are made. Having identified the student's level of mastery, the teacher should be able to adjust the learning environment of the lesson to accommodate the student; this is in the "folk" language of teacher education called "meeting the student where (s)he is." (On this point, see also the discussion in Mehan, 1979, pp. 122–124.)

Adjustments can be made across both dimensions of the lesson as learning environment—the Academic Task Structure (ATS) and the Social Participation Structure (SPS)—or across either dimension separately. The ATS can be simplified by lowering the level of difficulty of a given question or set of questions. The SPS too can be simplified through reallocation of rights toward speaking and listening. This will be illustrated in the analysis of an arithmetic lesson which follows. At this point it is sufficient to note that not only can the overall cognitive task of the lesson be made easier for a child by simplifying the ATS as well as the SPS, but that changes in social participation structure can also provide the teacher with opportunities to diagnose more fully the learning capacity of the child. Changing the SPS so as to allow the child to answer along with another child, or with the teacher, gives the teacher observational access to what Vygotsky (1978) terms the child's zone of proximal development—the range across which the child can perform successfully with help, as contrasted to the point at which the child's mastery stops when the child is performing the learning task alone.

Direct questions in lessons, then, are a way for the teacher to gain insight into what the individual child does or does not know. Admittedly, this central tenet of pedagogy is not universally shared among humans. There are sociocultural groups in which teaching is done without any direct questioning of learners (see the discussion of Native American learning and teaching styles in Erickson & Mohatt, in press; and Philips, 1972). Still, for Western Europeans and Americans, existence of the interactional lesson as a speech event presupposes that it is necessary for the teacher to ask direct questions of individual children because it is not certain whether the child knows the old information being reviewed, or the new information about to be taught.

The paradox is that various kinds of student mistakes in answering—even though some of them are essential as opportunities for teaching and learning—can play havoc with the maintenance of a coherent academic and social task structure in the lesson. Content mistakes in the ATS can cause troubles in the maintenance of the SPS, as in the case of a hesitation by a student that breaks the interactional rhythm. Mistakes of academic content that are correct in social form (SPS) can also cause trouble in the ATS, as in the case of a student providing a wrong answer that violates the expectations of the teacher and other students as to the logically sequential flow of ideas in the lesson, even though the answer is given in the socially "right" time and does not distort the smooth rhythmic flow of alternation between question and answer. Conversely, mistakes in terms of SPS can damage the ATS, as in the case of a student giving the academically "right" answer in the socially "wrong" time. Because of this, lessons are speech events characterized by the presence of frequent cognitive and interactional troubles and repair work.

When school lessons are compared with other speech events, according to the comparative frame of the "ethnography of speaking model" of Hymes (1964, 1974), it is apparent that lessons stand at a midpoint between formal ritual and informal spontaneity. In the most highly stylized speech the sequence of turns at speaking is prespecified, as is the allocation of turns among the various partners, the semantic content of each turn, and the appropriate non-verbal actions accompanying speech. Consider the following example of dialogue from the Roman Catholic mass:

PEOPLE: (rise as Celebrant turns to face them)
CELEBRANT: *The Lord be with you.* (hands open, arms extended)
PEOPLE: *And also with you.*
CELEBRANT: *Lift up your hearts.*
PEOPLE: *We lift them to the Lord.*

In contrast, the dialogue between an evangelical Protestant minister and congregation during the sermon is organized more loosely. Alternation of turns is not prespecified, the content of the minister's turns is not fully prespecified, although formulaic reiteration of what has just been said often occurs. The content of the turns for members of the congregation is not prespecified, although the optional "fillers" of the response slot (e.g., *Amen, That's right, Thank you Jesus, shout, break into song*) is narrower in range than is the range of options available to the preacher (see the discussion in Rosenberg, 1975).

The organization of speaking in a Quaker meeting (see Bauman, 1974) is even more loosely constrained in terms of turn allocation, turn sequence, and turn content. This organization is by no means random, however. Indeed, the principle that a speaker self-selects a turn, and the absence of a leader–follower relationship between audience and speaker are both features of interactional organization consistent with a more general social organizational principle underlying the whole of Quaker polity, the principle of the absolute equality of all individuals before God and one another.

Ordinary middle-class conversation among Americans (as discussed in Sacks *et al.*, 1974) is even more loosely constrained than a Quaker meeting. Speakers in ordinary conversation can designate next speakers as well as self-select their own turn. The range of topics is wider than in a Quaker meeting; for instance, a dirty joke told in ordinary conversation would be inappropriate in a Quaker meeting. Still, even in ordinary conversation the underlying order is not random, as the analysis by Sacks *et al.* suggests. What is distinctive about ordinary conversation, in contrast to the other examples, is the radically "local" nature of the order. The principles of order apply to the immediate moment—to adjacency pairs such as **this turn–next turn**. This is a very general kind of rule; indeed a better term is **operating principle** or **maxim**, to use

Grice's term (1975). The Gricean conversational maxim "be relevant" is advice that must be taken largely in terms of local context, within the conversation itself.

The generality of underlying operating principles and the locality of relevance for their application is what distinguishes speech events such as the Roman Catholic mass from speech events such as ordinary conversation. The mass as an encounter is radically nonlocal in its openness to influence from the outside, both across space and across time. In its Latin version, the sequence and content of the sample of dialogue previously presented has existed virtually unchanged for 1700 years. The usage began within the Christian congregation at Rome (which switched from Greek to Latin as its liturgical language ca. A.D. 300. Since then the Roman usage has spread throughout the world.

The mass is also amenable to modeling by highly specified sets of rules; indeed, by exact algorithms for its performance. Unlike Chomskyan rules of grammar, the rules for mass performance are not generative, but they share with Chomskyan rules the attribute of specificity of reference.

Neither the mass nor a sociolinguistic version of Chomskyan grammar can account for the organization of speech events such as school lessons. The mass has no room for accident—its algorithms are entirely nonlocal and define a closed system of options. All local happenings could be accounted for by a fully specified, nonlocal system of rules.

The school lesson, as a speech event, stands somewhere between the Roman mass and the evangelical sermon with audience participation. Some aspects of the academic task structure of a lesson are, like the mass, more predetermined than is the content of the evangelical preacher's sermon; the constraints on the content of student responses are narrower than those placed on the responses of the audience to the evangelical preacher. Yet the social participation structure of the lesson resembles the evangelical sermon more than it does the mass, in that the alternation of turn-taking is not fully prespecified, and in that the content of what is said by teacher and student is not fully prespecified, although much of it is influenced by cultural norms that stand, as it were, outside the situation of use. The lesson in its academic task structure is like the sermon in that it is conducted according to a moderately specified plan. Similar to a Quaker meeting and ordinary conversation, the lesson also is organized around operating principles that are quite general in reference. In consequence the lesson is moderately open to fortuitous happenings and it includes principles of both nonlocal and local organization in the production of interaction.

Thus the school lesson, as a speech event, is Janus-faced. Members of the lesson are able to take advantage of shared cultural norms of interpretation and performance that help to define structure points, and they are able to be open to the unique circumstances of fortuitous happening. This combination of local and nonlocal grounds for the organization of performance is what enables the lesson to be conducted as an improvisation. Chomskyan grammars do not provide material for improvisation—there is no limited set of constraints to provide a "theme" around which variations can be constructed. It is precisely the combination of the predetermined and formulaic along some dimensions of organization, together with openness to variation along other dimensions, that provides opportunity for improvisation. In 12-bar blues, for example, the sequence of harmonic changes is prespecified and the points in time at which the chords will change are prespecified, but melodic options at any point in time are very wide in range. The same was true for the improvisatory theater of the Italian Renaissance, the *commedia dell' arte*. The roles of stock characters were prespecified, certain bits of dialogue were patterned formulaicly, yet there was still much opportunity for locally situated variation around the nonlocally prescribed themes.

Turning now to consider the lesson in terms of theories of society and of socialization, it is extremely important to keep hold of the notion of the school lesson as an encounter, that is, a partially bounded social occasion, influenced by cultural norms and having within its own frame something of a life of its own.

Such a view of the lesson avoids the extremes of social or psychological determinism on the one hand, and radical contextualism on the other.[4] Functionally determinist theories of society, culture, and education, such as those of Durkheim, leave no room for human choice. The model is of an over-socialized individual who has learned to play every social scene as if it were the Roman mass. (In Durkheim's model, the individual has learned to **want** this.) A similarly oversocialized model of the individual can be seen in psychologically determinist theories, whether they be Skinnerian or Freudian. (In Freud's model, the individual resists the socialization, but is overcome by it.) Both the psychological and the sociocultural determinists locate the major causes of individual action outside the immediate scene of action. They presuppose an individual who is almost totally preprogrammed by prior experience; in Garfinkel's term, a "cultural dope" who operates as a robot (Garfinkel, 1967). Socialization is a one-way process in a world without freedom.

At the other extreme is the position of radical contextualism. Here the immediately local circumstances of production (e.g., this turn, next turn) are focused on so narrowly as to exclude the relevance, if not the possibility, of nonlocal influences, for example, culturally learned standards of expectation and performance, constraints from the wider society on the choices possible in the scene of action. There is no need for socialization in this theory.

[4] In the following discussion I am indebted to comments by Jenny Cook-Gumperz and by Hugh Mehan. See also his discussion in Mehan, pp. 126–130, and in Mehan and Griffin, 1980.

Virtually everything can be explained in terms of making sense in the immediate momentary scene of action. Taken to its logical conclusion, this theoretical position leads to solipcism. There is no oppression in such a world, but there is no freedom either, for there is neither an individual nor a society, only the interaction of the moment; there are no opportunities for choices that have consequences beyond the moment and the immediate scene.

Each extreme is untenable as grounds for a theory of education, which must presuppose at least three levels of organization—general society and culture, specific situations, and specific individuals—and some processes of relationship among the levels, one of which is socialization of the individual. What is argued for here is a middle way between the two extremes: a way that preserves the integrity of each level of organization in its own right and that enables us to view socialization as a two-way process.

This leaves us a place for a theory of school lessons as **educational encounters**; partially bounded situations in which teachers and students follow previously learned, culturally normative "rules," and also innovate by making new kinds of sense together in adapting to the fortuitous circumstances of the moment. Students are seen as active participants in this process, not simply as the passive recipients of external shaping. Teachers and students are seen as engaged in **praxis**, improvising situational variations within and around socioculturally prescribed thematic material and occasionally, within the process of improvisation, discovering new possibilities for learning and for social life.

Overview

What follows are excerpts from a mathematics lesson taught on the morning of the fourth day of school in a first-grade classroom.[5] It is a "shake-down cruise"—a practice version of a mathematics lesson, since it is so early in the year.

The students and the teacher in this classroom are bilingual in Spanish and English. The lesson is conducted almost entirely in Spanish. Because it is very simple in subject matter, however, the English-speaking reader does not need much knowledge of Spanish in order to follow the conduct of the lesson. The language of the academic task is simple. So, it would seem, is the social organization of the lesson's enactment. But that would be a mistaken assumption.

[5] The lesson comes from a study of bilingual classrooms currently in progress. For additional discussion of the overall study, see Cazden, Carrasco, Maldonado-Guzmán, and Erickson, 1980 and Erickson, Cazden, Carrasco, and Maldonado-Guzmán, 1980.

The lesson as a number activity involves the correct identification of numerals, both one by one and in a sequential set. There are a number of "turns" in the lesson. In each, a child or group of children is to count aloud the numbers one through seven while simultaneously pointing to the corresponding numeral written on the chalkboard. Then the child or group is to identify by saying and pointing to single numerals the teacher calls out.

Consequently the academic task structure involves, among others, the following logical operations and sequential steps:

Part A. Identify the numbers [1–7] as a connected set by reading aloud and pointing. Begin with the numeral 1 and continue through the numeral 7.

Part B. Identify numerals in the set [1–7] as individual numbers. Identify the numeral "out of sequence" as the teacher calls out, one by one, numbers that are not in adjacent series position within the set [1–7].

It is apparent that in Parts A and B, different kinds of cognitive skills are called upon from the student. The recognition and recall task in identifying the connected set of numerals differs from that in identifying the numbers presented in isolation and out of series position. Moreover, different sorts of discourse organization and social participation structures are involved in order to produce Parts A and B in a conversational arrangement. In Part A the answerer's role involves producing a connected series of information "bits," whereas in Part B the answerer's role consists of producing one information bit at a time. The questioner's role in Part A consists of a brief initiation followed by a period of "connected answering moments" as the answerer replies. In Part B the questioner initiates a connected series of question moments interspersed with brief moments of attending to the short answer. The result is two very different discourse routines in Part A and Part B. These can be represented schematically as follows:

A. 1. **Teacher** (questioner): Say Question 1 and designate answerer
    2. **Student** (answerer): Produce connected set of answer chunks a–g
       a. Say and point to first numeral of set [1–7]
       b. Say and point to second numeral of set [1–7]
       c. Say and point to third numeral of set [1–7]

B. 3. **Teacher** (questioner): (optionally) Evaluate previous, complete answer, evaluate incomplete answer, or ask next question
       a. Next question: Name any numeral in set [1–7]
    4. **Student** (answerer): Produce single answer
       a. Point to numeral previously named

5. **Teacher** (questioner): Ask next question
   a. Next question: Name any numeral in set [1–7] that is not adjacent to the numeral named in previous question
6. **Student and teacher:** Reiterate Steps 4 and 5 as often as desired by the teacher
7. **Teacher:** (optionally) Evaluate student's answers to Part B, or to Parts A and B, or proceed on to designate next answerer

This formalization helps one to see some relationships between the logic of subject matter exposition (academic task structure) and the social organization of discourse (social participation structure). The less cognitively difficult type of academic task is presented first, the more difficult type is presented second. The social tasks differ as well. Questioner role differs from answerer role within each of the two types of tasks and the questioner and answerer roles both differ across the two types of tasks (e.g., the answerer role in Part A involves both saying and pointing, whereas the answerer role in Part B involves pointing only).

The formal model is profoundly inadequate, however, as a guide to practical action in the actual enactment of the lesson. In order to "get through" Parts A and B in actual enactment, coordination is required in the (successively) reciprocal and (simultaneously) complementary actions of the teacher and student from moment to moment. Very little of this coordination is shown in the model. First of all, the model presumes that the student will only answer correctly. Second, the model presumes that there are no other actors in the scene besides the teacher and one student—it says nothing about the participation of other children present in the lesson. Finally, and most fundamentally, the model says nothing about the real-time character of enactment as a succession of strategically crucial "next moments" (see Erickson, 1981). Parts A and B and their constituent sequential "chunks" are moments in real time, with different practical exigencies from moment to moment that are often fortuitous, given the context of action at the time.

Formalization, taken by itself, misleadingly cleans up this messiness, ambiguity, and suspense in the moment of enactment. In Part A, for example, the regularly rhythmic timing and continuity of intonation in the answerer's speech are culturally conventional cues "telling" us that what is being produced are items in a connected list: uno, dos, tres, quatro (one, two, three, four). What if, having said *tres*, the child does not say *quatro* in the next rhythmic interval to come? Does this mean the child doesn't know the next item in the list? Does the child know the next item, but is distracted by something else going on? Should the teacher change the questioner role and insert a prompt at this point? Should the teacher give the child more time to answer? Will other children chime in as the teacher waits for the designated answerer to speak?[6] These are just a few of the contingencies involved in the actual enactment of the underlying plan or script for academic task structure and social participation structure. What is practically needed in the moment is not simply knowledge of the next canonical step in the sequential organization of the academic and social plan. What is needed, by teacher, designated answerer, and other students present, is the capacity to improvise collectively an enacted variation on the ideal theme, or plan. The subsequent texts and commentary will show that teachers and students do in fact improvise, and that their deviations from an ideal formal order are not just to be thought of as random errors (noise in the system), but are better characterized as adaptation to the exigencies of the moment—actions that make sense within an adequately specified context.

The ideal "theme" looks like this, when presented in quasi-musical notation. (The hypothetical example that follows should be read aloud, rhythmically.)

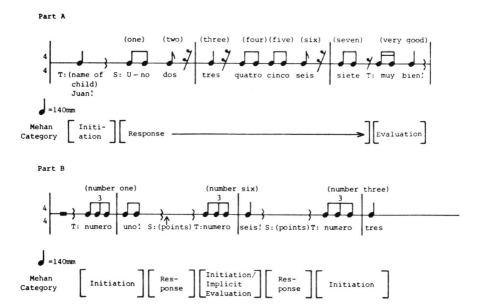

Before going on to review some of the actual variations on this ideal theme, it is necessary to discuss text transcription conventions more fully.

[6] These are not simply rhetorical questions. The genuine suspense is akin to that in questions the announcer asks at the end of the daily episode of a soap opera, or the spectator asks while watching a play for the first time. Will Hamlet kill himself, or his uncle, or his mother, and when? **Get on with it, Hamlet!** The tension of expectation is essential in theater, in music, and in everyday interaction as well.

In the transcripts, overlap (simultaneously occurring speech) is indicated by a vertical line with two "flags" facing to the right—[. "Latching," that is, speech by a second speaker which immediately follows that of the prior speaker with no pause, but also with no overlap, is indicated by a vertical line with an upper flag facing left and a lower flag facing right—⅂. Slanted lines indicate pauses; double slanted lines—//—indicate a sentence-terminal pause that is the equivalent of the quarter-note rest in musical notation. The single slanted line indicates a clause or breath-group terminal pause of approximately half the duration of the former pause, that is, the single-slanted line pause is the equivalent of the eighth-note rests in musical notation. Elongation of a pho-neme is indicated by successive colons—:::. Usually, in the transcript, each line of text represents one breath group in the speech stream. The first syllable of the line is usually the syllable that receives the greatest volume and/or pitch stress. If there are "anticipatory" syllables or words antecedent to the syllable receiving primary or secondary stress, those antecedent syllables or words appear at the rightmost edge of the previous line:

A-

yúdalo Carlos / donde es-

tá?//

Because the leftmost syllable on a line is usually the syllable receiving stress, and because there is often a constant rhythmic interval between points of stress, it is possible to read the transcript aloud, reproducing not only the stress points, but the rhythmic organization of speech, within and across speaking turns.

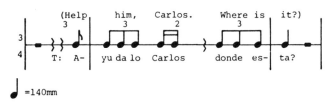

The reader is urged to read the examples aloud even if he or she does not speak Spanish.

LESSON I. VARIATION 1

Turning now to the actual enactment of the lesson, one sees that in almost every instance of the reiteration of a "turn" discourse routine consisting of Parts A and B, some variation on the ideal model is performed. Indeed, as the teacher introduced the academic–social task at the beginning of the lesson, Part A of the ideal theme was elided, and the turn of the first child designated as the answerer consisted only of Part B.

LESSON I. VARIATION 2

In a second "turn" of the lesson, both Part A and Part B were included, but the performance of the parts nonetheless involved variation on the ideal model (see Figure 9.1). In Part A, the variation consisted in alternation of the communicative rights and obligations involved in the answer role, and in the status of the persons occupying that role. The teacher was one of the "answerers" to her own question, and a group of children alternated with the teacher in answering, as the teacher took the whole group on a "shakedown cruise" or practice attempt at Part A of the turn. In addition, the rhythmic relationship between each information "bit" in the first answer (i.e., the saying and pointing successively to uno, dos, tres, etc.) is not a constant interval. Rather, the teacher and the chorus of children overlap one another in a call-response pattern. The children's overlapping is not held accountable as interruption by the teacher. At no point does the teacher sanction as a "violation" aspects of the variation from the ideal model. The teacher is behaving as if the variations make sense.

Notice the latching and overlapping of the answer segments between teacher and student in Part A. This overlapping and latching occurs at Points 21 and 22 in the transcript. Then at Point 23 the teacher initiates the first segment of the second discourse routine, Part B. The question is *Donde esta el numero uno?* (Where is the number one?). At Point 24 the designated answerer says *uno*, but does not point to the numeral written on the chalkboard. His answer is incorrect in both form and content, or at least it is ambiguous because one is not sure he is not simply repeating what the teacher just said. (The academic task here is to show knowledge of the numeral by pointing to it on the chalkboard.) At Point 25 the teacher reiterates the question, "Uno." Then at Point 27 the teacher asks another boy, Carlos, to help the designated answerer. At the end of Point 27, while another child is saying *en mi casa*, the designated answerer finally points to the numeral one on the chalkboard. Then at Point 29 the teacher continues to ask for individual numbers. But, unlike the ideal model, the teacher asks for successive numbers in the series. (Perhaps, because the child had so much trouble with the number one, the teacher simplifies the academic task. She could be using this variation to see if the child knows the complete set of numeral(s). In addition, the ideal rhythm pattern is broken; in the various question–answer pairs at Point 29 the teacher waits longer for an answer some times than she does at others, for example, the single sentence-terminal pause given to the answer slot after the number

(21) T: U:no:/   do::s   tre:s
          uno / do::s   ; maes-   One,   two,   three,
     CC: one, two,   three,
     C: tra me ayudo?   (another child) teacher,
                                               can I help you?

(22) T: cua:tro:/   ci::nco::   sei::::s: four,   five,   six,
     CC: /cua:tro / cinco   sei::s /   four,   five,   six,
     M: S::::iete   Seven   seven
     T and CC: sie:te

(23) CC: (talking at once)   (talking at once)
     T: Dónde está el número   Where is number one?
          uno?
     C: Uno   One
                                                one

(24) C: uno   one

(25) T:

(26) C: /// /// one   one

(27) T: A-   Help him Carlos, where is it?
          yúdalo Carlos dónde es-
          tá? /// /// A-   Let's see number one. (a child
          ver número   giggles loudly)
          uno (a child giggles loudly)

(28) C: En mi   At my house.
          casa
          A ver número   Let's see number two.
          dos // número   Number three. Number four. Number
          tres // número   five. Number six.
          cuatro // número
          cinco /// número   And seven. (Other conversations
          seis /// y el   occurring among groups of children.)
          siete //

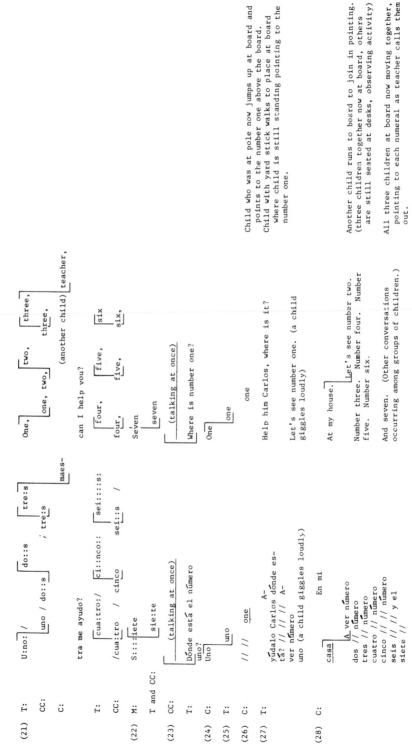

Child who was at pole now jumps up at board and points to the number one above the board. Child with yard stick walks to place at board where child is still standing pointing to the number one.

Another child runs to board to join in pointing. (three children together now at board, others are still seated at desks, observing activity)

All three children at board now moving together, pointing to each numeral as teacher calls them out.

172

(38) T: U::no

One

(39) CC: do::s / tre::s / cua::tro / ci::nco / sei::s / sie:te

two, three, four, five, six, seven

(40) T: Dónde está el número / cinco Carlos?

Where is number / five Carlos?

(41) C: Número / cinco

Number five

(42) T: Muy / bien / Dónde está el número / tres? //

Very good. / Where is number three?

(43) C: Tres? //

Three?

(44) T: Tres // // muy / bien // Dónde está el número // // siete

Three. Very good / Where is number .... seven

C: cuatro

four

C: cuatro

four

C: siete

seven

(45) T: Ex/ce/lente/Carlos

Stage directions:

T still at side of room, class observing Carlos at board.

Boy comes from off camera and walks toward board. Another child stands up at same time to point enthusiastically to something.

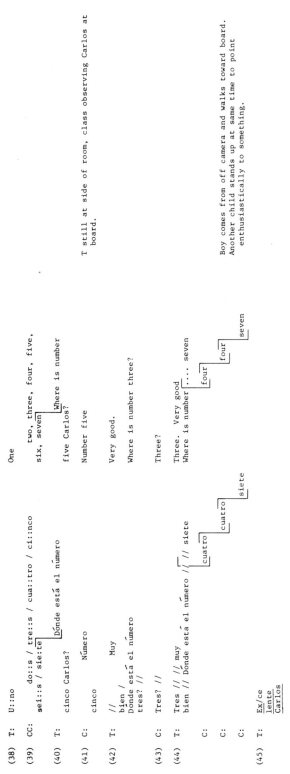

Figure 9.1. Transcript Example 1: Lesson I, Variation 2.

173

quatro (four), followed by a double sentence-terminal pause after the number cinco (five).

All these variations can be seen as responses to practical exigencies of the moment. The differences in wait time for answers at Point 29 seem to be in response to the child's hesitation in answering. The teacher adapts her action in asking to the reciprocal action of the child in answering. We see analogous social adaptation in timing between teacher and student at Point 21, in the echoing and call–response enactment of the segments of the first answer. Here, too, the teacher's permitting variation in the social organization of discourse—the social participation structure—simplifies the academic task structure. It is cognitively easier to say the list of numbers assisted by prompts from the teacher, and so by saying the answer together with the children in a call–response and overlapping way the teacher has changed the academic task structure by varying the social participation structure. Change in ways of speaking can thus be seen as providing opportunity for change in ways of thinking—differences in learning environment.

LESSON I. VARIATION 3

In the third reiteration of the "turn" in the lesson it is now Carlos's turn. During Part A of the turn, Carlos answers together with a chorus of other children, rather than alone. (This answer form simplifies the academic task.) The teacher initiates the answer herself with a prompt at Point 38 of the transcript, and the choral answer follows at Point 39. In Part B of the turn, beginning at Point 40, Carlos answers alone (see Figure 9.2).

LESSON I. VARIATION 6

Now the "turn" is given by the teacher to Janet (see Figure 9.2, Point 86). Janet recites the numbers in series, accompanied by a chorus of children. In this variation on Part A, the teacher not only does not hold the chorus accountable as interrupters, but asks them, including Janet, to say the series again, louder (see Point 88). Note also that as the chorus says the series of numbers, they stop at six (Point 87), yet the teacher gives this violation no negative sanction. Then at Point 90, as the children repeat the list of numbers, they go themselves one better (as if to "make up") by counting to eight. This too is a discrepancy from the ideal model of the task, but it is not sanctioned as a violation by the teacher. (Apparently at this point the two approximations of the task are "good enough.") Then at Point 91 Part B begins. As Janet completes this part of the task, Child E (Ernesto) is producing what seems to be literal "noise" in the system (see Points 92 and 94 in Figure 9.3). But this is not just random noise, as is apparent at Point 97. By this time Janet's turn is complete and the teacher has said (Point 95), *Daselo a alguien que no ha tenido opportunidad* (Give it [the turn] to somebody who hasn't had a chance). Ernesto, at Point 97, says he has not had a turn. He has been saying this for some time already during the lesson, as have other children, saying *Yo, Yo* (me, me). At Point 64 he had said, *Yo no he tenido ni un **tu::::rn*** (I haven't even had one **turn**), intensifying both syntactically (even had one) and prosodically (by volume and pitch stress), and by the lexical code-switch to English combined with the prosodic marker of elongation of a phoneme (*tu::::rn*).

So Ernesto's "noise" appears not just to be for fooling around. Getting the next turn is a matter of suspense. Ernesto seems to be protesting his exclusion from rights of access to the conversational floor. This apparent protest takes an even more interesting form during the next reiteration of the "turn," which was also not given to Ernesto. (Here the reader should continue in the transcript, beginning at Point 96 of Figure 9.2, before the next turn has begun, and continuing through Point 114 at which point Parts A and B have been completed. Notice Ernesto's exclamation at Point 104 after he has not been given the turn, and his "contribution" to the answer slots that are being given to the designated answerer at Points 109, 111, and 113.)

Finally, after the suspense of trying for the turn again and not getting it (Point 103), Ernesto exclaims at Point 104. Then, after the completion of Part A of the task (Point 107), during which a single child spoke as an answerer, Part B begins, consisting of the discourse routine of alternation between teacher question summoning single answer slot. Here Ernesto is apparently playing on his implicit knowledge (communicative competence) as a member of the classroom speech community. He apparently knows (not necessarily consciously) of the social organization of discourse in Part B that the short answer slots follow the previously adjacent teacher question slots, and that the adjacency relationship is enacted through regular rhythmic timing of the alternation between slots. Also, Ernesto apparently knows that the social form for communicating the semantic content of the answer is pointing, an answer form that by definition does not make noise. Hence, the nonverbally channeled answer slot can be occupied by some sort of noise on the auditory channel without "damaging" the discourse organization so much that the whole discourse sequence will have to be recycled. Therefore, Ernesto can get away with filling the other child's rhythmically defined answer slots with his own rhythmic "answer," consisting of drumbeats with his pencils on the desk. The drumbeats are timed perfectly to coincide with the turn-exchange transition points in the discourse pattern being enacted. The teacher seems to me to be collaborating by studiously overlooking what Ernesto is doing. This seems to me to be an absolutely brilliant situational variation on a normative social organizational "theme" element in the lesson. Ernesto can be seen here as a master of the social and academic task structure.

(86) T:

No puedo oír a uh
Janet (name said with English phonemes)
// // Per-
dón Janet.

I can't hear, uh, Janet
Excuse me Janet.

T still seated next to Carlos. T has ignored him since placing him in chair. Carlos is still shuffling through papers.

(87) CC:

(all together) uno / dos / tres /
cuatro / cinco / seis /

(all together) one, two, three,
four, five, six,

(88) T:

dilo otra vez sí huh // uh mas mas mas /

say it again yes huh, uh more more more

(89) T:

Class making a variety of noises in response to Elena's choice. Class reciting with Janet. T raises voice above noise of group.

(90) CC:

Uno / dos / tres / cuatro / cinco /
seis / siete / ocho

one, two, three, four, five,
six, seven, eight

(91) T:

cinco
Janet
Muy bien / número

Very good,   number
five Janet

(92) E:

Brrr::::(rolling tongue)

brrr::::(rolling tongue)

(93) T:

seis
Número

Number six

(94) E:

(makes snoring sounds then bangs
twice on desk. Continues banging)
Número

(makes snoring sounds then bangs
twice on desk. Continues banging)
Number

Teacher talks above noises of class.

(95) T:

seven // // Muy bien /
Janet // //
Dáselo a
alguien que no ha tenido oportuni-
dad //

seven. Very good
Janet.
Give it to somebody who hasn't had a
chance.

(96) C:

Maestra yo no te-
nía /

Teacher I didn't have one.

Janet walks slowly and timidly to center (near pole) and looks at class.

(97) E:

Yo no
tengo

I don't have one.

Janet stops near pole and looks from side to side at raised hands of children in class.

(98) CC:

Yo:: Yo::

Me, me::

(99) E:

Yo

me

(100) C:

Yo:: // // Yo::

me:: me::

(101) T:

Tangan las
manos su-
bidas

Have your hands
up.

	Spanish	English	Notes
(102) C:	Yo / yo	Me, me.	Janet hands yardstick to boy at table to right of T and immediately sits down.
(103)' T:	Okay	Okay	
(104) E:	Oh:::: BA: /	Oh:::: BA:	Boy walks with yard stick to board. As he passes another child who is seated, some interchange takes place (not clearly visible).
(105) T:	no ha tenido oportuni-dad // //	_____ hasn't had a chance.	
(106) C:	A mí	Me	
(107) C:	Uno / dos / tres / cuatro / cinco / seis / siete	One, two, three, four, five, six seven	Child at board identifies numbers which T requests.
(108) T:	Muy bien número cinco // //	Very good, number five.	E beats rhythmically on desk in between teacher's statements.
(109) E:	[musical notation] Número seis	Number six.	
(110) T:	[musical notation]		
(111) E:	[musical notation] Número cuatro	Number four.	
(112) T:	[musical notation]		
(113) E:	Muy	Very good.	
(114) T:	bien / escoge alguien que no ha tenido oportunidad / Dámelo	Choose someone who hasn't had a chance. Give it to me.	
(115) C:	Levantan las manos los que no han tenido oportunidad	Raise your hands, those that haven't had a chance.	
(116) T:	[Yo]	[Me]	T raises hands to demonstrate when she calls on class to raise hands. Several children raise hands. Child at board looks around area to determine whom he will select. He quickly hands yardstick to a child and returns to seat at the right of T.
(117) E:			

Figure 9.2. Transcript Example 2: Lesson I, Variation 6.

177

The ingeniousness and deftness of Ernesto's play can be seen even more clearly than in the transcript by displaying the sequence of quasi-musical notation:

(From Transcript, Points 108-113)

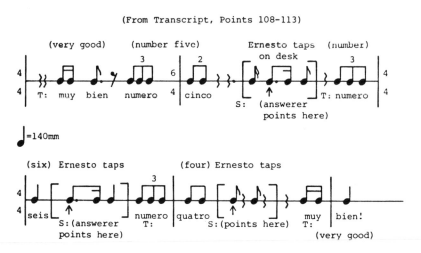

Discussion

From examination of a number of instances of the performance of a small lesson sequence, an underlying ideal model was inferred. The model outlines some salient aspects of the social participation structure and the academic task structure—what can be called the academic and social task structure. Looking closely at the performance of an instance of the lesson sequence, however, one sees that it is usually discrepant in some features of specific organization from the general, inferred model. If one is not simply to regard these discrepancies as random error (free variation), one has at least two options: to elaborate the formalization of the model by stating an embedded system of optional rules; or to assume that what is happening is adaptive variation, specific to the immediate circumstances of practical action in the moment of enactment.

I have taken the latter of these two courses. The interpretive analysis of instances from the lesson was done to argue that the discrepancies from the ideal model represent adaptive action taken by, in most instances, the teacher as instructional leader, and in one instance, the student Ernesto. Since lesson discourse, like all other face-to-face interaction, is jointly produced as various actors in the event take action in account of the actions of others, the variants chosen by the teacher have consequences for what the students will do and vice versa. Moreover, I have attempted to show how adaptive changes in the academic task structure have consequences for the social participation structure, and vice versa. This is an important point for pedagogy, and has been over-looked in much recent research.

References

Au, K. Hu-pei. Participation structures in a reading lesson with Hawaiian children: Analysis of a culturally appropriate instructional event. *Anthropology and Education Quarterly*, 1980, *11* (2), 91–115.

Bauman, R. Speaking in the light: The role of the Quaker minister. In R. Bauman & J. Scherzer (Eds.), *Explorations in the ethnography of speaking*. Cambridge, Mass.: Cambridge University Press, 1974.

Bellack, A., Kliebard, H., Hyman, R., & Smith, F. *The language of the classroom*. New York: Teachers College Press, 1966.

Bossert, S. T. *Tasks and social relationships in classrooms*. Cambridge, Mass.: Cambridge University Press, 1979.

Brazelton, T. B., Koslowski, B., & Main, M. The origins of reciprocity: The early mother–infant interaction. In M. Lewis & L. Rosenblum (Eds.), *The effects of the infant on its caregiver*. New York: John Wiley & Sons, 1974.

Bremme, D. W., & Erickson, F. Relationships among verbal and nonverbal classroom behaviors. *Theory into Practice*, 1977, *16* (3), 153–161.

Byers, P. *From biological rhythm to cultural pattern: A study of minimal units*. Unpublished doctoral dissertation, Columbia University, 1972. (Ann Arbor: University Microfilms, No. 73-9004).

Cazden, C., Carrasco, R., Maldonado-Guzmán, A., & Erickson, F. The contribution of ethnographic research to bicultural bilingual education. In J. Alatis (Ed.), *Current issues in bilingual education*. Washington, D.C.: Georgetown University Press, 1980.

Collins, J., & Michaels, S. The importance of conversational discourse strategies in the acquisition of literacy. *Proceedings of the Sixth Annual Meetings of the Berkeley Linguistic Society*, Berkeley, California, 1980.

Condon, W. Neonate movement is synchronized with adult speech: Interactional participation and language acquisition. *Science*, 1974, *183*, 99–101.

Duncan, S., & Fiske, D. *Face to face interaction: Research, methods, and theory*. Hillsdale, N.J.: Lawrence Erlbaum, 1977.

Erickson, F. Gatekeeping and the melting pot: Interaction in counseling encounters. *Harvard Educational Review*, 1975, *45* (1), 44–70.

Erickson, F. Talking down: Some cultural sources of miscommunication in inter-racial interviews. In A. Wolfgang (Ed.), *Research in nonverbal communication*. New York: Academic Press, 1979.

Erickson, F. *Stories of cognitive learning in learning environments: A neglected area in the anthropology of education*. Paper presented at the symposium "The Anthropology of Learning" at the Annual Meeting of the American Anthropological Association, Washington, D.C., December 1980.

Erickson, F. Timing and context in everyday discourse. In W. P. Dickson (Ed.), *Children's oral communication skills*. New York: Academic Press, 1981.

Erickson, F., Cazden, C., Carrasco, R., & Maldonado-Guzmán, A. *Social and cultural organization of interaction in classrooms of bilingual children*. Second Year Interim Report to National Institute of Education, Teaching and Learning Division, Project #NIE C-0099, 1980.

Erickson, F., & Mohatt, G. The cultural organization of participation structures in two classrooms of Indian students. In G. Spindler (Ed.), *Doing the ethnography of schooling*. New York: Holt, Rinehart, & Winston, 1982.

Erickson, F., & Shultz, J. When is a context?: Some issues and methods in the analysis of social competence. *The Quarterly Newsletter of the Institute for Comparative Human Development*, 1977, *1* (2), 5–10. Also reprinted in J. Green & C. Wallat (Eds.), *Ethnography and language in educational settings*. Norwood, N.J.: Ablex, 1981.

Erickson F., & Shultz, J. *The counselor as gatekeeper: Social interaction in interviews*. New York: Academic Press, 1982.

Garfinkel, H. *Studies in ethnomethodology*. New York: Prentice-Hall, 1967.

Goffman, E. *Encounters: Two studies in the sociology of interaction*. Indianapolis: Bobbs-Merrill, 1961.

Goffman, E. *Frame analysis*. New York: Harper Colophon Books, 1974.

Grice, H. P. Logic and conversation. In P. Cole & J. L. Morgan (Eds.), *Syntax and semantics III: Speech acts*. New York: Academic Press, 1975.

Griffin, P., Cole, M., & Newman, D. Locating tasks in psychology and education. In R.O. Freedle (Ed.), *Discourse Processes*, in preparation.

Gumperz, J. J. Sociocultural knowledge in conversational inference. In M. Saville-Troike (Ed.), *Linguistics and anthropology* (Georgetown University Roundtable on Languages and Linguistics). Washington, D.C.: Georgetown University Press, 1977.

Gumperz, J. J., & Cook-Gumperz, J. *Beyond ethnography: Some uses of sociolinguistics for understanding classroom environments*. Paper presented at the annual meeting of the American Educational Research Association, San Francisco, April 1979.

Hall, E. T. *The silent language*. New York: Fawcett, 1959.

Hymes, D. Introduction: Toward ethnographies of communication. In J. Gumperz & D. Hymes (Eds.), The ethnography of communication. *American Anthropologist*, 1964, 55 (5, Pt.2), 1–34.

Hymes, D. Studying the interaction of language and social life. In D. Hymes, *Foundations in sociolinguistics: An ethnographic approach*. Philadelphia: University of Pennsylvania Press, 1974.

Kendon, A. Some functions of gaze direction in face to face interaction. *Acta Psychologica*, 1967, *26*, 22–63.

McDermott, R. P. *Kids make sense: An ethnographic account of the interactional management of success and failure in one first grade classroom*. Unpublished doctoral dissertation, Stanford University, 1976.

Mehan, H. *Learning lessons: Social organization in the classroom*. Cambridge: Harvard University Press, 1979.

Mehan, H., & Griffin, P. Socialization: The view from classroom interactions. *Sociological Inquiry*, 1980, *50* (3–4), 357–392.

Mehan, H., & Wood, H. *The reality of ethnomethodology*. New York: John Wiley and Sons, 1975.

Michaels, S., & Cook-Gumperz, J. A study of sharing time with first grade students: Discourse narratives in the classroom. *Proceedings of the Fifth Annual Meetings of the Berkeley Linguistic Society*, 1979.

Philips, S. Participant structures and communicative competence: Warm Springs children in community and classroom. In C. Cazden, V. John, & D. Hymes (Eds.), *Functions of language in the classroom*. New York: Teachers College Press, 1972.

Rosenberg, B. A. Oral sermons and oral narrative. In D. Ben-Amos & K. S. Goldstein (Eds.), *Folklore: Performance and communication*. The Hague: Mouton, 1975.

Sacks, H., Schegloff, E., & Jefferson, G. A simplest systematics for the organization of turn-taking for conversation. *Language*, 1974, *50*, 696–735.

Schank, R. C., & Abelson, N. P. *Scripts, plans, goals, and understanding: An inquiry into human knowledge structures*. Hillsdale, N.J.: Lawrence Erlbaum, 1977.

Scheflen, A. E. *Communicational structure: Analysis of a psychotherapy transaction* (formerly Stream and structure in psychotherapy). Bloomington: University of Indiana Press, 1973.

Schegloff, E. A. Sequencing in conversational openings. *American Anthropologist,* 1968, *70,* 1075–1095.

Scollon, R. The rhythmic integration of ordinary talk. In *Georgetown University Roundtable on Languages and Linguistics.* Washington, D.C.: Georgetown University Press, 1981.

Shultz, J., Florio, S., & Erickson, F. Where's the floor?: Aspects of the cultural organization of social relationships in communication at home and at school. In P. Gilmore & A. Glatthorn (Eds.), *Ethnography and education: Children in and out of school.* Washington, D.C.: Center for Applied Linguistics, in press.

Sinclair, J. M., & Coulthard, R. M. *Toward an analysis of discourse: The English used by teachers and pupils.* Oxford: Oxford University Press, 1975.

Smith, B. Othanel, and others. *A study of the logic of teaching.* U. S. Department of Health, Education, and Welfare: Cooperative Research Project No. 258 (7257). Urbana, Ill.: Bureau of Educational Research, College of Education, University of Illinois, n.d.

Stern, D., & Gibbon, J. Temporal expectancies of social behaviors in mother-infant play. In E. Thoman (Ed.), *Origins of the infant's social responsiveness.* Hillsdale, N.J.: Lawrence Erlbaum, 1979.

Taba, H. *Thinking in elementary school children.* U.S. Department of Health, Education, and Welfare: Cooperative Research Project No. 1574. San Francisco: San Francisco State College, 1964.

Tannen, D. What's in a frame?: Surface evidence for underlying expectations. In R. O. Freedle (Ed.), *New directions in discourse processing* (Advances in Discourse Processes: Vol. 2). Norwood, N.J.: Ablex, 1979.

Vygotsky, L. S. *Mind in society: The development of higher psychological processes.* M. Cole, V. J. Steiner, S. Scribner, & E. Souberman (Eds.). Cambridge: Harvard University Press, 1978.

Weber, M. *Wirtschaft und gesellschaft* (Vol. 1). Tübingen, 1922, pp. 1–14. Translated as The nature of social activity. In W. C. Runciman (Ed.), *Weber: Selections in translation.* Cambridge, England: Cambridge University Press, 1978. Pp. 7–32.

Wilkinson, L. C., Clevenger, M., & Dollaghan, C. Communication in small instructional groups: A sociolinguistic approach. In W. P. Dickson (Ed.), *Children's oral communication skills.* New York: Academic Press, 1981.

10
Gaining Access to Learning: Conversational, Social, and Cognitive Demands of Group Participation[1]

JUDITH L. GREEN
JUDITH O. HARKER

This chapter offers a conceptualization of the process of teaching–learning as a communicative process. This conceptualization draws on theoretical constructs from anthropological linguistics, sociolinguistics, and cognitive and social psychology in its underlying premises and analytical methods. The model derived from this concept suggests that children acquire knowledge of social and communicative strategies needed to gain access to the academic content of lessons simultaneously with the acquisition of the academic content. From this perspective, knowledge of social norms and conversational demands constitutes a second type of curriculum, the curriculum of social processes and strategies for learning. Curriculum, defined in this manner, is tripartite in nature; it is composed of academic, social, and communicative demands (Wallat & Green, in press).

The acquisition of knowledge contained in any one of these components is a complex process. The complexity is compounded by the fact that these components often cooccur in actual practice. That is, as teachers present academic content, children are simultaneously receiving information about the social and conversational demands for participation from the ways in which teachers present information. Teaching–learning conversations, therefore, produce knowledge of social norms and knowledge of conversational demands as well as knowledge of academic content of lessons.

[1] The research presented in this chapter was supported by grants from the College of Education, Kent State University, 1977–1979.

183

In this chapter, we will describe the nature of teaching–learning as a communicative process from the perspective of both teacher and students. To illustrate the nature of knowledge about the teaching–learning process obtained from this conceptualization, we will present a series of analyses providing information that builds toward an ethnography of kindergarten for two sets of teachers and children.

The present discussion and data analyses extend previous work that has identified instructional and communicative demands in a storytelling lesson (Green, 1977; Green & Harker, in press), classroom contexts (Green & Wallat, 1979), and social and communicative demands in group time (Green & Wallat, 1979, 1981; Wallat & Green, 1979, in press). The overall goal of this work is to generate and test hypotheses about the nature of teaching–learning processes from the perspective of participants so that we may better understand the classroom as a social system and the nature of teaching–learning as communicative processes.

The series of questions that underlie both past and present work will serve as the frame for the following discussion. The questions include: (a) What are the communicative contexts of the classroom?; (b) What is learned from participation in classroom contexts?; (c) What is required to be a member of the ongoing events of the classroom?; (d) How is information transmitted?; and (e) What are the social, contextual, and thematic demands of classroom lessons? However, before we can consider the framework for the discussion of the findings, a discussion of the limitations, a description of the data base that served as the basis for the multiple analyses, and a discussion of the premises underlying the theoretical frame and analysis will be presented.

Limitations

Two limitations of this work must be acknowledged. First, although we are ultimately concerned with children learning the academic curriculum, we have chosen to concentrate on the social and communicative requirements for participation in the learning events of the classroom for the present chapter. We see this knowledge as both a prerequisite to and a concurrent part of the process of gaining access to the information contained in the academic curriculum. The findings, therefore, relate to only one part of the "cultural capital" of the classroom (see Cook-Gumperz & Gumperz, Chapter 2, this volume). Second, the analyses undertaken to date focus on less than the whole school day and, in some instances, on less than the school year. The study is primarily a hypothesis generating study; to date, hypothesis testing has been completed on a limited basis.

Data Base

The data gathered over a 3-year period in two kindergartens in northeast Ohio form the basis for exploring the social, conversational, contextual, and thematic demands of kindergarten. Year 1 consisted of informal participant observations (Spradley, 1980) for gaining access to the classroom for systematic videotaping of the ongoing classroom events, building trust between teacher and researcher, and developing an action research team (Conlin, 1980; Wallat, Green, Conlin, & Haramis, 1981). Years 2 and 3 involved systematic, ongoing participant observation, videotaping, and ethnographic interviewing. The focus of the data collection was the naturally occurring events of the first hour of the school day (Green & Wallat, 1979). Year 3 was included to explore, which, if any, requirements for kindergarten in each classroom were consistent across populations and which were idiosyncratic to a particular group of students in a particular time period, and the nature of similarities and differences in demands for participation and learning between these classrooms.

Teaching as a Communicative Process: Underlying Premises toward Developing Grounded Theory

Conceptualizing teaching as a communicative process shifts the research focus from attempts to examine the effects of psychological variables (e.g., motivation, self-concept, reinforcement) to sociolinguistic–psycholinguistic variables related to communicative participation of individuals in the teaching–learning process (e.g., communicative competence, social norms for participation, conversational rules). This shift is related to the first premise, to an unmet need in research on teaching, the need for grounded theory (Glaser & Strauss, 1967; Spradley, 1980); that is, theory "grounded in empirical data of cultural description [Spradley, p. 11]" (**Premise 1**). The definition of cultural description adhered to in this work is the classic definition of culture as a way of "perceiving and believing [Berger & Luckmann, 1967]." As Gumperz (1975) states: "The question of how actors communicate information and influence and persuade others in actual situations is still far from being resolved. Yet, an understanding of teaching as a process of verbal communication depends on a solution to this question. [p.1]."

Recent work on the ethnography of communication in classrooms and ethnomethodology has begun to develop such theory. This work, adapted from anthropology (e.g., Erickson, 1977; Gumperz & Hymes, 1972; Spradley, 1980) and sociology (e.g., Mehan, 1979; Mehan & Wood, 1975), provides a basis for identifying naturally occurring contexts and variables, and for identifying recurrent patterns of interaction within and across the differentiated contexts of the classroom.

ON THE NATURE OF EVIDENCE

In developing grounded theory and generating and testing hypotheses from the naturally occurring events, we must be concerned with what constitutes evidence. The second premise relates to the concept that evidence can be internal and external (**Premise 2**). This notion of evidence is adapted from the sociolinguistic work of Gumperz and Tannen (1979) and Tannen (1980). This approach suggests that once patterns have been identified (the internal evidence), this evidence can be tested by obtaining external validation of the findings from participants in the event or from members of the same social group. Once verification has been obtained, these variables can be formally tested in other similar situations using a type-case analysis model (Erickson & Shultz, 1977, 1981; Florio & Shultz, 1979).

The need to collect internal and external evidence of events leads to the construction of a multistep, multifaceted approach to the study of communicative processes in educational settings. In this approach, systematic data recording that includes videotape records, field notes, maps of the classroom, and photographs of student products is undertaken to obtain internal patterns. Once these records are obtained, a systematic search of the tapes for recurring contexts is then instituted. Such a search led to the selection of group discussion time for analyses since this activity represented both a recurrent activity within each classroom and an activity that occurred in both classrooms. In addition, this activity has distinct boundaries and physical characteristics; it was flagged in time within the day (discussion time), in space (on a rug), and in group organization (whole class as opposed to individual and small group worktime). (For other systematic ways of approaching this problem see Corsaro, 1981; Erickson & Shultz, 1977, 1981; Mehan, 1979; Mehan, Cazden, Coles, Fisher, & Maroules, 1976; Sevigny, 1981; Spradley, 1980.)

Once the general setting to be studied is identified, the evolving contexts and conversational structures are identified and described using a method of sociolinguistic ethnography developed by Green and Wallat (Green, 1977; Green & Wallat, 1979, 1981). This methodology produces a series of structural maps that form the basis for all subsequent analyses. (See Figure 10.1, for a sample map and Appendix A for an explanation of the map symbols.) In the present analysis, we added a system for semantic or discourse analysis developed by Frederiksen (1975) to our procedures. These methods are heuristic tools that help focus our attention on cues used in the construction of meaning (e.g., verbal, nonverbal, and prosodic cues used by participants). By concentrating on patterns of cues, we reliably isolate recurrent patterns that then

Tran-script Lines	IU	Message Units Transcript Text	Potentially Divergent Units	Thematically Tied Instructional Units
085		WE'RE GOING TO HAVE—		1 [8] ⟨R⟩ 23 16
086		REMEMBER YESTERDAY WE TALKED ABOUT		8 ⟨R⟩ 25
087		[off camera Shauna triggers something]	0 (r$^o_{nh}$) 24	
088		SHAUNA		17 [R] 24 18 25
089		NEWS AND VIEWS		18 [R] 25
090		AND IF EACH OF YOU WOULD LIKE TO HAVE A CHANCE TO SAY SOMETHING		8 [R] 25
091		AND WE TALKED ABOUT THE PROBLEM—		8 [R] 25
092		James You know what I'd like to	8 (r^o_j) 24	
093		JAMES, EXCUSE ME	17 [R] 24	
094 HV		James: [assess actions]	17 [r^+_j] 23	
095		WE TALKED ABOUT THE PROBLEM WE HAVE IF FIVE PEOPLE TALK AT A TIME		1 18 [R] 25
096		IS THERE A PROBLEM WITH LISTENING IF THAT?		10 [Q] 25 15
097		St. X: uh huh		10 [r^+_x] 25
098		WHAT HAPPENS IF ALL OF US TALK AT ONCE?		15 [Q] 25
099		All: I don't know. Can't hear.		15 [r$^+$]
100		WELL, IF ALL OF YOU TALK AT ONCE AND YOU CAN'T HEAR, IS THERE A WAY WE COULD DO IT SO WE CAN HEAR EACH PERSON?		10 [R] 24 15 25
101 102		All: Yes Peter: One at a time [said loudly]		10 [r$^-$] [r$^+$] 25 [Q] 15 P
103		WHAT DID YOU SAY PETER?		15 [r^+_p] 21
104		Peter: One at a time [said loudly]		
105		LET'S TRY YOUR IDEA.		10 [R$_P$] 24 [Q] 10 P 15
106		MAY WE TRY YOUR IDEA?		10 [r$^+$] 23
107		Peter: [shakes head yes]		
			END OF	PHASE I

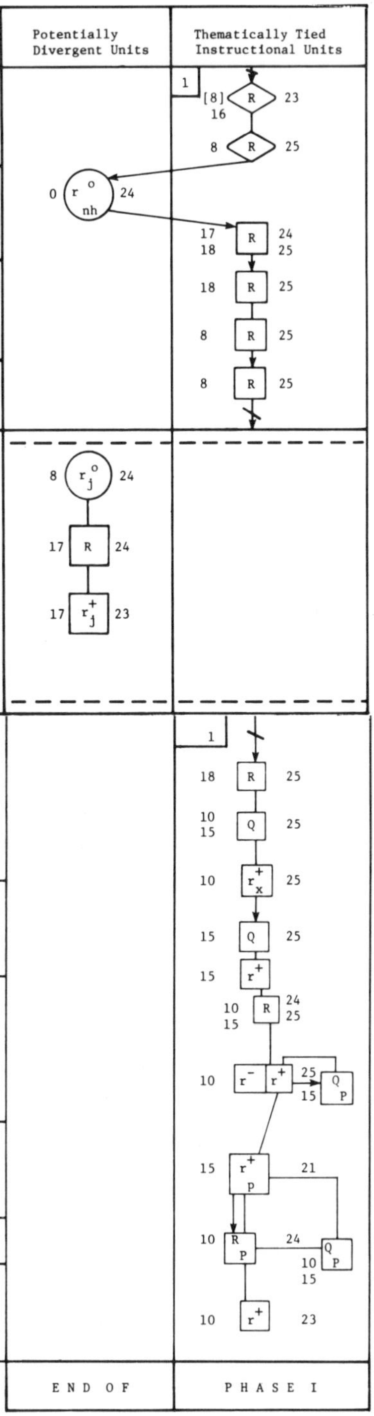

Figure 10.1. Map of the instructional conversation (Teacher M). Phase I of the day's news lesson (review participating rule).

become variables to be tested in later analysis (Green, 1977). Finally, by focusing in depth on when and how these variables occur within and across contexts, and on their purpose and interrelatedness, a description of classroom contexts and requirements for participation in these contexts are obtained.

Once this information is obtained, external evidence about the participants' perceptions is elicited. This information is obtained in a variety of ways: (a) audiotapes of teacher's goals are obtained using a structured interview after each day of taping (Conlin, 1980; Wallat et al., 1981); (b) face-to-face interviews are obtained with teachers focusing on the videotapes; (c) maps of the classroom are constructed by children; and (d) interviews of children are obtained focusing on the videotapes of the events and/or on the maps they constructed (Wallat & Green, 1979). (For another approach to eliciting teachers' perceptions, see Bussis, Chittenden, and Amarel, 1976; Mehan, Hertweck, Combs, and Flynn, Chapter 15, this volume).

The two types of evidence are then laid side-by-side and explored for consistency. If the findings are not validated by the teacher and/or children, we explore the descriptive analysis for factors that explain this conflict. To date, the teachers' and students' perceptions have validated our findings; that is, they agree that the descriptions obtained match their perceptions of classroom events, contexts, and requirements for participation in the classroom.

One further test of validity was suggested by Sanday (1973). She suggests that if a description is adequate, the researcher should be able to use this information to participate in the classroom so as not to break any of the rules. Although we cannot become children, the type-case approach, in which descriptive models of one day's events, contexts, and requirements are used to predict what will (or will not) occur on subsequent days, permits us to test further the validity of our findings. Figure 10.2 provides a flow chart of this procedure.

In this section, we have briefly overviewed both the premises underlying our approach and the general procedures these premises suggest. In the next sections, we will explore the specific premises underlying the conceptualization of teaching–learning as a communicative process.

ON CONVERSATIONAL STRUCTURE

Researchers must understand both the methodological approach being used, and the phenomena being observed (Birdwhistell, 1977; Corsaro, 1981; Lutz, 1981; Sevigny, 1981). Fundamental to a concept of teaching–learning as a communicative process is an understanding of the nature of face-to-face behavior (Erickson & Shultz, 1977, 1981; Goffman, 1974; Gumperz & Hymes, 1972; Kendon, Harris, & Key, 1975) that indicates conversations are rule-

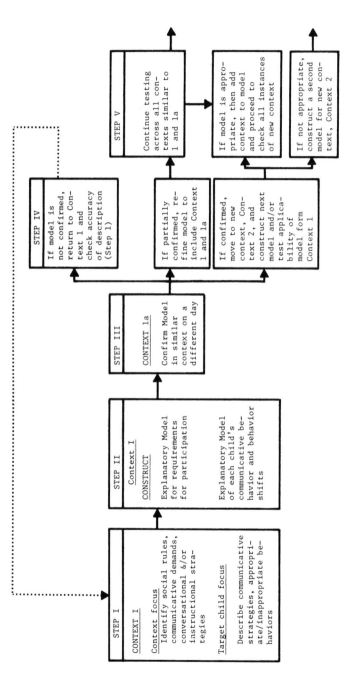

Figure 10.2. Type-case analysis toward model building: Hypothesis generation/confirmation design.

governed, constructed entities (**Premise 3**). They are constructed by people acting on and working with their own messages and behaviors and the messages and behaviors of others to reach communicative goals (e.g., Cook-Gumperz & Gumperz, 1976; Erickson & Shultz, 1977, 1981; Green, 1977; Green & Wallat, 1979, 1981; Gumperz, 1975; Gumperz & Tannen, 1979; Tannen, 1980) (**Premise 4**).

Within this constructivist view, messages in conversations can be verbal and/or nonverbal (**Premise 5**), and can be transmitted in more than one channel of communication, often simultaneously, within a single conversation (Barnes & Todd, 1977; Green, 1977; Knott, 1979) (**Premise 6**). For example, a teacher can engage in a conversation with the class in a primarily verbal mode, while transmitting a message in a nonverbal mode to an individual within the group (e.g., pay attention). The second message is backgrounded for the group, but foregrounded for the individual within the group. Such messages, although backgrounded, are part of the instructional conversation and provide information to the group about behavioral expectations (**Premise 7**).

The constructed nature of conversations is compatible with recent findings that context is not a given entity (e.g., a livingroom, a classroom); rather, context is constructed as part of the conversational process (Erickson & Shultz, 1977, 1981) and contributes to interpretation of meaning (Cook-Gumperz, 1981) (**Premise 8**). The key to determining both message and context is consideration of contextualization cues. These cues (verbal, nonverbal, and prosodic features of conversation) are the "means by which speakers signal and listeners interpret how semantic content is to be understood and how each sentence (behavior) relates to what precedes or follows [Gumperz & Tannen, 1979, p. 308]" (**Premise 9**). The products of conversational processes, therefore, are a series of constructed meanings, semantically and socially related to the definition of context (**Premise 10**).

Conversations, however, are not composed of strings of random messages. By considering how messages are tied interactionally, socially, semantically, thematically, and pedagogically, identification of various types of tied, hierarchically structured conversational units is possible (e.g., Green, 1977; Green & Wallat, 1979, 1981; Gumperz & Herasimchuk, 1973; Mehan, 1979; Mehan et al., 1976; Sacks, Schegloff, & Jefferson, 1974). See also Frederiksen (1981) and Gumperz and Tannen (1979) for conversational work and Barker and Wright (1966) for behavioral work (**Premise 11**). Lessons, viewed from this perspective, are not preset entities; however, they are constructed entities produced by teachers and children as they work together to reach instructional goals (Green, 1977; Green & Harker, in press; Green & Wallat, 1979, 1981) (**Premise 12**).

Conversations, and therefore lessons, are dynamic. Members in a conversation negotiate conversational structure, establish context, and construct shared meaning. Thus, conversations are not scripts to be followed rotely by teachers and students (**Premise 13**). That is, conversational construction is not linear in nature. During conversations, breaches in cohesion occur (**Premise 14**). Analysis of what participants do when a breach or potential breach occurs makes visible the interpretations of the event held by participants, the rules for participation, and the meaning intended by participants (Green & Wallat, 1979, 1981; Gumperz, 1976; Gumperz & Tannen, 1979; Mehan, 1979; Mehan et al., 1976; Wallat & Green, in press) (**Premise 15**).

This discussion suggests that conversations are complex entities and that participation in conversations is a complex process. Participants and researchers must not only consider what is said but also how it is transmitted. From participating in ongoing conversations and observing how meaning is transmitted, children have the opportunity to learn what is required for participation, to decipher the contextual requirements, and to learn how to gain access to the "cultural capital" of the classroom (**Premise 16**). This constructivist view of classroom communication is one of the central themes that runs through the chapters in this volume. (For a historical view of constructivist research, see Magoon, 1977.)

ON PEDAGOGICAL CHARACTERISTICS

The constructivist premises discussed previously apply to both instructional and noninstructional conversational contexts. Several characteristics of instructional–pedagogical settings, however, make communicative requirements and communicative competence somewhat different from those in noninstructional situations. First, in classrooms, the roles of teacher and student are specified (**Premise 17**). The teacher has the responsibility for determining when conversations can occur as well as the structure and direction of the conversation (Barnes & Todd, 1977; Green, 1977) (**Premise 18**). In addition, teachers and students are constrained by the curriculum goals of classrooms (**Premise 19**). Although all conversations are goal directed, the goal of instructional conversations is assumed to be more overt and less negotiable than conversational goals in noninstructional activities (**Premise 20**).

Although other premises and features of conversation may be important to a complete understanding of conversational structure, participation, and meaning, these premises provide an outline of the underlying view of the process adhered to in this research. With this frame in mind, we will now present a discussion of findings about the communicative, social, and thematic demands in two kindergarten classrooms.

Findings: Toward a Model of Teaching–Learning as a Communicative Process

Findings from five related, but separate analyses will be presented in this section. Each analysis began with the description of interaction between teacher and children displayed on conversational maps (Figure 10.1) obtained from the systematic method of sociolinguistic ethnography developed by Green and Wallat (1979, 1981). Once the maps were constructed, additional analyses of the graphically displayed data were undertaken. In the following section, a brief framework for each analysis, the data analyzed, the analysis procedures, and external validation findings will be specified.

CONTEXT IDENTIFICATION

In the previous section, we presented research that suggests that contexts are constructed as part of conversations and are not preset entities. To identify contexts from this frame, researchers have posed the question, "When is context? [Erickson & Shultz, 1977, 1981; Green & Wallat, 1979]." By considering factors such as what participants are doing at various points in time, the nature of group organization, the requirements for participation, and the theme (topic) of the conversation, these researchers identify various contexts of the classroom. One key to this analysis is the fact that demands for participation are similar within a context and shift when a new context is formed. For example, when children sing together, the context can be defined as group and the theme as singing; when, in the next activity, children are greeted individually, the context has shifted to individual within the group and the theme to greeting (Green & Wallat, 1979). Context, therefore, is defined by multiple criteria and not by general physical setting. This can be further seen in the fact that although two contexts are defined above, the general physical setting remained constant—the children and teacher sat around a rug in one part of the room.

In this analysis, the contexts that occurred during a 13-minute segment of group meeting time (rug–discussion time) were explored using this approach. This analysis demonstrates that group meeting time in the two classrooms was not a single context—Teacher M's discussion group consisted of five separate contexts and Teacher H's consisted of six.

Table 10.1 demonstrates that similarity exists between the two teachers on several levels. Both have approximately the same amount of talk (computed in terms of message units, not duration of time), the same number of completed contexts, lessons that include more than one phase, and similar types of grouping practices (total group structure and the individual within the total group).

Table 10.1
Distribution of Content, Context, Group Structure, and Messages (Group Meeting Time—Length: Thirteen Minutes)

Context number	Teacher M			Teacher H		
	Content	Group type	Total messages	Content	Group type	Total messages
1	Greeting song Welcome lesson (Phase I)	Total group	24	Defining individual space Welcome lesson (Phase I)	Individual within group	32
2	Individual greeting Welcome lesson (Phase II)	Individual Total group	38	Good day song Welcome lesson (Phase II)	Total group	29
3	Greeting song with Spanish words	Total group	22	Calendar and date	Total group + one child within group	74
4	Review of rules for participation: news and views (Phase I)	Total group	23	DUSO kit lesson (aborted)	Total group	2
5	News and views lesson (Phase II)	Individual within group	268	Individual greeting	Individual within group	115
6	—	—	—	Visual discrimination lesson and restructuring group	Individual within group	116
	Total student and teacher messages		375			368

Observation of this aspect of the school day across videotapes of the school year confirmed the differentiated nature of this period. When interviewed, both teachers verified the contexts identified and then specified that they used specific activities, for example, singing, as a means of establishing the group. Both teachers also stated that the purpose of group time was to help children develop a sense of group and to permit children to receive individual recognition within the group. In this analysis, external evidence (observations and interviews) validated our findings. The interview data added further information about the reason for these contexts that could not be obtained from the observations alone.

These contexts are interesting in that they are primarily social in nature and do not contain traditional academic content. In these contexts, children have the opportunity to practice the making of social events (Cook-Gumperz, 1973); that is, to extend their knowledge about the types of social and conversational demands for participation that will be placed on them as students. In these contexts, children are presented with information about how to differentiate their roles as individuals within the group and how to participate in a large group. They have the opportunity to discover when groups occur and how to behave and learn in groups; however, this knowledge is not assured by particpation. These situations provide input; factors such as past experiences, cultural frames, and developmental factors influence what will be learned (Cook-Gumperz & Green, in press; Cook-Gumperz & Gumperz, Chapter 2, this volume; Tannen, 1980).

The changes in expectations for participation in these contexts suggest that demands are placed on children to use and extend their communicative repertoires in a variety of ways. Exploration of expectations for group participation is one way to identify the communicative demands of and the communicative competence required in kindergarten, since communicative competence is knowing how, when, and with whom to talk and for what purpose (Hymes, 1974).

GAINING ACCESS TO LEARNING

The notion of communicative and social demands is further illustrated in the discussion of when children are permitted spontaneous access to group discussion. The theoretical frame for this analysis and for the one on social rules identification (discussed next) comes from a synthesis of work in social psychology and sociolinguistics. This frame has been presented in depth elsewhere (Green & Wallat, 1979, 1981; Wallat & Green, 1979, in press); therefore, only a brief discussion will be presented here.

The analysis presented in this section focuses on students' attempts to gain access to either the teacher or the group discussion at times other than their designated turn at talk or at times when the floor was open to anyone.

These bids for access are either verbal or nonverbal actions on the part of an individual in an instructional setting. To gain a turn, students must determine when, about what, and to whom they can talk. In other words, they must read the demands for participation, the rules governing this participation, and then select from their communicative repertoires appropriate ways of behaving (Green & Stoffan, 1980; Merritt, 1980; Merritt & Humphrey, 1979).

Like contexts, social norms governing participation are constructed as part of the ongoing interactions in classrooms. These norms may be viewed as expectations for behaviors or signals for social responsibility, since they act to guide and constrain behavior (Wallat & Green, in press). Social norms are also viewed as products of classroom interactions. In this approach, a norm is not assumed to be static; that is, once established it always exists and is followed without question. Rather, social norms must be established, maintained, checked, suspended, and reestablished (Blumer, 1969), not only across but within contexts. In addition, some rules or norms are negotiable whereas others are not.

As suggested earlier, children receive information about the norms from their interactions with the teacher, from observing the teacher's interactions with other students, and from observing what occurs when a breach in expected behavior happens. The breaches (unsuccessful bid attempts in this analysis) serve to highlight the rules; the successful or adherence behaviors tend to reinforce the expected or appropriate behaviors for the context. The purpose of this analysis was to explore whether children acquired one type of expected behavior, when to gain a turn at talk in group discussion time. Evidence of learning was defined a priori as a change in the proportion of successful to unsuccessful bids. We hypothesized that, if children had learned when they might obtain a turn at talk (other than at designated times) from participating in one set of contexts on one day, then on subsequent days, the number of unsuccessful bids would decline (Green & Stoffan, 1980).

To explore this question, data from group discussion time on Days 3 and 4 of the school year were explored in Teacher M's kindergarten. Bids were determined by observing both verbal and nonverbal actions of students and the cues to contextualization by teacher and group in which the individual student's actions were embedded. Tables 10.2 and 10.3 present the bid patterns of the group on 2 consecutive days in the first three contexts of group discussion time.

As indicated in Table 10.2 (Day 3), 7 bids were made during the first 3 contexts and the transition times between contexts; only 1 was successful. In contrast, on Day 4 (Table 10.3), 11 bids were made across the various contexts and transition times and 6 of these (64%) were successful. Exploration of these tables uncovered a pattern. On Day 3, bids were distributed across both contexts and transition times, whereas on Day 4, the bids occurred only at transition points between contexts. With this change in bid pattern comes

Table 10.2
Number of Student Bids for Access to Group[a] (Day 3, September 15, 1977)

Context	Number of bids (nonverbal–verbal)	Number of successful bids
Welcome song	2	1
Transition	1	0
Greeting: Individual	1	0
Welcome song (Spanish words)	0	0
Transition	2	0
Total	7	1

[a] Number of students present = 13.

an increase in the success factor of the bids. This pattern suggests that the children have extracted rules or norms for when they might gain access.

Another pattern can be identified when the nature of transitions between contexts is considered. The first three contexts (**welcome, greeting,** and **song**) are different phases of a single lesson, **greeting–welcome.** These contexts are followed by the phases of **news and views** lesson. Consideration of interactional rhythm (Erickson, Chapter 9, this volume), contextualization cues (e.g., pause time, kinesics, proxemic distance, intonational contours), and the nature of the lessons (e.g., theme, expectations for participation) lead to the conclusion that the transitions between Context 1 and 2, and between Context 3 and 4 were both qualitatively and quantitatively different. The increase in students' bids for access during the transition between Context 3 (**Spanish song**) and 4 (**preparation for news and views**) also suggests that the students are sensitive to the qualitative and quantitative differences in the transition times, and that the students were beginning to "read" the rules for gaining access.

Furthermore, analysis of successful bids (verbal and nonverbal content) suggests that successful bids tend to be thematically tied to content of the lesson. However, because a bid is thematically tied does not ensure its ac-

Table 10.3
Number of Student Bids for Access to Group (Day 4, September 16, 1977)

Context	Number of bids (nonverbal–verbal)	Number of successful bids
Welcome song	0	0
Transition	2	1
Greeting: Individual	0	0
Transition	0	0
Spanish song	0	0
Transition	9	6
Total	11	7

ceptance. When queried about this, Teacher M indicated she weighs bids against lesson frame, her goals for individuals, and the effect that permitting the bid would have on the lesson's direction and student participation. Although the teacher's statement indicates there is a degree of negotiation in whether a bid for turn will be successful, the data show that if the students adhere to certain rules (e.g., when to bid in time) the probability of success increases. Observation at the end of the school year (May 23, 1977) showed that during this same time frame, no student made a bid in an inappropriate place or in an inappropriate way. In addition, rules such as *each student gets a turn at talk during News and Views* were used spontaneously by students to inform others about their rights and obligations for participation.

Interviews of students focusing on maps constructed of the classroom and on videotapes of events produced direct statements about who could talk and when someone could speak. In addition, students provided information about the number of students who could be in an area, what the activities were across the day, and what types of behaviors were generally expected during an activity (e.g., *sit in your own space; cleanup your own materials; no more than three at the listening center*) (Wallat & Green, 1979, in press). Interviews with the teacher also confirmed these findings and provided information about why bids might be successful or unsuccessful, even when they appear to adhere to the rule that is generally functioning.

This section indicates that students and observers can extract the rules or norms for behavior that are functioning within and across contexts by observing the actions of students and teacher. In the next section, we will present the rules or expectations for behavior we identified in the transition time between arrival and group discussion time—that is, the transition just prior to the contexts discussed in the previous two sections.

SOCIAL RULES IDENTIFICATION

The theoretical frame on social norm construction presented in the preceding section outlines this analysis. The transition time prior to group discussion was explored across a portion of the school year (September 16, 19, 21; October 5; and February 8). This analysis permitted us to use an extended version of the type case analysis used in the previous section and described in Figure 10.2. A microanalysis of the conversational and behavioral structure of transition time on September 15 (Day 3 of school for Teacher M's class) was undertaken. Then, using the rules we obtained on Day 3, 4 additional days, both contiguous and noncontiguous, were analyzed for examples of the rules and for indications of additional rules.

Table 10.4 presents the frequency of occurrence of each verbally stated rule for the 5 days. As indicated on this table, some rules were verbally stated on each day sampled (e.g., Rule 1a, 2a, 4b, 5b) whereas others were not.

Table 10.4
Steps to Structuring and Restructuring Group Verbally Stated during Transition Times

Group coordination norms	Social behaviors	September				October	February	May
		15	16	19	21	5	8	23[a]
		Transition length in minutes						
		2:53	2:52	4:34	4:32	2:37	4:57	—
1. Signals for attention	a. Piano chords (nonnegotiable)	1	1	1	1	1	1	—
	b. Teacher identifies **individuals** who have interpreted meaning of signal (stop work, look to teacher, listen for directions) (nonnegotiable)	2	3	5	2	1	0	—
	c. Elicits meaning of signal (rule nonnegotiable)	0	0	0	1	1	1	—
2. Responsibility for work space	a. Finish work and clean space (context dependent)	2	1	1	1	1	1	—
	b. Clean up work space previously occupied (nonnegotiable)	3	0	0	0	0	0	—
	c. Leave work at space to finish later (negotiable)	0	3	2	0	0	5	—
	d. Plan ahead for choice of work (choice of activities negotiable)	0	0	4	0	0	0	—
3. Responsibility for work objects	a. Work object has own general space in room (e.g., arrival shelf materials) (nonnegotiable)	1	1	0	0	0	0	—
	b. Student's personal objects and/or projects are to be placed in a "safe" place by student and student	1	0	1	0	0	0	—

c. If individual has produced a product and wishes to share product a holding space is available (placement is negotiable)	1	0	0	0	0	0	—
4. Signals for change of group structure (e.g., meet in new area) (nonnegotiable)							
a. Directions addressed to group	2	4	2	1	1	0	—
b. Directions addressed to individuals	5	0	0	1	0	3	—
5. Responsibility for physical orientation							
a. The group has a specific physical structure (e.g., circle) (nonnegotiable)	0	2	6	1	2	0	—
b. Find and stay in individual space within the physical structure (negotiable)	9	9	10	7	4	1	5 (circle time)
c. There is a specific way to sit so that others can see (nonnegotiable)	0	2	0	0	0	0	2 (circle time)
6. Responsibility for cooperative effort							
a. During songs, everybody sings and works together (e.g., children sing with teacher and are not directly-overtly taught song) (nonnegotiable)	2	4	3	1	0	1	1 (circle time)
b. During discussion, we speak one at a time (nonnegotiable)	3	2	0	1	0	0	0
c. When someone is speaking, we listen to the speaker (nonnegotiable)	5	1	6	9	0	0	2 (circle time)

[a] The structure for this day was different due to the math program. A circle time was held at a later time than usual, and the transition from math to group meeting time merely included moving from the tables to the work area (i.e., the children did not need time to replace individual work). Selected findings are presented from this group meeting that illustrate the existence of the norms established for behavior within group.

Given Blumer's (1969) concept of norms as being established, maintained, checked, suspended, and reestablished, this finding is expected. If children are nonverbally adhering to rules and participating appropriately, there is no need to state rules verbally. Analysis of nonverbal behaviors on these days indicated that students were adhering to norms, thus rendering verbal statements of the rule unnecessary. In this analysis, both the overt, verbal statements and nonverbal indications of adherence to norms provide internal evidence of the existence of the norms presented in Table 10.4. This analysis and the previous one also indicate how type case analysis can be used in hypothesis generating and hypothesis testing within an individual subject (one classroom) across time.

External evidence from student and teacher interviews not only confirmed our observations and analysis, but provided further information about why these behaviors and actions occurred. For example, in her face-to-face interview, Teacher M spontaneously mentioned that she uses Elkind's (1979) concept of framing or centering an event to help her establish and maintain behavioral expectations. She stated that this approach helped establish a stable environment in which children could be permitted freedom of choice in the classroom. From this perspective, the existence or invocation of a rule indicates stability of behavioral expectations and the existence of a behavior frame. In addition, the lack of proliferation of new rules for behavior also suggests stability of behavioral expectations.

Both internal and external evidence indicate that students are able to extract the rules for participation from observations of what is occurring in their classroom. These rules become part of their communicative repertoires and norms for behavior remain stable across time. The question that must be tested is this: Do similar patterns exist in other classrooms? To begin to answer this, we will now compare this classroom with a second one. Rather than focus on the rules, however, we will concentrate on the nature of the communicative and instructional demands that result from the type and distribution of instructional talk by teachers.

PATTERNS OF INSTRUCTIONAL LANGUAGE USE

Social rules guide participation. Moment-by-moment participation, however, is also influenced by the instructional language strategies used by the teacher. In this section, we will explore the conversational–instructional demands for children's participation in two classrooms. The data for this analysis will once again be the group discussion time contexts presented in Table 10.1 for each teacher. The basis for the analysis is the strategies represented on the instructional maps (Figure 10.1 and Table 10.5). Strategy in this instance refers to verbal action on the part of individuals; these strategies result from some degree of conscious planning. Central to this perspective is the assumption that teachers have options, make decisions, and select desired actions from a repertoire of actions and ways of transmitting these actions (Green & Harker, in press); that is, teachers and students are not robots mechanically acting out a preset script. The specific strategies included in the sociolinguistic ethnographic system come from a synthesis of work in sociolinguistics and classroom interactions. These strategies are those that serve both pedagogical and conversational purposes (see, Green, 1977 for a rationale, Green and Wallat, 1979, 1981 for a definition of strategies, and Table 10.5 for a brief description of strategies).

Comparison of Talk: Molar Analysis

We began the analysis of instructional language use on a molar level. We explored the frequency of teacher messages to student messages. Teacher M's talk contained 50% of the total messages and her students' talk contained 50% of the messages. In contrast, Teacher H's talk contained 67% of the total messages, whereas her students' talk contained 33%. The two teachers, therefore, are quantitatively different with regard to the amount of teacher-to-student talk. On a molar level, the demands for verbal participation differ from these five contexts in the two educational settings.

Comparison of Teacher Talk: Microanalysis of Quantitative Differences

Consideration of molar differences such as these tells us little about the specific nature of the demands for student participation. Therefore, the question of teachers' instructional language was subjected to a closer, more sensitive examination. Before discussing the patterns reflected in the frequency distribution of instructional language use for these two teachers, one additional factor must be considered. That is, messages may contain more than one strategy. For example, the message "Shauna" (line 088, Figure 10.1), serves to both control Shauna's behavior (strategy code 017) and to refocus her attention on the lesson (strategy code 018). Determination of these multiple functions was obtained from analysis of contextualization cues and from consideration of how the participants work with and build on their own messages (behaviors) and those of others. In this instance, Shauna ceased her actions off camera and the teacher continued with the lesson. (Off-camera determinations are possible because the first author was the participant observer in the setting.)

When we considered the total number of strategies that each teacher used (277 for Teacher M and 349 for Teacher H), we found a difference of 72 messages. However, when the number of strategies were considered relative to the amount of teacher talk, no difference was found. Teacher M had 1.48 strategies per message and Teacher H had 1.42. This suggests no argument

Table 10.5

Summary of Quantitative Similarities and Differences between Teacher M's and Teacher H's Instructional Language Use

Variable/ Strategy and map number code	Characteristics	Nature of difference
Focus (8)	Brings attention to theme Brings attention to behavior expectations	No difference in frequency of occurrence
Frame ($\boxed{8}$)	Message (e.g., *OK, then, now*) to indicate *get ready to listen or act*	Not used by Teacher M Used throughout lessons and across contexts by Teacher H Low frequency item within data
Hold ($\textcircled{8}$)	Message (e.g., *OK*) to indicate *hold on a second, stay with me*	Not used by Teacher M Used by Teacher H at points of context shift, change in turn distribution, topic shift Low frequency item within data
Ignore (9)	No response provided to question, direction, etc.	Not used by Teacher H Used by Teacher M as response to student initiations at times when initiation not desired Low frequency item within data
Confirm + (10)	Positive feedback Requests for confirmation (positive)	Teacher H provides direct positive feedback statements more frequently Teacher M asks for positive confirmation from students more frequently
Confirm − (11)	Negative feedback about accuracy of response Negative feedback to a general question	No difference in frequency of occurrence
Continue (12)	Backchanneling (Yngve, 1970). Use of devices such as *um hum, yes*, head nods, to indicate attention on part of listener Serves to keep conversation going—encourages talk to continue	Not used by Teacher H Used by Teacher M during news and views Low frequency item within data
Extend (13)	Adds more information onto student's message	Used more frequently by Teacher H Low occurring item for Teacher M
Raise (14)	Changes level of comprehension required from lower level to higher level	No difference in frequency of occurrence Low frequency item within data
Clarify (15)	Makes clear previous message Requests more information to make previous message(s) clear	Teacher M uses clarification more frequently in terms of total Teacher M also uses requests for clarification more frequently

(continued)

Table 10.5 (*continued*)

Variable/ Strategy and map number code	Characteristics	Nature of difference
Edit (16)	Hesitation, false starts, repetition of words that indicate persons are monitoring what they are saying	Low frequency item within data Used more frequently by Teacher M
Control (17)	Direct statements of behavior control or expectation	Used more frequently by Teacher H
Refocus (18)	Redirects attention to theme or behavior expectation	No difference in frequency of occurrence
Restate (19)	Repetition of statement either directly or paraphrase	No difference in frequency of occurrence Low frequency item within data

can be made that one teacher's language is more complex with regard to the average number of strategies used.

This lack of difference in the average number of strategies used by the teachers does not mean that no difference exists regarding demands for participation. Analysis of the language use patterns presented in Figure 10.3 produced patterns of similarities and differences in terms of frequency of use of instructional–conversational language. The similarities and differences in Figure 10.3 are quantitative in nature; however, when the patterns that occur are considered, they suggest qualitative similarities and differences. To facilitate the discussion of the similarities and differences, a descriptive summary table of the findings was constructed (see Table 10.5).

To interpret the quantitative information presented in Figure 10.3, criteria for similarity had to be determined. In this analysis, similarity of use was defined arbitrarily as a difference of less than 10 occurrences in strategies for frequently occurring strategies and 5 or less for low occurring strategies. A low occurring strategy was defined as one whose frequency of occurrence in this data was 10 or less. With these criteria as a frame, we can now explore the similarities and differences in instructional language used by Teacher M and Teacher H and, thus, the nature of the demands for participation and communication in these classrooms.

No difference was found with regard to use of **focusing, negative confirmation, raising, refocusing,** and **restatement.** The similarities between the teachers, therefore, are striking. Both focus children's attention on the themes and task; both use this strategy more frequently than any other strategy; both use refocusing about equally; and both use limited amounts of restatement.

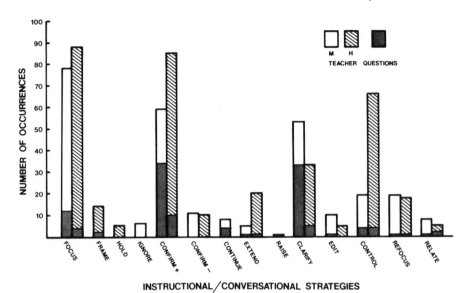

INSTRUCTIONAL/CONVERSATIONAL STRATEGIES

Figure 10.3. Distribution of questions to total talk by strategy type.

This pattern of similarity suggests that both teachers can be described as goal directed. This interpretation is supported not only by the use of focusing types of behavior (focusing, refocusing, restatement), but also by the fact that these strategies, when taken as a whole, occur more frequently than any other strategy.

External evidence obtained from teacher self-interviews and face-to-face interviews supports this interpretation as does information obtained from student interviews. The goals of the teacher's lessons were clearly provided. In addition, these goals interfaced with the participant observer's independent judgment and the student's knowledge of what was expected and what was occurring.

As striking as the similarities are, the differences between the teachers in terms of frequency of use are equally striking. Differences exist between the two teachers on six strategies: **clarify, frame, hold, confirmation +, extend,** and **control.** In terms of absolute frequency, the difference favors Teacher M on only one of these strategies, clarify; and more specifically, request for clarification (indicated by the high proportion of questions in this category). The remaining five strategies are used more frequently, in absolute terms, by Teacher H. The pattern of these differences suggests a difference between the two teachers regarding student involvement and expectations for participation in these five contexts. The pattern of use by Teacher H suggests she is more verbally directive than is Teacher M. Teacher H controls the direction and nature of the conversation directly; that is, she tells students to stay with her (use hold), provides direction, frequent confirmation of their responses (this strategy occurs almost as frequently as focusing), and uses direct statements of control and behavior expectation. She also builds on student responses (extends), thus involving students by acknowledging and using their contributions to the lesson. In contrast, Teacher M uses considerably less direct statements of control, extension, and confirmation +. She tends to clarify and request clarification of student messages. This pattern suggests that participation requirements in Teacher M's class contexts differ from those in Teacher H's.

The difference is further heightened when the frequency of question asking is considered. Teacher M uses question asking more frequently than Teacher H in absolute terms. When question asking is considered by strategy, we find that on all variables in which a difference occurred, the difference favored Teacher M. This pattern suggests that Teacher M desired more verbal involvement from students in these contexts than Teacher H. Her use of clarification and confirmation requests also supports this interpretation. This pattern, when added to the difference between the two teachers in terms of total teacher-to-student talk, indicates that expectations for student–conversational–instructional participation are greater in Teacher M's room than in Teacher H's for the contexts considered.

The patterns of quantitative differences begin to point to differences in requirements for general verbal participation in these classrooms. However, since these data are composite data, that is, data collapsed across all five contexts, we cannot determine whether the type of participation and language used were appropriate for the contexts (lessons) and goals of these lessons. To understand the differences between the teachers, we need to consider qualitative differences and the match between context and type of language.

Comparison of Teacher Talk: Microanalysis of Qualitative Differences

The data in Figure 10.3 and Table 10.5 are based primarily on verbal occurrences of behavior and strategies isolated from their contextual surroundings. In the premise of this chapter, we reviewed literature suggesting that meaning is situation specific. Therefore, to understand how particular strategies function in classroom conversation, we returned to the tapes and maps and explored how the different strategies were used and their place in the evolving conversations. This analysis suggested some qualitative differences between teachers and also pointed to the fact that while one teacher used verbal statements to indicate behavior, the other teacher used nonverbal and prosodic features to engage in a similar strategy. For example, Teacher H engaged in verbal framing by using terms such as *okay, then, now, next* to indicate *get ready to listen or to act* or *What I say next is important* (Sinclair & Coulthard, 1975). Teacher M, in contrast, signaled frames and frame shifts prosodically and nonverbally. The question, therefore, is not one of whether the teacher engages in a given behavior, but rather how this behavior occurs since differences in behaviors signal differences in demands. The difference in both frequency and type of occurrence indicates that children in the two classrooms are cued differently about context and focus shifts, and thus are exposed to different demands on their communicative ability.

The differences in demands and delivery can also be found in the use and signaling of cohesion and place holding for the two teachers. Teacher H, as indicated previously, uses direct statements such as *okay, now* to indicate it is still her turn, and the children are to stay with her between contexts. Teacher H uses these strategies to maintain interactional ties between events and to maintain the group. Teacher M achieves the same purpose by nonverbal cues (e.g., body position, interactional rhythm, head position, eye gaze, gesture). Thus, once again, children are cued differently and are faced with differences in demand of their communicative competence.

The qualitative differences in participation requirements are further reinforced when the strategy of continuance is considered. This strategy, often called **backchanneling** (Yngve, 1970), refers to the use of messages such as *uh huh, yes, mmm, and nonverbal head shakes,* to indicate *I'm listening* and *You can continue talking.* Teacher M uses this strategy primarily during News and Views; Teacher H, however, has no such context. The lack of context equivalence, therefore, raises the question of whether we can compare these teachers. The question of context equivalence (Florio & Shultz, 1979) led us to consider the match between language used, context, and teacher goals.

Teacher H's contexts contained more direct structuring than did Teacher M's. If we reconsider the contexts presented in Table 10.1, we find that two of the contexts for Teacher H included restructuring group as a goal and definition of the activity. These contexts are composed of a large amount of "control" strategies. Given the goals of these contexts, such strategies are expected since the teacher is moving children from one place to another. In contrast, Teacher M has two contexts in which student participation on a verbal basis is expected or required—review of rules for participation in News and Views, and News and Views itself. The teacher's goal in these contexts is to elicit student participation and student suggestions for participation rules. She does this by using question asking, continuances, and requests for confirmation and clarification.

This discussion suggests we need to consider the nature of language and the context in which it occurred, and that before we can compare across settings, we must consider whether the contexts within the settings to be compared are equivalent (Florio & Shultz, 1979). In the two classrooms we studied, the equivalent contexts were "greeting song." These can be defined as equivalent because the expectations for participation are similar, as is the structure of the context. The children were seated at the edge of the rug; the song was not taught directly (children learn to sing by singing with the teacher);

and children were expected to spontaneously join in. In these contexts, the demands for participation are similar.

The preceding discussion demonstrates that issues of similarities and differences between teachers and classrooms are complex. The pattern with regard to types of strategies used indicates that, in these two classrooms, differences in expectations for participation existed in the contexts studied, and that the teachers, in these contexts, had different interactional styles. However, when the nature of the context was considered, and the teacher's goals were reviewed, the differences were not unexpected. This discussion also suggests that although the two teachers had similar goals for participation and interaction on one level, they differed in how they achieved these goals. The delivery—or rather the paths—to the goals differed for the two teachers. This phenomenon suggests that although two teachers may have similar goals or stated expectations, they may not have similar social and communicative environments for children. Perhaps children in these classrooms are being socialized into different schooling processes; that is, the children are learning different ways of going to school and different requirements for becoming a member of the classroom society. This argument needs further exploration.

To test this hypothesis, studies need to be undertaken that explore communicative, social, and academic demands within and across other classroom contexts, between classrooms, between schools, and between different levels of schools. In other words, we need to investigate how children's learning in one context and one setting prepares them for participation in other settings.

Multiple Semantic Demands: Microanalysis of Discourse Structure

This section presents a detailed examination of the discourse structure of the context of Teacher M's lesson, referred to as "Phase I of the Day's News Lesson." The basis for the analysis is the videotape, transcripts, and structural maps developed in the prior sociolinguistic analysis of Teacher M's classroom (see Figure 10.1). The system of discourse analysis is adapted from Frederiksen's (1975) system of semantic representation. It is used here as a heuristic tool in order to make explicit the content of messages and the interrelationships among messages (such as conferences, inferences). The analysis of discourse structure builds on the sociolinguistic, ethnographic analysis that objectively specified the contextualization cues and conversational ties between messages. This information is used as a basis for making decisions about meaning. Part of the value of discourse analysis is the additional objectivity provided by the well-defined, explicit components that combine to form the propositional structure of the content of messages.

Before presenting the analysis, a brief discussion is necessary about the approach in general. A complete description of the system is presented in

Frederiksen (1975). (See Appendix A for a brief description.) The analysis focuses on propositional structure of the content of messages. The propositional structure is a network of propositions composed of concepts (e.g., John, ball, hit) that are connected by a set of relations (e.g., case relations: AGENT, OBJECT). The set of relations is finite. It includes: case relations, relations that describe events (e.g., time, goal, location, result, theme), attribute relations (e.g., member, category, attribute), and logical relations (e.g., conjunction, cause, condition). Logical relations operate on simple propositions to form more complex structures.

MESSAGE COMPLEXITY

By specifying the propositional structure completely, the internal complexities of messages can be shown (see Table A.1). For example, one kind of complexity is seen in the embedding of propositions within other propositions. The transcript line 095 (Table A.1) states: *We talked about the problem we have if five people talk at a time.* A much simplified representation shows that this sentence has three propositions embedded within it: (a) we talked; (b) THEME: (about) we have problem; (c) CONDITIONAL; (if) five people talk at a time.

This suggests a hypothesis that complex embeddings may be a source of misunderstandings where only a part of the message is interpreted correctly. Although the hypothesis remains untested in this chapter, the system we are presenting has the potential for investigating and testing it.

Another type of complexity is presented in the form of inferences expected of the participants. Ellipsis is a relatively common kind of conversational inference. For example, on transcript line 102 in Table A.1, Peter says loudly, *One at a time.* He is answering the question (line 100) *is there a way we could do it so we could hear each person?* We and the teacher infer that Peter is using ellipsis to mean, *We could do it one at a time.* Peter is also making proform substitution inferences that *it* in the question refers to doing "News and Views," and that *do* refers to talking during this time, not to other actions such as sitting down or handraising. He has also answered not the form of the question, but the intent; that is, **what** *is a way we could do it?* The evidence that Peter inferred both the correct intent and the correct referents for *do it* is that his answer was confirmed and selected by the teacher.

SYNTHESIS OF FINDINGS: CONTEXT, THEMATIC, AND SOCIAL TIES

Conversational structure and flow are also clarified by a propositional analysis of discourse by pointing out thematic ties between propositions and social ties as signals for group participation. Table 10.6 is derived from the propositional analysis. It illustrates how three types of ties connect different parts of the conversation.

The **context ties** (Column 2) describe the overall flow of the lesson and the functions different parts seem to play in it. The context ties include more global level functions such as P:009, which establishes a discussion context, and subparts within a context, as in P:010 or P:020 where the discussion is extended to listening and a solution to the problem is accepted.

The relation between P:009 and P:010 is important to note because first, it signals an extension of the "problem" to include both talking and listening; second, it is a yes–no question—the first of this lesson segment. It serves to shift the role of students from listener to participant. As shown in Column 2 (and continued in this category on the right half of Table 10.6), this pair of propositions serves to open the new discussion part of the context.

The discussion contains several teacher questions addressed to the class as a whole and then to an individual (Peter). The propositions P:012 through P:016 demonstrate the problem of everyone talking at once, because the whole class responds. The necessity for Peter to talk loudly and the teacher's request for repetition also demonstrate the problem at hand. The discussion ends with P:020, when the teacher suggests they try Peter's idea.

The final propositions (P:020–022) set the stage for the new context, the actual beginning of News and Views, while simultaneously closing the discussion part of the context. Proposition 001, although only a fragment, served the same purpose at the beginning of this segment. It marked the end of the Spanish song and the start of a new activity.

The **thematic ties** (Column 3) describe conceptual links between propositions. They parallel the context ties and provide a rough validation of both the flow within contexts and breaks between them. The THEME relation introduced in P:002, *talked about . . . News and Views* is tied via CONJUNC-TION relations, *and*, to the THEMES in P:004 and P:005 (and restated in P:009). Proposition 009 is tied to P:010 via an inferred IDENTITY relation: *the problem if five people talk at a time* is the same as the *problem with listening.* And, *problem with listening* is later identified in, and thus tied to, P:014, *can't hear*, which is also tied to P:015, 017, 019, and 020.

The thematic ties can also confirm where breaks in the coherence of the lesson occur, as in P:003 ("Shauna") and James's interruption at P:006–008. These propositions do not have thematic ties to the rest of the lesson. The teacher's suggestion, *Let's try your idea*, is also not tied to the **content** of the previous discussion, and marks a shift to complete this segment and begin the actual News and Views lesson. It is however, **structurally** tied, because *your idea* functions as a pronoun to substitute for Peter's *one at a time.* Thus, it is coherent in a way the interruptions were not.

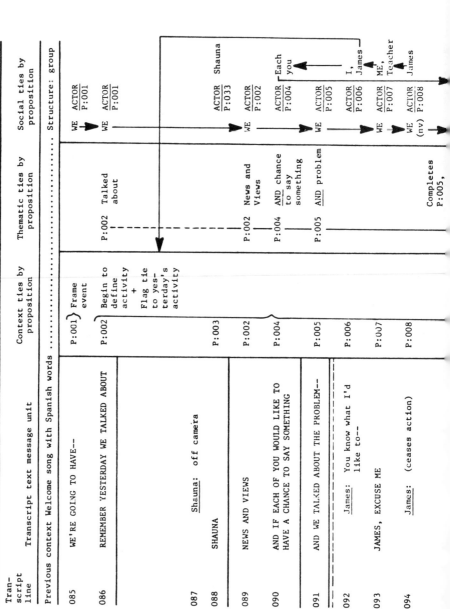

Table 10.6

Synthesis of Findings: Contextual, Thematic, and Social Ties (Teacher M. Establish Rules for News and Views)

Transcript line	Transcript text message unit	Context ties by proposition	Thematic ties by proposition	Social ties by proposition	Structure: group
Previous context Welcome song with Spanish words					
085	WE'RE GOING TO HAVE--	P:001 } Frame event		WE → ACTOR P:001	
086	REMEMBER YESTERDAY WE TALKED ABOUT	P:002 Begin to define activity + Flag tie to yesterday's activity	P:002 Talked about	WE ACTOR P:001	
087	Shauna: off camera				
088	SHAUNA	P:003		WE ACTOR P:033	Shauna
089	NEWS AND VIEWS	P:002	P:002 News and Views	WE ACTOR P:002	
090	AND IF EACH OF YOU WOULD LIKE TO HAVE A CHANCE TO SAY SOMETHING	P:004	P:004 AND chance to say something	WE ACTOR P:004	Each you
091	AND WE TALKED ABOUT THE PROBLEM--	P:005	P:005 AND problem	WE ACTOR P:005	
092	James: You know what I'd like to--	P:006		WE ACTOR P:006	I, James
093	JAMES, EXCUSE ME	P:007		WE ACTOR P:007	ME, Teacher
094	James: (ceases action)	P:008	Completes P:005,	WE (nv) ACTOR P:008	James

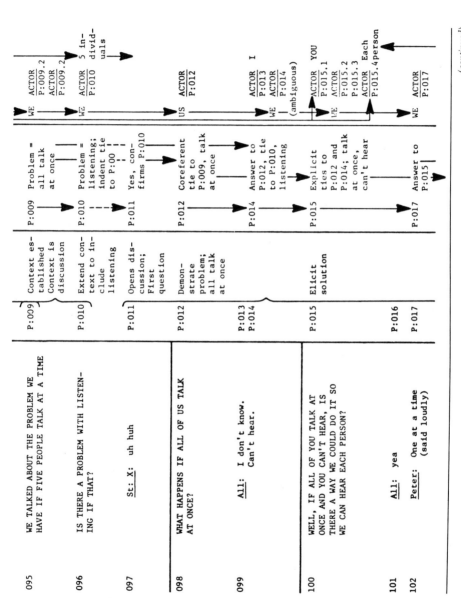

095	WE TALKED ABOUT THE PROBLEM WE HAVE IF FIVE PEOPLE TALK AT A TIME	P:009	Context established Context is discussion	P:009	Problem = all talk at once
096	IS THERE A PROBLEM WITH LISTEN-ING IF THAT?	P:010	Extend context to include listening	P:010	Problem = listening; indent tie to P:00
097	St: X: uh huh	P:011	Opens discussion; First question	P:011	Yes, confirms P:010
098	WHAT HAPPENS IF ALL OF US TALK AT ONCE?	P:012	Demonstrate problem; all talk at once	P:012	Coreferent tie to P:009, talk at once
099	All: I don't know. Can't hear.	P:013 P:014		P:014	Answer to P:012, tie to P:010, listening
100	WELL, IF ALL OF YOU TALK AT ONCE AND YOU CAN'T HEAR, IS THERE A WAY WE COULD DO IT SO WE CAN HEAR EACH PERSON?	P:015	Elicit solution	P:015	Explicit ties to P:012 and P:014; talk at once, can't hear
101	All: yea	P:016			
102	Peter: One at a time (said loudly)	P:017		P:017	Answer to P:015

ACTOR column:

WE — ACTOR P:009.2 / P:009.2 — 5 individuals
WE — ACTOR P:010
US — ACTOR P:012
WE — ACTOR P:013 / ACTOR P:014 (ambiguous) — I
WE — ACTOR P:015.1 — YOU / ACTOR P:015.2 / ACTOR P:015.3 / ACTOR P:015.4 person — I / Each person
WE — ACTOR P:017

(continued)

211

Table 10.6 (continued)

Transcript line	Transcript text message unit	Context ties by proposition	Thematic ties by proposition	Social ties by proposition
103	WHAT DID YOU SAY PETER?	P:018 Teacher selects solution	P:018 Request repetition	ACTOR You, Peter / P:018
104	Peter: One at a time (said loudly)	P:019	P:019 Repeats P:017	WE → US → WE ; ACTOR I, Peter / P:017 P:018
105	LET'S TRY YOUR IDEA.	P:020 Teacher accepts solution	P:020 Tie to P:015, Your idea = one at a time	ACTOR P:020
106	MAY WE TRY YOUR IDEA?	P:021 Obtain permission	P:021 Tie to P:020, coreferent	ACTOR Your, Peter / P:021
107	Peter: (shakes head yes)	P:022 Granted; close context	P:022 Answer to P:021	ACTOR Peter / P:022

The **social ties** are shown in the right-hand column of Table 10.6. They are based on the coreferences that occur in the propositional structure among speakers and addressees. A coreference occurs when a term or terms refer to a single object (Teacher M, the teacher, she). The "we" and "us" actors shown in Table 10.6, refer to the whole class including the teacher, and form co-reference ties among many of these propositions. The "we" ties are illustrated by arrows on the left; "I" ties are shown to the right.

The shifts between the "we" (group mode) and the "I" (individual mode) form a parallel lesson to the one discussed before under context and thematic ties. The social lesson for these children involves learning how to function as a group and as an individual within the group; an idea related to, but more general than, the problem of "everyone talking at once."

The teacher in P:001 (*We're going . . .*) and P:002 (*we talked . . .*) set the group mode. On line 087 (Table 10.6), Shauna, functioning in an indi-vidual mode, is required to join the group. This reinforces the group mode for the class. In P:004, *each of you* focuses on the individual within the group. The teacher moves back to *we* in P:005, but before this is completed, James interrupts. From James's perspective, he has read the *each of you* statement in that context as a signal to begin News and Views and is bidding for his turn. He will be first because of his placement in the circle when News and Views begins. James is attending not only to P:004 (*each of you*), but also to the previous day's context evoked in P:002 (*Yesterday . . . News and Views*). This is not a deliberate interruption by James, but rather a failure to read completely the available social, thematic, and contextualization cues. Specifically, he missed the teacher's shift back into "group" in P:005 (*we talked . . .*), and misread the present context as News and Views instead of *how to talk during News and Views*.

The teacher, as leader-member of group, denies his bid and continues P:009 in the "we" mode. James's behavior shows his compliance and returns to the "we" mode. The interchange with James also illustrates the expected norms for group participation to the other children.

Beginning with P:009, there is a series of shifts between group and individual. Proposition 009 contains dual components: group (the "we" prob-lem) and individual (if five "individuals" talk at once). These components function to maintain group identity and to preserve the role of the individual within the group. This and similar messages (P:020, P:021, P:022) also set the stage for the next context, the actual News and Views lesson, in which these rules for participation are followed—the rules that were elicited, negotiated, and also demonstrated during this segment of the lesson.

The synthesis of findings presented here highlights the complexity faced by teachers and students in structuring and participating in instructional con-versations. For children to participate appropriately, they must understand the cues available to them in three domains—contextual, thematic, and social. That is, they need to know what the nature of the activity (context) is, what thematic information is being exchanged, and what the social nature of the group is at any given moment. We argue that failure to read all of these demands may lead to inappropriate behavior (as in James's bid) or miscommunication.

Conclusion

The multiple analyses presented in this chapter indicated how complex the study of teaching–learning processes can be from the researcher's perspective. Fortunately, participants in these processes cope with the complexity as a matter of their everyday lives in kindergarten. We have shown that children produce observable signs of comprehension by following the rules or norms for behavior. Over time, analysis presented in the previous sections showed that children are sensitive to implicit shifts in expectations, are able to extract norms for behavior from the ongoing conversations between teacher and students, and are able to "read" the contextual, social, and thematic demands of unfolding instructional contexts.

The analysis also showed that children in different classrooms are faced with varying demands for participation and learning. From the teacher's perspective, we saw that although two teachers may have similar goals, the ways in which they implement these goals produce differing social, contextual, and thematic demands on students. The question of teacher effectiveness, then, must be one that looks at whether teachers meet their goals, the goals of the individual school, and the goals of the school's community. Although the analysis presented here focused on a microanalysis of classroom demands and expectations, future analyses need to explore the demands across classrooms within the school, demands within the community, the state, and so on. In other words, this analysis needs to be placed within other analyses of broader and broader contexts. However, by beginning with the classroom, we are concentrating on the everyday life of the teacher and children as they engage in teaching–learning as a communicative process.

Appendix A: The Propositional Structure

BASIC CONCEPTS OF DISCOURSE ANALYSIS

The system for discourse analysis used in this appendix has been adapted from that of Frederiksen (1975). Although the notation here is simplified, the definitions have not been changed. The initial step in discourse analysis is the identification of units called **propositions.** These are composed of a finite set of RELATIONS that connect and operate on an open set of possible concepts. Relations include the following:

Case relations: agent, patient, object, instrument, dative

Relations describing events: source, result, theme, goal, time, location, manner

Relations describing objects: number, category, attribute

Logical relations: conjunction, disjunction, cause, identity, conditional, equivalent, ordinal

The first three types of relations occur within a proposition. Logical relations usually join two or more propositions, although conjunction and disjunction may occur within a proposition as well.

The sentence *John hit the ball* is a proposition composed of two relations, AGENT, OBJECT: and three concepts, John, hit, ball:

P:sample   John, AGENT, hit, OBJECT, ball

Definitions of these relations can be found in Frederiksen (1975). The purpose of this discussion is not a full explanation of the system, but rather a brief description of the notation and major components in order that the propositional structure can be understood. It is important to understand that the propositional structure is a heuristic device for representing the meaning of this segment of instructional conversation. This is not necessarily a unique representation. Other possible ways exist to represent this information using this system or other systems (Kintsch, 1974). However, the value lies in developing a systematic, explicit, well-defined way to represent meaning in order to examine aspects of it that are of interest, such as complexity, inferences, and coreference ties.

Several notational symbols and concepts are presented:

UPPER CASE LETTERS	Represent relations
lower case letters	Represent concepts
AGENT	Relation connecting the actor and resultive actions, which are those having a result, for example, *I broke the window.*
PATIENT	Relation connecting actor and action when the action is a process, for example, *We were talking, I like candy.* Abbreviated as PAT.
THEME	Refers to the content of a cognitive action, e.g., *I thought about **this sentence,** or of cer-tain cognitive objects, for example, *I read a book about gardening.* This is not related to or defined as the "theme" of a lesson or conversation.

Table A.1
Prepositional Analysis of Lesson Segment

Tran- script line	Transcript text	Propo- sition number	Propositional structure
085	We're going to have . . .	001	We, PAT, have OBJ, < > . . . .
086	Remember yesterday we talked about	002 002.1	(class), PAT, remember, THEME, [2.1] we, PAT, talk, THEME, < >, TIME, yesterday
088	Shauna—	003	Shauna, (PAT, < >)
089	News and Views	002.1	News and Views
090	And if each of you would like to have a chance to say something	004 004.1 004.2	[002 THEME], CONJ, each, PAT, like, OBJ, [4.1], COND, < >, chance, CAT, [4.2] you, AGT, say, OBJ, something
091	And we talked about the problem	005	[002 THEME], CONJ, we, PAT, talk, THEME, problem
092	(James) You know what I d like to—	006 006.1	You, PAT, know, THEME, [6.1] I, PAT, like, OBJ, (?)
093	James, excuse me.	007 007.1	(Teacher, PAT, want, THEME, [7.1]) (James, PAT-neg, talk)
094	(James, nonverbal) Stops actions and talk	008	(James, PAT-neg, < >)
095	We talked about the problem we have if five people talk at a time.	009 009.1 009.2	(repeat 005) We, PAT, talk, THEME, [9.1] [We, PAT, have, OBJ, problem], COND [9.2] People, NUM, five, PAT, talk, MANNER, at once
096	Is there a problem with listening if that?	010	[(9.1 problem, IDENT), problem, CAT, [< >, PAT, listen]], ?, IF, [9.2]

097	(Student) Uh huh.	011	(yes), (Problem, CAT, [< >, PAT, listen])
098	What happens if all of us talk at once?	012	[(?), RELATION, (? happens)], IF, [12.1]
		012.1	[all of us, PAT, talk, MANNER, at once]
099	(Whole class) I don't know. Can't hear.	013	I, PAT-neg, know, THEME, [012]
		014	< >, PAT, neg, hear, OBJ, < >
		014.1	([problem 010], IDENT, [012], IDENT, [014])
100	Well, if all of you talk at once and you can't hear, is there a way we could do it so we can hear each person?	015	[12.1], IF, [14], TIME, when, [15.1]
		015.1	((class), PAT, do, OBJ, News and Views)
		015.2	way, CAT, [15.1], MANNER, [15.3]
		015.3	We, PAT, hear, OBJ, [15.4]
		015.4	Each person, (AGT, say, DAT, us, RESULT, < >)
		015.5	[015.2], PAT, exist, ?
101	(All) Yes.	016	([015.2], PAT, exists)
102	(Peter) One at a time. (said loudly)	017	(< >, PAT, talk), MANNER, one at a time
103	What did you say Peter?	018	Peter:You, AGT, say, DAT, (us), RESULT, what?
104	(Peter) One at a time. (said loudly)	019	[017, repeated]
105	Let's try your idea.	020	(teacher, PAT, want, THEME, [20.1])
		020.1	(class), PAT, try, GOAL, [20.2]
		020.2	[Peter, PAT, has, OBJ, idea], (CAT, News and Views)
		020.3	[020.2], IDENT, [017]
106	May we try your idea?	021	[Peter:You, AGT, allow, DAT, class, RESULT, [21.1], ?]
		021.1	[class, PAT, try, GOAL, [020.3]]
107	(Peter) Shakes head, yes.	022	Yes:[021]

End of Phase I of News and Views segment

CONDITIONAL	COND, a logical statement composed of two propositions, the antecedent and the consequent. It does not contrapose because all the antecedent conditions on which the validity of the consequent depends are not stated, for example, *I will open the umbrella if it rains.*
IF	Material conditional, where antecedent conditions are fully specified, for example, *Only if it rains will I open the umbrella.*
P:001	Propositions are numbered from P:001 to P:n. Each sentence receives a new whole number. Complex, embedded propositions receive sub-numbers, P:001.1, P:001.2, etc.
< >	Refers to an "open slot," a part of the structure which was not stated or implied in the transcript. *The ball was hit* contains an open slot in the AGENT position, since who or what hit the ball was not stated: < >, AGENT, hit, OBJECT, ball.
( )	Indicates an inference, and may include all or part of a proposition. *Remember yesterday we talked* contains an inferred PATIENT: (listener), PATIENT, remember, THEME, [we talked], TIME, yesterday.
[ ]	Indicates that a proposition is embedded in a concept slot of another proposition, as in the preceding example. This shows where complexities occur.
?	Indicates that a statement is a question. Wh-questions typically query the identity of a slot in the proposition. *Who hit the ball?* — ?, AGENT, hit, OBJ, ball; *What did John do to the ball?* — John, AGENT, ?, OBJ, ball; *Why did John hit the ball?* — [?], CAUSE, John, AGENT, hit, OBJ, ball. Yes–no questions query the truth of a statement, and are represented: ? [statement].

Several modifications have been made in this system that make it different from Frederiksen's (1975) system. The obvious change on the surface is that Frederiksen's system was presented as a network, whereas this is more clearly a list of propositions. This is largely a notational difference; the same concepts are presented in two different formats. This propositional list is easier to represent, and is thus preferred in this context.

Less obvious are the simplifications that were made. Tense information (past, present, future) and aspect information (inceptive, cessive, continuative, habitual) are not included in this representation. Also, Frederiksen broke down several relations into subtypes that we have simplified into a single relation here: OBJECT, DATIVE, LOCATION, and TIME. The level of detail available in Frederiksen's (1975) system was not really needed in these areas for our purposes. Their simplification did not lose critical information, but did make charts easier to read.

References

Barker, R., & Wright, H. *One boy's day.* Hamden, Conn.: Archon, 1966.

Barnes, D., & Todd, F. *Communication and learning in small groups.* London: Routledge & Kegan Paul, 1977.

Berger, P. L., & Luckmann, T. *The social construction of reality.* New York: Doubleday, 1967.

Birdwhistell, R. Some discussioin of ethnography, theory, and method. In J. Brockman (Ed.), *About Bateson.* New York: E. P. Dutton, 1977.

Blumer, H. *Symbolic interationism: Perspective and method.* Englewood Cliffs, N.J.: Prentice Hall, 1969.

Bussis, A. M., Chittenden, E. A., & Amarel, M. *Beyond surface curriculum.* Boulder, Co.: Westview Press, 1976.

Conlin, S. M. *Teacher as researcher: Teacher's view of classroom events and research process.* Paper presented at the American Educational Research Association meetings, Boston, 1980.

Cook-Gumperz, J. *Social control and socialization: A study of class differences in the language of maternal control.* Boston: Routledge & Kegan Paul, 1973.

Cook-Gumperz, J. Persuasive talk: The social organization of children's talk. In J. Green & C. Wallat (Eds.), *Ethnography and language in educational settings.* Norwood, N.J.: Ablex, 1981.

Cook-Gumperz, J., & Gumperz, J. J. Contex in children's speech. In J. Cook-Gumperz & J. Gumperz (Eds.), *Papers on language and context.* Berkeley: University of Califomia Language Behavior Research Laboratory, 1976.

Cook-Gumperz, J., & Green, J. L. Children's sense of story: Influences on children's storytelling ability. In D. Tannen (Ed.), *Spoken and written language.* Norwood, N.J.: Ablex, in press.

Corsaro, W. Entering the child's word: Research strategies for field entry and data collection. In J. Green & C. Wallat (Eds.), *Ethnography and language in educational settings.* Norwood, N.J.: Ablex, 1981.

Elkind, D. *Child and society.* New York: Oxford University Press, 1979.

Erickson, F. Some approaches to inquiry in school-community ethnography. *Anthropology and Education Quarterly*, 1977, VIII(2), 58–69.

Erickson, F., & Shultz, J. When is a context?: Some issues and methods in the analysis of social competence. *The Quarterly Newsletter of the Institute for Comparative Human Development*, 1977, 1(2), 5–10. Also reprinted in J. Green & C. Wallat (Eds.), *Ethnography and language in educational settings.* Norwood, N.J.: Ablex, 1981.

Florio, S., & Shultz, J. Social competence at home and at school. *Theory into Practice*, 1979, 18(4), 234–243.

Frederiksen, C. Representing logical and semantic structure of knowledge acquired from discourse. *Cognitive Psychology*, 1975, *7*(7), 371–485.

Frederiksen, C. H. Inference in preschool children's conversations: A cognitive perspective. In J. L. Green & C. Wallat (Eds.), *Ethnography and language in educational settings*. Norwood, N.J.: Ablex, 1981.

Glaser, B., & Strauss, A. *The discovery of grounded theory*. Chicago: Aldine, 1967.

Goffman, E. *Frame analysis*. New York: Harper Colophon Books, 1974.

Green, J. L. *Pedagogical style differences as related to comprehension: Grades one through three*. Unpublished dissertation, University of California, Berkeley, 1977.

Green, J., & Harker, J. Reading to children: A sociolinguistic perspective. In J. Langer & M. T. Smith-Burke (Eds.), *Reader meets author: Bridging the gap*. Newark, N.J.: International Reading Association, in press.

Green, J., & Stoffan, M. *Living in kindergarten*. Paper presented at the American Educational Research Association meetings, Boston, 1980.

Green, J. L., & Wallat, C. What is an instructional context? An exploratory analysis of conversational shifts across time. In O. Garnica & M. King (Eds.), *Language, children and society*. New York: Pergamon Press, 1979.

Green, J. L., & Wallat, C. Mapping instructional conversations. In J. Green & C. Wallat (Eds.), *Ethnography and language in educational settings*. Norwood, N.J.: Albex, 1981.

Gumperz, J. J. *Teaching as a linguistic process*. Paper presented at the National Institute for Education Conference on Language in the Classroom, Washington, D.C., 1975.

Gumperz, J. J. Language, communication and public negotiation, In P. Sanday (Ed.), *Anthropology and the public interest*. New York: Academic Press, 1976.

Gumperz, J., & Herasimchuk, E. The conversational analysis of social meaning: A study of classroom interaction. In R. W. Shuy (Ed.), *Sociolinguistics: Current trends and prospects, 23rd annual round-table*. Washington, D.C.: Georgetown University Press, 1973.

Gumperz, J. J., & Hymes, D. (Eds.). *Directions in sociolinguistics*. New York: Holt, Rinehart & Winston, 1972.

Gumperz, J. J., & Tannen, D. Individual and social differences in language use. In C. F. Fillmore et al. (Eds.), *Individual differences in language ability and language behavior*. New York: Academic Press, 1979.

Hymes, D. *Foundations in sociolinguistics*. Philadelphia: University of Pennsylvania, 1974.

Kendon, A., Harris, R. M., & Key, M. R. *Organization of behavior in face-to-face interaction*. The Hague: Mouton Publishers, 1975.

Kintsch, W. *The representation of meaning in memory*. Hillsdale, N.J.: Lawrence Erlbaum, 1974.

Knott, G. Nonverbal communicating during early childhood. *Theory into Practice*, 1979, *18*(4), 226–233.

Lutz, F. Ethnography: The holistic approach to understanding schooling. In J. Green & C. Wallat (Eds.) *Ethnography and language in educational settings*. Norwood, N.J.: Ablex, 1981.

Magoon, J. Constructivist research. *Review of Educational Research*, 1977, *47*(4), 651–693.

Mehan, J. *Learning lessons*. Cambridge: Harvard University Press, 1979.

Mehan, H., Cazden, C., Coles, L., Fisher, S., & Maroules, N. *The social organization of classroom lessons*. LaJolla: University of San Diego, Center for Human Information Processing, 1976.

Mehan, H., & Wood, H. *The reality of ethnomethodology*. New York: John Wiley and Sons, 1975.

Merritt, M. *Service-like events during individual work time and their contribution to the nature of communication in primary classrooms* (Final Report for Grant No. NIE G-78-0081). Washington, D.C.: Center for Applied Linguistics, March 1980.

Merritt, M., & Humphrey, F. Teacher, talk, and task: Communicative demands during individualized instruction time. *Theory into Practice*, 1979, *18*(4), 298–303.

Sacks, H., Schegloff, E., & Jefferson, G. A simplest systematics for the organization of turntaking for conversation. *Language*, 1974, *50*(4) (Part 1), 696–735.

Sanday, P. *Anthropology and education*. The Hague: Mouton, 1973.

Sevigny, M. Triangulated inquiry: A methodology for the analysis of classroom interaction. In J. Green & C. Wallat (Eds.), *Ethnography and language in educational settings*. Norwood, N.J.: Ablex, 1981.

Sinclair, J. M., & Coulthard, R. M. *Toward an analysis of discourse*. New York: Oxford University Press, 1975.

Spradley, J. *Participant observation*. New York: Holt, Rinehart & Winston, 1980.

Tannen, D. *A theory of conversational style*. Paper prepared for presentation at the conference on Psycholinguistic Models of Production: An Interdisciplinary Workshop, University of Kassel, West Germany, July 13–17, 1980.

Wallat, C., & Green, J. Social rules and communicative contexts in kindergarten. *Theory into Practice*, 1979, *18*(4), 275–284.

Wallat, C., & Green, J. Construction of social norms. In K. Borman (Ed.), *Socialization of children in a changing society*. Hillsdale, N.J.: Lawrence Erlbaum, in press.

Wallat, C., Green, J., Conlin, S., & Haramis, M. Issues related to action research in the classroom: The teacher–researcher team. In J. Green & C. Wallat (Eds.), *Ethnography and language in educational settings*. Norwood, N.J.: Ablex, 1981.

Yngve, V. *On getting a word in edgewise*. In papers from the sixth regional meeting of the Chicago Linguistics Society, 1970.

11
Distributing and Directing Attention in Primary Classrooms[1]

MARILYN MERRITT

A premise of this book is that a major part of the essence of classroom education inheres in the teaching and learning that takes place through the process of teacher–student communication. Two truncated examples might be when a teacher gives an explanation of a mathematical operation while students listen, and when a student asks a teacher how to spell a word, to which the teacher responds. Clearly, for such teacher explanations or student queries to result in teaching and learning there must be **mutual engagement** (see Merritt, in press) of teacher and student(s). If we grant that teachers and students are not so mutually engaged every minute of class time (for example, when students are silently reading or doing other kinds of seatwork), the question arises as to how mutual engagement is achieved. How does a participant signal wanting engagement, how is it secured, and how is it released?

Two facts about classrooms immediately become salient: (a) The roles of teachers and students are different, that is, asymmetrical; teachers are able to initiate talk with students at almost any time, but not vice versa. (b) The teacher's time is a scarce commodity; there is one teacher and many students, all of whom may want the teacher's attention at the same time. This chapter offers a conceptualization of how these facts interact with two features of human interaction generally:

[1] The work reported on here was supported in part by Grant No. 7800081 of the National Institute of Education, for which I was principal investigator.

223

1. Mutual engagement requires joint focus of attention within the frame of the same (for all participants) **vector of activity** (Merritt, in press); a vector of activity being conceptualized as a line of action engaged in by one or more persons.
2. Individual resources for communicative involvement are somewhat flexible, in that the modality resource of the "whole person" in a face-to-face setting can be "split" into nonverbal and verbal modalities, depending on the enactive demands of the vector of activity.

The investigative approach taken in this study relies on the selection of a naturally occurring locus of observation in which mutual engagement takes place. Such a locus is the **servicelike event**. Typically, servicelike events are interactional segments during which a student who is not currently working directly with the teacher in some way solicits the attention and "help" of the teacher (Merritt, 1979a, 1979b; Merritt & Humphrey, 1980). These are thus student-initiated engagements. These events occur most frequently during individualized instructional time, when the teacher is working with only one student or a small group of students.

The analysis reported here grows out of the aim to contextualize servicelike events in terms of the interactional demands and resources of primary classrooms generally. The educational theme of this chapter is the teacher's distribution of attention among all the students in the class and the teacher's direction of students' attention among all the possible vectors of activity in the classroom. After introducing the data base in the next section, the analysis will be developed under the headings of situational demands for distributing attention, communicative resources, directing attention, and ritual parameters and stylistic options. A recurrent theme is the **dual** (or multiple) **processing** and **dual participation** that seems to be required by competent students as well as competent teachers.

Data Base

The data chosen for analysis were a collection of audio- and videotapes (about 450 half-hours) compiled from a private, upper middle-class, urban primary school over the course of one school year. As part of a large study of children's functional language development and education in the early years, students and teachers had been observed in a variety of natural situations of social interaction. Ten classrooms were studied, 2 each at the 5 grade levels of nursery through third; the ages of the children ranged from 4 through 9 years. In each classroom there were about 20 students—half girls and half boys—and one female teacher with a resource specialist or aide occasionally present at the kindergarten through third-grade levels, and a second teacher always present at the nursery level. All of the participants in the study were English speakers. These data were extensively analyzed from a number of perspectives as part of the original study (Shuy & Griffin, 1981). Nevertheless, the quality and richness of the data has provided opportunities for further studies (see also Cahir, 1978; Humphrey, 1979).

The servicelike event study is based on a subset of the original data bank. For all 10 classrooms, videotapes were reviewed and segments selected for further analysis from all 5 of the original taping periods, which were designed to represent key periods over the course of the school year. This resulted in a total subset of about 50 half-hour videotapes.

The examples given in this chapter are all taken from verbatim transcripts of selected portions of these 50 tapes. It should be kept in mind that this chapter is primarily conceptual and descriptive. The focus is on transitions in the teacher's involvement with one child or activity to another. The thrust of the investigation has been to develop an interactional conceptualization of what happens when teacher involvement shifts—one that allows us to describe how the shift takes place and what some of the consequences may be.

Further, as with almost all naturalistic data, the examples are illustrative of much more than the text describes. Thus, one example may be discussed in terms of two points, but also be illustrative of a third point, which in the analysis is demonstrated by another example. Ideally, a collection of examples centered around one locus of observation should lend a resonating quality to the overall analysis.

Situational Demands for Distributing Attention

From the perspective of any individual, for an ideal model of participation, we might suppose that at any point in time each person uses the basic whole person modality to involve him- or herself completely in a single vector of activity. Such a model is, of course, more fantasy than reality for either students or teachers. In a busy classroom with many activities going on, teachers are rarely, if ever, free to involve themselves completely in one activity. Though they will ordinarily have one main or official vector of activity, the responsibility that teachers have for what goes on generally means they must constantly be attuned to happenings outside the main activity. Situational demands thus require teachers' **processing** of more than one activity even if they are **involved** in only one.

Further, given the fact that teachers' attention and involvement are probably the most valued "commodity" for the conduct of any classroom activity, they must be concerned with how involved attention is parcelled out among the student participants (see Cazden, 1974). Turn taking during sessions of whole-group activity is not the only mechanism for distributing teacher involvement.

Most teachers probably try to equalize involvement time "structurally" by organizing reading groups, math groups, and so on, such that each group is scheduled to receive an equal amount of teacher time. Although this seems like a good strategy for parceling out teacher involvement in group activities, recent work by Eder (Chapter 12, this volume) and McDermott and Gospodinoff (1978) has pointed out systematic problems in providing equitable teacher time for high and low ability groups.

Teacher involvement in individual tasks is usually less structured. Almost inevitably students solicit tutorial instruction, evaluation, and procedural guidance as they need it, and most teachers probably rely on students to make their needs known. These occurrences are servicelike events. Additionally, during periods of seatwork activity teachers often initiate individual contacts with students, usually seeking out those who rarely initiate talk as well as those the teacher expects to need help academically.

During these periods of non-whole-group activity, situational demands often require **students** as well as teachers to **process** more than one vector of activity even though each independently working child is **involved** in only one. There are at least two reasons for this: One is that the teacher wants and needs to have access to every child's attention, with minimum effort, more or less whenever the teacher demands it. Thus, although children may be expected to work independently and be "on task" and "involved with their work," they are also expected to pick up on the teacher's request for focused attention at any time. Of course, teachers are aware that for children to become sufficiently involved in their work to be really on task they must tune out a great deal of what is perceptually available to them. Children must learn the modalities through which they are to channel their participation and the relative "communicative loading [Merritt, 1979b]" of the entire repertoire of modalities involved in classroom communication.

Thus, to get children's attention teachers develop special communicative devices that intrude on those modalities the children have learned to work in. The most straightforward technique is for the teacher to suddenly speak in a much louder voice—usually with a discourse marker and terms of address (*All right, boys and girls; Okay, now, class*). But many teachers also develop idiosyncratic devices such as turning off the lights, shouting out *heads up, eyes up,* or *freeze* (see Cahir, 1978; Shultz, Florio, & Erickson, 1980).

The second reason that dual processing is a necessary feature of students' "working independently in the classroom" has to do with servicelike events, with getting help or soliciting monitoring behavior from the teacher. Frequently, when a child works independently, the nature of the task is such that the child may need help midway through (e.g., how to spell a word) or need to have his or her work checked over for mistakes (especially with math assignments). Exactly when these needs arise will be independent of what others are doing, including the teacher.

Needing the teacher does not guarantee the teacher will be responsive to a child's request at just that moment, however. The teacher will ordinarily **want** to be responsive to such a request whenever it comes. However, if the teacher is already involved with other students (ordinarily one or a small group of students) he or she will also want to preserve the integrity of the vector of this activity when the "outside" child's request comes.

In fact, one generalization that seems to hold for our data is the following: **Once teachers have actually engaged in a particular vector of activity, they will aim to preserve the integrity of that vector of activity and seem to "feel obliged" to stay within that vector of activity until it is resolved or until some degree of ritual closure has been achieved with respect to interrupting or departing from it.** The integrity of the vector does not inhere in the teacher's involvement or engagement, of course, but rather in the **students'** involvement. In many cases, however, this seems to require the teacher's coinvolvement.

This means that the teacher may or may not feel able to respond immediately to "outside" demands for involved attention. In our classroom data, children—in the older primary grades especially—are expected to share some of the responsibility for equitable distribution of the teacher's involved attention. The data illustrate how interruptions are not fair to the student(s) with whom the teacher is individually working and how outside students should avoid asking for help when the teacher is already busy. In one third-grade class that was observed, the teacher initiated a special class meeting about the problem of interrupting the teacher. She points out that interruptions are not fair to the student(s) with whom the teacher is working and that other students should avoid asking for help when she is already occupied. The data also allude to the **dual processing** expected of competent students. Students are most desirably expected to **wait until the teacher is free** and to **not just wait**, but rather to **do something else while waiting.**

Ideally, no teacher would ever need to divert attention from the vector of activity in which he or she is involved. However, our data show there are many times when the situational reality is otherwise. Thus we might ask, "What are some reasons for a teacher to attend immediately to a child who is not currently in the teacher's vector of activity?" The answer to this question depends not only on whether the child solicits the teacher's attention, but more so on why attention is needed. The teacher may want to return a child's first greeting of the day. There may be an emergency such as an injury or spilled paint, a display of misinformation, a brief inquiry, a "return" for clarification, checking, or direction in the next phase of activity, or simply a display that a child may not continue the designated vector of activity without attention. For example:

1. **Baking Session. Nursery. January. Mid Morning.** (Several children are at a table with the teacher who is letting various ones of them stir and "have a taste." Several children have been clamoring to be next, but not Brian who is farthest away from the teacher and seems to be starting to "act silly.")[2]

> TEACHER: *Let's let David have his turn now, and then somebody else can do it.*
>
> HOLLY: *It's **snack** time.*
>
> BRIAN: [to H] *No, it's not snack time, it's* (crackers) *time.*
>
> BRIAN: [pretends to spoon flour out of a bowl]
>
> BRIAN: *No, it's, it's flour time.*
>
> ALEXA: [to T] *Then can I {do it?}*
>
> → TEACHER: *{Brian,} do you want to help cook, in a minute?*

Given the fact that exceptions are made and teachers do sometimes attend to outside solicitations when they are busy, another question comes to mind: Why may a teacher not immediately attend to a child who is actively soliciting attention? Some reasons are that the teacher did not hear or notice the solicitation, the teacher may anticipate the child's reason for wanting attention does not really require or deserve attention, or the teacher will have to take too much time away from the current activity to address the child's problem. The major factor in not immediately attending to a child's active solicitation seems to be the degree of jeopardy to the teacher's primary vector of activity. This depends both on the anticipated nature of the soliciting child's request (especially, how long it is likely to take) and the phase of the teacher-involved vector of activity. This phase feature was also noted by Shultz (1976) in his analysis of a tic-tac-toe game and in various recent analyses by Erickson and Shultz (1977, 1981).

It also seems clear that teachers try to correct children's soliciting behavior, and in many cases make a decision to attend or not attend to a child partially on the basis of whether the child is compliant with teacher constraints on soliciting behavior. In the following example, the teacher asked if anyone needed her help before she began a group lesson, and stated that she did not want any interruptions unless it was an emergency. The soliciting child is so

---

[2] Transcription notations are as follows: (   ) refers to an unclear utterance, [   ] refers to nonverbal behaviors, numbers within [   ] indicate length of pause in seconds, - refers to an interruption without simultaneous talk, { refers to an interruption with simultaneous talk, = refers to a latched utterance (i.e., one utterance follows another with no pause), : indicates elongation of phoneme, boldface italics indicate extra loudness or stress on an utterance, and → in the left-hand margin indicates line(s) containing the phenomenon of interest.

persistent that the teacher does finally respond. Nevertheless, since the child's reason was not judged to be an emergency, and even though the lesson has already been interrupted, the teacher refuses to comply with the child's request for information.

2. **Dictionary Lesson. Third Grade. January.** (The teacher is working with three children on dictionaries. A fourth child, Robin, has approached the table and hovered around for several minutes, lingering near the teacher, who has not attended to her.)

TEACHER:	*Alright, let's see if you can look up the wor:d.*
ROBIN:	*(Excuse me) Mrs. Ixxxx?* [1.8″]
TEACHER:	[She looks up at Robin.] *What are you forgetting?*
ROBIN:	*Umm . . .* [1.2″]
TEACHER:	*Is this an emergency?*
ROBIN:	*(unclear)*
ROBIN:	*Kind of.*
TEACHER:	*Well let's hear it.*
ROBIN:	*Um where is the "Understanding Questions" answers?* =
→ TEACHER:	= *That's **not** an emergency.* [shakes head vigorously] [Robin turns and starts walking off.]
→ TEACHER:	*You can find something else to do.*
TEACHER:	[to group] *Alright, I want you to look up . . .*

Communicative Resources

At this point it may be useful to consider more specifically how participants cope with the communicative demands of a situation. Given the fact that involvement time with the teacher is a scarce commodity in the classroom, we can ask the following: Are there any particular communicative skills that teachers use to maximize, within fairly brief segments of time, the number of their involvements with children and activities?

One such communicative skill is what I have called "slotting" in previous discussions of how teachers handle servicelike events. Teachers slot-out of their main activity to attend to children needing outside help. This slotting-out is usually coordinated with verbal "down-time" in the teacher's main involvement. This is something that teachers do, with respect to the "host" or main-involvement activity, whether or not there is a child waiting at the teacher's elbow for attention. In the example following the teacher initiates use of down-time.

3. **Make an Arrow. Nursery. October. Early Morning.** (Teacher A-1 is sitting at a table with four girls. Alexa and Kathy are each working alone

on some drawings. The teacher is working with Emily on her drawing. Susan is watching the teacher and Emily.)

EMILY: *Make a, make a arrow because they, my parents want me*
TEACHER: ⎧*Do you want to*⎫ *make the arrow?* [points with marker at
             ⎨   ⎬ paper]
EMILY: ⎩(unclear)   ⎭
EMILY: *Okay.*
→ TEACHER: [She gives Emily the marker pen and as Emily leans down
             to draw, leans back in her chair and scans the table. The
             teacher looks at Alexa, who is staring with a blank ex-
             pression across the table.] [3.4″]
→ TEACHER: *Alexa, it looks to me like you're writing some of the*
             words that you see there, writing your name over (it).
ALEXA: [On the word *like*, Alexa's gaze shifts back to the
             paper and she begins drawing again with the marker pen.]
ALEXA: (I had) *to write my name because I covered it.*
TEACHER: *Ohh:, I see what you*   ⎧*mean.* ⎫
SUSAN: [to the teacher, about Emily] ⎨*Look at*⎬ *her arrow!*
TEACHER: [She looks at Emily and her paper.] *That's terrific.*
             Would you like to put this in a matte, so it's really
             special looking? Put some colored paper . . .

With this example we can see more clearly the impact of the instructional approach on patterns of interaction. It seems that, instructionally, these teach-ers are committed to working with students in a way that always involves the teacher as little as possible in actually doing part of the activity. This allows the child maximal participation in accomplishing tasks, which is highly de-sirable. This feature, however, creates interactional lags or "down-times" that are akin to "transactional pauses [see Adelman, 1976; Merritt, 1976a,b]" for the teacher. Because involvement in individual children's vectors of activity is so important, the teacher usually uses these down-times to slot-out to another vector of activity while waiting for the current child to get to the next phase of activity (for which the child needs the teacher's involvement).

This is a positive feature in that it allows the teacher to be multiply involved over a period of time. But if engagement in the secondary vector of activity turns out to take longer (especially if it is a lot longer) than the time needed for the child to complete the independent phase of the task, this feature can mean that the child(ren) in the teacher's "primary" vector of activity, her "official" involvement, turns out to be the one(s) waiting. A hint of this was seen when Susan explicitly solicited the teacher's reinvolvement with *look at her arrow!*

Sometimes, of course, the basic setup for the teacher's involvement is not that of one primary vector of activity (as with a reading group) and other secondary ones. The distribution of the teacher's involvement may, rather, be more of a "round," in which several children are individually working on a single, basic activity with many segments punctuated by brief teacher engagements. This was essentially the case with the "peanut game" in our nursery data.

In the peanut game, children seated around one table were asked to first say how many peanuts they wanted, then to count how many the teacher had given them, and then to say how many more they needed to have the number they originally said. In arrangements such as this, the teacher may sometimes specifically say something about her involvement with the child who is individually carrying out the activity. For example, as Ms. B-1 distributes peanuts she says to Allison, *You count these while I do something else, and then I'll be back to you.* And a few moments later she says to Catherine, *You count those while I come back* [to you]. The teacher involves herself with one child at a time, slotting-out to the next child when she gets to a point of down-time (here, waiting for students to count peanuts).

So far I have been talking about slotting as completely leaving—if only for a short time—one vector of activity to engage in another. This is not the teacher's only option for meeting the multiparticipation requirements of a busy classroom, however. In response to the many activities in the classroom, teachers often seem to develop a skill for "splitting" the communication channels and thereby multiplying the number of modalities with which they can participate communicatively at the same time.

Most obviously, there is a split between verbal and nonverbal modalities. Frequently, the verbal modality is again split by distinctions in tone of voice or rhythm (as cadence).[3] These multiple modalities serve to designate participation by the teacher with multiple sets of classroom participants and their attendant activities. In the following example Mrs. C. is helping Sam with a task that involves matching colors and letters. She has her back to the wall and is facing the door, as well as Sam, when a late student comes in. Mrs. C. slots-out in midsentence to greet Carter. (Here I have tried to indicate cadence with # under the rhythmically stressed items of the "split" sentence.)

4. *Hi Carter.* Kindergarten.

TEACHER: *What color is next to G?*
SAM: *White.*
TEACHER: *No, that's G. The letter G is white. But what*
                                                                          #

       is the color **Hi, Carter**   *next to it*
          #   [higher pitch]   #
           [looks at Carter]

[3] Another more obvious possible split in the verbal modality occurs in classrooms where there is more than one code or language available.

The possibility of splitting the verbal modality in this way depends on two things: (a) maintenance of the verbal rhythm of the primary vector of activity (with Sam), which preserves the integrity of the vector of activity; and (b) some nonverbal signal that directs attention toward some portion of the verbal modality as belonging to a second vector of activity (to avoid confusing participants in the primary vector). The latter is definitely akin to what others in this volume have called "contextualization cues" (see Cook-Gumperz & Gumperz, Chapter 2, this volume; Erickson, Chapter 9, this volume).

Nevertheless, the major modality split is between verbal and nonverbal. In certain teacher-dominated vectors of activity, such as reading, there seems to be an almost official split in the teacher's involvement. The verbal modality is reserved for the primary vector of activity (reading), whereas the nonverbal modality is largely available for secondary vectors of activity, including servicelike events. For instance, when reading is the primary vector of activity, the nonverbal modality is advantageous for two reasons: (a) the verbal modality must be available for oral reading; (b) reading involves the children's focused visual attention on the text, so that, ideally, if the teacher is gesturing with her hands to other children or nonverbally engaged in a servicelike event (e.g., checking a math assignment), this should be minimally disruptive to the reading vector.

In another example from the data a momentary breakdown in this systematic split occurred that pointed out the reading students' ordinary expectation that teacher verbal comments are directed to the readers. The teacher slotted-out of a reading vector using the verbal modality, Hunh-unh, Hunh-unh, as well as the nonverbal gesture of vigorously shaking her head. This was necessary to ensure swift and immediate action. However, it was also clearly confusing to the child who was reading (Billy), who commented, I thought you were saying I didn't read it right.

Another result of the teacher's slot-out using the verbal modality is that it stopped the reading vector. This was an impairment to the integrity of the reading vector. On the other hand, though, the teacher did not open up the Hunh-unh vector to the reading participants and Billy's query, What was he doing? was not responded to. Billy seemed to understand that the teacher did not want to let her sanctioning slot-out become a focus for the reading vector. He then waited poised (attending but uninvolved) until the teacher was almost finished with her other vector and then began reading again as though nothing had happened. The teacher also returned and the reading vector proceeded smoothly.

It thus becomes very important for teachers to develop consistent patterns of modality splitting for routine occurrences and to find ways of reconstituting redundancy for nonroutine ones. I recently observed an interesting instance of the latter from another third-grade classroom. A teacher slotted-out using the verbal modality, but she rapidly stood up before calling out, *Wait a minute, wait a minute* to an outside group. Not only was the act of standing a very perceptible nonverbal act, but it also changed her voice location creating a noticeable difference in the verbal modality ordinarily used for the reading group.

Directing Attention

Teachers participating in several vectors of activity can create communication problems for children, in that each child is expected to be involved in only some vectors of activity. Teachers thus have an important role in distributing equitably their own attention, and also in directing each child's attention to what he or she is expected to be involved in. This issue relates not just to the social aspects of teaching; rather it is closely related to more instructional aspects of teaching such as focus of attention. This is, of course, a crucial issue for teaching and learning and one that has been studied extensively by psychologists (see especially the work of Bruner [1973] and that of the Russian psychologist Vygotsky [1962]). I do not presume to enter into this psychological dialogue, but would merely like to point out the interface between focus in terms of task curriculum and focus in terms of social interactional enactment of a "teaching and learning sequence." An effective implementation of a task curriculum item, it seems, requires that teachers as well as students make adjustments in their orientation to "what is going on" in the current interaction. If the teacher merely assumes the students are focusing on a certain aspect of the curriculum, when in fact they are not, this results in the negative effect that Henry (1968) has called "anticognition."

Very clearly, what is involved is **inference.** Inferencing is based on the presumed focal aspect of new information or new moves in the interaction. Teacher and students sometimes do not share the same understanding of what constitutes the focal aspect of a new move as illustrated by the next example.

A group of children had informally been asked to think of imaginary items to go into an imaginary basket. The teacher first suggested fruit, which elicited many fruit names from the children. However, when the teacher asked, *How about spinach?*, the children failed to interpret this as a "test question [Cherry, 1980]" about whether spinach is a fruit. Instead, they thought the teacher was "opening up" and relaxing the previous constraint of what can go in the basket. The children responded creatively to this by expanding in a number of directions and including different vegetables, items other than either fruits or vegetables such as flowers, and going to get imaginery flowers instead of just saying it.

5. *How about spinach?* **Nursery Level.** (Nursery school teacher B-1 is sitting with a group of children on the floor after an enactment of "Little Red Riding Hood." She has asked the children to gather around for a "celebration" of the wolf's demise, and to think about what they will celebrate with—that is, what kinds of things "are in the basket.")

	TEACHER:	*Fruit, that's a good idea. What kinds of fruit shall we have in our basket?*
	ANITA:	*Apples.*
	TEACHER:	*Okay.*
	ALLISON:	*Bananas.*
	TEACHER:	*Bananas. Okay.*
	ELLIOTT:	*Oranges.*
	TEACHER:	*Okay.*
	DAVID	*Peaches.*
	TEACHER:	*Peaches, that's a good one.*
	EVE:	*Grapes.*
	TEACHER:	*Okay.*
	ALLISON:	[tapping the basket, which is in the center of the group]
→		*That's all.*
→	TEACHER:	*How about spinach?*
→	ALLISON:	*Okay.*
→	ELLIOTT:	*How about—uh—I'll get some flowers for you* [getting up].
→	TEACHER:	*How about carrots?*
→	ALLISON:	*Yeah.*
	ANITA:	*I'll get carrots now.* [getting up]
→	TEACHER:	*Are they fruits?*
	ALLISON:	*No.* [shrugging shoulders]
→	TEACHER:	*Not a fruit?*
	ELLIOTT:	[standing, holding out hand with imaginary bunch of flowers]
	ALLISON:	*No.* [intonational gloss, as if to say *of course not; so what?*]
→	TEACHER:	*All right, carrots.*
	ELLIOTT:	*Mrs. Jones, here're your flowers* [holding out hand]. *Here're your flowers.*
	TEACHER:	*Oh, thank you. How nice of you.* [with hand "taking" Elliott's bunch of flowers]
	EVE:	*And some broccoli?*
	TEACHER:	*Broccoli, that'd be good, wouldn't it?*

The teacher may well have decided that her introduction of the move, *How about spinach?* did not work the way she thought it would and so may have thought this sequence was not educationally successful. My own view is that it displayed very crucial teaching skills: When the teacher's query did not get the response she expected (that spinach is not a fruit), she actively pursued their line of thinking, and, in this case, made no effort to revert to her own initial focus. Most importantly, the teacher did not end the sequence with the misapprehension that the children thought spinach was a fruit.

Three features of directing focus of attention in primary classrooms can be mentioned here. First, in such informal (indirect) instructional contexts there seems to be some of what Cazden (1979) discussed for slightly more formal (direct) instructional contexts in her paper about "Peek-A-Boo" as an instructional model. Children use formats or paradigms for enacting, anticipating, and interpreting behavior in a teaching and learning sequence. Sometimes these formats are explicitly laid out by the teacher, but if not, children may "borrow" formats from another learning environment, or informally create or decide on a paradigm in the course of a teaching and learning sequence.

Second, teachers seem to develop these formats for directing and receiving attention along the lines of modality splitting. For example, the nursery school teachers especially seemed to be involved in directing students' attention to the verbal, and to the more "completely" (i.e., decontextualized) verbal form, as in the following example. This occurred during a session when the teacher was working with one child, Sara, on an experiment with water pouring.

6. *I want to color the water blue.* **Nursery Level. January.**
(Sara has just brought to the table a set of food coloring vials.)

TEACHER: *What color would you like to color the water?*
SARA: [points to one vial]
TEACHER: *What's the name of that color?*
SARA: *Blue.*
TEACHER: *All right. Can you say **I want to color the water blue?***
SARA: *I-want-to-color-the-water-blue* [said with "recitation" intonation].
TEACHER: *All right.*

7. *I didn't talk.* **Nursery Level. January. Midmorning.**
TEACHER: [to Sara] *Do they both have the same amount of water or does the glass have one and the vase have another?*
SARA: [ponders the question with elbows on table and chin in hands, but then points to the glass.] [6.5″]
SARA: [to teacher] *They both have the same amount.*
TEACHER: [quoting] ***They both have the same amount of water.*** *I'm very interested in your answer. Can you tell me how you figured that out?*
SARA: [nods] [1.6″]
TEACHER: [to Sara] *Tell me what you thought.* [Over the last few seconds some hysterical laughter has been coming from the children playing with clay at a nearby table.]

	TEACHER:	[gets up and walks over to the nearby table] [4.2″]
	TEACHER:	[to group] *I'm going to stop you* (unclear). *All right?*
	TEACHER:	[returns to Sara's table and sits down] [6.5″]
→	TEACHER:	*Sara, I'm sorry we were interrupted by the clay people just then, and I couldn't really* **hear,** *and I was very interested* ⎰ *because–* ⎱
→	SARA:	[to teacher] *I didn't* ⎱ **talk.** ⎰ [1.5″]
	TEACHER:	[nodding] *I know. But I want to have you talk to me about it, because I'm very interested in how you figured it out.*
	SARA:	*I know because it's* (over) *there to there, because, of–, this thing is bigger than this thing.* . . .

Third, although teachers want to have children know the "why" of what they are doing as much as possible, teachers do not want to be drawn into an explanation for something that the child may not have enough information (or in the teacher's estimation may not need to have) to process the explanation. In many of these situations, the teacher's role seems to be more explicitly that of "guide," whereby the child's focus of attention and activity is explicitly directed. These directions are also often dictated in terms of modality. Thus, although the teachers often encourage development of the verbal modality, they also sometimes direct students' attention away from it. In our data, this is most prevalent at the kindergarten levels with both teachers, though these two teachers were in any lay sense very different in style. Thus we noted a number of teacher admonishments such as the following, all from the kindergarten data.

Ms. D.:	*Don't talk about it, just do it.*
Ms. C.:	*Don't discuss it. Just do it.*
Ms. D.:	*Wait, Jenny. You're still listening. Put your head down.*
Ms. D.:	*Put your hands in your lap and think.*
Ms. C.:	*Stop talking and think. Your mind can't be thinking while your mouth is doing all that talking.*
Ms. D.:	*You know, some of you keep asking whaddaya do, whaddaya do* [deliberately mock whiney voice]. *Put your head down and stop asking questions.*

Ritual Parameters and Stylistic Options

In this section I would like to consider how the issues discussed previously interact with ritual considerations, and how the free variation in implementation can be seen as an arena for identifying stylistic options.

One use of the term "ritual" refers to a set of behaviors or ways of doing things that are routine, that are essentially expected forms or formats used to accomplish something in a "culturally" defined setting by members of that "culture." Thus, some researchers of classroom settings have referred to class-room routines as classroom rituals (for uses of the term applied to the classroom setting see Corsaro, 1979; Griffin & Mehan, 1979).

This routine aspect of the term ritual probably inheres to some extent in all uses of the term. Nevertheless, following the work of Goffman (1956, 1963, 1971), I use the term less as a noun and more as an adjective. Thus, I have included the concepts of ritual equilibrium and ritual closure in my analyses. Briefly (and here the reader is encouraged to seek out Goffman's more complete discussions), this use of the term derives from the noun use in that there is some large complex of behaviors alluded to, which in any given dyad of social interaction are expected or not expected, depending on the relative status and so on of the two cointeractants. **In our view, it is not so much the case that a PARTICULAR set of behaviors is ALWAYS expected to accomplish a goal (such a set comprising A ritual), but rather that a range of behaviors can be assigned a ritual INTERPRETATION—an interpretation of "proper" expectedness or appropriateness according to a range of inter-actional variables (relative status, nature of the setting, and so on).**

In searching for variation in **individual** actions or presentations of self that affect the ritual quality of some face-to-face interaction, Goffman (1956) distinguished two basic types: those having to do with deference and those having to do with demeanor. Deference involves displays of respect for the "other," whereas demeanor displays respect for the "self." The subtlety of this distinction is sometimes lost because often a single act may have both moti-vating forces driving it (as one grooms one's hair before coming to school, partly out of deference to the setting and other people, and partly out of proper demeanor or self-esteem). Most of the recent discussions in sociolinguistics concerning negative and positive politeness (Brown & Levinson, 1978; Gum-perz & Tannen, 1979; Lakoff, 1979) can be related fairly directly to concerns with displays of deference. This is also the major sense in which I have invoked the term ritual (as in ritual equilibrium between two interactants, ritual closure of a vector of activity).

The following short sequence from the classroom data illustrates a way in which the demeanor component comes into play. Presumably, when Mary-ann tells Joyce she hates her, the act is so socially unacceptable that Maryann has demeaned herself by it. Joyce, by rejoining in kind, has also demeaned herself. Linda makes this evaluation in contextual terms with *Now you're* **both** *fresh.*

8. **Kindergarten.** (Three girls are at a table. Maryann and Joyce have been arguing and the discussion has just escalated.)

MARYANN: *I hate you Joyce.*
JOYCE: *You're fresh, Maryann, and fresh means bad.*
LINDA: *Now you're **both** fresh!*

Returning to the issue of competing demands for the teacher's attention, we can note that the teacher has essentially three options for attending to a secondary vector of activity: (*a*) include the current participants in the teacher's departure (*Oh, look at Jackie's design*); (*b*) partially slot-out and use a split modality involvement (e.g., with reading groups use a verbal modality for reading and a nonverbal for secondary vectors); or (*c*) totally slot-out.

This third option means the teacher has temporarily left the "primary" vector. Note, however, that this does not necessarily mean the primary vector will stop. In fact, many teachers seem to be aiming for a group situation in which the group will keep working (the vector will keep going) whether or not they are involved. Other work in this volume has pointed out the value to teachers of child behavior that keeps the group involved even though teachers' participation may be interrupted.

When teachers leave a primary vector to attend to a secondary one they will ordinarily return a few moments later. The leave-taking and reentering can be accomplished in a variety of ways: (*a*) teachers may act as though they were never gone (e.g., the *Hi Carter* or *Huhn-uhn* examples); (*b*) they may formally stop the primary vector (*All right. Excuse me just a minute*); (*c*) they may leave without formally stopping, but reenter formally (*Sara, I'm sorry we were interrupted by the clay people.*). The latter two ways represent some ritual acknowledgment of the impairment to the primary vector. They are, in fact, **ritual brackets** that mark accessibility (not altogether unlike *Hi* and *Bye-bye*). We might, then, want to refine our analysis of leaving and reentering vectors with some further distinction in slotting to include slot-out, slot-in, bracket-out (*Excuse me*), and bracket-in (*Okay. Sorry*).

What we are dealing with here are issues of ritual closure or ritual boundedness of participant interchanges. It is my hunch that this is one aspect of teacher style that children must attune themselves to in order to operate successfully in terms of managing ritual equilibrium between themselves and the teacher (this notion extends to dealing with other students as well, of course). A given teacher may stylistically orient to a norm of maintaining a greater or lesser degree of ritual boundedness to the various pieces of interaction in the classroom.

Some beginnings and ends are, of course, less amenable to such stylistic variation. It is not inconsequential, for instance, that Ms. C's unusual slot-out to say *Hi Carter* seemed to be in response to Carter's first coming into class. These access rituals that bound off the entire day are fairly obligatory.

In another classroom (nursery), teacher B-1 also left her primary vector to greet a student for the first time that day. However, in this instance the teacher used a different option for leave-taking and reentering, perhaps because she anticipated a longer interruption. From the water-experiment table, in a slightly louder sing-song voice, the teacher called out *Catherine's just arrived. She's been to see the doctor this morning. How are you now, Catherine?* Verbally, Ms. B-1 at first included the current participants in her departure from the water activity, but at the same time she oriented her body away from the table where she was sitting. At least one child did not seem to understand that this body orientation constituted the teacher's signal of inaccessibility. Seth continued to address comments to her although she did not respond (*I'm stirring. I'm stirring*). When the teacher eventually left the table Seth seemed to finally understand her inaccessibility, and sarcastically intoned, as she walked away, *Excuse me.*

Unfortunately, the full text of this sequence is too long to include in this chapter. However, I would like to present the final portion of the transcript to point out how considerations of ritual boundedness become involved with instructional issues as well as social ones.

When the teacher returned to the table where Seth had been stirring and Caroline had been waiting for a turn to "do the experiment," she found that Martha, Catherine, and Harold had gathered around and Martha was sitting in the teacher's chair holding the food coloring. Ms. B-1 immediately reasserted her control by reclaiming the food color, and her sense of where things were by inviting Caroline's participation. From the larger context it seems very likely that Ms. B-1 wanted this activity to end as soon as possible, yet she took the time to see that the instructional sequence was properly bounded-off by allowing one more coloring (*All right. You put a little more in, then I'm going to put the coloring back.*). She also remedialized her previous, possibly negative, contact with Martha (taking the food color away) by specifically including her in the watching. Such a move not only restores ritual equilibrium between teacher and student, it also directs the child's involvement into an instructional activity.

9. *All right. You put a little more in.* **Nursery.** (The teacher has reapproached the table. She leans over Martha, takes the food color box from her, and says *Okay*.)

TEACHER:	*Did you want to put a little more blue coloring in it, Caroline? Is that what you have in mind?* [Caroline seems to nod.]
CATHERINE:	[to teacher] *Can I do that?*
→ TEACHER:	[to Caroline] *All right. You put a little more in, then I'm going to put the coloring* (back).
CATHERINE:	[to teacher] *Can I do that, what you're doing?*

HAROLD: [to teacher] *Can I do it after* (her)? [Carolina or Martha]
CATHERINE: [to teacher] *Can I do it* {*after?*
TEACHER: [to group]   {*I would like*} *to have*
               everybody {*have a turn if we can.* }
CAROLINE: [to teacher] {*I'm* (a) *put a little more*} *in.*
→ TEACHER: [to Caroline] *All right. You want a put a little more*
               in that one? [the measuring cup] *All right.* [Caroline
               does so.]
→ TEACHER: *Watch it for a minute.* [Teacher tugs at Martha's back to
               get her to stand up to look inside the cup.]
TEACHER: *Martha, watch that, for a minute so you can see what*
               happens. [Teacher walks away from the table, apparently
               to return the food color.] [2.9″]
CATHERINE: [to Caroline] *Why don't you stir it up?* [The children
               stare at the cup.]
(MARTHA):   *What's happening?*
CATHERINE: [toward Caroline] *It's turning blue.*

Ms. B-1 had also obviously succeeded in setting up this last phase of the
activity so that the vector of activity proceeded as was intended, even though
the teacher had already withdrawn her own participation.

Implications for Practice and Future Research

I began this chapter by invoking the canonical teaching and learning
sequence in the classroom—one in which there is mutual engagement of teacher
and student within the frame of the same vector of activity. Analytically, my
aim has been to provide a conceptualization of what parameters come into play
when engagement takes place, to illustrate different patterns of situational
demands and communicative resources, and to sketch out the arena of educational consequences.

As stated at the outset, the educational theme of the chapter is the
teacher's distribution of attention among all the students in the class and the
teacher's direction of students' attention among all the possible vectors of
activity in the classroom. The issue of **distribution** may be construed as one
of **educational equity;** the issue of **direction** as one of **educational efficacy.**
In these terms, it is hard to imagine any two aspects of classroom communication that have greater salience for educational practice. Yet, because the
issues are so complex, and because they are manifested so very differently in
traditionally structured whole group lessons than in classrooms that provide
individualized instruction, they are poorly understood.

First of all, certain difficulties seem to be misconceptualized or at least misnamed. For example, a major complaint of teachers with individualized instructional classrooms is that some students are unable to work independently. Oddly enough, however, it seems to me that often the very children a teacher may designate as unable to work independently are those who sometimes display great powers of concentration and involvement in individual tasks. The problem seems to be that working independently in a classroom with several other children does not necessarily mean great absorption in independent tasks. Rather, as I have tried to illustrate in this chapter, it means coordinating involvement in independent tasks with whatever else is going on in the classroom. Thus, children who are "unable to work independently" may need a different kind of help in becoming good students.

Second, in the arena of informal, non-whole-group classroom communication, many of us take for granted behaviorally adaptive patterns that may not be universal. For example, it is my hunch that the availability of modality splitting as a behavioral adaptation to competing demands for attention may vary considerably crossculturally. In discussing this recently with Livia Polanyi (personal communication, 1980), I was told that this kind of modality splitting does not seem to be typical in the Netherlands. She remarked, by way of example, that mothers do not pull up their children's pants while talking to other adults; they are either talking to the adult or pulling up a child's pants. My own early impressions of this phenomenon in India also seem at variance from mainstream middle-class American expectations. This kind of deep-seated cultural training in focusing attention may have important implications for educational programs with culturally heterogeneous teacher–student populations.

Third, although recently a number of researchers have pointed out the need to view social and instructional happenings within the same paradigm (especially the studies reported in this volume), very little work has tried to incorporate the importance of ritual constraints such as ritual boundedness (see Goffman, 1976 for an elaborate discussion of the distinction between communicative or system constraints and ritual constraints in social interaction). Attention to **ritual boundedness** can be directed along the lines of **who is participating,** along the lines of **appropriate modalities**, or along the lines of **what activity** or work is being undertaken. Thus, as was pointed out in the last example, the bounding-off of Caroline's interest in the water experiment was very important for establishing proper respect for work and work involvement. A student needs to develop a sense of its being good to stay involved, and yet to know when to release, to finish, involvement. We are, in a sense, speaking again of preserving the integrity of an instructional vector of activity. At another level, in a previous example, the teacher helped Emily to bound-off the completed product of her work involvement by suggesting she put her picture *in a matte, so it's really special looking? Put some colored paper . . .*

Fourth, the notions of attention and participation are inherently complex and interrelated. In this chapter, I have adopted the dichotomy of **uninvolved attention** (to refer to the nonparticipatory attention given to secondary or outside vectors of activity) and **involved attention** (to refer to the participatory attention given to main or primary vectors of activity). **Dual** or **multiple processing** refers to either involved or noninvolved attention to more than one vector of activity. **Dual** or **multiple participation** refers to involved attention to more than one vector of activity. Typically, in primary classrooms, it is only the teacher who does dual participation. At the beginning of the chapter, I pointed out that teachers are able to initiate talk with students at almost any time, whereas students are quite restricted. In fact, teachers are incipient participants in all instructional vectors of activity, whereas each student has very limited participatory rights in other students' activities.

Finally, given the fact that both teachers and students are occasionally interrupted in carrying out certain vectors of activity, a critical concern for the issue of educational efficacy is how effectively an interrupted participant **returns** to the interrupted vector of activity. In the examples given we saw teachers making very adroit returns to the interrupted activities. An unexplored issue, but one I believe is very important, is how **students** learn to return to interrupted activities. There are times, for example, when independently working students' attention is directed to a classroom announcement or to take an individual spelling test. How quickly interrupted children return to their work and what facilitates this return or redirection of attention is an educationally important issue.

Acknowledgments

I wish to acknowledge the support of the Center for Applied Linguistics and research associates Frank Humphrey and Stephen Cahir in carrying out the overall study. I am indebted to Erving Goffman for suggesting that I consider the issue of dual processing in the development of my analyses. He is in no way accountable, of course, for the way in which I have followed up on his suggestion.

References

Adelman, C. *The use of objects in the education of children of 3–5 years.* Final report HR3234/1, HR3661/1 to the Social Science Research Council, 1976.

Brown, P., & Levinson, S. Universals in language usage: Politeness phenomena. In E. Goody (Ed.), *Questions and politeness.* Cambridge: Cambridge University Press, 1978.

Bruner, J. S. *Beyond the information given.* Ed. J. M. Anglin. New York: W. W. Norton, 1973.

Cahir, S. R. *Activity within and between activity: Transition.* Unpublished doctoral dissertation, Georgetown University, 1978.

Cazden, C. B. Two paradoxes in the acquisition of language structure and functions. In K. Connolly & J. Bruner (Eds.), *The growth of competence.* New York: Academic Press, 1974.

Cazden, C. B. Peekaboo as an instructional model: Discourse development at home and at school. *Papers and Reports of Child Language Development,* 17, 4. Stanford University, 1979.

Cherry, L. A sociocognitive approach to language development and its implications for education. In O. Garnica & M. King (Eds.), *Language children, and society.* New York: Pergamon Press, 1980.

Corsaro, W. A. "We're friends, right?": Children's use of access rituals in a nursery school. *Language in Society,* 1979, 8(3), 315–317.

Erickson, F., & Shultz, J. When is a context?: Some issues and methods in the analysis of social competence. *The Quarterly Newsletter of the Institute for Comparative Human Development,* 1977, 1 (2), 5–10. Also reprinted in J. Green & C. Wallat (Eds.), *Ethnography and language in educational settings.* Norwood, N.J.: Ablex, 1981.

Goffman, E. The nature of deference and demeanor. *American Anthropologist,* 1956, 58, 473–502.

Goffman, E. *Behavior in public places: Notes on the social organization of gatherings.* New York: Free Press, 1963.

Goffman, E. *Relations in public: Microstudies of the public order.* New York: Basic Books, 1971.

Goffman, E. Replies and responses. *Language and Society,* 1976, 5, 257–313.

Griffin, P., & Mehan, H. Sense and ritual in classroom discourse. In F. Coulmas (Ed.), *Conversational routing: Explorations in standardized communication situations and prepatterned speech.* The Hague: Mouton, 1979.

Gumperz, J., & Tannen, D. Individual and social differences in language use. In W. Wang & C. Fillmore (Eds.), *Individual differences in language ability and language behavior.* New York: Academic Press, 1979.

Henry, J. Anti-cognition. Paper prepared for United Nations special report on children and youth (mimeographed). St. Louis: Department of Sociology–Anthropology, Washington University, 1968.

Humphrey, F. *"Shh!": A sociolinguistic study of teachers' turn-taking sanctions in primary school lessons.* Unpublished doctoral dissertation, Georgetown University, 1979.

Lakoff, R. T. Stylistic strategies within a grammar of style. In J. Orasanu, M. K. Slater, & L. L. Adler (Eds.), *Language, sex, and gender.* New York: New York Academy of Sciences, 1979.

McDermott, R. P., & Gospodinoff, K. Social contexts for ethnic borders and school failure. In A. Wolfgang (Ed.), *Nonverbal behavior.* Toronto: Ontario Institute for the Study of Education, 1978.

Merritt, M. *Resources for saying in service encounters.* Unpublished doctoral dissertation, University of Pennsylvania-Philadelphia, 1976. (a)

Merritt, M. On questions following questions (in service encounters). *Language in Society,* 1976, 5, 315–357. (b)

Merritt, M. Building "higher" units and levels: The case for the strategic locus of observation. In P. R. Clyne, W. F. Hanks, & C. L. Hofbauer (Eds.), *The elements: A parasession on linguistic units and levels.* Chicago: Chicago Linguistic Society, University of Chicago, 1979. (a)

Merritt, M. "Communicative loading" and intertwining of verbal and nonverbal modalities in service events. *Papers in Linguistics,* 1979, 12(3–4), 365–392. (b)

Merritt, M. Repeats and reformulations in primary classrooms as windows on the nature of talk engagement. Special issue on the language of the school age child, Ed., L. Cherry Wilkinson. *Discourse Processes,* in press.

Merritt, M., with Humphrey, F. *Service-like events during individual worktime and their contribution to the nature of classroom communication.* Final Report for Grant No. 78-00081 of the

National Institute of Education, 1980. To be published in a revised version under the title, *Children asking the teacher*, by the Center for Applied Linguistics, Washington, D.C.

Polanyi, L. *Personal communication*, 1980.

Shultz, J. *It's not whether you win or lose, it's how you play the game* (Working Paper No. 2, Newton Classroom Interaction Project). Cambridge: Harvard Graduate School of Education, 1976.

Shultz, J., Florio, S., & Erickson, F. "Where's the floor?": Aspects of the cultural organization of social relationships in communication at home and at school. In P. Gilmore & A. Glatthorn (Eds.), *Ethnography and education: Children in and out of school*. Philadelphia: University of Pennsylvania Press, 1980.

Shuy, R., & Griffin, P. What do they do at school any day: Studying functional language. In W. P. Dickson (Ed.), *Children's oral communication skills*. New York: Academic Press, 1981.

Vygotsky, L. S. *Language and thought*. Cambridge: M.I.T. Press, 1962.

12

Differences in Communicative Styles across Ability Groups[1]

DONNA EDER

The recent interest in communicative competence has been centered around the development of communication skills in nursery school and elementary classrooms. Not only are communication skills important in and of themselves, but they are also necessary for gaining and demonstrating academic knowledge. In addition, a child who can communicate effectively demonstrates an understanding of the basic norms of classroom interaction.

Most of the research so far has examined communication patterns during lessons involving the entire class (Erickson & Schultz, 1977, 1981; Fisher, 1979; Griffin & Humphrey, 1978; Mehan, 1979; Wallat & Green, 1979). However, much instruction takes place in small, ability-based groups (Austin & Morrison, 1963; Weinstein, 1976). Not only are communication norms in these groups likely to differ from those found in larger groups, it is possible that different norms exist for different ability levels. If this is the case, students might be socialized to different communication styles depending on the level of the group to which they are assigned.

The aim of this chapter is to examine the development of communication styles in ability-based reading groups in a first-grade classroom. The degree to which students initiate conversation and the topical relevance of their comments will be examined first. Then the extent to which students interrupt other students' reading turns will be considered as well as the teacher's dif-

[1] This research was supported by the Spencer Foundation, Grant No. 44–329–01.

245

ferential response to these interruptions across ability levels. Students' comments during reading lessons in the fall will be compared with their comments during lessons in the spring to determine which different communication styles were developed during the year across group levels.

Participating in Small Group Lessons

To participate successfully in group lessons students must make topically relevant comments that are appropriately timed (Mehan, 1979). Although there is evidence that children as young as 3 or 4 years of age can carry on coherent conversations (Cook-Gumperz & Corsaro, 1977; Keenan & Schieffelin, 1976), classroom lessons often involve new and greater topical constraints. Specifically, children need to learn that the teacher has certain rights regarding the initiation of topics during classroom lessons and that their comments must be in line with those topics. In addition, since classroom lessons consist of a number of topically related sets, students need to learn that new topics can only be initiated at certain junctures in the lesson (Mehan, 1979). In his study of lessons involving an entire class, Mehan found that students' comments were responded to more favorably if they occurred at these junctures and that students became more successful at identifying such junctures throughout the year.

Students also need to acquire knowledge regarding turn-taking rules in order to participate successfully in classroom lessons. Although there has been some attempt to identify universal rules for turn-taking (Sacks, Schegloff, & Jefferson, 1974), others have argued that these rules vary across cultures (Philips, 1976) and speech events (Ervin-Tripp, 1979). According to Ervin-Tripp, turn-taking varies depending on the amount of interest in others' speech and the degree to which speech is predictable. Thus, in situations where children are uninterested in the comments of others, there are likely to be more overlaps in their conversations. Gearhart and Newman (1977) have argued that turn-taking, in general, may differ for children. They found more competitive refusals to attend and longer gaps between utterances in conversations among 3-year-olds.

Although the existence of universal turn-taking rules has been debated, there is agreement that turn-taking is much more complicated in groups of three or more where participants must identify **who** is to speak next as well as **when** to change speakers (Ervin-Tripp, 1979; Sacks et al., 1974). Although the choice of the next speaker becomes increasingly more difficult as groups become larger, it is somewhat less difficult in lessons involving an entire class due to the highly structured nature of turn allocation in such lessons (Griffin & Humphrey, 1978; Mehan, 1979; Wallat & Green, 1979). Consequently, turn-taking may be more difficult in small group lessons than in large group lessons. At the same time, because small instructional groups are larger than the groups children typically play in (Corsaro, 1979), they need to acquire more turn-taking skills to participate effectively in small group lessons.

Method

In order to examine differences in communicative styles across reading groups, a sociolinguistic analysis of videotaped interaction was conducted. Such analysis is necessary to accurately code such detailed behaviors as reading turn interruptions and to best determine how an utterance is related to both previous and future utterances (Cherry, 1978; Mehan, 1979; Streeck, 1980). Besides collecting videotaped data, the classroom was observed an average of twice weekly for an entire academic year. Ethnographic data collected during these observations are essential for interpreting the meaning of utterances and are particularly important for determining the extent to which students' remarks are topically relevant (Cicourel, 1980; Corsaro, in press; Keenan & Schieffelin, 1976).

DESCRIPTION OF CLASSROOM

The research setting was a first-grade classroom with 23 students (13 boys and 10 girls) primarily from middle-class backgrounds. Most of the classroom instruction occurred in four ability-based reading groups. Students were assigned to these groups during the first week of school. The teacher relied mainly on kindergarten teachers' perceptions of students' reading aptitude. Each group met every day for approximately 20 minutes. Although a given reading group lesson often involved a number of activities including unison reading from charts, periods of silent reading, discussion of workbook assignments, and so on, the primary instructional activity in all four groups was taking turns reading aloud. During this activity the teacher assigned turns at reading to one student at a time. When this student completed a turn, a new reading turn was assigned until all or most of the group members had an opportunity to read. The entire class also gathered for a general meeting each morning. During this time the teacher took roll and the lunch count and described the work that students would be doing at their desks that day. On some days the work was introduced with a brief lesson or discussion. On others the meeting included a short period of sharing time.

COLLECTION OF VIDEOTAPED DATA

Reading lessons from all 4 groups were taped on 4 days in the second and third months of the school year at approximately 2-week intervals. Taping was done on different days of the week to obtain data representative of that period. A similar procedure was followed in the spring when each group was again taped on 4 days, approximately 2-weeks apart. This resulted in a total of 32 videotaped reading lessons (8 lessons for each of the 4 groups). General meetings were also videotaped on 6 of the 8 days. All of the reading lessons and general meetings were transcribed.

CODING DEFINITIONS

The coding of topical and nontopical acts was guided by definitions developed by Corsaro (1978). These definitions were modified to more closely reflect issues specific to classroom lessons:

1. **Topical initiation:** Any comment that is relevant to the current topic and is not simply a response to a previous topic-relevant act. Once the teacher begins the lesson, this becomes the topic. Anything pertaining to the lesson is considered topical.

Examples:	TEACHER:	*Turn to page sixteen.*
→	STUDENTS:	*We've already read this page.*
	STUDENT:	*"Big dogs jump."*
→	STUDENT:	*I know you have a big poodle.*

2. **Nontopical initiation:** Any comment that is not relevant to the current topic and is not a response to a previous nontopical act. Nontopical initiations include comments about activities not related to the reading lesson once it begins (e.g., other students in the class, lunch or recess, personal information unrelated to the lesson content). They also include unnecessary comments about instructional material.

Examples:	STUDENT:	*"I like big dogs."*
→	STUDENT:	*We went to the beach yesterday.*
→	STUDENT:	*Someone scribbled on my page.*

3. **Reading turn interruption:** Any comment by a student after the teacher has nominated another student to read.

4. **Topical interruption:** Any topical initiation or response including reading aloud that occurs during another student's reading turn.

5. **Nontopical interruption:** Any nontopical initiation or response that occurs during another student's reading turn.

Teacher responses were coded into four categories: reprimand, interrupt, ignore, and acknowledge.[2]

---

[2] These categories are similar to those used by Mehan (1979) except that "interrupted" was added and two of his categories (i.e., "bound off" and "incorporated") were combined for the "acknowledged" category since very few initiations or interruptions were incorporated.

1. **Reprimand:** The teacher explicitly discourages the student from responding further.

Examples:	STUDENT:	*I know.*
→	TEACHER:	*Just count to yourselves.*
	STUDENT:	*My marker's ripped.*
→	TEACHER:	*Well, don't worry about it.*

2. **Interrupt:** The teacher starts talking about something different before the student has completed his or her utterance.

Example:	BECKY:	*How come we don't—*
→	TEACHER:	*A little louder, Cynthia.*

3. **Ignore:** The teacher does not respond positively or negatively to the student's comment (i.e., the teacher does not say anything or does not orient her next comment to that student).

Examples:	GARY:	*Boy that was a hard one.*
→	TEACHER–JEFF:	*What did the girl see?*
	SARA:	*"Run."*
→	TEACHER–PETER:	*Starts with r.*

4. **Acknowledge:** The teacher makes at least one comment related to the student's comment while oriented to that student.

Examples:	MELINDA:	*There was a big jungle gym, with a bridge, and I went there in Hawaii.*
→	TEACHER–MELINDA:	*Oh, when you were in Hawaii.*
	OTIS:	*What smells like fish around here?*
→	TEACHER–OTIS:	*Maybe they're cooking something.*

DATA ANALYSIS

An interactionist approach was used combining the strengths of both qualitative and quantitative analyses. A qualitative, or sociolinguistic, analysis was conducted first. A given utterance was examined within the context of previous and past utterances to interpret its meaning and determine its effectiveness (Cook-Gumperz, 1977; Corsaro, 1978; Philips, 1974; Streeck, 1980). In addition, the institutional context in which the utterance occurred was also considered (Cicourel, 1980; Fisher, 1979; Mehan, 1979). In this respect, this study goes beyond many sociolinguistic analyses that often do not consider the effect of social context on interaction.

At the same time, an attempt was made to indicate how representative each style and response was by reporting frequencies of specific acts across group levels. Although such frequencies provide some idea of how typical different behaviors are, they have certain limitations. For example, when utterances are counted no indication is generally made regarding the length of an utterance, whether or not it is a repetition of a previous utterance, and so on. These frequencies are useful, however, for indicating general trends and for providing information regarding the degree to which differences in behaviors and sequences across group levels are representative of the time period being analyzed. Also, by combining quantitative with more qualitative analyses, the results should be more useful than those of studies reporting only behavioral frequencies and providing little information about the context in which the behaviors occurred (e.g., Allington, 1980; Weinstein, 1976).

The first stage of the analysis involved coding all student initiations and teacher responses during the four reading group lessons on the first videotape. Since the number of student initiations might differ depending on the activities that occurred during reading lessons and since this might vary across groups, student initiations during a class meeting on the same day were also coded.

The second stage consisted of examining all reading turn interruptions and teacher responses during reading lessons on 3 days in the fall (a total of 12 lessons). One day was excluded as one group did not take turns reading aloud that day. In the next stage, reading turn interruptions that occurred in the fall were compared with reading turn interruptions for 3 days (or 12 lessons) in the spring. Again, one day was excluded since all groups did not read aloud that day.

Findings

Communicative competence includes, among other skills, the ability to obtain the floor. During classroom lessons, access to the floor is typically under the teacher's control. Several studies have found that much classroom conversation follows a pattern of teacher initiation, student response, and teacher evaluation, with little opportunity for student initiations (Mehan, 1979; Sinclair & Coulthard, 1975).

The first analysis examines how often students contributed to classroom conversation by focusing only on those utterances that go beyond a simple response to the previous utterance. Table 12.1 shows the number of student initiations during each reading group. Students in the high group were clearly more capable of gaining access to the floor than were students in the other three groups. This is due, in part, to the fact that more lesson time in the high group was spent discussing related topics, a less structured activity than

Table 12.1
Number of Student Initiations by Ability Group Level[a]

Student's group level	Number of student initiations		Number of student initiations acknowledged	
	During reading group	During class meeting	During reading group	During class meeting
High (6)[b]	54	17	18	11
Medium-high (6)	17	4	4	2
Medium-low (6)	17	4	3	3
Low (4)	8	0	3	0
Total	96	25	28	16

[a] Includes all initiations during reading groups and the morning class meeting on the first videotape (the 5th week of school).
[b] Group size.

reading. This was, however, not unique to the lesson on this particular day as the high group, in general, spent more time engaged in discussions. Also, this pattern of participation was similar to that found during the morning class meeting, where all students participated in the same activities. In both the reading lesson and the class meeting, over half of all student initiations were made by high group members.

Gaining access to the floor is of little consequence if one's utterance is not acknowledged. Since conversations during classroom lessons were mainly teacher-controlled, a response by the teacher is essential for having one's remarks incorporated into the conversation (Mehan, 1979; Philips, 1974). Table 12.1 also shows the number of student initiations that received at least a minimal response from the teacher. First of all, most of the student initiations were not acknowledged. Again high group members had the most teacher-acknowledged comments, primarily because they made many more initiations.

In general, this first set of results indicates that early in the year, students differed considerably in their attempts to participate actively in classroom conversation. Whereas high group members made the majority of all student initiations, low group members made very few. In fact, during the class meeting none of the low group members made a single attempt to initiate conversation.

TOPICAL RELEVANCE

As mentioned previously, an important aspect of communicative competence is making topically relevant remarks. Related to this, students need to learn the respective rights of teachers and students regarding topic initiation, that is, it is the teacher's right to determine the topic during classroom lessons.

Whether a remark was topically relevant was an extremely important factor in determining whether the teacher acknowledged it. Although she acknowledged 44% of the topically relevant remarks during reading lessons, she acknowledged only 12% of the nontopical remarks.

Although students in all groups made some nontopical comments, the majority of the initiations in the two higher groups were topical (61% in the high group and 59% in the medium high). Often their initiations helped to promote the teacher's topic as in this example from the beginning of the medium-high group lesson:[3]

Example 1: Medium-High Group

The teacher (T) has just called the group up for their reading lesson. Irene, Yale, Nancy, Eric, and Larry are all members of this group, whereas Gary and Dale are not. "All" refers to all of the group members.

	T–I:	*Uh,* {*Irene, why don't you move over here, please.* [Points]
→	Y–T:	{*Here's what page we're on.*
→	N–T:	*I thought Robin was greens.*
	T–N:	*What?*
	N–T:	*I thought Robin was* (*in greens*).
	T–N:	*No.*
	E:	*I know.*
	N:	*Good this is still at my page.*
	L–I:	*Hey, you just passed the page.*
	T–G,D:	*Uh, Gary and Dale, back at* **your chairs** *. . . Bring me your papers, please, OK?*
	T–All:	*All right, we're on page twenty-nine.*
	Y:	*That says "Jump in. Jump"* –
	T–All:	*"Jump" where?*

Although the teacher sometimes had difficulty getting students in the lower groups to concentrate on the lesson, the comments of students in this group actually helped focus the group's attention. Yale's comments, in particular his second one, were directly related to the activity of reading. He frequently made topically relevant initiations during reading group that may have influenced the teacher's decision to move him to the high group 3 weeks later.

---

[3] Examples 1 through 4 are from the fifth week of school and examples 5 through 10 are from reading lessons in the fall. The following notations are used: (   ) refers to an unclear utterance, [   ] refers to nonverbal behaviors, - refers to an interruption without simultaneous talk, { refers to an interruption with simultaneous talk, = refers to a latched utterance (i.e., one utterance follows another with no pause), " " refers to reading aloud, and → in the left-hand margin indicates line(s) containing the phenomenon of interest.

In the next example, Melinda's comments help keep the group's attention on reading during an interruption from a student who is not a group member.

Example 2: High Group

The students are reading in unison from a reading chart. Melinda is a member of the high group, whereas Sara and Cynthia are not.

T–ALL:	OK. Uh, where are they now?	
ALL:	At the park.	
S–T:	Cynthia's bothering me. [Comes over to the group.]	
→ M:	I know what **that**	says. "Park." [Points to word on chart.]
T–C:		Cynthia, Cynthia. Let's not Let's not bother Sara.
→ M:		"Park. Park. Park."
T–M:	All right, they're at the park, and uh, Melinda can read.	
	Who is this?	

Melinda's comment helped keep the group's attention on reading until the teacher's attention was returned to the group. The teacher then rewarded Melinda by assigning her the next reading turn.

In contrast to the higher groups, only 29% of the student initiations during the medium-low group lesson were topically relevant. Instead, students often attempted to bring up their own topics during the lesson, as in this example.

Example 3: Medium-Low Group

The teacher has just passed the reading books out. Jeff, Gary, and Dale are all group members.

T–J:	Jeff, turn one more page, now.	
→ G:	How many more days until we get out of school?	
D:	We're gonna stay in school for . . .	thirteen days,
T–J:		Good, all right.
	Jeff, let's start on page **two-four.**	

Whereas more student initiations in the low group were topically relevant than in the medium-low group, half of them were nontopical. In the next example, Cynthia makes two nontopical comments during Robin's reading turn.

Example 4: Low Group

The teacher has just assigned a reading turn to Robin. Cynthia is also a group member.

T–R:	*You can read the first line over there. . . . You want a marker?* [Gives her a book marker.] *Put your marker under the first row of words.*
T–ALL:	*What's she telling* {*them now?*
→ C–T:	{*I want a yellow marker?*
T–C:	*That's all right, for today.*
→ C:	*I don't want a green one.*
T–C:	*Well the next time we change, I'll give you the color* {*you want.*
R–T:	{*"You can run."*

Neither Gary's comment in Example 3 nor Cynthia's comment in Example 4 helped to promote the teacher's topic. In both cases the teacher either ignored or reprimanded their nontopical remarks. She said nothing in response to Gary's comment and failed to comply with Cynthia's request for a green marker instead of a yellow one. In addition they were more likely to be reprimanded and somewhat more likely to be interrupted or reprimanded.

To summarize, in the fifth week of school, members of the two higher groups made more topically relevant initiations than members of the two lower groups. The greatest percentage of nontopical comments occurred in the medium-low group where students frequently brought up their own topics during the reading lesson. The teacher responded to nontopical initiations in a similar manner across group levels. Not only were nontopical comments less likely to be acknowledged at all levels, they were more likely to be reprimanded.

TIMING OF UTTERANCES

A second important aspect of communicative competence concerns the appropriate timing of one's comments. Knowing when to talk is as important as knowing what to talk about. Wallat and Green (1979) found that turn-taking during entire class meetings was based on two rules: (a) one speaker at a time, (b) once someone's turn has begun we do not interrupt. Mehan (1979) found that students were expected to wait until the completion of an "initiation–response–evaluation" sequence before talking.

The main turn-allocation strategy used during reading group lessons was having students take turns reading aloud, which is a common practice in most reading groups (Austin & Morrison, 1963). This activity is relatively new for most first graders and rather difficult since it requires students to maintain interest in an activity they cannot participate in directly. Thus it is not surprising that students at all levels frequently interrupted other students' reading turns during reading lessons in the fall.

In some cases, students read along with the reader as in this example from the high group.

Example 5: High Group

Aaron is reading from a reading chart. Melinda and Otis are also group members.

	A:	"*the*" =
→	M:	"*the*"
	A:	⎧"*bus*"
→	M:	⎩"*bus*"
	T–ALL:	*Let him do it.*
	A:	"*to . . . the*"
→	O:	"*park.*" =
	A:	"*park.*" =
→	O:	"*park.*"
	T–ALL:	*Let's just let Aaron do it.*

In other cases, students made comments related to the story they were reading or were otherwise topically relevant as in the next example.

Example 6: Medium-Low Group

Dale is reading; Peter and Gary are also group members.

	T–D:	*That's right, Dale. Read the last line . . . Go ahead, Dale.*
	P:	"*I like big dogs. They jump.*"
→	G–P:	*I know you have a big poodle.*
	D:	"*Big dogs . . .*"
	T–D:	"*Big dogs . . .*"
	D:	"*jump.*"
→	G–P:	*You can't even handle it.*
	T–D:	"*jump.*" *Very good.* [Nods.]

At other times students brought up topics that were not related to the story or the activity of reading, as in the following example where Becky asks the teacher why the reading groups do not meet in a different order.

Example 7: Low Group

Krystal has just asked the teacher if she can read next. Cynthia and Becky are also group members, whereas Larry is not.

	T–K:	No let's let Cynthia read on the next page. You can do the last one.
→	B–T:	How come we don't–
	T–C:	A little louder, Cynthia.
	C:	"Janet"
	T–C:	Good.
	T–L:	Larry.
→	B–T:	Teacher, how come we don't start with Greens first, then the Yellows, then these last ones?
	T–B:	We do sometimes.
	T–C:	All right, Cynthia, "Janet . . ."

Whereas the teacher responded to nontopical comments in a similar manner across group levels, her response to reading turn violations varied dramatically across groups. When students in the high group talked or read during another student's turn, they were often reprimanded as in Example 5. Students in the other groups were reprimanded far less often, especially when their interruptions were topically relevant. In these groups, interruptions were usually ignored as in Example 6. When students spoke out of turn in the low group, however, the teacher did not reprimand their interruptions, and often acknowledged them.

Usually the teacher's responses were brief and did not expand on the students' comments as in Example 7 where she answers Becky's question but does not pursue the topic. Becky used several strategies to get a reply from the teacher. Not only did she repeat a question previously interrupted by the teacher, she added a summons (i.e., *Teacher*) at the beginning.

Occasionally the teacher pursued a comment of a low group member even though it occurred during another student's turn as in the next example from the same lesson.

Example 8: Low Group

The group is in the middle of reading a story about Mark's bunnies. Becky, Krystal, and Cynthia are all group members.

1	T–ALL:	All right, let's turn the page. See what
2		she's looking for.
3	B:	Aw-aw-aw-aw.
4	T–ALL:	See what she's found?
5	B:	Yeah.
6	T–B:	What?
7	B–T:	Bunnies.
8	T:	{ Bunnies.
9	K:	(Bunnies.

10	T–B:	*All right, Becky* ⎰*you can start reading.*
11	C–T:	⎱*We got a bunny at home.*
12	T–C:	*Do you? Just one?*
13	C–T:	*Yeah.* ⎰*Can I bring it to school?*
14	B–T:	⎱*That looks like "come."*
15	T–C:	[Nods.] *Ask your mother if you can bring it.*
16	T–B:	*All right, Becky. "Come"* [Points to her page.]
17	B:	*"Come* ⎰*here . . . Mark."*
18	C–T:	⎱*If she has to work tomorrow ( )*
19	T–C:	*All right, but when she doesn't she can.*
20	T–B:	*"Come here, Mark." Good, "Come . . ."* [Points to her
21	B:	page.] *"here."*

Here the teacher responds to Cynthia's interruption by asking for further information. Cynthia responds with yet another question, which the teacher answers (line 15), even though Becky has started trying to read. The discussion between the teacher and Cynthia continues (lines 18 and 19) with Cynthia talking as Becky is reading. Finally the teacher successfully returns her attention to Becky in line 20.

Cynthia's comment occurs at the beginning of Becky's turn, which may be why the teacher pursued it. When students talked at the beginning of a high group member's reading turn, however, the teacher's response was very different.

Example 9: High Group

The students are about to read a story entitled "On the School Bus," which begins on page 18 of their book. William, Otis, Melinda, and Yale are all group members.

T–W:	*William, since it's your birthday, you can start reading first today.*
T–O:	*Otis?*
M–T:	*My birthday will be* ⎰*the last day of school.*
Y:	⎱*On the school bus,*
	eighteen, eighteen,
T–W:	*William, wait a minute.*
T–Y:	*Yale? Ready?* [Points to Yale.]
T–W:	*Uh-huh. All right, William.*
W:	*"I go to school on a bus."*

Examples 8 and 9 illustrate very different responses to reading turn interruptions in the high and low groups. One explanation for these markedly different responses stems from the fact that high group members were much more verbal than low group members early in the year (refer back to Table

12.1). Thus the teacher may discourage high group members from talking, while at the same time encourage discussion from low group members.

Furthermore, the teacher is probably concerned about maintaining the interest of low group members during other students' reading turns. Because reading turns were usually much longer in the lower groups, there would be a greater likelihood of losing the other members' interest. Also, the teacher might perceive low group members as having less interest in reading in general and would not want to discourage any expression of interest in the lesson. If this is the case one would expect the teacher to acknowledge primarily topically relevant interruptions in lower groups, and to discourage nontopical interruptions of any of the groups.

Table 12.2 shows the percentage of reading turn interruptions the teacher acknowledged, ignored, interrupted, and reprimanded across all group levels. Although the majority of these interruptions were ignored at all levels, interruptions in the low group were acknowledged more and reprimanded less often. When the interruptions were divided into topical and nontopical categories, it is evident that this differential response applied only to topical interruptions. These latter interruptions were acknowledged almost twice as often in the low group as in any other group and were never reprimanded in the low group. There was also a tendency to acknowledge topical interruptions more often in the medium-low group and somewhat more often in the medium-high group than in the high group. On the other hand, nontopical interruptions were seldom acknowledged in any group and were often reprimanded in all but the medium-high group where they were typically interrupted or ignored.

This differential response by the teacher is apt to contribute to different communicative styles across reading groups. In other words, reading turn interruptions are likely to become infrequent in the high group and increasingly more frequent in the lower groups. The average number of reading turn interruptions per lesson is compared across group levels at fall and spring time points in Table 12.3. Although both high groups show a decrease in interruptions between fall and spring, both low groups show an increase. The greatest change occurred in the high group where there was a 56% decrease in interruptions. The next greatest change occurred in the low group where there was a 47.5% increase. The greatest difference in teacher response occurred in these two groups.

When topical and nontopical interruptions are examined separately, it is clear that only topical interruptions increased in the lower groups. Nontopical interruptions, which were discouraged at all levels, decreased at all levels. Thus the main difference in communicative style developed in the classroom across groups concerned the timing of utterances and not their topical relevance.

The fact that low group members were not developing an understanding of reading turns as being inviolable was also evident from their own comments:

Table 12.2
Teacher Response to Reading-Turn Interruptions by Ability Group Level[a]

Group level	Percentage of all interruptions				Percentage of topical interruptions				Percentage of nontopical interruptions			
	Acknowl-edged	Ignored	Inter-rupted	Repri-manded	Acknowl-edged	Ignored	Inter-rupted	Repri-manded	Acknowl-edged	Ignored	Inter-rupted	Repri-manded
High (6)[b]	9	65	7	20	9	68	3	21	8	58	17	17
Medium-high (6)	11	65	10	13	13	72	0	15	7	40	47	7
Medium-low (6)	14	68	5	15	17	68	2	13	5	68	5	21
Low (4)	28	56	8	8	33	59	7	0	11	44	11	33

[a] Includes all reading turn interruptions during reading lessons on 3 days in the fall (i.e., the 5th, 7th, and 9th weeks of school).
[b] Group size.

Table 12.3

Average Number of Reading-Turn Interruptions Per Lesson by Ability Group Level[a]

Group level	Average number of reading-turn interruptions			Average number of topical interruptions		Average number of nontopical interruptions	
	Fall	Spring	Percentage change	Fall	Spring	Fall	Spring
High (6) (7)[b]	15.3	6.7	−56.0	11.3	6.0	4.0	.7
Medium-high (6) (7)	23.0	19.3	−17.0	18.0	17.3	5.0	.7[c]
Medium-low (6) (6)	23.0	31.7	+38.0	15.7	26.7	7.3	5.0
Low (4) (3)	12.0	17.7	+47.5	9.0	15.0	3.0	2.0[c]

[a] Includes all reading turn interruptions during reading lessons on 3 days in the fall (i.e, the 5th, 7th, and 9th weeks of school) and 3 days in the spring (i.e., the 24th, 28th, and 30th weeks of school).

[b] Group size in fall and in spring.

[c] The sum of the average of topical and nontopical interruptions does not equal the average number of all interruptions for two groups since it was impossible to determine topicality for four interruptions in the medium-high group and two interruptions in the low group.

Example 10: Low Group

Krystal is reading; Becky and Cynthia are also group members.

> T–K: *And what's her name?*
> B: ⎰ *Janet.*
> K: ⎱ *Janet.*
> T–K: *Good. All right, go ahead.*
> K: *"Here I go."*
> T–C: *Watch your book.*
> → B–C: *Did you say "Janet" at* ⎰ *the same time?*
> T–K: ⎱ *Good.*
> K: *"See the . . ."*

Becky addresses a question to Krystal who is in the middle of her reading turn. This suggests that Becky is not only unaware that reading turns should not be interrupted, but is also unaware that the reader cannot engage in discussions with other members while reading. In general, Becky demonstrates her lack of knowledge concerning the speech event of reading aloud.

Discussion

The findings reported here indicate that students had different levels of communicative competence at the beginning of the year. Specifically, high group members gained access to the floor much more often than did members of other groups, especially low group members. In addition, members of the two higher groups made more topically relevant initiations early in the year. On the other hand, reading turn interruptions were relatively common in all groups at the beginning of the year.

Although the teacher did not encourage nontopical comments in any of the groups, she responded very differently to interruptions. Interruptions were often reprimanded in the high group while being acknowledged in the low group. Because norms regarding interruptions differed so dramatically across group levels, high group members made many fewer interruptions in the spring than did low group members.

Consequently, low group members did not develop an understanding of reading turns as a speech event in which other members do not speak or engage the reader in discussion. Erickson (1981) found a similar confusion among kindergarten students concerning the speech event of an interview. Unaware that she was not to speak or talk to the interviewer, another student continually interrupted the interview and attempted to engage the interviewee in discussion.

The fact that low group members made more interruptions in the spring does not indicate they had less communicative competence. They had simply learned a different set of rules regarding participation in reading group lessons. However, if low group members apply those same rules to other speech events in the classroom, they may be judged as having less competence. In addition, they may be judged as being less competent when they interrupt in their own groups if the teacher is unaware that she has, perhaps inadvertently, developed different norms for different groups.

This has some parallels with Philips (1972) study of cultural differences in classroom participation. She found that although Indian students were competent participants in student-run groups and other speech events with participation structures similar to those in the Indian community, they were less competent participants in speech events such as class meetings with very different participation structures. In other words these students were "competent" by certain criteria, that is, they could participate actively in familiar events, and "incompetent" by other criteria, that is, they seldom participated in class meetings. The results of both Philips' and this study indicate the importance of viewing communicative competence in the classroom as a complex phenomenon. Thus, students following certain norms when speaking may be viewed as being incompetent if judged according to other norms.

In general, these findings suggest that students are being socialized to different communicative norms depending on their assigned group level. Other studies have found similar differences in teachers' behaviors across group levels. McDermott (1976) found the teacher in his study of first-grade reading groups used different turn-allocation strategies in the low group. In a study of 20, first- and second-grade classrooms, Allington (1980) found teachers were more prone to interrupt low group readers on oral-reading errors. Similarly, Cook-Gumperz and Gumperz (personal communication) found the teacher made more extensive interruptions during reading turns in the low reading group than in the high group. Consequently, the low group members developed a halting, staccato style of reading whereas the high group members read in connected phrases. The greater amount of interruptions by the teacher during reading turns in the lower groups has also been found to result in an increased likelihood of having other students read during one's turn (Eder, 1981, in press).

It should be emphasized that the teacher's differential behavior across group levels is understandable. Erickson (Chapter 7, this volume) found other teachers do not always follow an ideal turn-taking model, simplifying the participation structure at times to allow children to focus on academic tasks. If teachers perceive academic tasks as being more difficult for low group members, it is not surprising that they allow more turn-taking violations.

These findings, thus, imply a need for changes in teaching activities as much as in teacher perceptions. Specifically, the common practice of taking turns reading aloud should be questioned. The turn-taking demands are difficult for all students, but especially so for students in lower groups where reading turns are generally longer and more difficult to follow.

Finally, the implications of the differential communicative styles developed in this classroom for other communicative skills should be considered. Students who learned to respect reading turns probably learned more respect for speaking turns in general. Also, although the teacher pursued some reading turn interruptions, most were only briefly acknowledged. Thus high group members learned to bring up comments after reading turns when they were more likely to be pursued whereas low group members did not. This may explain, in part, why the high group had more frequent, longer discussions than the other groups. These discussions could be useful for developing additional communicative skills.

In summary, due to initial differences in communicative competence across groups as well as to perceived differences in student interest, the teacher responded differently to reading turn interruptions. Not only were interruptions less likely to be reprimanded in the low group, they were often acknowledged. Consequently, students developed further differences in communicative styles by the spring with high group members interrupting turns much less often than low group members. Thus, depending on the group to which they were assigned, the students were exposed to and learned different communicative norms. Further research that examines other ways children receive subtly different academic and social instruction is needed to better ensure equal educational experiences for all students.

Acknowledgments

I would like to thank Bill Corsaro, Sue Fisher, Bud Mehan, Peter Schreiber, and Louise Cherry Wilkinson for their helpful comments. I would also like to thank Bud Mehan, Rebecca Cooper, and Kriss Drass for their assistance in transcribing and coding the data, and Karen Frane for typing the manuscript.

References

Allington, R. Teacher interruption behaviors during primary-grade oral reading. *Journal of Educational Psychology*, 1980, *72*(3), 371–377.

Austin, M., & Morrison, C. *The first R: The Harvard report on reading in elementary school*. New York: Macmillan, 1963.

Cherry, L. A sociolinguistic approach to the study of teacher expectations. *Discourse Processes*, 1978, *1*, 373–394.

Cicourel, A. Three models of discourse analysis: The role of social structure. *Discourse Processes*, 1980, *3*(2), 101–132.

Cook-Gumperz, J. Situated instructions: Language socialization of school age children. In S. Ervin-Tripp & C. Mitchell-Kernon (Eds.), *Child discourse*. New York: Academic Press, 1977.

Cook-Gumperz, J., & Corsaro, W. Socio-ecological constraints on children's communicative strategies. *Sociology*, 1977, *11*(3), 411–434.

Corsaro, W. Sociolinguistic patterns in adult–child interaction. In E. Ochs & B. Schieffelin (Eds.), *Developmental pragmatics*. New York: Academic Press, 1978.

Corsaro, W. "We're friends, right"?: Children's use of access rituals in a nursery school. *Language in Society*, 1979, *8*, 315–336.

Corsaro, W. Something old and something new: The importance of prior ethnography in the collection and analysis of audiovisual data. *Sociological Methods and Research*, in press.

Eder, D. Ability grouping as a self-fulfilling prophecy: A micro-analysis of teacher-student interaction. *Sociology of Education*, 1981, *54*, 151–162.

Eder, D. The impact of management and turn-allocation activities on student performance. *Discourse Processes*, in press.

Erickson, F. Timing and context in children's everyday discourse: Implications for the study of referential and social meaning. In W. P. Dickson (Ed.), *Children's oral communication skills*. New York: Academic Press, 1981.

Erickson, F., & Shultz, J. When is a context?: Some issues and methods in the analysis of social competence. *The Quarterly Newsletter of the Institute for Comparative Human Development*, 1977, *1*(2), 5–10. Also reprinted in J. Green & C. Wallat (Eds.), *Ethnography and language in educational settings*. Norwood, N.J.: Ablex, 1981.

Ervin-Tripp, S. Children's verbal turn-taking. In E. Ochs & B. Schieffelin (Eds.), *Developmental pragmatics*. New York: Academic Press, 1979.

Fisher, S. Revealing students' reasoning practices. *Classroom Interaction*, 1979, *15*, 16–24.

Gearhart, M., & Newman, D. Turn-taking in conversation: Implications for developmental research. *ICHD Newsletter*, 1977, *1*(3), 7–9.

Griffin, P., & Humphrey, F. Task and talk. In R. Shuy & P. Griffin (Eds.), *The study of children's functional language and education in the early years*. Arlington, Va.: Center for Applied Linguistics, 1978.

Keenan, E., & Schieffelin, B. Topic as a discourse notion: A study of topic in the conversation of children and adults. In C. Li (Ed.), *Subject and topic.* New York: Academic Press, 1976.

McDermott, R. P. *Kids make sense.* Unpublished doctoral dissertation, Stanford University, 1976.

Mehan, H. *Learning lessons.* Boston: Harvard University Press, 1979.

Philips, S. Participant structures and communicative competence: Warm Springs children in community and classroom. In C. Cazden, V. John, & D. Hymes (Eds.), *Functions of language in the classroom.* New York: Teachers College Press, 1972.

Philips, S. *The hidden culture.* Unpublished doctoral dissertation, University of Pennsylvania, 1974.

Philips, S. Some sources of cultural variability in the regulation of task. *Language in Society,* 1976, 5, 81–95.

Sacks, H., Schegloff, E., & Jefferson, G. A simplest systematics for the analysis of turn taking in conversation. *Language,* 1974, 50, 696–735.

Sinclair, J. M., & Coulthard, R. M. *Toward an analysis of discourse.* New York: Oxford University Press, 1975.

Streeck, J. Speech acts in interaction: A critique of Searle. *Discourse Processes,* 1980, 3(2), 133–154.

Wallat, C., & Green, J. Social rules and communicative contexts in kindergarten. *Theory Into Practice,* 1979, 18(4), 275–284.

Weinstein, R. Reading group membership in first grade: Teacher behavior and pupil experience over time. *Journal of Educational Psychology,* 1976, 68, 103–116.

13

What Is Writing For?
Writing in the First Weeks of School
in a Second–Third-Grade Classroom[1]

SUSAN FLORIO
CHRISTOPHER M. CLARK

*Let us envision a class of students asked to write on the
subject to which school teachers, jaded by summer,
return compulsively every autumn: "How I Spent My
Summer Vacation."*
—Walter Ong, *Interfaces of the Word,* 1977

*The biggest problem with second graders is that a lot of
them forget how to write over the summer.*
—An elementary school teacher commenting on the
first weeks of school

It is easy to malign writing instruction in the elementary classroom.
Critics have, for example, chided the stereotypic teacher holding a bundle of
yellow, lined newsprint in front of a group of squirmy children and exhorting
them to describe in prose the summer that has just come to an untimely end.
But is that what teachers really do? And, if it is, what does the deadly September
scenario tell us about the functions of writing as communication in the
classroom?

The image is probably overdrawn and unfair. Writing and its instruction
can be difficult tasks. And, in fact, we know very little about the best ways
to teach writing and even less about the writing already undertaken in classrooms everyday. Prerequisite to improving writing instruction, it would be
useful to discover how writing presently functions in both the school and
nonschool lives of teachers and children.

This chapter is about writing in school life. We describe some of the
uses to which writing is put in the first weeks of school in one second/third
grade classroom. In so doing, we speculate on the writing curriculum in elementary school and on the realization of that curriculum by means of teacher

[1] The work reported here is funded by the National Institute of Education (Grant No.
90840). The opinions expressed in this chapter do not necessarily reflect the position, policy, or
endorsement of the National Institute of Education.

265

planning and the interaction of teacher and students in the course of everyday school life. The aim of this chapter is to discover whether there is anything else to writing in school than uninspired essay topics, dull pencils, and yellow newsprint.

Background of the Problem

In the past few years interest has grown among researchers from many disciplines in the process of writing as functional communication and in the social contexts in which writing is undertaken (e.g., Basso, 1974; Goody, 1968). Like their colleagues in anthropology and psychology, educational researchers rarely considered writing. When they did, researchers often overlooked the composing process and the communicative functions of writing in classrooms. They focused instead on the written traces left by individuals or groups. The writings of children typically were used in educational research and evaluation as artifacts from which to draw inferences about the cognitive abilities of the writer or about the adequacy of formal writing instruction. Moreover, the writings examined were almost exclusively the products of classroom activities called "English" or "language arts," and instruction was construed largely as drill and correction in the surface features of grammar (Moffett, 1968).

Although there has been some speculation and much concern about the quality of writing and writing instruction in classrooms, little investigation of this writing has actually taken place. In addition, what we know about the social and intellectual functions of spoken language in classrooms has rarely been applied (Cazden, John, & Hymes, 1972) to a consideration of school writing—the reasons it is undertaken, its many manifestations, the norms for its appropriate use. Indeed, there has been precious little of this sort of documentation of writing in any part of the lives of teachers or children (Hymes, 1979).

This study serves the ultimate aim of understanding the communicative worlds of teacher and child by examining classroom writing and its instruction. Writing is construed in this research as one expressive alternative available to members of a community. Having chosen that alternative, the writer has access to a repertoire of ways of writing. One of the places in which children gradually learn what that repertoire is and how to apply it is the classroom. By documenting communicative choice related to writing in one of the important social settings in a child's life, we may later be able to compare and contrast the uses of writing in that setting with their uses in other settings navigated by the child. In the end, these efforts may lead to a better understanding of the classroom as one environment for learning to write, of the teacher as one adult responsible to meet and nurture the child–communicator, and of the child as a "natural symbolist [Gardner, 1980; Vygotsky, 1978, p. 112]" and emergent writer.

The Study

OVERVIEW

The research reported here is part of a yearlong descriptive field study of school writing. Two classrooms in a small city in central Michigan were the sites for the research; the classes studied were a second–third grade in an elementary school and a sixth grade in a middle school. Each class was taught by a team of two teachers, and in both cases one of the teammates served as a focal informant in the study. Data collected in the course of the study included the following:

1. Field notes of classroom participant observation
2. Periodic videotapes of classroom activity
3. Viewing sessions in which focal teachers discussed and analyzed videotapes made in their classrooms
4. Interviews with both teachers and students about the writing done in their classrooms
5. Weekly journals kept by focal teachers recording their thoughts about the process of writing in their classrooms
6. Naturalistically collected samples of student writing

The study was interdisciplinary in nature. Data collection and analysis reflected theoretical perspectives and employed methods from ethnography, sociolinguistics, and cognitive psychology (see Clark & Florio, in press, and Florio & Clark, 1979, for details of the study).

This chapter limits the scope of the larger study to the uses of writing in only the elementary classroom. Data used in the examination include only the field notes, interviews, journals, and student writings produced in this classroom. The report considers only one part of the school year—the first few weeks—when participants negotiate the transition from home and summer vacation back to school and when the class becomes established as a working social unit. Finally, the report highlights one particular occasion for writing, the "safety posters," to exemplify the multiple functions served by writing in the classroom and the roles played by teacher and students in undertaking them.

LOCATING LITERACY IN THE CLASSROOM

Analysts have written about the opacity of the process of acquiring spoken language—about the fact that children are rarely taught directly the rules of the grammars and ways of speaking they gradually acquire (e.g., Brown, 1973; Cazden, 1972; Hymes, 1974). We have come to understand that language is acquired in use, and that one practices speaking as social interaction, not as preparation for it. In a sense, children and their parents accomplish something extraordinary when language is acquired, but they do it by behaving in quite ordinary ways (Cook-Gumperz, 1975).

The process of acquisition of written literacy is equally opaque. We know, for example, that writing arises in communities at least in part because it enables members to perform the social and intellectual operations that literacy makes possible (Goody, 1968). People begin to write because, within their communities, they need to keep records, engage in commerce, or extend their social relations over time and distance. In addition, writing may profoundly alter the social and intellectual lives of its users once it is established, changing their vision of what is and of what can be accomplished in human life (Goody, Cole, & Scribner, 1977). But although this remarkable social and intellectual process may be unfolding as the individual or the community becomes literate, writing itself is undertaken in ordinary ways in the course of everyday life and commerce. The profound changes wrought by writing are rarely discussed or reflected on by its users.

This state of affairs challenges the analyst interested in the process of acquisition to locate literacy in everyday life. Since the process is so largely unremarked on, it must be sought by closely examining the occasions on which it is undertaken and the relation of its use to the life of the individual and the community. For the educational researcher, the challenge is to locate those school situations in which children come to know that writing is an available expressive option and that, having chosen it, one particular way of writing will best accomplish the social or intellectual function called for in a particular situation. Subsequently the analyst must examine what is newly possible for the child—and for the classroom group—as a result of having written. This is the sort of information, taken for granted by members of the educational community, that is neither addressed in teacher preparation nor accounted for in curricular descriptions, nor even "counted" as writing and writing instruction by educators, children, or parents. Yet it is precisely this everyday use of language that is at the heart of the process of becoming a competent communicator—in speaking or in writing (Hymes, 1974, 1979).

Addressing the problem they have termed "locating literacy," Scollon and Scollon have pointed out that the phenomenon of literacy is "located in a complex of behaviors, attitudes, situations, values, institutions, and personal roles [1979, p. 6]." Although there may not be precise agreement among members about the unique location of literacy in the social life of any community, there is some typification of the activities involving reading and writing among members of a group. The Scollons contend that "this typification of literacy becomes clearer as we observe both the socialization process and as we contrast variations of socialization [p. 6]."

In our society, the classroom is one of the places in which socialization into literacy occurs. By thinking of writing in the classroom in terms of acquiring communicative competence, the analytic task becomes one of identifying the occasions when writing is typically the preferred expressive mode and of discovering the attendant social roles and expectations of teacher and students on those occasions. It is within the medium of these social occasions that the analyst is likely to discover the values and beliefs about writing imparted implicitly and explicitly to the child in formal education.

The following questions therefore guide inquiry into the use of writing in the elementary school classroom: What types of occasions for writing are presented to or perceived by the child upon entry into school? What ways of writing are available to the child for use on those occasions? How does the child begin to differentiate among the functions of writing and the written forms appropriate to them? What role does the teacher play in this process? What other contextual forces are operant? To answer these questions it is helpful to begin at the beginning—to observe writing early in the school year, when it is most likely that the teacher will make manifest norms for the use of writing in school and when young students, fresh from home and summer, may make illuminating transgressions.

DESCRIPTION OF SETTING

Room 12 is the only room of its kind in the Conley Elementary School.[2] Its special nature has important implications for the initial uses of writing that can be observed there. To locate literacy meaningfully in its social context, it is useful to briefly consider Room 12 as an environment for learning.

Occupying an entire wing of the school building, Room 12 houses four teachers and four cross-age homerooms—two at the second–third grade level and two at the fourth–fifth. The room has movable walls, a large common area, and four classroom alcoves that can be isolated from one another or merged (see Figure 13.1). Mixed age interaction, independent and small group learning in centers, and a team approach to planning and teaching have been associated with Room 12 since its creation in 1976.

---

[2] To ensure the privacy of informants in this study, pseudonyms are used throughout when referring to school, teachers, or students.

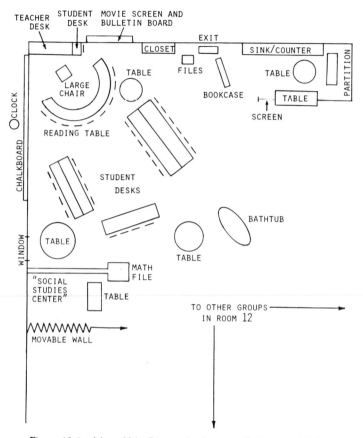

Figure 13.1. Map of Ms. Donovan's classroom (field notes, 9/5/79).

The school itself is known in the community as a lively and active place particularly effective in instructing children from a range of ethnic and economic backgrounds. Conley School receives Title I aid, and although many children attending the school come from the middle-class households of employees and students of the nearby state university, many others are poor. Some children live in a large, government-subsidized apartment complex or in winterized summer cottages near the school. Many families are employed in local agriculture or the automotive industry, and unemployment has been increasing recently. A large number of Conley children from all economic levels live in single-parent households.

A controversial place since the wing was built, Room 12 receives mixed reviews from teachers and parents. Some teachers consider it a challenge and a professional opportunity to work there, whereas others shun the room's potential disorder and lack of privacy in which to teach and plan. Similarly, some parents prefer less open environments for their children. However, it is not uncommon for parents from all backgrounds to inquire of the principal how their child can be assigned to Room 12. In fact, the Room 12 teachers assert that many parents think only the most able children are assigned there; assignment to Room 12 is a status symbol of sorts.

Although Room 12 has changed over the years, the vestiges of the open education movement that inspired it are still apparent in its spatial arrangement and in the teachers' approaches to instruction. During the year, students have the opportunity to make choices about the timing and format of their academic and social activities. In addition, children work in a variety of interactional arrangements including teacher-led large groups, small student groups, mixed-age tutorials, and learning centers.

Room 12's openness, the large number of mixed-age students who occupy it (nearly 100), its special status in the building and community, and its ethos of student choice in learning give rise to many occasions on which writing is used to serve important social and academic functions.

OCCASIONS FOR WRITING IN ROOM 12

Addressing the transition from oral to written ways of communicating in the life of schoolchildren, Cook-Gumperz and Gumperz have suggested that

> the move into literacy requires children to make some basic adjustments to the way they *socially* attribute meaning to the events and processes of the everyday world in order to be able to loosen their dependence upon contextually specific information and to adopt a decontextualized perspective [Cook-Gumperz & Gumperz, 1978, p. 16].

Schoolchildren move toward decontextualization in language as they begin to share thoughts in writing rather than in talk. In writing, they must often communicate with an absent audience, and lack the prosodic and kinesic channels that have heretofore been an integral part of expression (Cook-Gumperz & Gumperz, 1978). More generally, children are called on to elaborate thoughts and intentions in written ways as they navigate a world of new personal relationships, new surroundings, and new interactional goals. In school, the children cannot necessarily rely on shared understandings and expectations that may have abided in the home (Florio & Shultz, 1979; Shultz, Florio, & Erickson, in press). More will have to be made explicit in school, and writing will be one of the appropriate ways to share one's thoughts with others.

Observing that "all people have their uses for literacy in the context of their social needs [Cook-Gumperz & Gumperz, 1978, p. 29]," and that school in our culture may err in too narrowly defining literacy's functions and requisite skills, Cook-Gumperz and Gumperz advocate school experiences sensitive to issues of the transition from the primarily oral culture of family and childhood to the primarily written culture of school and work. They support writing experiences that "favor the learning of written culture through the *medium of the oral culture* [Cook-Gumperz & Gumperz, 1978, p. 28]." Ideally, in school, these experiences arise meaningfully in response to social and intellectual needs occasioned by the new environment of the classroom.

When second and third graders return from summer vacation to Room 12 of Conley Elementary School, they encounter many new occasions calling for just such gradual adjustments from oral to written expression. Some of these occasions are planned by Ms. Donovan, their teacher, who is experienced in helping children manage the transition back into school—and back into writing. Others arise naturally, as part of the process of establishing the class as a social unit with routines for management of time, activity, and social relations. Finally, some arise simply as part of getting to know a group of strangers.

What follows is the story of an occasion for writing in Room 12. The story is offered to give the reader a feeling for the kind of data collected and analytic approaches used in this study. In addition, the story is intended to show the following: (*a*) that writing arises in classrooms open to its possibilities; (*b*) that it helps to know about teacher plans, intentions, and beliefs to make sense of writing instruction; and (*c*) that writing occasions can be negotiated and multifaceted.

The Safety Posters: Turning the Unexpected into an Occasion for Writing

The following paragraph is an excerpt from notes taken during an interview on Monday, September 17, 1979, the eighth school day of the year:

> In our interview, Ms. Donovan described how she used an unexpected traffic safety assembly as an opportunity to do a writing excercise. The assembly included a film on bicycle and pedestrian safety and a talk on the same subject. After Ms. Donovan and her students returned to Room 12, she asked them to recall some of the safety rules that they had just heard about. Ms. Donovan said that she was very surprised at the terrific difficulty that the children had in remembering the safety rules. At first, they could remember only the general topic of the assembly. With some coaching and reminding, several of the rules were recalled. Then Ms. Donovan asked the students each to choose one safety rule and draw a picture illustrating the rule. These poster-size pictures, with the safety rules as captions, will be posted in the hallways as a service and a reminder to the other students in the school.

The "safety posters activity," as we have come to call it, is an early and telling example of occasions for writing in our primary grade classroom. It began with the unexpected: a schoolwide assembly that Ms. Donovan learned of only on arrival at school Monday morning. What began as an unexpected interruption of the school day grew into an elaborate series of learning experiences that extended over several days and, to some degree, involved children and adults throughout the entire school. What happened and how did it come about? To answer this question, let us "unpack" the preceding paragraph from the interview notes of September 17:

In our interview, Ms. Donovan described how she used an unexpected traffic safety assembly as an opportunity to do a writing exercise.

Commentary

This assembly was a schoolwide event presented in the gym by two uniformed young women employed by the local police department. The young women were known by some of the children, as their summer jobs had involved monitoring bicycle safety. The assembly is a clear example of formal contact between the larger community and the school population. Bicycle and pedestrian safety are topics that are very relevant to elementary school children, and responsibility for the safety of school children is shared by school personnel, parents, public safety officers, and the community at large. Safety is a fundamental issue, and, in this case, a safety assembly took priority over classroom and academic issues. The fact that the assembly was unexpected, yet easily incorporated into the morning was, in part, a function of the flexibility of the early weeks in school, when the daily and weekly schedules are not yet fully developed into relatively fixed routines. Ms. Donovan learned about the safety assembly before the children arrived and included it as the first entry (*) on the daily schedule written on the chalkboard (Field Notes, 9/17/79):

On the board, JD has written the "plans for today." They are as follows:

Today is Sept. 17, 1979

Schedule		
9:20–10:05 Assembly*	12:15–12:50 Lunch	2:45–3:00 Cleanup
10:05–10:30 Gym	12:55–1:15 Centers	3:00–3:10 Diaries
10:30–11:00 Reading	1:15–1:55 Math	
11:00–11:15 Recess	1:55–2:10 Recess	
11:15–11:30 USR	2:15–2:45 Science (2) Social Studies (3)	
11:30–12:15 Language Arts		

The assembly included a film on bicycle and pedestrian safety and a talk on the same subject.

Commentary

The 9/17/79 field notes describe the assembly as follows: "The young women talked about and showed several film strips about safety in walking or bicycling to school." The field worker who attended the assembly also noted that this was the first schoolwide assembly of the year, that some students were loud and disorderly and were brought back to order by the school principal, and that the safety presentation was not smooth and spellbinding. One of the filmstrips actually burned up as it was being projected. In short, this assembly had as much to do with learning how to behave at an assembly as it did with safety rules.

During the assembly Ms. Donovan had the idea of using this experience as the basis for a writing activity later in the morning. We do not know what triggered the idea, but our earlier interviews and observations suggest that Ms. Donovan was predisposed to make the most out of the unexpected. She valued writing and believed that school writing activities must have a clear purpose if they are to be successful. On the second day of school, Ms. Donovan and her students did another writing activity that began with the "common experience" of a film. She describes this activity in her journal entry of September 9:

> I was pleased with Friday's writing lesson. Motivation was movie on word families, then students wrote and illustrated sentences utilizing a word family (e.g., Jim **Rice** slid on **ice** and landed on **lice**.) This type of open-ended lesson seems to be the most effective. Children with differing abilities can be as simplistic or sophisticated [as they want to] depending upon their creativity. Instruction is to the group, but the results are individualized without isolation from the total group.

As we shall see as the safety posters activity unfolds, the structure of this occasion for writing includes an initial shared experience (the safety assembly), a clear purpose and audience, and an open-ended opportunity for children to produce something that reflects their ability, creativity, and sophistication. The most advanced students are not held back, and the least advanced students can still achieve a measure of success. In short, the safety assembly probably triggered the plan for the safety posters activity because the assembly fit Ms. Donovan's pattern or set of criteria for a good writing activity. It seems this "spontaneous planning" that Ms. Donovan engaged in is more frequently seen in curriculum areas such as language arts, where there are few published series or kits, than in subjects like math, reading, and science, which are largely structured by published materials.

After Ms. Donovan and her students returned to Room 12 she asked them to recall the safety rules that they had just heard about. Ms. Donovan said that she was very surprised at the terrific difficulty that the children had in remembering the safety rules.

Commentary

Again, the field notes give us a clearer picture of what actually happened on that Monday morning. Ms. Donovan's students stayed in the gym after the safety assembly for physical education (10:15–10:30 a.m.). When the children returned to Room 12, they worked on reading worksheets, went to recess, then did 15 minutes of silent reading. It was not until 11:35 a.m. (language arts time) that the children were asked to recall the safety rules taught in the assembly. Given so many interpolated activities, that the assembly itself was full of interruptions and distractions, and that the children did not know in advance they would be expected to remember the specific wording of the safety rules, it is not surprising they had difficulty. The safety assembly was an experience removed in space and time from the classroom. The children had no props or memory aids to stimulate their recall.

At first, they could remember only the general topic of the assembly. With some coaching and reminding, several of the rules were recalled.

Commentary

In attempting to bring her plan into action, Ms. Donovan had to take on the role of "class memory" and "memory coach." She had assumed the safety assembly experience would be sufficiently recent and vivid to serve as the common experience basis for the language arts activity. When Ms. Donovan discovered (to her surprise) the children did not remember the specific safety rules, she changed her plan on the spot. The teacher's task now became to recreate the common experience in a form, place, and time such that all the students had it available to them for use in the next part of the activity. The field notes (9/17/79, p. 3) show how this was done:

> As part of language arts, Ms. D asks students to "re-run" this morning's safety program and recall what they learned. At a piece of large white paper up front, Ms. D prints what they recall. The format is that an individual raises her/his hand. Ms. D writes down what (s)he says. Another student is asked to read it back.
> Ms. D writes down what students say in multicolor magic markers:
> 1. Don't run on the street without looking.
> 2. Don't take shortcuts you don't know.
> 3. Don't cross the street when the light is red.

4. When you ride your bike, keep your hands on the handlebars.*
*This formulation arrived at after several revisions. Ms. D has said,
Take your time and re-state it, how you want to say it. In coming up with
this one, students chime in with alternatives; Ms. D asks them to let her
re-state it.

(This activity resembles others I have seen so far. It is the generation
of general information posters by the whole group with Ms. D acting as
scribe.)

In coming up with sentences, Ms. D says, *Sometimes does it take a
couple of times to get out what you want to say? That's OK.* The person who
offers the original ideas has the final say as to how it is written down.

This process continues until 10 safety rules are recorded. Notice that Ms.
Donovan goes to some length to see that every student has a chance to be
involved actively in the rule generation part of this process. Oral editing,
friendly amendments, and reading aloud are all used to produce a document
that every child has had a hand in and understands. Mechanics such as spelling and penmanship are taken care of by the teacher acting as scribe. The
use of a rough draft is foreshadowed as Ms. Donovan says, *Sometimes does it
take a couple of times to get out what you want to say? That's OK.* In short, this
part of the safety posters activity constitutes a **collective** and largely **oral**
preparation for writing that makes visible how the solitary, silent author could
prepare to write.

**Then Ms. Donovan asked the students each to choose one safety rule and
draw a picture illustrating the rule. These poster-size pictures, with the safety
rules as captions, will be posted in the hallways as a service and a reminder
to the other students in the school.**

Commentary

This was the point at which the full plan was first communicated to the
children, that is, the part of the plan that had to do with transforming what
the students "knew" into graphic form. The students were given a choice,
within a clear and limited set of alternatives, and this element of student
choice seems to have been an important part of Ms. Donovan's beliefs about
effective learning activities, particularly in writing. The combination of drawing
and writing is also a striking aspect of this task, as illustrated in Figure 13.2.
Other researchers have commented on the close and mutually supportive relationship between drawing and writing, especially in the early grades (Clay,
1975; Cook-Gumperz & Gumperz, 1978; Ervin-Tripp & Mitchell-Kernan,
1977). The field notes give a vivid and more complete portrayal of the
writing–drawing phase of the safety posters activity (Field Notes, 9/17/79, pp.
4–5):

Next Ms. D asks students to think of ways to help remind the rest of the school of these rules. The students suggest the following:

take them around
*put them up on the hallway**
tell them not to do it

*This is response to Ms. D's question: *How could each one of you help remind them of one rule?*

(It is interesting to note that, in response to the charge, the students do not generate any means that are specifically writing-related. They **do,** however, offer symbolic alternatives that are largely visual.)

After the students make their suggestions, Ms. D says, *I had an idea, too. Each (person) could make a poster with one rule and put it in the hallway.* The students say, *Yeah!*

Ms. D: *Do a picture and write the rule on the bottom.*

Before getting started, an additional rule is generated:

11. Don't ride a bike too big for you.

At **11:50,** as students go to their seats to start, Ms. D says, *At the end I'll write the rule for you or you can write it yourself in magic marker. The picture has to be done in crayon.*

The students sit quietly at first. Overheard is the following exchange:

S: *What are you going to do?*

S: *I don't know; I'm still thinking.*

Some students prefer to write the rule first; others make pictures first. Several students found the task difficult for several reasons, e.g., they did not want to do a rule that they found out a lot of other students were doing; they couldn't draw what they needed to illustrate the rule (such as a bicycle). The upshot of these difficulties was that by the end of the available time, some students were completely finished while others were just getting started.

Notice that both the **purpose** of the posters and the **audience** for the posters are specified before crayon touches paper. The students were guided by their teacher to participate in "coming up with the idea" of drawing safety posters. All of the necessary elements were now in place: the list of rules on what Ms. Donovan calls "experience paper," crayons, poster paper, an opportunity for choice and originality, a sense of shared ownership of the project, and the dual motivation of having one's work displayed in the hallway (a place of honor) and of doing good (perhaps even saving a life) by reminding other schoolmates of the safety rules. Ms. Donovan takes a further step to minimize threat by offering to write the rule herself on the bottom of the posters of those students who want or need that help.

The time allowed for drawing and safety rule writing was about 45 minutes (11:30–12:15). As the field notes indicate, there were wide individual differences in task completion. This is an issue that Ms. Donovan returns to again and again during the course of the year. For example, the issue was first raised in the September 17 interview (p. 4):

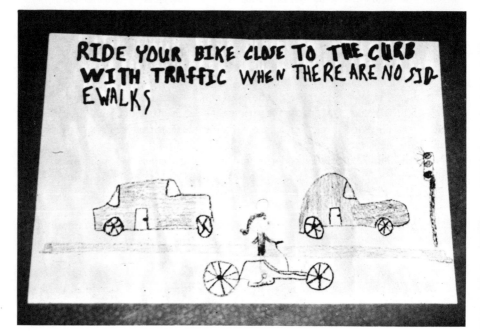

Figure 13.2. Sample safety posters (field notes, 9/19/79).

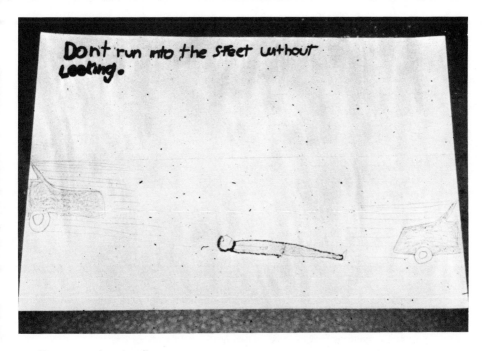

Don't run into the street without looking.

Figure 13.2. (continued)

In discussing planning and diagnostic testing, Ms. Donovan raised a perennial problem for teachers: how to deal with the relatively large differences in the speed at which children work when they are working independently. *What should I do with the kids who finish fast? When I give them fun and extension activities to do I feel that the children who finish more slowly are being gypped. I like closure—everyone must finish. I don't want the slower students to get farther and farther behind.*

(It is interesting to note that this problem of individual differences in working speed has shown up so early in the year. We should take care to note the ways in which Ms. Donovan deals with this issue as she tries to resolve an apparent conflict between her personal philosophy on equal opportunity and the practical realities of a mixed ability class. She seems to recognize that faster is not always better. This might be especially true in writing.)

Epilogue

The safety poster activity continued to develop, as though it had a life of its own. By Wednesday, September 19 (2 days after the safety assembly) all of the posters were finished. That day, in a conversation at lunch with the kindergarten teacher, Ms. Donovan had the idea that her students should make small group presentations of their posters to the kindergarten children as a prelude to displaying the posters in the school hallways. Arrangements were made to do this on Thursday, September 20. During the morning and afternoon that day, groups of three or four of Ms. Donovan's students were sent to the kindergarten room to show their posters and teach the younger children the safety rules. The field notes for September 20 and 21 show how this process developed:

(9/20, p. 1): At **9:20,** students gather in the center. Ms. D says, *The kindergarteners are just learning to get along together.* This comment is prelude to her sending several students to kindergarten to hang posters and tell about them. (Yesterday at lunch, Ms. D negotiated the time and purpose of the safety poster sharing with Mr. B, the kindergarten teacher.)

(9/20, p. 1): Dani returns from the kindergarten and says that she was scared to read her poster to the children. She says that, *the kids didn't even listen,* but that she read it and showed them her drawing anyway.

(9/20, p. 3): [At about **11:00**] Before the students left for pictures, they began to talk about their experiences of sharing the safety posters with the kindergarten earlier this morning. Some said they found it *embarrassing* and *scary.* Some students said they thought it might have helped to practice beforehand. They agree that students who will go this afternoon should practice first. Ms. D tells the other students to help them practice by asking questions *that you think the first graders would ask.* As a few students stand up to do it, their peers applaud their efforts.

(9/20, p. 4): At **12:55** the students reconvene in the center. Ms. D, who had a chance to talk to Mr. B (the kindergarten teacher) at lunch, says, *Mr. B said that you guys did a really good job this morning, even if you were nervous.* Then five students leave with their posters to talk to Mr. B's afternoon class, saying that they are nervous (Lea has a stomach ache).

(9/21, p. 3): At **12:55,** after lunch, the students gather in the center. Afternoon roll is taken and one of the students reads the "afternoon plans." Three students leave for the kindergarten with their safety posters. Ms. D asks them, *Do you know what yours says?* She has them read back what's written on the posters before leaving.

(9/21, p. 3): At **1:05,** students return from kindergarten.
JD: *How'd it go?*
S: *Terrific.*
S: *Not very many questions, though.*

Oral presentation of the safety posters to the kindergarten children added to the safety posters activity. The second and third grade authors' sense of audience was undoubtedly heightened. They saw very clearly that it was useful to reexamine, edit, and rehearse what they had written if an audience was expected to understand their messages. They learned that writing and drawing could be used to focus oral communication (in this case, teaching), and that a graphic product could serve the author as a reminder and illustration of his or her message. Ms. Donovan's students also learned from one another's experience and served as a constructively critical audience for the dress rehearsals. And finally, this phase of the project served as a meaningful connection between two groups of children within the school, showing on a small scale how writing can contribute to the building of a social system when members are separated in space and time.

Conclusion

The safety posters activity was just one of literally hundreds of occasions for writing that took place in the two classrooms in which we worked during a full school year. Our analysis of and commentary on the safety posters activity have raised a number of issues about how, why, and under what circumstances written literacy is acquired in schools, and what role the teacher plays in this process.

Like many other occasions for writing noted in the earliest weeks of school, the safety posters activity began with a shared experience not originally planned by Ms. Donovan. Also, like many other early writing occasions, this one had importance in both the school and nonschool lives of the students. It was an expressive enterprise that moved the students beyond the boundaries of Room 12. Ms. Donovan seized the opportunity to turn an unexpected event into an occasion for writing. Her engagement of students in a series of related expressive activities, both written and oral, involved her in a special sort of pedagogical role. Ms. Donovan extended her planning and teaching beyond the bounds of prepared instructional materials and district mandates for the language arts. She created writing curriculum with her students as the class jointly produced a situation that would both support the practice of writing and be supported by that writing. Ms. Donovan and her students participated in an extended communicative enterprise that involved the practice of written literacy as they prepared and shared documents they called "the safety posters."

Acknowledgments

The authors acknowledge Janis Elmore, June Martin, Rhoda Maxwell, and William Metheny for their contributions to the study on which this chapter is based.

References

Basso, K. H. The ethnography of writing. In R. Bauman & J. Sherzer (Eds.), *Explorations in the ethnography of speaking.* London: Cambridge University Press, 1974.

Brown, R. A first language: The early years. Cambridge: Harvard University Press, 1973.

Cazden, C. B. Child language and education. New York: Holt, Rinehart & Winston, 1972.

Cazden, C. B., John, V., & Hymes, D. Functions of language in the classroom. New York: Teachers College Press, 1972.

Clark, C. M., & Florio, S. Understanding writing in school: Issues of theory and method. In P. Mosenthal & S. Walmsley, Research in writing: Principles and methods. New York: Longman Press, in press.

Clay, M. M. What did I write? New Zealand: Heinemann Educational Books, 1975.

Cook-Gumperz, J. The child as practical reasoner. In M. Sanches & B. G. Blount (Eds.), Sociocultural dimensions of language use. New York: Academic Press, 1975.

Cook-Gumperz, J., & Gumperz, J. From oral to written culture: The transition to literacy. In M. F. Whiteman (Ed.), Variation in writing. New York: Lawrence Erlbaum, 1978.

Ervin-Tripp, S., & Mitchell-Kernan, D. Child discourse. New York: Academic Press, 1977.

Florio, S., & Clark, C. M. Occasions for writing in the classroom: Toward a description of the functions of written literacy in school. Paper presented at the annual meeting of the American Anthropological Association, Cincinnati, Ohio, 2 December 1979.

Florio, S., & Shultz, J. Social competence at home and at school. Theory into Practice, 1979, 18(4), 234–243.

Gardner, H. Artful scribbles: The significance of children's drawings. New York: Basic Books, 1980.

Goody, J. (Ed.). Literacy in traditional settings. Cambridge: Cambridge University Press, 1968.

Goody, J., Cole, M., & Scribner, S. Writing and formal operations: A case study among the Vai. Africa, 1977, 47, 289–304.

Hymes, D. Foundations in sociolinguistics: An ethnographic approach. Philadelphia: University of Pennsylvania Press, 1974.

Hymes, D. Language in education: Forward to fundamentals. In O. Garnica & M. King (Eds.), Language, children and society. Oxford: Pergamon Press, 1979.

Moffett, J. Teaching the universe of discourse. New York: Houghton Mifflin, 1968.

Ong, W. Interfaces of the word. Ithaca: Cornell University Press, 1977.

Shultz, J., Florio, S., & Erickson, F. Where's the floor?: Aspects of the cultural organization of social relationships in communication at home and at school. In P. Gilmore & A. Glatthorn (Eds.), Ethnography and education: Children in and out of school. Washington, D.C.: Center for Applied Linguistics, in press.

Scollon, R., & Scollon, S. The literate two-year old: The fictionalization of the self. Working Paper of the Native American Language Center, Fairbanks, Alaska, January 1979.

Vygotsky, L. S. Mind in society: The development of higher psychological processes. M. Cole, V. John-Steiner, S. Scribner, & E. Souberman (Eds.), Cambridge: Harvard University Press, 1978.

14

Instructional Language as Linguistic Input: Second-Language Learning in Classrooms[1]

LILY WONG FILLMORE

Introduction

For non-English speaking students, the language used by teachers serves a double function: It conveys the subject matter to be learned at school, and it provides an important source of the input such students need in order to learn the school language. Not every instance of instructional language works in this way, however. Speech becomes usable as input for language learning only when it has been produced with the learners' linguistic needs and limitations in mind. Specialists who have studied the language that qualifies as input for language learners have found that it tends to be more restricted structurally and topically than ordinary language (Ferguson, 1977; Snow & Ferguson, 1977). Topics unrelated to the immediate speech situation tend to be avoided, and often the discussion is limited to topics that can be seen or experienced by the learner. Such speech frequently is accompanied by actions, gestures, and other nonverbal demonstrations and cues; thus, the learners—if they are at all observant—can figure out what is being said, even if they know little of the language being spoken.

[1] Support for this work was provided by the National Institute of Education Grant #NIE-79-0118 to the University of California, L. W. Fillmore, principal investigator, and S. Ervin-Tripp, Coprincipal investigator.

By contextualizing the language being spoken in this way, speakers make it possible for learners to assume a tight relationship between what is being said and the situation in which the speech is taking place. The situational information and cues make it possible for the learner to make guesses as to what is being talked about. This is an essential process in the learning of a new language. Further, the kind of language that serves efficiently as input to language learners is often structurally simpler than ordinary language. Speakers tend to avoid complex structures, and to stick with simpler ones. Utterances are likely to be repeated or paraphrased, with small modifications, as learners give indications of understanding, or of not understanding. These modifications are usually tailored to the needs of specific learners, with the speakers basing their adjustments on feedback provided by the learners as to whether they understand what is being said or not (Berko-Gleason, 1977; Phillips, 1973; Shatz & Gelman, 1973; Snow, 1972).

Considering the double function played by instructional language in classrooms serving non-English speaking students, certain conflicts in educational goals can be expected to arise. It is not easy to limit language use in classrooms to simple structures when teaching complex subject matter, any more than it is possible to limit topics to present experiences when the curricular materials that must be covered set out the topics that must be dealt with in instruction. Similarly, it is difficult to build in the repetitiveness and contextual redundancies needed by language learners when there are other students in the class (as there almost always are) who are fluent speakers of the language. The amount of modification needed by the learners would render the language used in the classroom to an inappropriately low level, where these fluent speakers are concerned. Many teachers find it impossibly difficult to handle the special needs of language learners in their classrooms. They deal with the competing goals of helping the language learners learn the school language and of teaching them subject matter, by concerning themselves only with teaching subject matter rather than with making themselves understood to the students in the class who have difficulty understanding the language in which the subject matter is being taught.

From the language learner's perspective, the ideal situation for language learning is one in which there are many fluent speakers of the target language with whom to interact. In a classroom, the more classmates around who can speak the new language, the better it is for the learner, especially if they are willing and ready to provide language input and help of the appropriate sort for the learner. A major problem for language learners involves getting enough exposure to the new language, and getting enough practice speaking it with people who know the language well enough to help them in their efforts to learn. If, in the classroom, there are English-speaking students with whom they can interact, then the language learners do not have to depend as much on the teacher's success in using language in such a way that it works as input. But even when there are classmates around who might be able to provide help, not all learners are able to avail themselves of this kind of assistance. Some learners simply lack the social skills needed to initiate contact with these English-speaking classmates, or to sustain interaction with them once they have made contact. Thus, the language used by teachers is an important source of linguistic input for most, if not all, students who find themselves having to learn the school language as a second one.

Classroom organization, that is, how teachers organize students for instruction, can affect the amount and quality of exposure learners will have to the new language. There appears to be two basic ways teachers organize and structure learning activities. The traditional way is for the teacher to control and direct actively the instructional activity. For example, the teacher presents the lesson, controls what is done during the lesson, and exercises a high degree of influence over what gets talked about and by whom. In such teacher-directed learning activities, the verbal exchange is largely between the teacher and class, as opposed to being between the teacher and individual student, or the student and fellow student. In contrast, a learner-centered organization or more "open" classroom is one in which teachers accomplish instruction largely through individualized learning activities, with much of the instructional interaction taking place between teacher and individual students, or among students in peer-teaching arrangements (see Peterson, 1979, for a review).

In this chapter, I report on an observational study of the instructional language used in four bilingual classrooms. Instructional language that apparently works as linguistic input is distinguished from language that does not work in this way. Different approaches to instructional language use in bilingual classrooms will be shown to affect the opportunities non-English speaking students encounter in these classrooms. This work is part of a larger NIE-sponsored study Susan Ervin-Tripp and I are currently conducting that examines some sources of individual differences in second language acquisition. The project involves a longitudinal investigation of the learning of English by some 60 young non-English speaking children. About half of these are Cantonese speakers, and the rest are Spanish speakers. We began following these children just as they began kindergarten, and we observed them through their first grade year. Although we are chiefly concerned in the larger study with establishing the extent to which individual characteristics of a cognitive and social nature affect language learning, we have not limited ourselves to looking only at such learner characteristics. It has become quite clear to us after two years of observing these children learning language that the instructional programs to which these children have been exposed also affect the success of their efforts.

Methods

The 60 children who served as subjects attended 4 kindergartens in 1979–1980. Three of these were officially designated as "bilingual" kinder-gartens; one was not, although the students in that class were nearly all non-English (NES) and limited-English speakers (LES) and there was a bilingual teacher assisting the English-speaking teacher in that classroom. The subjects began their kindergarten year with no English, that being a major criterion for selection as subjects in the study. Designation of students as NES was made after repeated (4 to 8 times) interviews by two or more investigators. In many cases, students said to be NES by their teachers were found to know some English, and they were consequently reclassified by the researchers as LES, and dropped as subjects from the study.

In addition to the 14 to 18 non-English speakers who qualified as subjects in each of the four kindergartens, there were also a number of children who were limited-English speakers. They were rejected as subjects because we had to establish a baseline for comparison, and the only sure way of doing this was to start with a group of subjects who were total novices to English. However, in many cases, some of these limited-English students knew so little English that it was difficult to distinguish them from the ones we were able to determine were true non-English speakers.

The four classes, however, were noncomparable with respect to the proportion of students in each that could be described as English speakers; that is, students who were either English monolinguals or fluent bilinguals. In one of the classes there were two English speakers to every limited or non-English speaker. (This was a double kindergarten, bringing together a Spanish bilingual class and an English monolingual class in a large double classroom.) In the other Spanish bilingual class, there were equal numbers of English and limited or non-English speakers. The two Chinese classes were quite different. There were few students in either who could be described as fluent English speakers—1 out of 5 in one class, and only 1 out of 12 in the other. Table 14.1 shows just how noncomparable these classes were in student composition.

The classes differed in another major dimension, that is, in the manner in which they were organized for instruction. Two of them, Classes 1 and 3, could be described as "open classrooms," although Classroom 1 had some teacher-directed activities incorporated in a basically open format. Classroom 3 had virtually no teacher-directed activities, whereas in Classes 2 and 4, most of the day was organized around teacher-structured lessons in which the students were either taught as a whole class or in large groups. Table 14.2 shows how the classes are categorized by student composition and classroom organization.

Table 14.1
Student Language Composition by Classes

Class	Type of program	English speakers N	English speakers Percentage	LES/NES speakers N	LES/NES speakers Percentage	Totals
1	Spanish bilingual	35	66	18	34	53
2[a]	Spanish bilingual	17	52	16	48	33
3[a]	English (with Cantonese assistant)	5	21	19	79	24
4[a]	Cantonese bilingual	2	8	24	92	26

[a] Several non-English speakers were added to each of these classes in the spring of the kindergarten year, but are not included in the figures shown in this table.

We acknowledge, of course, that there can be serious problems in studying the language learning of students whose main exposure to the new language was in classrooms differing as much in composition as these. Our justification for this selection was that the classes in which our subjects were enrolled reflect accurately the conditions under which such children are learning English, at least in the communities where we are carrying out this research. We recognized that if we are to look for the sources of individual differences in language learning, then we have to consider the conditions under which the kinds of learners we are interested in are learning language. We have tried, in addition to studying their language learning per se, to record their language learning experiences as accurately and completely as we can, and in so doing, to determine what effects the situational differences to which they have been exposed are having on their learning of the new language.

PROCEDURES

The findings reported in this chapter come from the observations carried out in our four classrooms during the first year of the study. One observer, and often two, was in each of the classrooms nearly everyday throughout the school year. These observers were testing and observing the children on the language

Table 14.2
Classification of the Four Classrooms by Student Composition and Classroom Organization

Classroom organization	Student composition Mixed NES–English speaking	Student composition High NES
Open	Class 1	Class 3
Teacher directed	Class 2	Class 4

learning and social style characteristics we are studying, and tape-recording samples of our subjects' language use as they acquired English. They were also observing the uses our subjects made of the opportunities to hear and use the new language in the classroom. These observations were both formal and informal. As the researchers carried out other kinds of data-collection activities, they were able to informally observe a great deal about the way the children went about learning the new language.

Formal observations were carried out on a monthly basis, with each child observed during a major learning activity in that class for about a half hour each month. These were audio-recorded, and detailed notes were made during the observations of the child's participation in the activity. The audio-recordings and the notes are enabling us to reconstruct the events, and to get a fairly good picture of what seems to make sense or not make sense to language learners. In addition to these regular observations of all subjects in the study, we also videotaped some all-day observations of a smaller number of subjects. We selected four subjects from each classroom and followed each of them for a full day with a video camera, recording all of the interactions involving that individual during the day.

What we have, then, is a record of the opportunities that exist in each classroom for learning language, at least from the perspective of several learners in each. We also have a record of the uses individual learners make of these opportunities to hear and use the new language.

The purpose of these observations was to examine the process by which our subjects are learning English. Our aim is to establish how each of the students whose language and social styles we are measuring and observing, and whose language development we are tracking, is approaching the learning of English. These observations have helped us to make sense of a rather unexpected finding.

At the end of the school year, we assembled ratings of the extent to which our 60 students had learned English. Each of the two or three members of the research team who had worked with the subjects in each site rated the English skills of the subjects in that classroom, and ranked them with respect to one another and with respect to all of the other children in the class. In each class, there were several children we knew to be fluent speakers of English, and several we were certain knew no English at all, since they were new immigrants who had arrived in the classroom near the end of the school year. These children provided known ends on a scale along which their classmates could be placed. The teachers and teacher assistants in each classroom were also asked to rate and rank the children in their class. These judgments augmented the "hard data" we had collected during the year in the form of language samples and proficiency test scores and gave us an additional assessment of the second language proficiency our subjects had achieved during their first year of exposure to English.

Results

In two of the classrooms, all or nearly all of the children who began the year with no English had learned some by the end of the first school year. There were individual differences among them in how much they had learned, to be sure, but just about everyone had learned enough English that they could be described at least as limited-English speakers. In the other two classes, no more than 60% of the non-English speakers had learned any English to speak of by the end of their first school year. The others were judged by all of us as not having learned any English. These ratings have largely been confirmed by our language tests and samples.

What made the difference between these classes? Apparently, the differences in classroom composition described earlier in this chapter did not by themselves determine whether the children learned English or not. The two classrooms in which almost everyone learned some English include the one with the largest proportion of limited and non-English speakers, and the one with the smallest proportion. Table 14.3 shows how the learners in the four classes fared. Nor did the differences found among these classes relate to the first language background of the students. Class 1, with all but two NES students learning some English by the end of the year, was a bilingual class serving Spanish speakers; Class 4, in which all of the NES students learned English, was a bilingual class serving Cantonese speakers. Instead, the differences appear to stem from the way language was used in each of the four

Table 14.3
Comparison of Students Who Failed to Learn English

	Beginning of the year		End of the year	
Class	Number of NES[a] in class	Percentage LES/ NES in class	Number of NES[a] in class	Percentage NES who learned no English
1	14	34	2	14
2	15	48	6	40
3	18	79	7	39
4	14	92	0	0

[a] Only those children who entered school prior to December 15 of the kindergarten year with no English at all are included in these figures. The LES children are represented in the LES–NES figures shown, but not in the NES figures.

Table 14.4
Comparison of Students Who Failed to Learn English

Classroom organization	Group composition
Open	Class 1 (14%)[a] Class 3 (39%)
Teacher directed	Class 2 (40%) Class 4 (0%)

[a] Percentage of students who learned no English after 1 year in the class.

classrooms, and this, in large part, was affected by the way each was organized for instruction, and by the student composition in each class. By examining the observations we made throughout the year in these classrooms, we have begun to piece together a picture of types of situations that appear to promote language learning, and to distinguish them from those situations that appear not to.

We believe we have found evidence that language use, stemming from the way in which the classrooms were organized for instruction, interacted with situational variables, such as classroom composition, to affect the ability of students to learn the new language. Table 14.4 shows how the classes compared on language learning, in relation to student composition and classroom organization. Figure 14.1 pictures the interaction between group composition and classroom organization.

Discussion

Let us consider language use situations in classrooms in which learners apparently have difficulty finding adequate opportunity to learn the new language. In open classrooms, such as 1 and 3, organized around individualized learning activities, the use of instructional language is more diversified than in teacher-directed classrooms. Instructional language can be used between students in peer-teaching or group-learning activities, or it can be used by the teacher in giving students individual instruction.

Learners in such classrooms have to play a greater role in getting needed exposure to the target language than do those in teacher-directed classes, since there are fewer occasions when the teacher is actually talking to the whole class. Such language is, in a sense, free input since the individual does not have to do anything special to get the exposure. In open classrooms, interaction between the teacher and students tends to be one-on-one. Some interaction will be initiated by the teacher, but there is a limit on how much any individual can expect without making any effort. If more contact is needed, either with

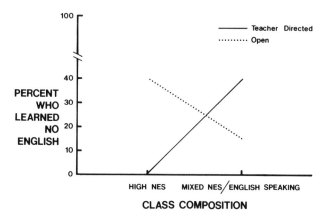

Figure 14.1. The interaction between group composition and classroom organization.

the teacher or with peers, the individual learner will have to solicit it. This requires a certain amount of social competence on the part of the learners, an attribute which varies among children. Hence, some learners have more contact than others with those who can help them learn their new language.

The importance of classroom organization is particularly obvious in cases where there is a marked imbalance between language learners and proficient English speakers in the class. In those situations where nearly all of the class are limited-English or non-English speakers, the teacher and aide (if there is one) are likely to be the only sources of second language input. Although one-on-one interaction is ideal for language learning purposes, there is only so much of it to go around in such classrooms. And with perhaps 30 children competing for this kind of interaction, the amount each receives may not be adequate to sustain language learning efforts.

A major problem for language learners who find themselves in such classes involves their having enough contact with people who can interact with them in the new language. In many cases, they will be encouraged to use English in speaking to their fellow classmates. But if all the children in the class are imperfect speakers of English, and they use English among themselves, they will end up practicing imperfectly learned forms, possibly with the result that these will become permanent aspects of their "internal grammars" of the new language. Researchers looking at the second language acquisition of French taking place in some of Canada's bilingual immersion programs have found that language learned on the basis of such input is likely to be a pidginized version of the target language, rather than a standard form of it (Selinker, Swain, & Dumas, 1975). Of course, children in such situations are more likely to speak to one another in their home language, a language in which they can communicate freely and easily, but this means they will not get adequate practice in hearing and using the new language.

This is precisely the situation that existed in one of the classrooms in which well over a third of the non-English speakers failed to learn any English. The children were interacting with one another as they went about their largely individualized learning activities each day, but they were doing so in their first language. Although the learning activities were in English (i.e., they were dealing with phonics and beginning mathematics in English rather than in their first language), they used little or no English in the classroom. Some of the non-English speakers could get by for an entire day with no direct contact with any English-speaking classmate. They had direct contacts with their English-speaking teacher each day, but those were brief and for some students relatively infrequent. The children were able to get by well enough since they were able to figure out what the teacher wanted them to do or to learn. She generally accompanied what she had to say with a nonverbal demonstration, and was conscientious about making herself understood. The children seldom said much during these interactions, but were nevertheless able to communicate their needs to her by nonverbal means. The children in that class who were unable to participate verbally in this kind of interaction, generally turned to the teaching assistant who was able to communicate with them in their first language.

Apparently, the amount of contact children can get with the target language in such situations, without special effort on their part, is not enough to support language learning. Children who make it a point to interact frequently with the teacher, or with the few English-speaking students in the class, learn English well enough. Those who are unable to initiate this kind of interaction, or who are uninterested in having it, generally have a harder time learning English.

The second type of situation that appears to limit the effectiveness of language used as input for language learning has to do with the range of language abilities represented in the classroom. If all, or nearly all, of the students are language learners, the problem of adjusting the language used for instruction so it serves as input is not a great problem for the teacher. Where everyone is a language learner, teachers tend, when using the target language for instructional purposes, to do what is necessary to help the learners understand what is going on. Whether what they do actually helps the students to learn the language is another question, of course. It will depend on whether the teachers are able to modify their language use in ways that make it work as language input.

From our observations, the language used by teachers in this type of situation tends to be geared to the needs of the learners. Generally, this requires that the actual content of the instructional program be geared down as well, with the subject matter goals set aside during the period when teachers and students work on learning the school language. Where a range of language proficiency is present among the students, the instructional situation is harder to manage.

Teachers find it considerably more difficult to tailor instructional language to the needs of language learners in classrooms where there are both language learners and fluent speakers of the target language. This was especially evident in Class 2. In addition to the 16 limited-English and non-English speakers, there were 17 fluent speakers of English (10 of whom were English monolinguals). For the teacher trying to use English as the medium of instruction for teaching subject matter, this kind of variation in the language ability of the students can be extremely difficult to handle. It is hard to make the adjustments the language learners need for figuring out what is being said in the presence of others who find such efforts unnecessary and boring. The tendency for most teachers in a mixed language situation is to talk to the students who understand best rather than in a way that can be understood by everyone. Often, the easiest solution is to aim at a point somewhere in the middle of the various abilities, and hope for the best. Indeed, this is what we have frequently observed during group instruction in mixed classes. Such language is modified somewhat, but not enough to allow children who do not know the language well to figure out what is being said. The consequence is that the English used instructionally is not very useful to learners as input data.

Of course, this leaves the teachers with another dilemma: How can they make sure that the children having difficulty with English are learning what they are supposed to be learning of the subject matter? It is quite apparent that when teachers do not make necessary adjustments for the sake of these children, the children will get little out of subject matter instruction.

We have observed several solutions teachers adopt that appear to be **unsuccessful,** at least from the perspective of the language learners in the class. One solution is to group the children by language and to teach each group separately in its own language. The trouble with this approach is that the non-English speaking students are not exposed at all to English.

A second solution is to translate, whereby the teacher presents the materials to be learned in English, and immediately afterward gives the students who have difficulty understanding English a translational equivalent in the language they do understand. This is a popular solution for teachers in bilingual programs who are trying to deal with the problem of teaching students who represent a wide range of language proficiency in the two languages of the classroom. In using both languages for instructional purposes, however, some students at all times will have a limited ability to comprehend whichever language is being used. In Class 2, for example, the non-English speakers had difficulty understanding the subject matter whenever English was the language serving as the medium of instruction. When Spanish was used, the 10 English monolinguals in that class had difficulty understanding what was being taught. The solution of using both languages, then, seems to be a sensible one, at least from the perspective of the teachers. In this way, both groups are hearing the subject matter in language they understand and both are being exposed to the language they do not understand.

This particular approach may work well for the teaching of subject matter, but our research leads us to believe that it does not enhance second language learning for either the non-English speakers or the English monolinguals, who presumably could be making use of the Spanish, for instance, as linguistic input for learning that language as a second one. By always giving the same information in both languages, the teacher relieves the learners of the need to make an effort at figuring out what is being said. This, I believe, is a vital step in the learning of a new language: A language cannot be learned as a second one unless the learner is trying to make sense of it. Furthermore, because the translation presumably made it possible for both groups to understand what was being said, modifications that would have qualified the language used as input were not made. Hence, the learners, even when they tried could not easily figure out what was being said.

Thus, the translation approach appears to short-circuit the two-way process that must take place between the person who speaks the target language and the one who wants to learn it. Teachers using this approach assume they are making it possible for both groups to learn the subject matter being taught and to learn, as a second language, the one they do not know. Presumably, for example, the juxtaposition of English with Spanish makes it possible for the non-English speakers to figure out how the English is being used. But, instead, students apparently learn to ignore the language they do not understand.

We have numerous video-recorded observations of students in this kind of instructional situation. They were alternately attentive and inattentive as the teacher switched between languages in their lessons. When the language they did not understand was being spoken, the students simply stopped listening because they could count on getting the information in the language they knew. Hence they were able to get along without having to deal with the problem of learning English so they could understand what was going on. This was a major factor in one of the two classes in which over a third of the children learned virtually no English after a year in school.

What situations appear to promote language learning? A common assumption held by opponents of bilingual education is that if non-English speakers are to learn English they must be taught exclusively in English. The assumption is that if students are not learning English it is because they are being taught in the first language. Obviously, there is an element of truth in this, but matters are much more complex than they appear. A critical difference between situations that promote language learning and ones that do not lies not only in the amount of exposure to the new language, but also in how the language is used.

In the two bilingual classrooms that promoted language learning, the teachers rarely mixed the languages of instruction. In Class 1, where a wide range of language ability was present among the students, the children were grouped by language ability for instruction—the Spanish speakers were in one group; the English speakers were in another. Each group was not taught exclusively in the familiar language, however. Some subjects were taught to each in the unfamiliar language as well, and when this language was used, the teachers made special efforts to use the language in a way that made it possible for the children to understand the content, and also to make use of that language as input for language learning purposes. The children, of course, were not totally segregated by language. Since English speakers and non-English speakers were members of the same large class, there were numerous occasions each day for members of each group to interact with the others, and they did to a certain extent. Hence, the students were not only getting exposure to the language to be learned from teachers, but from fellow classmates as well.

In Class 4, with few English speakers, a different solution was necessary. Here, teachers were main sources of the new language. They needed to structure the instructional program so the learners were provided with ample exposure to the language to be learned, and this language had to work as input. The teacher in the class in which every child learned English managed this by organizing the class around highly structured, teacher-directed activities. These included both whole-class and small-group learning activities, which were nearly always teacher directed. The instruction provided in these teacher-directed lessons was either in English or in the home language of the students—it was seldom mixed. When English was the medium of instruction, its use was judiciously shaped with the learners' needs in mind. The children were called on frequently to respond, either as individuals or as a group. The teacher occasionally used the other language to explain concepts that could not be demonstrated nonverbally and would otherwise be difficult for the children to understand in English. But on such occasions, the language was used for explanation, it seemed to us, rather than for translation. By structuring the class in this manner, the problem of the children practicing imperfectly learned forms on one another was minimized. There were drawbacks, of course: The children did not have as much opportunity to interact with one another as they did in the other three classes, and the English they learned tended to resemble teacher-talk rather than children's language—but they all did learn some English.

Conclusion

Clearly, the way teachers use language in classrooms serving non-English speaking students does affect the ease with which these children learn that language as a second one. It should be pointed out, however, that our observations are preliminary ones and should be regarded as such. Our next research step is to look at the way instructional language functions in a more formal way as language learning input. During the next several years, my colleagues and I will be investigating the problem more directly in larger numbers of classrooms.[2] This work has important consequences for bilingual education, I believe. At present, the future of bilingual education is in question throughout the country. Its proponents are being called on to demonstrate that this kind of approach works well for most children in achieving the only goal that educational policymakers in this country regard as valid where non-English speaking children are concerned—that of teaching these children the societal language. We recognize that bilingual education has other important instructional goals as well, but this particular goal is the one on which it is being judged, fairly or not. Finding out what does or does not work for language learners is a first step in improving the instruction that occurs in classrooms serving non-English speakers in this country.

References

Berko-Gleason, J. Talking to children: Some notes on feedback. In C. Snow & C. Ferguson (Eds.), *Talking to children.* New York: Cambridge University Press, 1977.

Ferguson, C. Baby talk as a simplified register. In C. Snow & C. Ferguson (Eds.), *Talking to children.* New York: Cambridge University Press, 1977.

Peterson, P. Direct instruction reconsidered. In P. Peterson & H. Walberg (Eds.), *Research on teaching: Concepts, findings, and implications.* Berkeley: McCutchan Publishing Corporation, 1979.

Phillips, J. Syntax and vocabulary of mothers' speech to young children: Age and sex comparisons. *Child Development,* 1973, *44,* 182–185.

Selinker, L., Swain, M., & Dumas, G. The interlanguage hypothesis extended to children. *Language Learning,* 1975, *25,* 139–152.

Shatz, M., & Gelman, R. The development of communication skills: Modifications in the speech of young children as a function of listener. *Monographs of the Society for Research in Child Development,* 1973, *38*(152).

Snow, C. Mothers' speech to children learning language. *Child Development,* 1972, *43,* 549–565.

Snow, C., & Ferguson, C. *Talking to children.* New York: Cambridge University Press, 1977.

[2] Paul Ammon, Mary Sue Ammon, Louise Cherry Wilkinson, Barry McLaughlin, Michael Strong, and I are currently (1980–1983) engaged in a large-scale classroom study funded by National Institute of Education on the effects of instructional practices on language learning.

15

Teachers' Interpretations of Students' Behavior[1]

HUGH MEHAN
ALMA HERTWECK
SAM EDWARD COMBS
PIERCE JULIUS FLYNN

In this chapter, we explore the relationship between what teachers say about students' classroom behavior and what students actually do in classrooms. This investigation provides information about theories of perception and categorization of people that guide teachers in their interpretations of students' classroom behavior.

The topic of this chapter is somewhat different from others in this collection. Although we have all been influenced by developments in the "ethnography of communication [Gumperz & Hymes, 1964, 1972]," the other chapters are primarily concerned with descriptions of communicating **in** the classroom. Ours is concerned with communicating **about** the classroom. Whereas some describe the organization of events in the classroom (e.g., DeStefano, Sanders, & Pepinsky, Chapter 7, this volume; Erickson, Chapter 9, this volume; and Green & Harker, Chapter 10, this volume) and others describe the organizational consequences of the distribution of certain speech functions (Eder, Chapter 12, this volume; Fillmore, Chapter 14, this volume), we have taken the context of the classroom and the instructional events that occur there as a starting place. Our purpose is to describe the social meanings that teachers assign to the student participants in these events.

[1] Support for this work was provided by the National Institute of Education Grant #8-0497, UCSD #3433; the statements expressed are solely the responsibility of the authors.

COMMUNICATING IN THE CLASSROOM

Theories of Category Formation

All people partition their environment into categories for establishing equivalence among objects and events. Two theories concerning the process by which instances are placed into categories are: (*a*) a "critical features" theory and (*b*) a "family resemblance" theory.

CRITICAL FEATURES THEORY

The critical or classical (Smith & Medin, 1979) view of category formation is based on an assumption of "literal measurement [Cicourel, 1964]" or "literal description [Wilson, 1970]" derived from a correspondence theory of meaning. The critical features theory assumes:

> (1) Membership is fully determined by possession of a small set of singly necessary and jointly sufficient features or attributes; (2) all members possess all of these critical features, and therefore, are equally qualified as members of the category; (3) there are distinctive boundaries between categories and hence no ambiguous examples that fit in more than one category at the same level of abstraction in the taxonomy; and (4) the possession of certain critical features cannot ameliorate the absence of any other critical features in the membership test—therefore, all critical features are equally important for determining categorization [Cantor & Mischel, 1979, p. 9].

FAMILY RESEMBLANCE THEORY

Critical features theory may be an appropriate guide to categorizing objects in the abstract world of formal, logical systems (Carnap, 1939). However, when one turns from the formal world of artificial systems to the concrete world of everyday categories—to songbirds and furniture, to appropriate and inappropriate classroom behavior—people may not apply the criteria of literal measurement found in critical features theory.

Wittgenstein (1953) was one of the first to point out that the members of everyday categories do not share all or a set of singly necessary and jointly sufficient features critical for category membership. When one examines a set of objects all labeled by one general term, one will not find a single set of features shared by all members of the category, but a "pattern of overlapping similarities," a structure of "family resemblances [Cantor & Mischel, 1979; Rosch & Mervis, 1975]." In Wittgenstein's (1953) words:

> We see a complicated network of similarities, overlapping and criss crossing, sometimes similarities of detail. I can think of no better expression to categorize these similarities than "family resemblances," for the various resemblances between the members of a family: build, features, color of eyes, gait, temperament etc., that overlap and criss cross in some way [pp. 66, 67].

Smith and Medin (1979) further specify the family resemblance view of category formation with their descriptions of "abstract prototypes" and "exemplar prototypes." The abstract prototype or "polythetic [Shweder, 1977]" view assumes that the representation of a concept is an abstraction from the specific exemplars of the concept, and this summary is used to decide whether a particular instance belongs to the category. It further assumes that different instances can vary in the extent to which they will embody the concept. A single description of some object may suffice, but the properties of the description are now only true for most, but not all of the members. Some instances of the class will possess more of the critical features than will others. Those instances possessing more critical properties are said to be more representative of the concept in question.

The exemplar prototype view assumes that the representation of a semantic concept consists of separate descriptions of some of its exemplars. Categorization is assumed to be basically an inductive or analogical process. The exemplars used to represent a concept are more likely to be typical rather than atypical exemplars (cf. Cicourel, 1980b). They are the "clearest cases" and "best examples," such that a chair is seen by speakers of our language and members of our culture to be a mere reasonable exemplar of the category **furniture** (Rosch & Mervis, 1975).[2]

The Locus of the Structures of Perception

These two theories of category formation hold competing views about the ontological locus of the categories people use to make sense of objects and each other. The question is: Do the structures of perception reside in the particular stimulus object or do they reside in the head of the perceiver?

STRUCTURES IN THE HEAD OF THE PERCEIVER

Those theorists who place the structures of perception exclusively in the head of the perceiver adopt a mentalist perspective on category formation. They treat the stimulus environment as an unstructured mass of undifferentiated information that must be tamed and differentiated by the linguistically alert child. According to this view, the world for the child at the outset is some version of James' "booming buzzing confusion." The child is taught in due course to impose upon this confusion a kind of discriminating grid that serves to distinguish the world as being composed of a large number of separate

[2] See Goodenough (1956) and Schneider (1965) for analogous treatments of the genealogical dimensions of blood and marriage in the kinship domain.

"things," each labeled with a name. This position has the individual, as a member of a culture, engaged in personal reality construction work, creating coherence out of chaos, order out of disorder.

STRUCTURES IN THE OBJECT OF PERCEPTION

Those theorists who place the structures of perception exclusively in the particular stimulus object adopt a realist position on category formation. Rosch and her colleagues (Rosch & Mervis, 1975; Rosch, Mervis, Gray, Johnson, & Boyes-Braem, 1976) are representative of this position. Although acknowledging the role of construction in perception, Rosch is critical of views that conclude categorization is entirely arbitrary. She says that such a view of categorization would be tenable only if the world as presented to the perceiver were entirely unstructured, that is, if the world formed a set of stimuli in which all possible stimulus attributes occurred with equal probability combined with all other attributes.

Rosch does not find that the world contains intrinsically separate things. Instead, real world attributes, unlike those stimuli often presented to experimental subjects, do not occur independently of each other.

> Creatures with feathers are more likely also to have wings than creatures with fur, and objects with the visual appearance of chairs are more likely to have functional sit-on-ableness than objects with the appearance of cats. That is, combinations of attributes of real objects do not occur uniformly. Some pairs, triples, or n-tuples are quite probable, appearing in combinations with one, sometimes another attribute; others are rare; others logically cannot or empirically do not occur [Rosch et al., 1976, p. 383].

Educational Correlates of Category Formation Theories

These positions on the formation of categories have correlates in the educational context, albeit the categorizer and the objects being categorized are considerably different. Instead of experimental subjects being asked to classify dot patterns, artificial faces, colors, dogs, furniture, or songbirds in contrived circumstances, we have classroom teachers classifying students' behavior as a matter of course in naturally occurring educational contexts. Accounts of students' success and failure abound, but the dominant ones cluster into versions of the realist and mentalist perspectives discussed previously.

REALIST ACCOUNTS OF STUDENTS' SCHOOL PERFORMANCE

The realist set of explanations accounts for students' success and failure in terms of students' characteristics. These "traits and states" theories are similar because they place the causal locus within the object of perception, the students themselves. Jensen (1969), who accounts for the failure of black and other ethnic minority groups in terms of a genetically provided, general lack of intelligence, provides an example of a realist account of school performance.

States and traits assumptions are also found in the "medical model [Mercer, 1979]" inherent in PL 94-142, the federal law that governs the education of handicapped students. The medical model, developed to understand and combat pathological conditions, assumes that symptoms are caused by some biological condition in the organism: "In the medical model, the organism is the focus of assessment and pathology is perceived as a condition in the person, an attribute of the organism. Thus, we say a person *is* tubercular, or *has* scarlet fever [Mercer, 1979, p. 95]."

The Education For All Handicapped Children law has specific provisions for answering questions about the **physical** state of the organism, for example, measures of "health, vision, hearing . . . and motor activities [Federal Register 121a532 [3] F]." However, the underlying assumptions of the medical model have been extended beyond the physical aspects of students considered for special education, such that "intelligence," "aptitude," "potential," or "mental ability" are also treated as internal states, attributes, or personal possessions of the individual.

The assumption that school success or failure can be attributed to the states or traits of the individual also guides "cognitive styles" research (Bereiter & Engleman, 1966; Bernstein, 1971; Hess & Shipman, 1965; Ramirez & Castaneda, 1974). Thus Bereiter and Engleman (1966) conclude that the language of ethnic minority and lower-class preschool children is "inadequate for expressing personal or original opinions, for analysis and careful reasoning, for dealing with anything hypothetical or beyond the present or for explaining anything very complex [p. 32]." This linguistic deficiency, they reason, is the basis of the poor school performance of "disadvantaged children" and forms the basis of such increasingly popular instructional packages as DISTAR, which teach poor and ethnic minority children by drill and practice, rote learning, and by dispensing tangible positive reinforcements.

MENTALIST ACCOUNTS OF STUDENT ACHIEVEMENT

A second set of accounts of students' school achievement shifts the reason for students' success or failure from the body of the students to the head of the teacher. The most notable example of this mentalist account of school performance is "expectancy theory [Bar Tal, 1978; Rosenthal & Jacobsen, 1968]." In its most extreme and simplistic form, expectancy theory assumes that it is not the students' characteristics or behavior that leads to success or failure, it is the expectations that teachers have about students' behavior that is influential.

Expectancy theory bears a strong family resemblance to labeling theory (Griffin & Mehan, 1980), especially as that theory has been applied to the identification of mentally retarded students (Mercer, 1974) and the study of rule breaking in classrooms (Hargreaves, Hester, & Mellor, 1975). According to labeling theorists (Becker, 1963; Kitsuse, 1962; Lemert, 1951), the main difference between normals and deviants is that deviants have been apprehended and processed by formal institutions (e.g., courts and hospitals), whereas so-called normals have not, in spite of having committed similar deviant acts in many cases. Thus, from the point of view of labeling theory, and its cousin expectancy theory, the reasons for students' success or failure are not to be found in the acts or characteristics of students themselves. Rather, they are to be found in the teacher's reactions to student behavior. Students are successful and unsuccessful not because of the inherent characteristics of their actions, but because they have been labeled or defined by others as such.

We are interested in the viability of these alternative theories for understanding teachers' interpretations of students' behavior. A naturally occurring feature of schools, the special education referral system, provided us with a routinized setting for a study of these contrasting views of success and failure.

The Special Education Referral System

Under normal circumstances, students enter school in the kindergarten, and at the end of each school year, are promoted to the next higher grade. One deviation from this normative pattern involves the "special education referral system," in which students are removed from the regular classroom during the school year, and are placed in a variety of special education programs. The process of identifying, assessing, and eventually placing students in special educational programs is a rich environment of naturally occurring, routine decision making, instances of which are difficult to create in laboratory settings.

We have been following the progress of students' cases through the special education referral system by examining decision making at a number of major decision-making points, including "referral," "appraisal," "assessment," "reappraisal," "evaluation," and "placement." The various career paths that result from this decision-making process, the adaptations that the school system makes to the constraints imposed by the practical circumstances imposed by too many cases and too few resources, are beyond the scope of this chapter. They have been described elsewhere (Mehan, Meihls, Hertweck, & Crowdes, 1981). What is of interest for our present purposes is the initial phase of the referral process.

The referral system is most often activated by a referral from a classroom teacher who fills out a standardized referral form that includes the reason for referral and biographical information about the student. Analyses of 165 referrals made during the 1978–1979 school year in one southern California school district show that students are referred for a host of reasons, including unusual academic performance, discipline for misconduct, physical handicaps, or behavioral problems. Once this referral form is completed it is reviewed by the School Appraisal Team (SAT). The referral case of which this form is now a part can then be resolved at different points in the system (e.g., after appraisal, after assessment, in the placement committee). For more details see Mehan et al. (1981).

The Data Base

The materials for this exploration of teachers' accounts and students' behavior come from two sources: student records maintained by the school district and "viewing sessions." The records of the 2781 students in the district were reviewed during the 1978–1979 school year. This records review provided us with information about the age, grade, and sex of the student, as well as the official reason for, and date of referral, the person making the referral, educational test results, and final disposition of the case.

After the referrals were made, we contacted the classroom teachers and scheduled observations if they agreed to participate in the study. A total of 27 teachers who referred 55 students agreed to participate in this aspect of the study.[3] Once permission was obtained, a member of the research team observed the classroom to obtain a sense of classroom routine and typical patterns of classroom life. Once general observations were completed, representative classroom events, including the student referred as part of a regular work group, were videotaped. On completion of the taping, "viewing sessions [Cicourel, Jennings, Jennings, Leiter, MacKay, Mehan, & Roth, 1974; Davies, 1978; Erickson & Shultz, 1981; Florio, 1978; Mehan, 1979; Shumsky, 1972; Shuy & Griffin, 1978]" were scheduled.

Thus, the order of events that form the basis of the following analysis is teacher referral, teacher contact, videotaping, and viewing session. Hence, the viewing session occurs after the referral has been made. This "chronology [Cicourel, 1980a]" means our methodology is, of necessity, reconstructive. We are trying to approximate a delicate decision-making process, one in which teachers make determinations about students' performance and single out certain students for referral. Although the lapse in time between referral and

[3] The data base of this report is 11 students referred by 7 teachers. As we analyze more protocols, we will revise our conclusions if necessary.

viewing, the differences in the demands of the classroom in which the decision is made, and the demands of the viewing session in which the decision is recounted make it impossible to duplicate the teachers' actual perceptual process by which they identify referral students, we are attempting to create a kind of natural experiment in a natural setting (D'Andrade, 1981a) to recreate as closely as possible what might have happened at the time of referral. We believe this reconstructive approach is preferable to other methodological alternatives because in striking a balance between fidelity to and control over the spontaneity of the original situation in which the referral decision was made, a certain ecological validity is achieved (cf. Cicourel, 1980b; Cole, Hood, & McDermott, 1978).

The Viewing Sessions

During the course of this far-ranging interview (see Combs & Hertweck, 1979, for details), teachers were first asked for general information about their classroom. Then, they were asked about the reasons they referred students. In the following analysis, we refer to these as the "interview reasons" in contrast to the "official reasons" for referral obtained from the students' school records. Next, teachers were invited to watch videotapes of events from their classroom. They were given the general instruction to "stop the machine whenever something interesting that you want to report on appears on the tape [cf. Erickson & Shultz, 1981]." Teachers were also given the following specific instructions for asking the interviewer to stop the tape:

1. When the child who was referred is doing something about which you would like to comment
2. When you or the children other than the referred are doing something about which you would like to comment
3. When you see a comparison between behavior and/or ability of the child referred and other members in the group
4. When you see some of the behavior on the tape which could have caused you to refer the child

The teachers' "identifications," (i.e., noting by comment or pointing) of referral behavior in response to the interviewer's instruction to point to instances of referral behavior on the tape were juxtaposed to an independent analysis of the taped classroom events conducted by Combs, Flynn, and Hertweck. The official and interview reasons for referral were used as a template or emic grid to search for equivalent instances of behavior elsewhere on the tape.[4] First, the team noted each teacher's categories for referring a student, for example, "low academic performance," and "poor peer relations." Second, the team noted the instances of behavior associated with each category, such that "poor pronunciation" and "hesitation in reading" were instances of "low academic performance," and "not joining in group activities" was an instance of "poor peer relations." Third, the entire tape was reviewed to see if other instances of these behaviors were visible in the conduct of both the referral and nonreferral students.

Teachers' Accounts and Students' Behavior

The teachers' comments during the viewing session, especially their responses to the questions listed previously, plus our independent analysis of the taped classroom events and school records form the basis of the following analysis.

TEACHERS' IDENTIFICATION OF CATEGORIES AND INSTANCES
OF REFERRAL REASONS

Analysis of the school records and viewing session transcripts reveals the following:

1. Teachers did not point out every reason they referred a student on the videotape. Teachers pointed to an instance of their "official" referral reason 48% of the time and to instances of their "interview" reasons 40% of the time.

2. Teachers did not favor particular referral reasons by uniformly identifying behavior only within particular categories. Table 15.1 lists the major referral reason categories, the number of referral reasons given in those categories, and the number of times the teacher pointed to one or more examples of that particular behavior during the viewing session.

This table indicates that teachers pointed to instances of academic, behavioral, psychological, and social categories approximately 50% of the time and to physical reasons 25% of the time during the viewing session. An "academic difficulty" such as "poor handwriting" or "working below grade level in reading and spelling" was as likely to be pointed to as a "behavioral problem" such as "disruptive classroom behavior."

3. Although teachers in general were not more likely to identify particular

---

[4] We are indebted to Jürgen Streeck for suggesting that we view the behavior of referral and nonreferral students in this way.

Table 15.1
Teacher Identification of Referral Reason Categories During Viewing Sessions

Referral reason categories	Number of referral reasons in category	Number of times teachers identified examples on tape	Percentage
Academic	16	9	56
Behavioral	4	2	50
Psychological	4	2	50
Social	4	2	50
Physical	4	1	25
Total	32	16	48

categories of referral reasons, categories had more salience for particular teachers. Teachers located at least one, and frequently more, instances of a particular referral category, while not identifying any instances of other referral categories. Although teachers may have given a referral reason within a particular category, they may or may not have pointed out an instance of that category.

We find the same pattern in the way teachers identified instances of specific categories of referral reasons as we did in the way teachers identified entire categories of referral reasons.

4. Teachers did not point to each instance of behavior that constituted a referral category. Table 15.2 shows the instances of referral behavior identified by the teachers and the number of occurrences identified by the research panel.

Percentage of identification ranges from 20.8% (teacher 2) to 110.2% (teacher 8), with the latter teacher identifying more behavioral occurrences than were apparent to the research panel. Compared to 362 total behavioral occurrences noted by the research panel, the teachers identified 133 behavioral occurrences (36%).

Table 15.2
Teacher Identification of Behavior on Videotape

	Teacher-identified behavior	Researcher-identified behavior	Percentage
Teacher 2	10	48	20.8
Teacher 3	31	106	29.2
Teacher 5	14	30	46.7
Teacher 8	43	39	110.2
Teacher 11	12	69	17.4
Teacher 15	11	13	84.6
Teacher 17	12	57	21.0
Total	133	362	36.7

5. The instances of behavior identified by the teacher were usually the first ones that appeared. The teachers did not watch the entire tape, which includes a number of instances of behavior, and point out the last one as the example of the referral reason.

In short, the teachers used exemplars to identify referral categories and instances of referral behavior. The process of categorizing by exemplars is analogous to what Mannheim (1952) called the "documentary method of interpretation." According to Mannheim, the documentary method consists of the search for "an identical homologous pattern underlying a vast variety of totally different realizations of meaning [Mannheim, 1952]." Garfinkel (1967) elaborates the use of the documentary method as follows:

> The method consists of treating an actual appearance as "the document of," as "pointing to," as "standing on behalf of" a presupposed underlying pattern. Not only is the underlying pattern derived from its individual documentary evidence, but the individual documentary evidences, in their turn, are interpreted on the basis of what is known about the underlying pattern. Each is used to elaborate the other.

For the teachers, one or two instances exemplify, "stand for," and "document" the referral category and the category is represented and elaborated by the exemplars. This spiral of a part-for-whole, whole-for-part relationship (Mehan & Wood, 1975) is signaled in the teachers' discourse by expressions such as, *That is a frequent response of his* or *So watch what he does during the videotape, it's typical . . .*

TEACHERS' IDENTIFICATION OF REFERRED STUDENTS' BEHAVIOR AND
NONREFERRED STUDENTS' BEHAVIOR

In this section we contrast teachers' identification of referral behavior with both students who have been referred and who have not been referred for special education. The critical features theory of category construction discussed previously generates the following propositions about teachers' referrals:

1. There are instances of student behavior (e.g., *dropping a book, hitting a child*).
2. Every instance of student behavior is collected into a category (e.g., "small motor control," "antisocial behavior").
3. All instances of a behavior in a category are treated in the same way (e.g., as an instance of referral behavior).
4. Every instance of referral behavior is noticed.
5. Every child who engages in such behavior is referred.

This set of statements has a causal quality. The behavior of the child is said to be the cause of the referral, for example, the student's action of throwing down a book is the reason the teacher makes the referral. The inverse of this set of statements is that every behavior not identified by the teacher is "not referral behavior."

Table 15.3 shows the number of instances of behavior located on tape by the research team and the number of instances of behavior identified by the teacher.

All of the teachers except one (Teacher 3) identified more behavior for referral students than for nonreferral students. In fact, in three cases, teachers did not point to any behavior displayed by nonreferral students. Of a total of 254 referral behaviors displayed by referral students, 118 were identified. Of 108 referral behaviors displayed by nonreferral students, only 15 were identified by teachers. Thus, although 46.4% of the behaviors by referral students were identified, only 13.9% of the behaviors by nonreferral students were identified. That is to say we have many instances of the following sort:

1. The teacher identifies a certain set of categories of behavior as reasons for referral, and identifies some of them in the behavior of the referral student on the tape during viewing sessions.
2. Instances of the same sort of behavior are apparent in the behavior of other students in the same event on the tape, but the teacher does not identify them as instances of referral behavior, nor is the child identified as a referral student.

The following teacher–student exchanges exemplify this point. In the event used in the viewing session with Teacher 11, two of the children are referral children. In fact, the reasons they were referred were practically identical. The teacher said, "they both lacked self-confidence," that is, "they continually expressed concern over getting their work done and the difficulty of their work."

In the course of the viewing session, four different segments of the tape elicited comments from the teacher regarding this lack of self-confidence. We present three of the segments, followed by the teachers' verbatim comments regarding the "lack of self-confidence" referral reason.

Segment 1. (Scene: A math lesson, in which students are arranging geometric shapes, called tangrams, into a pattern on a page. T = teacher, Ss = students, S1 and S2 are referral students. S3 and S4 are other students engaged in the taped lesson. I = Interviewer.)

> 5   T   *Okay. We're going to do something a little different today. I'm going to have you cut these out and you're going to do some puzzles, make some puzzles with them.* [Shane returns to group.] *And I want to **watch** how you do it, and we'll talk about how you're putting these puzzles together. The first thing you need to do is each*

Table 15.3
Teachers' Identification of Referred and Nonreferred Behavior

	Referred students			Nonreferred students		
	Instances of behavior on tape	Instances of behavior identified by teacher	Percentage	Instances of behavior on tape	Instances of behavior identified by teacher	Percentage
Teacher 2	29	10	34.5	19	0	0
Teacher 3	98	23	23.5	8	8	100
Teacher 5	22	14	63.4	8	0	0
Teacher 8	27	40	148.0	12	3	25
Teacher 11	43	12	27.9	26	0	0
Teacher 15	7	8	114.0	6	3	50
Teacher 17	28	11	39.3	29	1	3
Total	254	118	46.4	108	15	13.9

of you are going to get a colored square like this [draws shape on card] *and cut out on all the lines very, very carefully.*

6 Ss *Um hum.*

7 T *Because you need them really straight. Okay? Do you see that? So I'll give each of you a different color.* [Passes out material.] *Cut out the whole thing, uh huh. The whole thing. Along all the lines now.* **Yes** *go ahead and do that.* [Students begin cutting shapes.] *Okay, cut out on all the lines. And* **then** *you're going to be working with these pieces and trying to put them in a picture. Make a puzzle. Have you done these before?*

8 S3 *I have.*

9 T *Very good. Be sure you cut carefully on each line, okay?*

10 S1 *Can we go out of the line?*

11 T *A little bit but try to keep on the line as much as possible. All right? I think I'll do one too. Let me get the scissors.* [Stands up.] *Billy, well just try to make a little outline of it. Shane, you want to sit down? Make a sketch of it. I'll know what you mean.*

12 S1 *Miss Phane, could we just cut like* **this**?

13 T *Yeah, yeah. But don't lose any of your pieces though. Put the pieces behind you when you cut these off and don't lose any of those little pieces, okay?*

14 S3 *My little pieces are right there.*

15 S1 *Some people are going to have different kinds of shapes, aren't they?*

16 T *No. Everybody will have the same shapes. These are all start out from the same square.*

17 S1 *But we won't be cutting out the same way.*

18 T (To group) *Okay, put your scraps behind you and your scissors behind you* **so,** *you've got room to work in front of you there.*

19 S1 *We won't be cutting the same way. We won't be cutting the same way.*

20 T *What do you mean?*

21 S1 *Some people might be cutting different.*

22 T *But, we're all starting out with the same square and the same shape. Right? See that? Look.*

Teacher's Commentary on Segment 1:

TAPE STOPS

11–118 T: *I've been noticing all along what's coming out with Christian. He's the blond one.*

11–119 I: *The blond-haired one. Okay.*

11–120 T: *And, um, that's one of the things that I've been concerned about with him, is that he constantly needs to know whether he's doing it right . . .*

Segment 2. (Scene: The same lesson; the teacher has passed out a new pattern.)

72 T *I'm going to give you different so that you can stand out, yeah.* [Everyone speaks out at once here about colors.]

73 S4 *I want this color.*

74 T *They'll all fit, I assure you. It's the same house. Okay. Okay. Try and fit the shapes so that they fill in the house.* [Students begin working.]

75 S2 **No way.**

Teacher's Commentary on Segment 2:

TAPE STOPS

11–125 I: *Who said that?*

11–126 T: *"No way." Shane said that.*

11–127 I: *Okay.*

11–128 T: *He's the one back here.*

11–129 I: *Okay. Okay.*

11–130 T: *Yeah he, he starts out like that with a lot of things. It's like, I can't do it. He's just glancing at it. . . . He's very apprehensive about approaching, anything. But once he gets into it, and, or finishes something he's just so pleased with himself. And I'll say, hey, I thought you said, "No way." "Well."*

Segment 3. (Scene: The same lesson; the teacher has passed out a new pattern.)

131 T *Yeah. You keep the shapes, you're going to use the same shapes all right.* [Passes out materials] *I want you and try and make a whale.*

132 S1 *Okay, that's . . .*

133 T *You try and make an "E."*

134 S2 **Oh, no, me and my big mouth.** [Sings]

135 T *An arrow.*

136 S3 *Ohhh.*

137 S2 **Me and my big mouth.** [Sings]

138 S4 *What are you trying to make?*

139 S3 **Uh oh.**

140 T *They're each working on something different now.*

141 S2 *See if this fits. Oh goodies.*

142 S4 *I don't know if that fits.*

143 T *Well does it leave you a triangle space for the other one? Switch it around somehow so that it will leave you a space for that other triangle.*

144   S2   ***It's impossible, Mrs. Phane,*** *to do one like this way. To do an*
           E with one of these shapes.
145   T   *You think so?*
146   S2   *Uh huh.*
147   S1   *Nooo.*
148   T   *Just try. Move them around.*

Teacher's commentary on Segment 3:

TAPE STOPS

11–406   T: *I mentioned before, yeah, that whenever he's given some new*
            task to do it's always like, too hard, no way I can do it, until we,
            oh, come on, you just get into it and try it. When he finishes, I
            mean it's like fantastic, you know, that he did it . . .

The teacher did not stop the tape or comment on it when other students
said similar things at numerous places in the lesson. For example:

(Scene: The same math lesson, in which students are arranging geometric
shapes. S1 is a referral student; S3 is not.)
89   T   *So you move the other pieces around and see if you can get the*
          bottom part of the building.
90   S3   *That bottom part's hard.*
91   S1   *This part can't get filled.*

In this exchange, both a student who has been referred (S1) and a
student who has not been (S3) expressed concern over the difficulty of the
task, yet the teacher did not stop the tape nor comment on it while it was
running. In fact, the difficulty of the task was a constant concern for all
students during the lesson. The two referral and two nonreferral students all
commented on the difficulty of the task an equal number of times. Nevertheless,
the teacher did not treat the comments by the nonreferral students as instances
of the "concern over work difficulty" referral category during the viewing
sessions, although she did treat similar comments by the referral students as
exemplifying this referral category.

A second example concerns behavior displayed by a referral student and
a nonreferral student. "Rich" had been referred for many reasons, one of which
was "hitting other people." At the opening of the videotaped reading lesson,
Rich began hitting the student seated beside him. During the viewing session,
the teacher stopped the tape at that point and said this was an example of
the "hitting behavior" for which Rich had been referred. Later in the same
reading lesson, a nonreferral student was ejected from the lesson for misconduct.
As this student departed, he struck Rich on the head. The teacher did not
stop the tape at this point, nor comment on it in terms of the hitting behavior
referral category.

These examples suggest one way expectations lead teachers to treat a piece of behavior produced by one student differently than when it is produced by another student. One interpretation of this apparent differential treatment, one that would be consistent with the critical features theory of category construction, would be that there is a pygmalion or teacher expectancy effect working, such that the teacher concentrates on the behavior of one child and ignores the behavior of the second child. Our analysis to this point suggests an alternative interpretation. Teachers do **not** seem to be separating students' behavior (e.g., "hitting the child " or saying *it's too hard for me*) from the actor (the student), the situation (the particular classroom task or event), and the observer (the teacher). Instead of attending to **behavior in isolation,** teachers are attending to **action in context,** which includes the student, the task, the lesson, and the situation in which the action transpires.[5] That is to say, the teacher is not interpreting or perceiving discrete or finite pieces of information.

A musical analogy may make this point clear (see Erickson, Chapter 9, this volume for a more extensive elaboration of the musical metaphor). When a musical sequence is heard, one receives, in addition to the sensory elements (the notes), a certain overall impression, to which the term "melody" is attached. This overall sense of melody is not attributable to any of the single notes taken alone. The melody presents itself as an immediately perceivable whole. So, too, the students' action in a context presents itself to the teacher as a unified whole, an "ensemble" of perceptual particulars (Gurwitsch, 1966).

Because the teacher is attending to organized configurations and not discrete elements, a piece of behavior is not the same when it is conducted by different people in different contexts. *Johnny hitting Mary during math* is not the same as *Mary hitting Billy at recess*. So, too, Duke saying *this is hard,* is not the same as Shane saying *this is hard.* In the same way that the perceptual particulars of the vase–face illusion (see Figure 15.1) take on different meanings when seen as constituents of different configurations, a *slap in the face* takes on different classroom meanings when embedded in different contexts.

Thus, instead of saying that the teacher is attending to the **same** behavior in **different** ways, we are suggesting that the teacher is attending to **different** behavior in the **same** way.

Implications for a Teachers' Theory of Interpretation

We have found that teachers do not enumerate all the features that make an instance of behavior a member of a certain category of referrable behavior.

[5] Here, "action" is meant in Weber's terms: "action is . . . all human behavior when and insofar as the acting individual attaches a subjective meaning to it. . . Action is social, insofar as, by virtue of the subjective meaning attached to it by the acting individual (or individuals), it takes account of others and is thereby oriented in its course [1947, p. 80]."

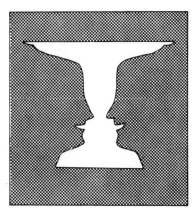

Figure 15.1. Vase–face illusion.

We have also found that teachers do not locate each of the reasons they referred students on videotape during viewing sessions. These observations have a number of implications for a theory about teachers' interpretations of students' classroom behavior.

TEACHERS' CATEGORY FORMATION

The teachers' patterns of observing students' behavior on tapes of classroom events suggests to us that the "critical features" theory is not a teachers' theory of person perception and category formation. It does not seem that teachers code categories of referrable behavior by means of a list of the formal criteria necessary and sufficient for category membership. All the features of referrable behavior are not equally important for the teacher; some features are more important for determining categories than others. Instead of applying the criteria of critical features theory, teachers are coding categories of referrable behavior in terms of prototypes of typical category members (cf. Rosch *et al.*, 1976; Smith & Medin, 1979). The teachers' use of prototypes and exemplars suggests that teachers' theories of perception and categorization have more of a "family resemblance structure" than they do a "critical feature structure."

THE LOCUS OF TEACHERS' PERCEPTUAL STRUCTURES

The fact that teachers do not locate each of the reasons they referred students on videotape during viewing sessions is also an indication that the reasons for referral are not to be found exclusively in the behavior of the students referred. The teacher's decision to refer students is only partially grounded in the students' behavior; it is also grounded in the categories that

the teacher brings to the interaction, including the expectations for academic performance, and norms for appropriate classroom conduct. But, what the teacher brings to the interaction is **not** independent of students' behavior as some versions of expectancy and labeling theory would lead us to believe. Rather, what the teacher brings to the interaction with the students seems to be as important as what the students do with the teacher in classroom interaction.

Thus, neither the mentalist nor the realist perspective has an adequate account of the teachers' interpretations of students' behavior. A third, interactional perspective, seems to be supported by the data. The interactional perspective maintains that perceptual structure exists neither in the head of the perceiver, nor in the object of perception. Instead, basic object groupings result from "an interaction between the potential structure provided by the world and the particular emphasis and state of knowledge of the people who do the categorizing [Rosch *et al.*, 1976, p. 430]." Cantor and Mischel (1979), summarizing a long line of research in implicit personality theory and person perception, come to a similar conclusion: "structure exists neither 'all in the head' of the perceiver nor 'all in the person' perceived; it is, instead, a function of the interaction between the beliefs of observers and the characteristics of the people observed (pp. 45–46)."

THE TEACHER AS A PRACTICAL REASONER

Schutz (1962) and Garfinkel (1967) distinguished "commonsense reasoning," the form of reasoning employed by people in everyday life, from "scientific reasoning," the form of reasoning employed by people in the practice of science. Commonsense reasoners conduct their affairs with a practical interest in the world, whereas scientific reasoners adopt a theoretic attitude toward the world. That is, scientists attempt to achieve a clarity of expression and conduct their investigations in accordance with the canons of formal logic, whereas practical theorists take the world as given, employ indexical modes of explication, and do not submit their investigations to the criteria established by formal logic. First Cicourel (1973) and then Cook-Gumperz (1975) extended the notion of "practical reasoning" to the realm of the child by describing the interpretive processes involved in the developmental acquisition of children's interactional skills.

The "practical" or "commonsense reasoner" has also been described as constrained by limitations on short-term memory (Miller, 1956; Wallace, 1961).[6] The practical reasoner relies on the positive cooccurrence or juxtaposition of events rather than considering the combination or all possibilities

[6] See D'Andrade (1981b) for a discussion of the parallels in the work of Miller and Wallace on short-term memory limitation.

(Jenkins & Ward, 1965; Smedslund, 1963). Shweder (1977) employs heuristic reasoning strategies rather than formal operations (Bartlett, 1958; Polya, 1957; Wason & Johnson-Laird, 1972), and "satisfies" instead of "maximizes [Simon, 1976]."

The teachers' behavior in our study seems consistent with these descriptions of "practical reasoners." Although our discovery that the rationality of teachers is "limited" or "bounded" would not be surprising to cognitive scientists who have explored the limitations of human information processing capacity (e.g., Norman & Dobrow, 1975), we still need a way of talking about the implications and consequences of characteristics about practical reasoning for the practice of teaching.

One thing is certain. Because of the cognitive and organizational constraints on human information processing alluded to in the preceding paragraphs, we cannot propose that teachers become more rational, "do more," or possess **more** information. They cannot be expected to stop forming categories with family resemblances and begin to use a critical features theory of category formation. The teachers' use of prototypes and exemplars in the interpretations of students' behavior is not a matter of inexactness or sloppiness. These are the procedures that practical reasoners employ to process information about their environments.

The contours of practical reasoning do not present a problem for the teacher within the context of the classroom because the teacher's practical project there is the education of individual children. These contours do present a problem when the teacher must deal with children in terms of institutionally provided sets of categories. At such times, the teacher's pragmatic project is transformed from one of education to one of record keeping or category construction.

The organization of classroom life presents teachers who have to fill out referral forms or report cards, or make reports at special education placement meetings with problems of information overload similar to those that are presented to researchers who want to use on-line coding schemes like those of Flanders (1970) or Stallings (1973) (Cole, personal communication).[7] Overwhelmed with information, the teacher has to average, work from memory, and construct a prototype of behavior when filling out referral forms or other official records. However, the pattern of classroom life does not map onto the categories provided in institutionalized record-keeping devices such as referral forms and school records because the institutionally motivated textual representations have been derived from different sources and constructed for different reasons (Cicourel, 1975). The day-to-day categorizations are rich in context

---

[7] See Griffin, Cole, and Newman (in press) for a more detailed discussion of the use of on-line coding schemes in classroom research.

cues, whereas the institutionalized categories provide few, if any, ways to express this richness and diversity.

What starts as a "teacher's puzzle," a problem with the education of a child that cannot be solved immediately, becomes transformed and increasingly reified as it is represented by more and more stable institutional categories. When the teacher asks special educators for help, the "puzzling student" becomes a "referral student," a member of a loosely defined, but institutionally consequential category. With the administration of standardized tests and decisions by a placement committee, the "referral student" becomes a "learning disabled" (LD) or "educationally handicapped" (EH) student. The official category LD or EH becomes both a social fact about the child and an object with a fixed, stable meaning for the school. The official category takes on a life of its own, its origins hidden (Bordieu & Passeron, 1977), even though it is a social product of its own practices. Because official categories are divorced from the lived experiences of classroom life that spawned them, what starts as a specific learning problem can be transformed into a generalized deficiency. We have found (Mehan et al., 1981) educators conclude that students who display "poor reading comprehension" must also have other academic deficiencies, poor peer relations, and a complex of other factors because these factors are institutionally associated with the specific learning disability.

How then can the institutional consequences of these categorizing practices be countered, especially in light of the cognitive and organizational constraints on information processing? Instead of asking educators to process **more** information in different ways, it may be possible to ask educators to process **different** information in the **same** way. One possibility is to provide teachers access to information about the children they are categorizing for teaching purposes that is currently available in school contexts, but is seldom made available to teachers. Moll, Diaz, Estrada, & Lopes (1980) are finding that the "English language model" teacher in a Spanish–English bilingual team-teaching situation is modifying her teaching behavior toward the Spanish language dominant students based on information she received about these students' performance by observing them in the Spanish half of the teaching situation.

Another possibility is to provide teachers with information about their students that is currently unavailable. Here we have "context specific" information in mind. The performance of children and experimental subjects on intellectual tasks varies considerably from context to context (Laboratory of Comparative Human Cognition, in press). For example, students' verbal performance varies when discourse in classrooms and supermarkets is compared (Hall, Cole, Reder, & Dowley, 1977; Isotomina, 1974–1975). Making cross-context comparisons is difficult for teachers, because of the paradox of observation (Labov, 1972), and because schools are not routinely organized to provide this kind of information. But, if teachers could see students in school-related contexts and in out-of-school contexts, they may be less susceptible to adopting a generalized deficit view of children who are not succeeding in classrooms. The teachers in the Kamahamaha Early Education Project (Au & Jordan, 1978; Jordan, 1977) and in the Odowa classroom project (Erickson & Mohatt, 1982) have been successful in this respect. By incorporating information about students' performance outside of school, mutual accommodations in curriculum organization have been made to the advantage of students' improved school performance.

Acknowledgments

We appreciate the special efforts of Margaret S. Crowdes and J. Lee Meihls who collected materials and helped organize the ideas that comprise this chapter. Courtney B. Cazden, Jenny Cook-Gumperz, Dell Hymes, and Louise Cherry Wilkinson provided helpful comments during the conference at which this chapter was first presented. Aaron V. Cicourel, Michael Cole, Peg Griffin, and Denis Newman also provided penetrating criticism and detailed comments that assisted us in the revision of this chapter.

References

Au, K. H., & Jordan, C. T. *Talk story in Hawaiian classroom.* Ethnographic and Sociolinguistics Research in Classrooms Symposium, American Anthropological Association meetings, Los Angeles, 1978.

Bar Tal, C. Attributional analysis of achievement-related behavior. *Review of Educational Research,* 1978, 48(2), 259–271.

Bartlett, F. D. *Thinking.* New York: Basic Books, 1958.

Becker, H. *Outsiders.* New York: The Free Press, 1963.

Bereiter, K., & Engleman, S. *Teaching the disadvantaged child in the preschool.* Englewood Cliffs, N.J.: Prentice-Hall, 1966.

Bernstein, B. *Class, codes and control: Theoretical studies towards a sociology of language* (Vol. 1). London: Routledge & Kegan Paul, 1971.

Bordieu, P., & Passeron, J. C. *Reproduction in education, society and culture.* Beverly Hills: Sage, 1977.

Cantor, N., & Mischel, W. Prototypes in person perception. *Advances in Experimental Social Psychology,* 1979, 12, 3–52.

Carnap, R. *Foundations of logic and mathematics.* Chicago: University of Chicago Press, 1939.

Cicourel, A. V. *Method and measurement in sociology.* New York: The Free Press, 1964.

Cicourel, A. V. *Cognitive sociology: Language and meaning in social interaction.* London: Penguin, 1973.

Cicourel, A. V. Discourse and text. *Versus,* 1975, Sept.–Dec., 33–84.

Cicourel, A. V. Three models of discourse. In *Discourse Processes,* 1980. (a)

Cicourel, A. V. Notes on the integration of micro and macro levels of analysis. In K. Knorr & A. V. Cicourel (Eds.), *Advances in social theory and methodology: Toward an integration of micro- and macro-sociologies.* London: Routledge & Kegan Paul, 1980. (b)

Cicourel, A. V., Jennings, S. H. M., Jennings, K. H., Leiter, K. C. W., MacKay, R., Mehan, H., & Roth, D. R. *Language use and school performance.* New York: Academic Press, 1974.

Cole, M., Hood, L., & McDermott, R. P. *Ecological niche picking: Ecological invalidity as an axiom of experimental cognitive psychology.* Laboratory of comparative human cognition newsletter, La Jolla, Cal., 1978.

Combs, S., & Hertweck, A. *The format for viewing sessions* (Working Paper No. 4). La Jolla, Cal.: Laboratory of Comparative Human Cognition, University of California-San Diego, 1979.

Cook-Gumperz, J. The child as a practical reasoner. In M. Sanches & B. G. Blount (Eds.), *Sociocultural dimensions of language use.* New York: Academic Press, 1975.

D'Andrade, R. G. *Cultural meaning systems.* Address given to the Social Science Research Council Conference on Conception of Culture and its Acquisition. New York City, May 1981. (a)

D'Andrade, R. G. The cultural part of cognition. *Cognitive Science,* 1981, *5* (3), 179–195. (b)

Davies, P. *Assessing others:An interactional study of the discourse and text of juvenile assessments.* Unpublished doctoral dissertation, University of California, San Diego, 1978.

Erickson, F., & Mohatt, G. Cultural organization of participation structures in two classrooms of Indian students. In G. D. Spindler (Ed.), *Doing the ethnography of schooling.* New York: Holt, Rinehart & Winston, 1982.

Erickson, F., & Shultz, J. J. *The counselor as gate keeper: Social interaction in interviews.* New York: Academic Press, 1981.

Flanders, N. A. *Analyzing teacher behavior.* Reading, Mass.: Addison-Wesley, 1970.

Florio, S. *Learning how to go to school.* Unpublished doctoral dissertation, Harvard, 1978.

Garfinkel, H. *Studies in ethnomethodology.* New York: Prentice-Hall, 1967.

Goodenough, W. Componential analysis and the study of meaning. *Language,* 1956, *32,* 195–210.

Griffin, P., Cole, M., & Newman, D. Locating tasks. In *Discourse Processes,* in press.

Griffin, P., & Mehan, H. Sense and ritual in classroom discourse. In F. Coulmas (Ed.), *Conversational routine: Explorations in standardized communication systems and prepatterned speech.* The Hague: Mouton Janua Linguarum, 1980.

Gumperz, J. J., & Hymes, D. (Eds.). The ethnography of communication. *American Anthropologist,* 666(II), 1964.

Gumperz, J. J., & Hymes, D. *Directions in sociolinguistics: The ethnography of communication.* New York: Holt, Rinehart & Winston, 1972.

Gurwitsch, A. *Studies in phenomenology and psychology.* Evanston, Ill.: Northwestern University Press, 1966.

Hall, W. S., Cole, M., Reder, S., & Dowley, G. Variations in young children's use of language: Some effects of setting and dialect. In R. Freedle (Ed.), *Discourse production and comprehension.* Norwood, N.J.: Ablex, 1977.

Hargreaves, D. H., Hester, S. K., & Mellor, F. J. *Deviance in classrooms.* London: Routledge & Kegan Paul, 1975.

Hess, R. D., & Shipman, V. C. Early experience and the socialization of cognitive modes in children. *Child Development,* 1965, *36*(4), 869–885.

Isotomina, Z. M. The development of voluntary memory in preschool-age children. *Soviet Psychology,* 1974–75, *13,* 5–64.

Jenkins, H. M., & Ward, W. C. The display of information and the judgment of contingency. *Canadian Journal of Psychology,* 1965, *17,* 93–241.

Jensen, A. R. How much can we boost I.Q. and scholastic achievement? *Harvard Educational Review,* 1969, *39*(1), 1–123.

Jordan, K. H. *The Kamahamaha early education project.* Paper presented at American Anthropological Association meetings, Houston, 1977.

Kitsuse, J. Societal reaction to deviant behavior. *Social Problems,* 1962, 9(3), 247–256.

Labov, W. *Sociolinguistic patterns.* Philadelphia: University of Pennsylvania Press, 1972.

Laboratory of Comparative Human Cognition, University of California-San Diego. Intelligence as cultural practice. In W. Sternberg (Ed.), *Handbook of intelligence.* New York: Cambridge University Press, in press.

Lemert, E. *Social pathology.* New York: McGraw-Hill, 1951.

Mannheim, K. On the interpretation of Weltanschauung. In P. Kecskemiti (Ed.), *Essays on the sociology of knowledge.* New York: Oxford University Press, 1952.

Mehan, H. *Learning lessons.* Cambridge: Harvard University Press, 1979.

Mehan, H., & Wood, H. An image of man for ethnomethodology. *The Philosophy of the Social Science,* 1975, 5, 365–376.

Mehan, H., Meihls, J. L., Hertweck, A., & Crowdes, M. S. Identifying handicapped students. In S. B. Bacharach (Ed.), *Organizational behavior in schools and school districts.* New York: Praeger Press, 1981.

Mercer, J. *Labelling the mentally retarded.* Berkeley: University of California Press, 1974.

Mercer, J. Protection in evaluation procedures. In L. G. Morra (Ed.), *Developing criteria for the evaluation of protection in evaluation procedures provisions.* Philadelphia: Relations for Better Schools, 1979.

Miller, G. A. The magic number seven plus or minus 2: Some limits on our capacity for processing information. *Psychology Review,* 1956, 63, 81–97.

Moll, L., Diaz, E., Estrada, E., & Lopes, L. *The organization of bilingual lessons:* Implications for schooling. Laboratory of comparative human cognition newsletter, La Jolla, Calif., 1980.

Norman, D. A., & Dobrow, D. G. On data-limited and resource-limited processes. *Cognitive Psychology,* 1975, 7, 44–46.

Polya, G. *How to solve it.* Garden City, N.Y.: Doubleday, 1957.

Ramirez, M. A., & Castaneda, A. *Cultural democracy, biocognitive development, and education.* New York: Academic Press, 1974.

Rosch, E., & Mervis, C. B. Family resemblances: Studies in the internal structure of categories. *Cognitive Psychology,* 1975, 7, 573–605.

Rosch, E., Mervis, C. B., Gray, W. D., Johnson, D. M., & Boyes-Braem, P. *Basic objects in natural categories.* New York: Academic Press, 1976.

Rosenthal, R., & Jacobsen, L. *Pygmalion in the classroom.* New York: Holt, Rinehart & Winston, 1968.

Schneider, D. M. American kin terms and terms for kinsmen. *American Anthropologist,* 1965, 67 (5, Pt. 2), 288–308.

Schutz, A. *Collected papers I: The problem of social reality.* The Hague: Martinus Nijoff, 1962.

Shumsky, M. *Encounter groups: A forensic science.* Unpublished doctoral dissertation, University of California-Santa Barbara, 1972.

Shuy, R., & Griffin, P. The study of children's functional language and education in the early years. *Final Report to the Carnegie Corporation of New York.* Arlington, Va.: Center for Applied Linguistics, 1978.

Shweder, P. A. Likeness and likelihood in everyday thought: Magical thinking in judgments about personality. *Current Anthropology,* 1977, 18, 637–648.

Simon, N. *Administrative behavior.* New York: The Free Press, 1976.

Smedslund, J. The concept of correlation in adults. *Scandanavian Journal of Psychology,* 1963, 4, 165–173.

Smith, E. E., & Medin, D. *Representation and processing of lexical concepts.* La Jolla: Paper presented at the Sloan Conference at University of Calfornia-San Diego, March 1979.

Stallings, J. *Follow-through program classroom observation evaluation.* Menlo Park: Stanford Research Institute, 1973.

Wallace, A. F. C. On being just complicated enough. *Proceedings of the National Academy of Sciences*, 1961, *47*, 458–464.

Wason, P. C., & Johnson-Laird, P. N. *The psychology of reasoning.* Cambridge: Harvard University Press, 1972.

Weber, M. *The theory of social and economic organization* (A. M. Henderson & T. Parsons, trans.). New York: The Free Press, 1947.

Wilson, T. P. Conceptions of interaction and forms of sociological explanation. *American Sociological Review*, 1970, *53*, 697–709.

Wittgenstein, L. *Philosophical investigations.* New York: Macmillan, 1953.

16

Conclusion:
Applications for Education[1]

LOUISE CHERRY WILKINSON
FRANCESCA SPINELLI

The implications for education of the work presented in this volume are numerous. Selected applications for evaluation, teaching, and learning are discussed briefly in this concluding chapter.

Implications for Assessment

Understanding individual differences among students in communicative competence is the purpose of assessment. Research suggests that an accurate assessment of students' knowledge of language usage in the classroom should be examined in relevant, multiple contexts. One problem with previous work is that assessment has been made of a particular language function or discourse unit in only one particular context. We cannot assume that performance of the appropriate behavior in that context necessarily predicts whether the student will perform the same behavior in another context. The generalizability of performance assessed in only one context is dubious. Ervin-Tripp (Chapter 3) observes that the forms of requests vary with context, and therefore, language should be evaluated in the context of concern, or else be evaluated in a context

[1] The work reported in this chapter was funded by the Wisconsin Center for Education Research, which is supported in part by a grant from the National Institute of Education (Grant No. NIE-G-81-0009). The opinions expressed in this chapter do not necessarily reflect the position, policy, or endorsement of the National Institute of Education.

323

which attempts to duplicate the context of concern. Mehan, Hertweck, Combs, and Flynn (Chapter 15) point out that behavior varies with context, and they suggest observation of a given behavior in multiple contexts so that conclusions about generalized deficit will be drawn cautiously. The background of the assessed individual must also be considered because, as Cook-Gumperz and Gumperz (Chapter 2) note, the judgment of behavior as appropriate varies with context.

Given the importance of context, it is difficult to specify the observational unit within which assessment of an individual student should be conducted. Thus, there is a problem of how to focus the assessment. The authors of this volume seem to agree that communicative competence cannot be broken down into isolated fragments of behavior for assessment or teaching in any one single context. Mehan, Hertweck, Combs, and Flynn (Chapter 15) point out that isolated behaviors do not necessarily carry their own meaning and the gestalt must be considered. An isolated utterance is regarded as a fragment without its linguistic and nonlinguistic context, which is necessary for the interpretation of meaning. Cook-Gumperz and Gumperz (Chapter 2) believe that communicative competence cannot be assessed as isolated skills, because of its very definition. It is composed of complexities in conversation and highlights the variety of factors that must be considered and how they change with context. According to their view, if behaviors are isolated, communicative competence would no longer be what is being measured. Cook-Gumperz and Gumperz pose the question of whether it is possible to isolate one single path to a given communicative goal. They believe that the traditional assessment procedures make that assumption, which is antithetical to the sociolinguistic perspective. One must ask what the tests are designed to reveal. Some of the authors have identified gestalts of behavior that have been found to differ for students, and these could serve as foci for assessment.

The work reported in this volume suggests that multiple methods of assessment are necessary. Observing that a student has produced a behavior conforming to the rules of language use in the classroom often is not sufficient for knowing whether the student has, in fact, achieved communicative competence, in the broad sense. In addition to the multiple descriptions in a number of contexts, we need to develop tools which help us assess what a student does and does not know about the use of language in the specific classroom situations. The importance of careful observation of students communicating and interacting in a variety of contexts that differ on a variety of dimensions is a fundamental implication of this work. In addition, it may be possible to create contexts with high communicative demand, such as Dickson (Chapter 8) suggests, or to manipulate contexts to see how a student responds to communicative error (Ervin-Tripp, Chapter 3).

After such information is gathered for individual students, the question arises of the norms to be used for comparison. Should they be those of a given culture? Should they reflect the environment of the student during the school day? Thus, the findings of a particular assessment cannot themselves be isolated from the values, expectations, and purposes for which the evaluation is to be used. The background against which the evaluation is being compared is as important as the data revealed in the evaluation itself.

Implications for Teaching and Learning

Research findings revealing individual differences in classroom communicative competence provide practical implications for teaching and learning. Two questions arise: Should individual differences in competence be encouraged or discouraged? How can individual differences be utilized to maximum advantage in the classroom? A description of differences and a consideration of the purposes that they serve is useful in attempting to address these questions. Differences that originate or are promoted in the classroom may not be in the best interest of the student. They may result from self-fulfilling prophesies on the part of the teacher, or be a consequence of variable behavior initiated by the teacher (e.g., Mehan et al. Chapter 15). For example, Eder (Chapter 12) found that the teacher's encouragement of lower ability children to participate in discussions may have led to her greater use of topical interruptions.

Regarding the purposes for changing individual differences, clearly it would not be appropriate to attempt to reduce differences among students to make them conform to an arbitrary convention, particularly when that convention conflicts with the students' self-concept or lowers self-esteem. However, there may be times when a difference among students leads to interference in learning. In this case, an intervention aimed at modifying the students' behavior may be appropriate. Reducing the differences among ineffective communicators and other students in the classroom may break the "rich get richer" cycle, in which the effective communicators, who are often high achievers, command and receive more of the teachers' attention than do the ineffective communicators (e.g., De Stefano, Pepinsky, & Sanders, Chapter 7; Eder, Chapter 12; Merritt, Chapter 11).

Individual differences in competence can be utilized to the advantage of both students and teachers. Flexibility in using and understanding language can be encouraged by interaction among those whose behaviors differ from one another (e.g., Florio & Clark, Chapter 13). Interaction among students with differing communicative styles and abilities could create "communicative pressure" that could encourage students to try a variety of strategies to make themselves understood and to obtain clarification from others (e.g., Cooper, Marquis, & Ayers-Lopez, Chapter 5; Genishi & DiPaolo, Chapter 4; Wilkinson & Calculator, Chapter 6).

Clearly, students' individual differences need to be taken into account in any attempt to teach communicative competence. Teachers need to become aware of the different characteristics of students, including their ability level, personalities, and social styles. We do not know what is best for students in the long run, however, present research suggests that there may exist an optimal match between the student and the instructional technique. There are probably many choices to achieve this match for a particular student (e.g., Eder, Chapter 12; Fillmore, Chapter 14).

Individual differences among students cannot be separated easily from instructional contexts, and this fact has implications for teaching and learning (e.g., Green & Harker, Chapter 10; Erickson, Chapter 9). Two types of instructional contexts have been discussed in the research reported in this volume: the large context of the classroom and school and the immediate context of the classroom at a given moment. Fillmore's findings suggest that teaching methods need to be varied according to large contextual factors, such as the composition of the student population, whereas the research of Merritt, and of Genishi & DiPaolo suggest that teachers should vary the form of their language according to the particular characteristics of the classroom, such as the activities engaged in by the students.

Stimulating students' development of communicative competence should be a goal of teaching. Using consistent routines may be a useful teaching technique. Routines are used in classrooms (e.g., Genishi & DiPaolo; Merritt) and recent research suggests that children may learn larger units of language, such as the discourse structure of a routine, prior to learning component parts (Fillmore, in press). Studies reported in this volume strongly suggest that instruction should not consist of teaching discrete, isolated, pieces of language, such as the utterance. Communicative competence in the classroom cannot be broken down into fragments out of context, without destroying the essence of the phenomenon (e.g., Cook-Gumperz & Gumperz). Routines may be particularly useful for bilingual children and in situations where the classroom context is unfamiliar such as at the beginning of the school year and with younger children first entering school.

An effective method, suggested by recent research in developmental psycho- and sociolinguistics, may be to encourage children to develop communicative competence by creating opportunities for them to model, practice, and receive feedback on their communicative performance. Teachers can emphasize such key communicative experiences and make them more frequent. These experiences should vary in complexity and diversity, including planned variation in participants, goals, and location. For example, contexts should be used that include and exclude the teacher. Genishi and DiPaolo suggest that the presence of teachers may interfere with the independent resolution of conflicts by children.

Several studies reported in this volume suggest that the peer system should be used to a larger extent in promoting communicative experiences. Peer-teaching, for example, would increase the opportunities for students to use language to exchange information and regulate their interpersonal behavior (e.g., Eder; Cooper et al.; Wilkinson & Calculator). Composition of peer groups and dyads could be varied according to the communicative competencies of the students. All of the students would benefit from the experience of using language in a variety of ways, including attempting to resolve misunderstanding and miscommunication. Students who have not achieved competence in this context yet may benefit from having more effective communicators as role models in a mixed-ability group. Those, however, who have achieved competence in this context may learn from taking the role of teacher (Cooper et al.) and they may exercise control over other students, by winning arguments (Genishi & DiPaolo). One variation of this experience is the teachers' manipulation of the context, in order to provide key communicative experiences for students who typically do not have them. The teacher could change the students' social status by designating a student as an "expert" by providing information that is both desired by yet unavailable to other students in the peer group (Cooper et al.).

Teachers may incorporate any of the techniques described into the ongoing instructional activity; or alternatively, they may set up separately planned communicative experiences for students, such as those described by Dickson and Ervin-Tripp. Clearly, teaching should involve encouragement of students' use of a variety of language forms and functions in a variety of classroom communicative contexts, so that flexibility and generalizability of competence can be promoted.

The results reported in this volume suggest that there is a paradoxical relationship between teaching and learning: Some students learn communicative competence even though it is not taught explicitly. The obvious resolution to this apparent paradox is that communicative competence is taught by both teachers and students in an implicit and unplanned way. Further research is needed to unravel the complexities of this process, including aspects amenable to intervention, and experiences that promote learning. We hope that this work, both past and future, will be helpful to teachers in their efforts to stimulate students development of communicative competence.

Reference

Fillmore, L. Wong. The second time around. New York: Academic Press, in press.

Author Index

Subject Index

LANGUAGE, THOUGHT, AND CULTURE: *Advances in the Study of Cognition*

Under the Editorship of: E. A. HAMMEL

DEPARTMENT OF ANTHROPOLOGY
UNIVERSITY OF CALIFORNIA
BERKELEY

Michael Agar, Ripping and Running: A Formal Ethnography of Urban Heroin Addicts

Brent Berlin, Dennis E. Breedlove, and Peter H. Raven, Principles of Tzeltal Plant Classification: An Introduction to the Botanical Ethnography of a Mayan-Speaking People of Highland Chiapas

Mary Sanches and Ben Blount, Sociocultural Dimensions of Language Use

Daniel G. Bobrow and Allan Collins, Representation and Understanding: Studies in Cognitive Science

Domenico Parisi and Francesco Antinucci, Essentials of Grammar

Elizabeth Bates, Language and Context: The Acquisition of Pragmatics

Ben G. Blount and Mary Sanches, Sociocultural Dimensions of Language Change

Susan Ervin-Tripp and Claudia Mitchell-Kernan (Eds.), Child Discourse

Lynn A. Friedman (Ed.), On the Other Hand: New Perspectives on American Sign Language

Eugene S. Hunn, Tzeltal Folk Zoology: The Classification of Discontinuities in Nature

Jim Schenkein (Ed.), Studies in the Organization of Conversational Interaction

David Parkin, The Cultural Definition of Political Response: Lineal Destiny Among the Luo

Stephen A. Tyler, The Said and the Unsaid: Mind, Meaning, and Culture

Susan Gal, Language Shift: Social Determinants of Linguistic Change in Bilingual Austria

Ronald Scollon and Suzanne B. K. Scollon, Linguistic Convergence: An Ethnography of Speaking at Fort Chipewyan, Alberta

Elizabeth Bates, The Emergence of Symbols: Cognition and Communication in Infancy

Mary LeCron Foster and Stanley H. Brandes (Eds.), Symbol as Sense: New Approaches to the Analysis of Meaning

Willett Kempton, The Folk Classification of Ceramics: A Study of Cognitive Prototypes